Preface

IN the more than two decades since the Kremlin ordered its many-pronged attack on the West's nuclear secrets, millions of words have been written on atomic espionage. When I began work on this book, however, I realized why much of the story remained untold. Many of the salient facts jutted out of newspaper accounts, but they were isolated. Reporters, under the pressure of deadlines, could only take a brief look at the peaks. Magazine writers tried to encompass too much material within the limits of their assigned space. Two excellent books—*The Atom Spies* by Oliver Pilat and *The Traitors* by Alan Moorehead—were written before the returns were in.

Those who tried to tell the story of atomic espionage were, moreover, brought up short by a series of dead ends. The ordinary uses of research do not suffice in telling this fascinating and shocking story. True, the voluminous transcripts of Congressional hearings, trials, the inquiries of government bodies, and the reports of special commissions offered a bewildering number of facts. But significant areas, never opened up for public scrutiny, remained unexplored. Much of the information necessary for a rounded account was locked away in the secret files of Counter-Intelligence and counter-espionage—and these are seldom opened to writers. Security still outranks curiosity or the often proclaimed right-to-know.

There was one major source to be tapped, the experienced memories of Soviet espionage agents who defected to the West. For the most part, these men and women tell what they know to the Central Intelligence Agency, to the Federal Bureau of Investigation, to Britain's MI-5, and/or to the French Deuxième Bureau—and then pray that they will be allowed to disappear from sight. If their existence is known, they do not respond to the queries of reporters and writers they have never before met. In fact, they devote themselves to forgetting, not remembering. For every ex-agent who is caught in the focus of public attention, there are many whose existence never becomes known except to specialists in Soviet espionage. Even those who shared the glare of sensational events speak fully only to their governmental questioners—and in private —or to people whose background and knowledge they trust. Igor Gouzenko, who years ago gave me what I believe to be his first interview with a newsman, was willing to let down the barriers because he knew me by reputation. "You will understand," he said.

What he meant was that he could employ with me the special shorthand of a special world. I have seen two former Soviet agents, meeting for the first time, plunge into what seemed like an interrupted conversation. There was no need to find a point of reference. Each knew immediately what the other was talking about, without any explanations. Never having been a Communist, I am in a sense an outsider. But I still remember the surprise of Whittaker Chambers when, after he got to know me well, he discovered that I was never a member of the underground party. Knowledge of the espionage world's shop talk has been invaluable to me in putting together this account of the greatest plot in history. Even in the testimony of former *apparatchiks*, there is much that remains meaningless to the untrained ear.

My major task in writing this book was to sort out the great mass of unrelated public information—including what was ignored or misunderstood when it flashed across the screen of our contemporaneity—to fill in the gaps with material from my own files, to consult my notes and my recollection, and to place it all in context. Because every chapter could of itself have been a small book, a second task was to boil away the fat of nonessential though interesting material.

Of necessity, I read many hundreds of news stories even though they merely echoed one another. There were, however, rewards in this—for buried away among the twice-told tales I found a fact or an allusion which lit up a dark corner of spying's netherworld. Much-plowed ground, like the Report of the Royal Commission which studied the documents taken out of the Soviet Embassy in Ottawa by Gouzenko, yielded important insights. Of considerable value were the reports and hearings of the House Un-American Activities Committee, the Senate Internal Security Subcommittee, and the Joint Congressional Atomic Energy Committee—not available when the earlier books on this subject were written. The Report of the Royal Commission in Australia which sifted the disclosures of Vladimir Petrov was also of value. Wherever it would not be improper or indiscreet, I have identified other sources in the course of my narrative.

I am deeply indebted to two books which guided me in recounting the history of nuclear research and in describing the complex problems of technology solved by the Manhattan Engineer District: *Men and Decisions* by Lewis L. Strauss and *Now It Can Be Told* by Leslie R. Groves. Security reports and testimony, buried away in the 992 pages of *In the Matter of J. Robert Oppenheimer: Transcript of Hearing Before Personnel Security Board*, corroborated what had previously been subject to controversy.

A final word:

This book is a tale of many men and many cities—of mixed motives, misplaced idealism, and ruined lives, of duplicity and innocence. For communism is not the monopoly of traitors. It reaches out in its many disguises to honorable men who do not know why or how or even that it has touched them. Subversion in our time does not lurk in Jacobin cellars: it openly manipulates hopes and causes before betraying them. In narrating actions and effects, my intent is not accusatory. Knowledge of what is past can deflect the course of future events. Since communism, as a paramilitary philosophy and a plan of attack, gains its strength by compounding the weakness and ignorance of others, a delineation of its methodology may serve to increase the will to resist it.

Contents

"Espionage is a distinct and principal Soviet industry."

Vladimir Petrov, former NKVD chief in Australia

"Every member of the Communist Party is an agent to execute the Communist program."

Mr. Justice Jackson, in *American Communications Association* v. *Douds*

"When security is found to be excessive, it can always be cured by relaxing it. There is no cure for inadequate security. Information once compromised is information broadcast forever."

Lewis L. Strauss, in *Men and Decisions*

1 The Bridegroom Cometh

The date: May 17, 1938.
The place: Buffalo, New York.
The mission: Espionage.

ON THAT DAY, Arthur Alexandrovitch Adams, whose alias combined the ludicrous juxtaposition of a blatantly Russian middle name and an honored American patronymic, crossed the Canadian border into the United States. Immigration officials took only routine notice of him, paying but casual attention to the Canadian birth certificate he carried with him. Customs officials had no reason to suspect that the sole contraband in his possession was a master plan, well-memorized, for penetrating the secrets of his host country. The United States was at peace, and to most people the potential enemy spoke with a German accent.

Arthur Alexandrovitch Adams was but one more traveler crossing the unguarded frontier which separates the United States and Canada. It would be years before American security agencies would know that the birth certificate he carried was fraudulent, obtained from a secret member of a Toronto Communist cell who bore the portentous name of M. S. Milestone. It would be years, too, before these agencies learned that a group of Americans in New York, on instructions from the Fourth Section of Red Army Intelligence, had already prepared for Arthur Adams a safe cover for espionage. But at that moment neither Adams nor his superiors in Moscow could have known that he would play a key role in history's greatest plot: the theft of America's most closely guarded nuclear secrets and the formation of an effective apparatus which, in its Phase Two, would confuse public thinking on atomic energy, influence the deliberations of Congress, and muddy up the waters of international policy.

Only in the eyes of a handful of scientists, working in their laboratories, could the gleam of an atomic age a-borning be detected. Yet it was easily foreseeable that the American-British-Canadian project, once it was discovered, would be the target of Communist spying. The catalogue of military and diplomatic espionage by the Soviets was in the late 1930s grim and long.* The

---

In the June 19, 1951, issue of Look magazine, the Washington correspondent for the Cowles newspapers, Fletcher Knebel, compiled a partial list of "the secrets Russia got":

"Military: H-bomb theory, A-bomb theory and plans, Panama defense details, proximity fuse, data on Oak Ridge gaseous diffusion plant, cosmic ray research, facts about Chalk River atomic plant, details on Hanford atomic plant, Uranium-235, Los Alamos atomic layout, identity of atomic scientists, mathematics of atomic aircraft, date of A-bomb test, plans for earth satellite, RDX high-explosive, turbo-prop aircraft data, Jeep plans, Edgewood Arsenal research-equipment blueprints, radiation data, B-29 plans, aircraft production figures, date of Normandy invasion, our progress in breaking Russian codes, 'Dina' explosive, sonar anti-sub devices, Torpex explosives, anti-sub aircraft radar, guided missiles progress, battleship radar, airborne distance indicator, scanning radar, waterproof maps, production, distribution and storage of weapons.

"Industrial: Photographic processes, high-octane gas, synthetic rubber, industrial sol-

9

Communists had given it new dimension by including in this time-dishonored practice industrial, technological, and scientific espionage—preying on the private sector by stealing patented processes which they could as easily have bought in the open market. They enlisted in this activity on a mass basis the nationals of Western countries whose loyalties were subverted and whose idealism was corrupted. No longer was a spy a shameful creature stealthily lurking in the back alleys of society. The Soviet *apparat* could claim men of stature and intellectual attainment—men who spurned money and justified their acts as moral. But the master Soviet accomplishment—an operation which Vladimir Ilyich Lenin would have lustily applauded—was the manipulation by trained agents of world opinion and of the scientific community, at a time when the cold war had barely begun to form its icicles.

In 1938, no reader of spy thrillers would have looked twice at Arthur Alexandrovitch Adams or considered him a menace. He was a frail man, obviously racked by pain, who seemed incapable of the taxing pursuit of espionage. A doctor would have said he was arthritic. He himself attributed his ailments, in the privacy of the *apparat*, to the beatings he had received at the hands of the Tsarist police during the abortive Russian Revolution of 1905. This was his small boast. On a higher plane, he spoke of an intimate association with Lenin in the early days of Communist revolutionary activity—a claim which must have had some basis in fact, since it was accepted by his superiors at the Center in Moscow. The extent of his disability was later described by one of his accomplices:

> He was a pretty sick man. . . . Many is the time I had to send my secretary down to get him out of bed. He was rheumatically crippled and had fallen out of bed and injured his eyes. So we were always under the impression that he would injure himself. . . . It would paralyze him completely. He would have great difficulty . . . in sitting in one position, and he would be all hunched up, and it would take at least one hour before he would come to himself.

Yet Adams was a man to watch. He was an Old Bolshevik, one of the elite of Soviet communism until Stalin began to slaughter them by the thousands in the grisly cellars of Moscow's Lubianka prison. More significant, he was a highly trained agent—a veteran and charter member of the secret police created by Felix Dzerzhinsky under orders from Lenin when the Bolsheviks overthrew the democratic government of Alexander Kerensky. Known originally as the GPU, the organization took many names over the years, but its function was always the same—to inspire terror in the Russian people and to prey on the non-Communist world.* In 1924, Dzerzhinsky would report confidently on the success of his efforts:

---

vents, hundreds of chemical formulas, sugar-refining processes, layout of United States and Canadian research laboratories.

"*Diplomatic and political: Secret Far Eastern dispatches, secret European dispatches, secret messages from embassies in Moscow, secret sessions of the Canadian Parliament, Justice Department espionage files.*"

* In 1923, the GPU (Gosudarstvennoye Politicheskoye Upravelenye) became the OGPU by the addition of the word Obedyedinnoye *to its name. In 1934, the entire name was changed to NKVD (Narodyny Komisariat Vnutrennikh Dyel), by which it is still popularly known. By 1946, when the Kremlin dropped the term "commissariat" for the more respectable "minis-*

The OGPU not only works energetically by paralyzing the espionage of foreign citizens in the USSR, but it also has succeeded in creating a network of information Intelligence agencies in all other large centers of Europe and North America. Responsible workers of the OGPU are detailed to all the diplomatic and trade missions of the USSR abroad. The total strength of the Foreign Department of the OGPU is 1,300, including employees of the foreign section in Moscow. The OGPU has rendered service to the Commissariat of Foreign Affairs and the staff of the Red Army in supplying secret information both of a political and military nature.

At the time Arthur Adams entered the United States, however limpingly, that modest 1,300 had grown into an army of some nine thousand highly-trained "master spies," almost 200,000 subordinates, and half a million *novators*—the dupes, innocents, and (as the NKVD calls them) the "in-the-dark" informants who consciously or otherwise supplied information to the Center in Moscow. Adams had been part of this operation as it grew and refined its techniques, his particular specialty the United States. As early as January 1919, he had been assigned to an espionage mission in this country. But the Soviets, full of revolutionary arrogance, were clumsier than they needed to be. Adams was caught red-handed, and was forced to leave New York "voluntarily" two years later. Only slightly deterred by this contretemps, he returned in 1927, ostensibly as the official representative of Amo, the Soviet Union's first and still inefficient automobile plant. A smattering of engineering and technical lingo helped him maintain this cover, as it did in all his other missions. The year 1932 saw him back again in New York, this time as a member of a group then negotiating with Curtiss-Wright for the purchase of airplanes—with side trips for the apparatus.

His next venture, in 1936, was an assignment from both Red Army Intelligence and the NKVD. In the glow of the Popular Front and as a reaction to Hitler's rise, Soviet espionage had taken a great leap forward. Young men in the federal government, researchers and technologists in American industry, and graduate students in the great universities had made the blinding discovery that Utopia and the Soviet Union were synonymous. In the darkness of their blazing noon, they were eager and ready to make a compound of moral treason and sophistry, excusing the betrayal of principle and common decency with the argument that they were "helping the working class" or "fighting fascism." The blow to American complacency delivered by the great depression still shook them and furnished additional rationalization. But though they contributed to the flow of information into the Soviet Union, they were for the most part rather poor agents. Only the innocence abounding in most Americans had prevented more than random discoveries of Soviet espionage, and these made such little impact on the public consciousness that

try," the NKVD became the MVD (Ministerstsvo Vnutrennikh Dyel). At the same time, because of some division in function, the MGB (Ministerstsvo Gosudarstvennoy Bezopasnosti) was created. After Stalin's death, Malenkov placed internal security in the hands of the KGB (Komitet Gosudarstvennoy Bezopasnosti). There is often some confusion as to whether a particular agent is NKVD or Red Army Intelligence. This is due to the overlapping of activities. Often the agent himself does not know who are his masters.

until the Gouzenko disclosures there were still people who insisted that it existed only in the minds of "Red-baiters."

The slips which occurred troubled Moscow, however impervious to their significance this country might be. Though the Soviets have put espionage on a mass-production basis, precisely because they rely on quantity to make up for quality, security remains an important factor. It was "to inspect the posts" in New York, Washington, Pittsburgh, Detroit, and points west that Arthur Alexandrovitch Adams was sent on his penultimate trip to the United States, in the guise of visiting relatives. Discipline had to be imposed, procedures tightened, and the small seed of fear planted in the minds of those who held professional rank in the Soviet Union's proliferating underground cells. The possibility of defection had to be scotched—and it was very real. Though the West had yet to understand the meaning of the great purges, or even to be really aware of them, they were a topic of much talk among the *apparatchiks*, who learned every day of the disappearance of this or that official in the Soviet hierarchy. For them, the need for exegesis was not necessary.

Like every espionage service, both the NKVD and Red Army Intelligence knew the drill. Stalin, through the Center in Moscow, decided to crack the whip. It is an index of the importance of Arthur Adams that he was selected to do the cracking. His orders were specific. No matter how ingenuous Americans might be, the network was to operate with the same care, using the same methods that obtained in London, Paris, or Berlin. An espionage apparatus, if it is properly organized, is like a chain that can be tugged in only one direction. This means that if Counter-Intelligence discovers one agent or link, and if that agent talks, he can only give information about his subordinates. The higher, and critical, links in the chain cannot be pulled in or arrested.

The Center in Moscow has all the pertinent, and some impertinent, facts about the entire network—the table of organization, so to speak. But it communicates directly only with its representatives in Soviet embassies and consulates. It maintains contact via the diplomatic pouch and short-wave radio. Messages are sent in code (at the Soviet Embassy in Ottawa there were five cipher clerks, each one using a code not known to the other four) and a set of cover names is used for individuals, organizations, and places. An embassy is known as *metro*, the NKVD is *the Neighbor*, passports are *shoes* (and those who supply forged or fraudulent passports are *shoemakers*), a legal front for espionage such as the Amtorg Trading Corporation in New York is called *a roof*, local Communist parties are referred to as *the corporation* (members are *corporants*). A hide-out or hiding place, such as the house on Gay Street in New York's Greenwich Village, where couriers off the ships brought messages for processing in the early 1930s, is a *dubok*. Anyone working for the apparatus is *nash*—"ours."

The Center divides any apparatus into two parts, the "legal" and the "illegal." This has nothing to do with the nature of the work being done, but of those who are doing it. A Soviet national, protected by a diplomatic passport and the immunity it gives, is a "legal" agent. So, too, is any Russian on official business—the member of a purchasing mission, a dance troupe bringing ballet and enlightenment to the Americans, or anyone who can offer a "legiti-mate" reason for being in the host country. The "illegals" are agents traveling under false papers who have submerged their identities—the "faceless men"—or natives of the country in which the network has been set up. If caught, they have no protection and expect to be sacrificed.

There is a free two-way communication between the Director at the Center in Moscow and the resident directors, but it stops there. The resident director is known to his agents by a cover name—"Al" or "Carl" or "Fred"—though he knows exactly who they are. They in turn use these cover first names with their subagents unless they are dealing with people known to them pro-fessionally or socially. If an agent is apprehended or defects, he can merely give the cover name to the authorities and supply some sort of description. At the time that Arthur Adams was "inspecting the posts," Whittaker Chambers knew the identities and histories of those who supplied him with information. But security was so lax within the apparatus that he knew the name and much of the personal background of his superior, Colonel Boris Bykov. It is ironic that in time Adams, the inspector, should make the same mistake of talking too much to his sources. But even during its most secretive phases, Soviet Intelligence failed to observe all the rules. As Igor Gouzenko once remarked to this writer:

"What does it matter? They work on such a mass-production basis that the loss of one agent is sometimes beneficial. The Americans arrest him, and they are lulled into thinking that they've broken up the whole network. Mean-while, nine or ten other networks remain untouched."

From the detailed confessions of Soviet agents to United States security agencies, it is known that in 1936 procedures were tightened, minimizing, though not eliminating, the continual threat of ideological defectors, double agents, and inadvertent discovery. As the *apparatchiks* grew into their new discipline, fewer and fewer of them were able to learn, as did Whittaker Chambers and Hede Massing, of the personnel and scope of parallel appara-tuses in the United States and abroad. The veterans of the October Revolution who had been subverted into the dirty business of spying either accepted the new ways, or, if they persisted in their romantic notions, were eliminated—to be replaced by younger professionals "academically" trained, for whom 1918 was but a childhood memory. If there were still intramural leaks, they ceased to be the rule and became the exception.

When Arthur Adams returned to Moscow, the relatives he had been "visiting" knew only that he was involved in "important work." If they had any educated guesses as to the nature of that work, they did not confide them to the Federal Bureau of Investigation. His superiors at the Center were, however, given a full report on the strengths and weaknesses of the organiza-tion in America and an evaluation of the agents there. Possibly as a result of his findings, at least one Soviet agent was "eliminated" in New York because of his weakness for female companionship and the bottle. This much is certain: Moscow was convinced that Arthur Adams had done his job well, that he was capable and trustworthy enough to be given another American assignment.

After a period of observation, mandatory after an agent has been exposed to the corrupting influences of capitalist society, he was tapped by the Red Army General Staff, Military Intelligence, Fourth Section, for what was to be his most important and most delicate mission: to head the "illegal network" in the United States.

This was not a snap decision. It was made at a very high level and for reasons the world would not guess until more than a year later. To get a false passport and to lay the groundwork for adequate cover both take time. The preparations began on December 19, 1937, when one Samuel Novick, a naturalized American citizen in the radio and electronics business, wrote to the Immigration and Naturalization Service that Arthur Adams ("a skilled radio engineer") had been working for him in Canada for ten years—a falsehood Novick would attempt to deny under oath many years later. Behind the plan to install Adams in the United States as a resident director was a long-range projection of Joseph Stalin himself. At that time, the Soviets and the Nazis had already put out the first feelers for what would burst on the world as the Hitler-Stalin Pact in the late summer of 1939.

Communist leaders were fully cognizant that this pact would be the signal for a Nazi attack on the West. And Stalin, who always assumed that others would act as he did, took it for granted that this would lead to a diplomatic rupture between the United States and the Soviet Union. Under those circumstances, the entire "legal" apparatus—the Embassy, the consulates, and Amtorg would be forced to shut up shop. The "illegal" apparatus would therefore become Stalin's only way to continue plundering the United States of its industrial techniques—an operation vital to the backword Soviet economy, which was struggling to drag itself back to the position Russia had held in 1913, before World War I and the 1917 Revolution had crippled it. Stalin knew that his overtures to Hitler, though more than reciprocated, would not be consummated in the pact for some time. He could afford to plan carefully.

The Center did not foresee that events beyond its control would compel it to act on a crash basis—to send Arthur Adams to his new assignment ahead of schedule. Those events concerned Whittaker Chambers, like Adams an "illegal," whose battle with his conscience had led him to break with the Soviet underground early in April of 1938. His defection had caught the Communists flat-footed and sent agents throughout the United States diving for cover. Colonel Boris Bykov, resident director of several groups and Chambers' superior, was immediately summoned to Moscow, disgrace, and a bullet in the back of the head. For a brief period, everyone even remotely connected with Chambers was put "on ice,"* and even those who were relatively safe lived in a period of panic. They had no way of knowing that Chambers would remain silent—or that when he spoke up, goaded by the implications of the Hitler-Stalin Pact, his disclosures would be brushed aside by President Roosevelt.

When Arthur Alexandrovitch Adams was given the order to salvage what he could of the demoralized American apparatus, he was already in Canada.

---

* The underground phrase is to "go private."

The dates would so indicate, for there was little over a month between the time that NKVD "disciplinarians" began looking for Chambers and the day that Adams crossed the border. Air travel was rare in those days, and the Center would have been reluctant to catapult Adams from Moscow to Buffalo so rapidly. This would be particularly true in an operation where Stalin was concerned. (In a totalitarian state, there are no excuses for failure.) In any case, Adams had been thoroughly briefed as to the nature of his original assignment. The necessary cover had already been provided and reliable contacts alerted. All of American industry, with its techniques, processes, and know-how—what Stalin lacked after twenty years of revolutionary misman-agement—awaited his plundering fingers.

In a city like New York, a man preserves his anonymity so long as he pays his rent, does not get too friendly with bartenders, and avoids trouble with cab drivers. But a spy, watching the reflections in store windows at all times to see if he is followed, feels that he must establish himself as a solid citizen, as if he were in Paris and had to account for himself to a prying *concièrge*. Adams checked in at the Peter Cooper Hotel and, almost before his bags were un-packed, had given the identification signal to Jacob Aronoff, a lawyer with offices at 165 Broadway. The two men, with Philip Levy, a small businessman who knew only that there was a profit in it somewhere, set up Technological Laboratories, Inc.—a business which was all name and no activity. Years later, Levy complained to a Senate committee that the deals with Adams, Aronoff, and his associates netted him no cash.

There were others on hand to make solid the Adams claim that he was an engineer and a machine designer. Eric Bernay, whose record shop just east of Times Square featured domestic Communist and Soviet music, went into "partnership" with Adams. Bernay was also the head of Keynote Records, whose musical social protest was financed by party funds and at least one Park Avenue angel. This was no surprise, for Bernay had at one time been business manager of the *New Masses*. His contribution was to put Adams on his payroll for seventy-five dollars weekly, a not ungenerous sum in 1938. Adams also used as a base Novick's Electronics, Inc., a company which received six million dollars in defense contracts for secret radar equipment—and a Navy accolade, the coveted "E" for excellence in production. To pad out Adams's income, a Hollywood businessman and secret party member was given $1,875 by Adams. This money was dutifully paid back, seventy-five dollars a week, as "salary." But none of these precautions were really needed. The idea that the Soviet Union indulged in espionage, using the Communist Party as a base, was then being received by most Americans with laughter or indignation. Even during the period of the Hitler-Stalin Pact, it was considered a sign of paranoia to think of the Communists as anything other than overzealous idealists.

The Arthur Adams apparatus, which grew and grew until it included well over one hundred agents, began modestly enough. There was Julius Hei-man, a millionaire businessman. Like a good father, he inculcated his daugh-ter with his ideas and put her to work at the Soviet Embassy. Heiman's mink-lined beliefs included a fierce hatred of the system which had given him his wealth and a fatuous love of the "worker's fatherland." The underground snapped the whip, and Heiman went into the steel business. This gave him a legitimate excuse to run courier errands for the network, particularly to Stockholm, then a leading transfer point for Soviet agents delivering information or taking out instructions.

A touch of glamour which Alfred Hitchcock would have appreciated was furnished by Leon Josephson. His brother Barney "owned" Café Society, a large and pleasantly decorated nightclub on New York's Sheridan Square, which provided some of the best jazz music of the period. While the greatest of hot musicians beat it out on the bandstand to the applause of college boys and jazz buffs, other business was transacted in the back rooms. There was, however, nothing romantic about Leon Josephson. He had earned his wound stripes and hash marks in Stalin's secret service. His associate at one time had been George Mink, one of the NKVD's peripatetic executioners. This sinister man's prime coup had been the ambushing of Ignace Reiss, who had incurred Stalin's displeasure by breaking with the espionage *apparat* and denouncing the Great Dictator as a "murderer." In 1935, an espionage arrest for Josephson ended happily when the Danish police released him.

One Rebecca Victoria Singer Stone was also involved, though her day of glory did not come until Adams was on the run from the FBI and needed willing confederates to help him evade arrest. Victoria Stone ran a jewelry shop on Madison Avenue—it is still in business—which she had set up with funds furnished by Julius Heiman. When the House Un-American Activities Committee questioned her in the late 1940's, her answers were vague and contradictory—and a report to the Congress in 1948 stated that she would be cited for perjury. She never was.

This was the nucleus. Before the apparatus could be worth its salt, Adams needed men and women with roots in the government and industry— the unsuspected *novators*, who were already in a position to deliver the facts, figures, and secrets demanded by the Center in Moscow and designated by the schoolboy term of "tasks." The documents which Igor Gouzenko, file clerk at the Soviet Embassy in Ottawa, turned over to the Royal Canadian Mounted Police show how tidily the Center assigned these tasks and how conscientiously the agents did their homework.

It is popularly believed that a resident director, filling his manpower requirements, turns to the local Communist Party for recruiting suggestions. This is not so. The Center has only contempt for non-Soviet party members. The local parties have done their job when they have enticed idealistic or warped people into membership or the "front" periphery. The selection is done by the Center, which submits a list of candidates to the "Comintern rep"—Moscow's gauleiter—much as Classification in the United States Army will furnish the names of riflemen or typists to the units that need them.

The mission of the resident director is known, of course, in Moscow. And at the disposal of the Center is the largest file in history of possible talent. This is what the NKVD, Red Army Intelligence, the Comintern, and subsidiary espionage groups innocuously call the Central Index. Millions of dossiers—

zapiski—are kept up to date for the use of enterprising recruiters. Every party member, past or present; every fellow traveler; every sympathizer who has put his name to petitions or contributed to party causes; every person who has had dealings, business or social, with officials of Iron Curtain countries—each one has a personnel folder in the acres of filing cabinets kept by Central Index.

Also the subject of Moscow's solicitous interest are foreign politicians who are considered vulnerable, trade unionists active on labor's left bank, intellectuals infected by the more polite forms of the Marxist virus, business-men who put profit above the national interest. The strenuous efforts of Communists in the United States, Canada, and Western Europe to organize "unions" of scientists had but the secondary purpose of mobilizing for agitation. The primary motivation was to search out men and women adept at the white magic of our time, to sound them out, to learn their weaknesses—all for the benefit of that *zapiska* which at the proper moment could provide the name of a strategically placed individual. The system worked when atomic espionage became the Kremlin's major area of interest.

Another myth, that the Soviet espionage apparatus shies away from party members in its recruitment of spies, is also untrue. The Center prefers them. Of course, once one of the faithful has been tapped, he breaks off all connection with the open party, cuts himself off from Communist friends, and may even pose as a critic of the Soviet Union. But even here there are major exceptions. Steve Nelson, a "hero" of the Abraham Lincoln Brigade and the Spanish Civil War, doubled in brass as commissar of California's Alameda County party and as an operative in the atomic spy ring.

The Center will reach out in any direction as it invades a given sector of "capitalist" society. But it prefers the indoctrinated Communist, whose background has been thoroughly investigated, who has been observed by his superiors, who has been tested in a thousand small ways, and whose loyalty to country, family and friends has been thoroughly compromised. Whittaker Chambers was selected for a highly sensitive assignment in 1933 even though he had been an editor of the *Daily Worker,* editor-in-fact of the *New Masses,* and author of a short story widely acclaimed by Moscow as representative of the true Bolshevik spirit and dramatized for agitprop use. And the Center has been vindicated during the four decades of its depredations. Cash-on-the-barrelhead operatives, like our own Francis Gary Powers of U-2 fame, feel no compunction about bowing to the inevitable. But given the army of Communist spies, the number who have defected (or talked when arrested) has been miniscule.

This, as Stalin used to say, is no accident. Every party member has filled out an exhaustive questionnaire giving a host of biographical detail. He is told that this is for the exclusive use of his immediate superiors, but it ends up always at the Central Index, where it is thoroughly studied, then placed in the *zapiska*. The questionnaire is then supplemented by the judgments and evaluations of fellow Communists—and becomes a better guide for psychological analysis than any of the tests devised by our own Central Intelligence Agency. Further light is cast on the "subject" by the comments elicited from him on party associates. One questionnaire issued by the Communist Party USA to its members began with:

DEAR COMRADE:

Below you will find a questionnaire to be used as a guide in writing your biography. Please be advised that the Central Commission wants a detailed and frank statement from you, one that will enable it to know you as well as you know yourself. Please use as much paper as necessary (on one side only) and be assured that this document will be treated in strict confidence and properly safeguarded.

The suggested topics delved not only into the member's background but also into that of his family and friends. It demanded one kind of important information: "Name all your recruits into the party, giving their present whereabouts and functions, as well as their social and occupational background. State whether they are at present in the party and if they dropped out, why." If any of the member's recruits later defected, this would be a warning to the Center. Defection can sometimes have a chain reaction. The Center is also deeply interested in the sexual habits of the people it honors by inclusion in the Central Index. Sexual deviation in a party member, sympathizer, or a likely subject for espionage recruitment is of more than considerable interest to the Center. It is not so much a question of blackmail as of exposing a man's weaknesses. Repeatedly the Center's queries to resident directors, as it seeks to develop outside sources, are directed to information on sex, liquor, and love of money. Agents, in reporting on their "contacts," are asked to give:

Personal positive and negative characteristics:

(a) Inclination to drink, women friends—or good family man;
(b) Lover of good things—or inclination to solitude and quietness;
(c) Influence of wife on actions—or independence in making own decisions;
(d) Circle of acquaintances and brief character sketches of them.

When the Center ran through likely possibilities for the new Adams network, it was armed with its *zapiski*. The validity of its judgments was such that not a single one of the people chosen reported Adams' approach to American security agencies. What little is known about the ring was discovered by the Federal Bureau of Investigation in its ceaseless check on suspected agents. Because the original target was industrial espionage—not involving the federal government—almost nothing is known of who did what to whom by Arthur Alexandrovitch Adams and his agents. When their activity impinged on the military—the ring was successful in stealing American bombsight secrets—more became known.

But forces and events were on the move. In university laboratories, scientists had begun their long battle to penetrate the secret of the atom and to harness their discoveries. A scientific revolution which would eventually bring obsolescence to weapons systems and military strategy was in the making. Agents throughout the West picked up the signal and reported it to the Center. The Kremlin was informed, though in the early stages it showed but small interest. When it became clear that the atom contained within it physical and political forces which could reshape the world, Stalin pricked up his ears. The orders went out for the espionage vacuum cleaner to suck in every fact, every technique. Perhaps by accident, the assignment in the United States to organize the operation which would transmit this new theory and technology fell to Arthur Alexandrovitch Adams, friend of the Lenin who had midwifed an equally earth-shaking revolution.

2 Target: Atomic Know-How

SIMPLICITY is the mother of confusion. In the debate over atomic energy which has raged since Hiroshima, some have claimed that the Soviets knew nothing until Klaus Fuchs and other espionage agents alerted them. Others have argued that the phalanx of atomic spies in the West contributed nothing to the Soviet state of the art. To this latter point, many scientists and intellectuals added a corollary, demonstrating that their logic was in this instance in inverse ratio to their Intelligence Quotient. They insisted that the secrecy demanded by the Manhattan Engineer District and the Atomic Energy Commission "aided" the Soviet advance and "hurt" the United States. And accepting Soviet claims of success, they simultaneously failed to observe that, if true, these achievements had occurred behind a hermetic wall of secrecy.*

The extremes of opinion have oversimplified the facts. In general theory, the Soviets were in the mid-1930s not far behind the Western nations. Russian science, when not tied to a Marxist-Leninist *mystique,* has ranged from adequate to excellent in its theoretical aspects. In the experimental and the practical, however, they have been hindered by the weaknesses of the Soviet economy. This was particularly true in the nuclear field, where great amounts of capital, a highly sophisticated industrial plant, and the willingness to risk time and materials on what may be a dead end in research are required. Soviet science has always moved timidly and taken the safe course. Soviet technology

---

*To this day, Western scientists do not really know if the Soviet Union has been exploding nuclear devices or bombs. Having little knowledge of their atomic weaponry, we assume for safety's sake that they are bombs. Those who chronically assert Soviet superiority also forget that in the "scale of violence" two twenty-megaton bombs are far more effective than one fifty-megaton device such as the U.S.S.R. recently set off in the atmosphere.

has "made do" with what it had at hand, never striking out boldly but relying on the pioneering of the West.*

Until the very late thirties and early forties, Soviet scientists could read all the journals of Western scientists. These were imported by the Soviet Academy of Science and carefully studied. And from them, the Kremlin's scientists could, by theoretical induction, arrive at accurate conclusions. But it was never a question of knowing that atomic fission could release energy in quantities hitherto unknown. (Einstein's theoretical $e=mc^2$ was never classified information.) The question was how to release and harness that energy, how to produce in sufficient quantities the elements necessary to bring this about—and what those elements were—and how to squeeze from the lemon of the Soviet economy sufficient funds to experiment in a field where billions of dollars were merely a down payment.

Given these circumstances, the Kremlin took a calculated risk that it could allow the West to expend the intellectual and financial blood and sweat of harnessing the atom. What was being done in American, Italian, and French laboratories was open to the world until shortly before the outbreak of World War II. And the Soviets always had a friend in the scientific court—Frédéric Joliot-Curie, a French Communist and one of the elite corps of nuclear scientists who could describe and annotate what the West had wrought. When secrecy was demanded—first self-imposed by the scientists themselves and later systematized as atomic energy became a military matter—the Kremlin knew that through the Center in Moscow it could reach out to some of the men involved, thumbing through the *zapiski* of the Great Index for leads and approaches. Aiding the network were the garrulous propensities of the scientific fraternity which to the very end could not quite believe that Big Brother was watching—and sometimes manipulating—them.

The mistake that the men of science made was that they confused ideas with techniques and capabilities. Dr. J. Robert Oppenheimer verged on an understanding of this when he told the Joint Committee on Atomic Energy in 1949: "History time and again shows that we have no monopoly on ideas, but we do better with them than most other countries." The idea of nuclear fission, and ultimately of the bomb, was never a monopoly or a secret. But translating that concept into an acutal device was a monopoly and would have remained so for many years were it not for the wholesale theft of atomic secrets by the Soviets—and the leg up given to their scientists by those of Oppenheimer's colleagues who insisted that the mechanics of the bomb should be fully disclosed to the whole world after Hiroshima and Nagasaki.

In 1933, two years after Dr. Harold Urey and his associates at Columbia had discovered heavy water, one of the first major breakthroughs on the road to nuclear fission and the bomb, the Soviets were still groping in theoretical areas which German, British, and American scientists had long passed. In July of that year, W. A. Sobolov and M. G. Gurevich were announcing a "sensa-

---

* The one Soviet leap forward in rocketry, the development of a powerful booster which gave it a temporary lead in space, was conditioned by an inability to keep pace with the West in miniaturization and transistorization. With far less rocket thrust, the United States has been able to cram many times the number of instruments in far smaller capsules.

tion" in atomic research which our own scientists must have considered quaintly old-fashioned. The "sensation" was duly reported in the English-language *Moscow Daily News:*

"Our discovery is only a preliminary step," Sobolov modestly explained. "It will provide a basis for developing new theories and guiding future research. Science is still far from penetrating the secret of the atom. But once it is grasped, new and undreamed sources of energy will be placed at the command of man.

"One gram of radium, for example, in its disintegration, emits 2 billion calories of energy. So far, however, we have made little progress toward harnessing this reservoir of power. The case with other elements is similar."

At the time Moscow "modestly" boasted of its scientific achievement, Dr. Enrico Fermi was working in Italy with a group of brilliant assistants, including the spy-to-be Bruno Pontecorvo. This group was already well on its way to the discovery of a process for making elements radioactive by bombarding them with slow neutrons—a step of such importance to science (and in time to the Manhattan Engineer District which created the atomic bomb) that the United States government was later forced to pay $300,000 in royalties to the Italian scientists. The "idea" behind the process was in the public domain, but the incentive and know-how of Fermi and his assistants were needed to give it concrete form. The idea for the next great step in atomic exploration was also known to Soviet scientists, but it took two German scientists to make it, and a third German scientist to understand it.

Science had become a kind of detective story in 1938, when Dr. Otto Hahn and Dr. F. Strassmann, two chemists, determined that when uranium is exposed to neutrons under the right conditions, an isotope of barium is created. Not fully comprehending what they had discovered, Hahn wrote to the physicist, Dr. Lise Meitner, whom he had smuggled out of the Third Reich, where she had been persecuted for her Jewish antecedents. From Copenhagen, Dr. Meitner wrote back explaining the significance of the experiment. "She pointed out," Hahn later told Lewis Strauss, the inspiration and financial backer of much early nuclear study, "that what had happened was that we had fissioned the uranium atom. The use of the word 'fission' in that connection, I think, was made for the first time."

As a physicist Dr. Meitner was also able to do the computation necessary to a full comprehension of the experiment. She nailed home mathematically the fact that in splitting the uranium atom, a minute amount of matter had been transformed into tremendous energy. Applying and confirming Einstein's formula, Dr. Meitner reported to Hahn that the energy released (e) equaled the mass of matter (m) times the square of the speed of light (c^2). (Light travels at the rate of 186,000 miles per second.) This discovery, as Lewis Strauss has pointed out, was "more exciting than anything which had occurred in physical science since the discovery of radioactivity by Becquerel forty-two years earlier." The atomic scientist Leo Szilard reported that the Physics Department at Princeton was "like a stirred-up ant heap." Szilard, a Hungarian refugee, had none of the reservations of the "modest" Soviet scientists about the future of nuclear energy. He wrote immediately to Strauss that the new discovery "might lead to a large-scale production of energy and radioactive elements, unfortunately, also perhaps to atomic bombs." His letter is dated January 25, 1939.

From that day on, nuclear research was sicklied over by the morbid cast of this thought. Szilard was not the first man to consider the explosive possibilities of the atom. But he had seen immediately the import of Dr. Meitner's calculations. His ideas spread quickly to others in the scientific community, if only because Szilard sought them out to discuss ways and means to push the work. Among those who shared his confidence—and in time his enthusiasm—were Dr. Edward Teller and Dr. Enrico Fermi. They were top-rank men, respected by their colleagues. (It was only when Teller triumphed over Oppenheimer in 1950 and won President Truman's assent to build the hydrogen bomb that Teller's reputation was assailed by politically minded scientists.)

Henry Adams wrote many years ago that, in scientific research, a "law of acceleration" applies. Knowledge is gained slowly at first, but the progression is geometric, not arithmetical. On February 13, 1939, Szilard was again writing to Strauss that "almost every day" new knowledge became available, forcing him to change his projected course of action. Yet in that same letter, he could prophetically outline what direction academic and government-sponsored nuclear research would take:*

Slow neutrons seem to split a uranium isotope which is present in an abundance of about 1% in uranium. If this isotope could be used for maintaining chain reactions, it would have to be separated from the bulk of uranium. This, no doubt, would be done if necessary, but it might take five or ten years [it took five] before it can be done on a technical scale . . . We would have the task immediately to attack the question of concentrating the rare isotope of uranium.

By February 22, 1939, Szilard and Fermi were hard at work, fairly certain that they could create a chain reaction with U-235, and Szilard was "beginning to give attention" to a process for concentrating this isotope. Early in March, the two scientists had advanced far enough in their experiments to believe that there was a fifty-fifty chance of success, and Strauss had agreed to finance the purchase of a quarter ton of uranium oxide for their use. And now the question of security arose. It is significant in view of the later controversy that the scientists thought of it first and tried to win agreement for some kind of voluntary secrecy. They had a healthy respect for German science. They were also aware, like most people at that time, that war with the Nazis could come at any moment. Being many of them refugees from Hitler or Mussolini, they were dedicated to the idea of keeping their work out of the hands of the Axis Powers. Their American and British colleagues, commendably anti-Nazi, though tending to be myopic in the left eye, concurred. The major leak was Joliot-Curie in France—conceited, selfish, a Communist, and ambitious. He, of

---

* *Lewis L. Strauss*, Men and Decisions (*Doubleday, 1962*).

all the Western scientists, insisted on publishing those results of nuclear research he knew—which were considerable.*

At this point, it was a matter of time, money, and adequate facilities before the bomb became a reality.

Had not war and the MED (Manhattan Engineer District) intervened, it is probable that the first use of nuclear energy would have been in the power plant of a submarine. On March 17, 1939, Enrico Fermi met with the Navy's Technical Division to brief its members on the new discoveries. Fired by his speech, the Naval Research Laboratory immediately began experiments to separate U-235. This laboratory, under Admiral Harold G. Bowen, leaped the decades and was working on the basis of a technical memorandum written by Ross Gunn days after Fermi's talk. It set forth plans for a nuclear reactor which, by providing power for submarine propulsion, would liberate underwater craft from the dangers of surfacing in order to recharge their batteries. It also made a submarine's range almost limitless and removed the need of a rendezvous for refueling with surface vessels. In that memorandum, the atomic submarine was, at least theoretically, born. Under President Roosevelt's directive, however, all nuclear research was assigned to the MED under the crash program that produced the bomb. It was not until the war's end that the United States Navy could resume its work.

The first alert for the Soviet Union that something might perhaps be added to the dimensions of war came in July 1939, when Leo Szilard and Edward Teller visited Albert Einstein, then vacationing at Peconic Bay, Long Island. The scientists engaged in nuclear research had arrived at several conclusions: (1) their own experimental chain reaction had reached a point where further studies could not be privately financed; (2) success in manufacturing an atomic bomb had moved from the realm of possibility to that of probability; and (3) government action was needed to corner the most important source of uranium, the mines in Katanga, then part of the Belgian Congo. Strauss had been urged to intercede with President Roosevelt, but he had wisely absented himself from that felicity by pointing out to the eager scientists that his close association with Herbert Hoover would make him *non grata* at the White House. The intermediary most likely to impress the President, it was decided, would be Einstein.

The Einstein letter to Mr. Roosevelt, dated August 2, 1939, was not delivered until two months later—the President was too occupied by the impending war to see Dr. Alexander Sachs, who had been chosen to present it. But the ideas and urgent requests it made appealed to the Rooseveltian temperament. Not only did he have confidence in Einstein, but the element of the bizarre and innovational made the proposed action precisely the kind of gamble to stimulate and intrigue a man of such far-ranging interests. In fairly short order, President Roosevelt had set up a high-level advisory group made up of

---

* *Under pressure from Joliot-Curie and the British scientist P. M. S. Blackett (later to be quoted approvingly by the Kremlin for his support of its position on international "control" of atomic energy), an important paper by Szilard and Walter H. Zinn,* Instantaneous Emission of Fast Neutrons in the Interaction of Slow Neutrons With Uranium, *was published despite their protests.*

himself, Vice President Henry Wallace, Secretary of War Henry Stimson, Chief of Staff George Catlett Marshall, Dr. Vannevar Bush, and Dr. James B. Conant. The Navy had already begun its researches, but since it was not represented on the policy committee, the assignment for building the plant and creating the bomb fell under the jurisdiction of the Army's Corps of Engineers.

From that point on, everything about the research project was presumably so hush-hush that even mention of atomic energy was kept out of the newspapers. The American public and the Nazis remained thoroughly in ignorance. The same cannot be said of the Communists. Starting in the early 1930s, the Center in Moscow, working through Red Army Intelligence, Four (Industrial) Section, had been systematically placing its operatives in orbit around the great men of science in the West. J. Robert Oppenheimer, not quite out of the top drawer scientifically but a man with great administrative and public relations talents, had by his own admission joined "just about every Communist front" in the country and gave his money and prestige to party causes. Dr. Einstein never quite realized that his incomparable mathematical genius made him no match for the casuistry of those who camped on his doorstep. In the middle echelons there were the naïve to offer cover and the committed to hide behind it.

In the early stages of the atomic project, the Center's interest was routine and precautionary. For many years the conscious agents and their unwitting *novators* had run a vacuum cleaner over the complex of American industry and government, sucking in whatever information came close to the nozzle and dumping it in Moscow. The atomic project became one more area of operations with a not very high priority. According to a former *apparatchik*, moreover, "if in 1942, the Soviets had been handed a complete blueprint of the nuclear process, they wouldn't have been able to do a thing with it. They were too busy preventing disaster on the military front, industry was being transferred helter-skelter to the Urals, and the main question for Stalin was survival. Nevertheless, the Communists knew, because that is their nature, that they would live to fight another day. And so every scrap of information on our atomic progress was important to them—to save them time, to give them a know-how they lacked, and to permit them to catch up quickly once the Nazis had been defeated."

From the start, the apparatus foresaw no great difficulties in plundering the atomic project. In the earlier phases, it was imbedded in an academic community too thoroughly conditioned by the Popular Front and the Spanish Civil War to doubt that the Soviet Union was idealistic, misunderstood, and more sinned against than sinning. The apolitical members of that community tended to judge their colleagues by themselves, and they failed to realize that in the ideological struggle the criteria of science do not apply. The problem of security was further complicated when the entire program was placed in the hands of the Corps of Engineers. For General Groves, who was tapped to head the MED, though justifiably suspicious of Soviet and home-grown Communists, was never really able to understand the language of the scientific club or

comprehend its ingrained bias. In surmounting the tremendous physical obstacles of building the bomb, he did an excellent job. He was a first-class
administrator, and he knew how to avoid the bureaucratic pitfalls of wartime
Washington. But he was a military man dealing with civilian prima donnas
unaccustomed to security restrictions. That he rubbed them the wrong way
was probably inevitable. But that he gave in to their quirks—grudgingly, to be
sure—as if the scientists on the atomic project were not bound by the same
rules of conduct as others involved in the war effort, led to serious trouble.

In justifying his espionage activities, Klaus Fuchs told British security
officers that "General Groves regarded scientists as long-haired eggheads whom
it was necessary to humor because scientists had to produce something which
the Army wanted." This was only part of the story, though it discloses more
about the scientists than it does about General Groves. He considered them a
breed apart, to be accepted on their own terms. He was, moreover, somewhat
dismayed that many of them were "foreigners." Had he been handed an all-
American team, his reaction to their shenanigans about security would have
been different.* But precisely because the scientists were what they were, General Groves sat uncomfortably on the point of his ambivalence—and the Center in Moscow profited thereby.

Colonel John Lansdale Jr., security officer for the MED, had been one of
those who urged more stringent measures to protect the techniques of atomic
production, but he was overruled by General Groves. Years later, he gave his
views of the problem. "I certainly can't overemphasize the extremely frustrat-
ing, almost maddening, let me say, tendency of our more brilliant people to
extend in their own mind their competence and independence of decision in
fields in which they have no competence," he said. "The scientists," he
noted, with some of the old bafflement still in his voice, "believed that their
judgment as to what people needed to know, as to what was security and the
like, was as good or probably better than [that of] others."

The scientists acted on a series of principles. The first of these was that
the military had no sense and no brains—and therefore could be justifiably
ignored; the second that compartmentalization of information, a prime rule of
security, was ridiculous. The directive at Los Alamos, as well as the other MED
installations, made it clear that no man on the project was to know any more
than was absolutely necessary for him to carry out his work. Many of the
scientists were irritated by this violation of their sacred right to hold bull
sessions. As a result, even the technicians were privy to facts which would be
valuable to those whose interest might be suspect. The scientists also had a
tendency to put personal loyalties above security and on a number of critical
occasions withheld derogatory information from the military. Finally, they
refused to believe that communism was anything more than political theory.

---

* In describing his relations with the scientists on the project, Groves complained: "If
I went to a laboratory or on to a plant and failed to speak to somebody who was there or
didn't see him [there was trouble] . . . even at Oak Ridge I had to go back at the expense of
about three hours one day to speak to a superintendent that I had failed to see when I went
through the plant, and when he spoke to me, I had not answered him . . . I say that so you see
why certain people were not removed."

In this, they had support from the very military they deplored. Colonel Lansdale, who considered the 1954 investigation of Dr. Oppenheimer a "manifestation of hysteria" and McCarthyism, described his wartime experiences with the Pentagon brass:

In the War Department I was being subjected to pressure from military superiors, from the White House and from every other place, because I dared to stop the commissioning of a group of fifteen or twenty undoubted Communists. I was being vilified, being reviewed and re-reviewed because of my efforts to get Communists out of the Army and being frustrated by the blind, naive attitudes of Mrs. Roosevelt and those around her in the White House which resulted in serious and extreme damage to this country. . . . I stood up in front of General McNarney, then Deputy Chief of Staff of the Army, and had him tell me that I was ruining people's careers and doing damage to the Army because I stopped the commissioning of the political commissar of the Abraham Lincoln Brigade, and the guy was later commissioned on direct orders from the White House.

To a degree, the same thing was true on the Manhattan Project. Though General Groves was personally anti-Communist, he arrived at the formula that once a man had been attached to the work it would be more dangerous to fire him than to keep him on. The first major security decision dumped in the lap of Groves involved Dr. Oppenheimer, director-in-fact of the preliminary experiments and deeply involved in the project. Few people have questioned Oppenheimer's loyalty. But as a "security risk," he presented a real problem. By his own admission, he had contributed regularly through the party to Communist causes, lent his name to Communist fronts, and attended Communist meetings. His wife numbered among her friends a high-ranking Communist activist and espionage agent. His former mistress, whom he still visited, was a member of the party. This is the bare skeleton of his record. The security people in the MED, moreover, were opposed to granting him clearance, as this colloquy between Colonel Lansdale and Roger Robb, counsel for the Gray Board, which investigated Oppenheimer years later, will attest.

MR. ROBB: Mr. Lansdale, it is true, is it not, that the security officers down the line below you in the Army hierarchy were unanimous in their opposition to the clearance of Dr. Oppenheimer?

MR. LANSDALE: Virtually so, yes. I say virtually so because I cannot precisely now recall that it was unanimous . . . I should think that the answer was yes. Let me add this: That had I been confined to the bare record, I might possibly have reached the same conclusion. In other words, if Dr. Oppenheimer had not been as important as he was, I would certainly have stopped with the record and used my every endeavor to persuade the General [Groves] that Dr. Oppenheimer ought to be dispensed with. However, in view of his importance to the project, we made a tremendous effort to reach a settled conclusion in our own minds. At least I did, and I am sure the General did.

MR. ROBB: You mean if he had not been an important figure you would just have discarded him as a nubbin and gone on to something else?

MR. LANSDALE: Oh, absolutely.

General Groves, however, overruled his own security officers and approved the appointment of Dr. Oppenheimer to the top position in the atom-bomb project. It is a decision he still defends—and the wisdom of it will never be known until the records of the Center in Moscow are opened to public scrutiny. Given the need of success at any cost (and the conviction among scientists that Hitler's much-touted "secret weapon" was the A-bomb), the Groves decision may have been justifiable. But the fact remains that Groves condoned breaches of security by Oppenheimer subsequent to his clearance and brushed aside later reports of his security officers which should have been sufficiently disturbing to cause a review of this decision. Groves stood firm on his original directive that clearance be granted "irrespective of the information you have concerning Dr. Oppenheimer."

The second serious mistake in those early days of the MED was the appointment of Dr. Edward U. Condon, a physicist then employed by Westinghouse, to handle administration and personnel. Groves wanted a man with an industrial background to relieve Oppenheimer of detail and to serve as liaison between the harassed military and the touchy scientists. But from every standpoint, Condon was a dead loss. Colonel Lansdale testified secretly to the House Un-American Activities Committee years later that he considered Condon a security risk. His ambiguous role during and after the war led the Committee to brand him "the weakest link in our atomic security"—a charge which gave him a cachet in certain circles. Though Oppenheimer recommended Condon, Groves has since said that "the responsibility was primarily mine."

From the start, Condon was a troublemaker. He was dissatisfied with the primitive living conditions at Los Alamos and complained because he was not given a big enough house. He had a small coterie of young scientists—many of them members of the Communist cell at the University of California's Radiation Laboratory at Berkeley. And his cantankerous behavior antagonized the military without satisfying the scientists. At the Oppenheimer hearing in 1954, Chairman Gordon Gray asked this question of Groves:

MR. GRAY: You said that Dr. Condon had been unsatisfactory in every respect. Does that include security? Did you have anything in mind on security in that regard, or loyalty?

GENERAL GROVES: I would say not in giving any information, but in setting up. He set up the rules at Los Alamos—at least I always felt that he was the man responsible for the rules—that tended to break down compartmentalization. He was the man who was primarily responsible at Los Alamos for the friction which existed. There would have been friction anyway. But the intensity of the friction that existed between the military officers who were trying to do the administrative operations out there so as to enable the scientists to work at science—Condon was the one who built all that up.

Condon lasted six weeks, then submitted his resignation. It was gratefully accepted, though Groves warned Oppenheimer to get Condon to put his reasons down in writing. To this day, Groves is convinced that Condon wanted out because he did not believe that the bomb could be constructed. But this was not the end of it. Every time a friend of his was being nudged off the project for security reasons, Condon would write a blistering letter to Oppenheimer, or telephone him, protesting the outrage in highly intemperate language. (In the postwar years, when some of these scientists were called to testify, they took the Fifth Amendment, but Condon still considered any investigation of their backgrounds a violation of the Constitution.) Condon, however, was later brought back to the project and placed in charge of certain experiments at Berkeley. That these experiments led to a dead end may have been fortunate. Groves has testified that Condon "just didn't do an honest day's work in our opinion"—running off to Pittsburgh for "his own family convenience."

Just before the first bomb was exploded at Alamogordo in 1945, Groves learned that a group of scientists had been invited to the Soviet Union. His firm rule was that no one connected with the MED should go for fear of an inadvertent leak. Just before the plane was to leave, Groves discovered that Condon had wangled an invitation. Groves objected strenuously and had Condon's passport withdrawn. "He made a terrific battle to go," Groves told the Gray Board. "That battle was so unrealistic and so completely lacking in appreciation of what was the best interest of the United States that you couldn't help but feel that either he was such an utter fool that he could not be trusted, or else that he put his personal desires above those of the welfare of the country." It should be noted that Dr. Oppenheimer shared Groves's distaste for Condon after the Los Alamos fiasco.

Whoever may have been responsible for it, one fact was obvious from the start: the MED leaked like a sieve. There was an unwarranted exchange of information, men were repeatedly kept on despite the protests of the security officers, and compartmentalization was disregarded. The breakdown of security was not restricted to intramural activities. When the atomic pile at Hanford, in Washington, suddenly quit (because of bad experimental techniques at the University of Chicago Metallurgical Laboratory) it became known to people in New York within forty-eight hours—people who were not on the project. Given this situation, it is no wonder that "information was pouring out"—to use Colonel Lansdale's phrase—to the Soviets from the very start. The MED was tailor-made for the Center in Moscow, and it took full advantage of this state of affairs.

3 The Slow Beginning

FROM THE MOMENT that Dr. Einstein wrote to President Roosevelt, the Center in Moscow knew that the United States had embarked on the greatest scientific adventure since the beginning of time. The Kremlin, however, gave the matter little more than passing attention. Stalin, who considered himself a military expert, did not believe that wars were won by physicists. Like the old-line British military men, he thought of combat in terms of massed troops, bayonets, and artillery. Even the German concept of fast-moving *Panzer* units—an application of old calvary tactics to a mechanized age—did not impress him. Not long before World War II broke out, he "liquidated" Marshal Tukhashevky, the greatest strategic mind ever developed by the Soviet Union, and scrapped the in-depth defense, which would have been able to cope with a Nazi onslaught—in favor of heavy troop concentrations at his borders. He also rejected Western concepts of strategic bombing.

If the Americans and the British wanted to play with test tubes, abstruse equations, and "atomic piles"—whatever those may have been—it was all right with Comrade Stalin. He was at peace with Nazi Germany, and a plan for the division of the world, one part Hitlerite and the other part Communist, was safely locked away in the Kremlin vaults. Reports to the Center indicated that even if the Western scientists could effect a controlled chain reaction, the means of applying this knowledge in time to change the course of the war were remote. The possibility of packaging nuclear fission in a bomb was beyond the ken of his own scientists. His intelligence confirmed this in the opinions it received from some physicists in the United States and Britain who were perfectly willing to conduct their experiments at government expense though convinced that the atomic age would be a long time in dawning. One such was Dr. Condon—and he was far from being a voice in the wilderness. Einstein, Szilard, Fermi, Teller, and Oppenheimer—to name but a few of the optimists—disagreed, but Stalin knew better.

This, of course, did not deter the Center from paying attention to the facts and figures it received. Good Intelligence services operate on the pack-rat theory. And any information which the enemy tries to conceal is of interest and significance, and isolated facts which in themselves seem meaningless can often be pieced together to form an important pattern. As a matter of routine, the great Index in Moscow was combed for the names of Western scientists who might be involved in the atomic effort, and trained analysts began a study of the *zapiski* to determine which of them could be approached. How these scientists could be reached, and what their weaknesses might be, was the subject of a careful report to both Red Army Intelligence and the NKVD.

29

In October 1941, the Center began having some long second thoughts. Dr. Klaus Fuchs, a German scientist who had taken refuge from Hitler in England, was active in nuclear developments. In that month, he had reported to the Center that experiments in nuclear fission were moving ahead at a pace few would have previously considered possible—and with Stalin's approval, tentative mobilization of an atomic spy ring was begun. On December 2, 1942, Fermi and a group of his fellow scientists made the breakthrough. In a primitive uranium and graphite pile, built under the stands of the athletic field at the University of Chicago, they succeeded in achieving the first controlled—and sustained—chain reaction. It was now a question of refining the knowledge gained, of making the necessary calculations, and of designing a bomb which was small enough to be carried by the planes of that time. When this information reached Moscow, it could not be ignored. The implications were too clear. Stalin knew that his beleaguered country could not compete in any race for the bomb. But from that day on, the Center gave high priority to the theft of atomic information.

It is one of the major ironies of the great plot that, had Stalin made a forthright demand for inclusion in the atomic project, he would probably have won President Roosevelt's assent. Harry Hopkins might have carried his battle to the White House and, as he usually did in such matters, convinced the President that to refuse would harm the American war effort. (There is no instance on record of a firm United States refusal of a Moscow request once it reached Hopkins.) But the Communist mind tends to be highly suspicious of goals too easily attained. (Walter G. Krivitsky, head of Soviet Intelligence in Western Europe, was promoted to the rank of general for stealing from a safe in the Nazi Foreign Office the text of the Berlin-Rome-Tokyo pact which created the Axis, even though Richard Sorge in Japan had already delivered it to the Center.)

Stalin never quite accepted the extent of American naïveté, good will, and/or submission to Moscow. Marx and Lenin had predicted the openhanded response of the "capitalists" to the Revolution, but Stalin was certain that any friendly gesture from the West was a trap. Having been a bank robber, he elevated theft to a national policy. Instructions were therefore forwarded to the resident director in New York, Arthur Alexandrovitch Adams, and to the "legals" at Amtorg, the Soviet consulate in New York, and its counterpart in San Francisco, to get cracking. The co-ordinator in the early stages was Adams, equipped with some technical knowledge and, as chief of industrial espionage in the United States, having a smattering of contacts in the scientific community.

Adams did not have to seek for recruits. The apparatus was in being, though semidormant. The great Index had already been combed for the dossiers of men considered likely prospects for invitation to the espionage and subversion waltz. At the University of California in Berkeley, the Radiation Laboratory which was to figure in the creation of the bomb had already been infiltrated. The Federation of Architects, Engineers, Chemists, and Technicians—whose local organizer was Marcel Scherer—served as invaluable cover both for Communist activity and for party recruitment. The FAECT had its members at the University of Chicago's Metallurgical Laboratory, which produced the first atomic pile, and at Columbia's SAM laboratory, which developed the gaseous diffusion process for Oak Ridge.*There was a small Communist cell at Berkeley, made up of scientists whose names would figure in later investigations of atomic espionage. Dr. Clarence Hiskey, one of the few caught red-handed (and a "protégé" of Adams) worked at both SAM and the Metallurgical Lab.

(In 1941, the FAECT was thoroughly "interlocked" with the special section of the Communist Party which worked among scientists. Secret minutes of an FAECT meeting early that year indicate how great was the interest in the Radiation Laboratory at Berkeley:

Ray Dunn stated that it would be necessary to obtain complete personnel list of employees with the Radiation Lab, and that this could best be obtained from the personnel office * * * raised an objection to this procedure stating that filching of such a list would probably come to the attention of the FBI and would cause trouble for the FAECT ...

A confidential report on the FAECT, moreover, quoted Scherer as having stated that many FAECT members had been accepted for jobs in the Radiation Laboratory. And, the report continued, "Incidentally, all personnel is directed through Scherer. He has an office on the campus and interviews people all the time ... It is not farfetched to say that all applicants are either members of the FAECT or have to become members before or after they are accepted as employees of the Lab. Scherer told a girl that he would guarantee her a job if she would join the FAECT—a job at the Lab.")

Of considerable significance was the presence in California of Steve Nelson—"hero" of the Spanish Civil War, high-ranking party functionary, and an honor graduate of the Lenin Institute in Moscow, whose curriculum includes techniques of espionage, subversion, guerrilla warfare, and revolution. Nelson had other qualifications. He was a friend of the Oppenheimers, or more precisely of Mrs. Katherine Oppenheimer, whom he had intercepted in Paris as she prepared to go to Spain in 1937 to learn what she could about the death of her Communist husband, Joseph Dallet. It has been reported that Dallet was executed for showing signs of political deviation, a common practice in that sanguinary conflict. Nelson, however, convinced the widow of what may be the truth, that Dallet had died bravely in combat—then sent her back to the United States. From this episode had grown a friendship which persisted after the Mrs. Oppenheimer-to-be drifted out of the Communist Party. This friendship was a windfall for the apparatus. Dr. Oppenheimer's sympathies were well known to the Center, but his importance required that he be handled with the utmost care.

In addition to the scientists already imbedded in the nascent atomic project, there were trained consular officials who could act as the recipients of all information gathered by the agents. In San Francisco, Gregory Kheifets and

* SAM stood for the initials of the laboratory's code name "Substitute Alloy Metals."

Peter Ivanov, both vice consuls, handled this chore. In New York, Pavel Mikhailov, also a vice consul, was of sufficient rank and stature in Soviet Intelligence to be sent to Canada to inspect the operations of the spy ring later exposed by Igor Gouzenko's defection to the West. Adding the Mata Hari touch was Louise Bransten, the blonde and green-eyed heiress to a two-million-dollar fortune, who was on intimate terms with Kheifets. Mrs. Bransten's home was used to entertain important party functionaries and to impress party members or fellow-travelers vital to the party's undertakings. On trips to New York, she would visit Mikhailov, leading security officials to believe that she may have doubled as a courier. When the Los Almos project was begun, the apparatus reached out to less exalted "contacts" such as David Greenglass, who succumbed to the pressure of his sister and brother-in-law, Ethel and Julius Rosenberg. In time, Harry Gold, perhaps the hardest-working agent in the Soviet espionage corps, was taken off industrial spying and assigned to work with Klaus Fuchs.

The over-all boss of the Center's Operation Atom was Vassili Zubilin, Third (later Second) Secretary of the Soviet Embassy in Washington. Zubilin, like Adams, was an old pro, carrying the credentials of both Red Army Intelligence and the NKVD. Particularly beloved because of his part in the assassination of Ignace Reiss in Switzerland, Zubilin held the rank of major general in the secret police. In Europe, he had frequently used the cover name "Peter." In the United States, his *nom d'espionage* was "Cooper."* Zubilin (real name: Zarubin) was familiar with the American scene, having traveled to this country on several occasions between 1934 and 1937, carrying a false passport made out to the name of Edward Joseph Herbert.

Zubilin could not have had much of a life. His wife, Elizabeta, was also an Intelligence agent of some importance, and her job was to keep an eye on him. This may explain his major weakness. In 1953, Lieutenant Colonel Yuri Rastvorov, who broke with the apparatus, told the Senate Internal Security Subcommittee that Zubilin "was fired from the service in 1947 because of alcoholism, and now he is retired, drinking peacefully." Only Zubilin himself or the Pavlovian specialists of the NKVD know whether he drank because he enjoyed it—or to forget the events of his full and jolly life. But alcohol had not dimmed his perceptions or slowed his hand during the four and one-half years that he ruled the apparatus in the United States. The now famous 1945 FBI report to President Truman detailing the ramifications of Soviet espionage in the United States, from Alger Hiss and Harry Dexter White to the atomic ring, recounts one meeting between Zubilin and Steve Nelson in San Francisco. The "source" of the information was a microphone planted in Zubilin's room:

Nelson advised Zubilin that his work on behalf of the apparatus had been predicated upon a note from Moscow which had been brought to him by a courier from New York and that Earl Browder was fully cognizant of the fact that he, Nelson, was engaged in secret work for the Soviets . . .

---

* *The Center in Moscow is not given to irony, but it is interesting that "Peter" and "Cooper" Zubilin's chief agent, Arthur Adams, lived at the Peter Cooper Hotel in New York.*

Nelson also discussed thoroughly with Zubilin what were vaguely described by him as "Russian activities" to distinguish them from the political and propaganda work of the Comintern. In connection with these "Russian activities" he pointed out that a number of the officials of the Communist Party were alarmed by the fact that Soviet representatives would approach party members in California and give them specific assignments, presumably of an espionage nature, and would instruct them to say nothing to their superiors in the party regarding the assignments given them by the Soviets. Nelson suggested to Zubilin that in each important city or state, the Soviets have but one contact who was trustworthy, and to let that man handle the contact with party members who were to be given special assignments by the Soviets.

At the time of this meeting, Nelson complained to Zubilin about the inefficiency of two persons working for the apparatus. (These persons who later were identified through investigation . . . as Getzel Hochberg and Mordecai Rappaport were relieved of their duties and actually transferred to other cities from those in which they had been working—Hochberg from New York to Detroit, and Rappaport from San Francisco Bay area to Los Angeles, Calif.)

Another entry in the report indicates how Arthur Adams transmitted information to Mikhailov in job lots:

Adams is known to be a contact of Pavel Mikhailov, acting Soviet consul general in New York City, who has been identified heretofore to an agent of this Bureau by Igor Gouzenko as the head of an important group of Red Army Intelligence espionage agents. For example, on the night of 25 October 1944, Adams was seen by Bureau agents to leave the residence of Jacob Broaches Aronoff carrying an extremely large and heavy case. Mikhailov drove an automobile up to the curb. Adams carefully put the case in the trunk compartment and drove off with Mikhailov.

But these instances of Soviet activity, and others to be described in later chapters, are hardly necessary to demonstrate the extent and success of Soviet espionage. There is far more concrete proof. When the Soviet Union began to build its atomic installation, its plutonium plant (PRS) was almost identical in size and specifications to "secret" Reactor 305 at Hanford, Washington. (As Admiral Strauss has pointed out, "The odds are astronomical against such a neat series of coincidences.") Comparing the figures, the conclusion is inescapable that Soviet engineers could have walked blindfold through the Hanford plant, so fully informed were they.

	Reactor 305	*Russian PRS*
Power	10 watts	10 watts
Diameter	19 feet	19 feet
Lattice spacing	8½ inches	8 inches
Loading	27 tons uranium	25 tons uranium
Rod diameter	1.4+ inches	1.6 inches

The Soviets were not only able to get the specifications of reactors. One of the messages transmitted by Gouzenko when he was the cipher clerk at the Soviet Embassy in Ottawa gave the exact amount of U-235 being used daily at the Metallurgical Laboratory. Another reported when the first test at Almogordo was held. Greenglass supplied the design of the implosion lens used in the bomb. Fuchs turned over every scrap of information he could lay his hands on—which was a great deal. Donald MacLean, when he was stationed at the British Embassy in Washington, had a permanent pass to the Atomic Energy Commission Headquarters, which allowed him to move in and out alone. Bruno Pontecorvo carried in his head much experimental and theoretical knowledge. The Communist cell at Berkeley was a constant source of information. Dr. Hiskey not only passed on top-secret data about the work at Columbia and the University of Chicago, but helped Arthur Adams in recruitment work.

So up to the minute were Soviet scientists that they even picked up the slang and jargon of the MED and adopted it as their own. A few indiscretions during the postwar period, when Bernard Baruch was attempting to work out United Nations control of nuclear energy with the Soviets, indicated to him— more than all the security reports—that the Communists had stolen the secret and the techniques. In his book *Men and Decisions* Lewis Strauss recounts one anecdote demonstrating this point:

Dr. Charles Allen Thomas, chairman of the board of the Monsanto Chemical Company, who was a key figure in the early years of the Manhattan Project, recalls another of these interesting coincidences. Scientists at that time were intrigued by the ease with which some atoms could stop certain neutrons. "One of them," said Dr. Thomas, "compared the process with the ease of hitting a barn when it presented a broadside target. As a result of this chance remark, the unit of measure for nuclear capture cross-sections became known as the 'barn' and this function of atoms is still measured in 'barns,' just as distance is measured in miles. When we first learned of Soviet nuclear technology some years later, we were surprised to hear *they* were measuring these same cross-sections in terms of 'barns,' even though the closest word to 'barn' in the Russian language is 'bahrahn,' which means mutton . . . I leave it to you to say who has been whose lamb chop," concludes Dr. Thomas. This incident only suggests that there was a fairly free flow of scientific information—in one direction.

Adding to this scientific free flow was Joliot-Curie, later to become head of France's atomic project. (He was fired in 1950 because of his membership in the Communist Party and his participation in a Communist "civil disobedience" campaign among French scientists.) Shortly after the liberation of Paris, MED agents were flown to France to meet with Joliot. Their job was to determine just how far along the Germans were in their own nuclear experiments. He was the man who would know. All during the occupation, he had allowed Nazi scientists to make use of his cyclotron in Paris—working along with them. The fact that the United States and the British were so pressingly curious about what the Germans had achieved in atomic energy was enough of a clue for Joliot-Curie.

Joliot and several German refugee scientists had developed some patents in the nuclear field just before the Nazis captured Paris. The refugee scientists, who had fled to England, freely assigned their rights to the British—but Joliot held out for payment. In November 1944, he began to clamor for his money and insisted that one of these refugee scientists visit him in Paris to discuss the matter. The British agreed, instructing the scientist, Hans von Halban, to give Joliot only the "barest outline" of what was being done in the United States, Canada, and Great Britain. But Joliot was able to pry loose considerably more than that. General Groves, who had not been informed of the Halban trip, assesses the significance of the visit in these terms: "Vital information relating to our research had been disclosed—information that had been developed by Americans with American money and that had been given to the British only in accordance with an agreement [under which they had committed them-selves not to divulge anything to a third country]. It confirmed facts that Joliot might have suspected but which he otherwise could not have known. The information had always been scrupulously regarded as top secret." From this point on, Joliot began throwing his weight about. He demanded full partnership with the United States and Britain in the atomic project—some-thing which war-torn France could not have afforded at the time—and threat-ened to go to the Soviets if he were turned down. It is a fair certainty that he had already confided what he had learned from Halban to one of the Soviet Union's many agents in France.

With Allied security so lax, Communist curiosity so great, and the stakes so high, the wonder is that it took the Soviet Union as long as it did to make and explode its first nuclear device. The exigencies of war and the country's industrial backwardness are in part responsible. So too was the operative Red axiom: There is an American way and a Soviet way in technology—and the Soviet way is to copy the American way. Stalin wanted American money and American know-how to cross every "t" and dot every "i" before he joined the atomic age. The decision was made for him.

On July 16, 1945, the test bomb was exploded at Alamogordo. President Truman and Secretary of State Byrnes were at Potsdam for the Big Three Meeting, and it took several days for the news of this success to reach them.

On July 24, Mr. Truman decided to inform Stalin. Byrnes described the scene in his memoirs:

At the close of the meeting of the Big Three [that afternoon], the President walked around the large circular table to talk to Stalin. After a brief conversation the President rejoined me . . . He said he had told Stalin that, after long experimentation, we had developed a new bomb far more destruc-tive than any other bomb and that we planned to use it very soon unless Japan surrendered. Stalin's only reply was to say that he was glad to hear of the bomb and he hoped we would use it.

Byrnes was surprised at Stalin's "lack of interest" and expected to be questioned at length the following day. Stalin never brought up the subject again. It is indicative of American innocence that Byrnes concluded that "be-cause the Russians kept secret their developments in military weapons, they thought it improper to ask us about ours."

But on July 22—two days before President Truman "broke the news" to

Stalin and not many hours after he himself had learned of the success at Alamogordo—the Center in Moscow cabled to its chief spy in Canada, Colonel Zabotin (cover name, "Grant"):

Take measures to organize acquisition of documentary materials on the atomic bomb!
The technical process, drawings, calculations.

On August 9, 1945, three days after the bomb had been dropped on Hiroshima and even before President Truman had returned from Potsdam, the Center in Moscow received this message from Colonel Zabotin in Ottawa:

Facts given by Alek [Allan Nunn May]: (1) . . . The bomb dropped on Japan was made of uranium 235. It is known that the output of uranium 235 amounts to 400 grams daily at the magnetic separation plant at Clinton [Oak Ridge].

The Center had zeroed in on the project.

4 The Assault on Berkeley

ON MARCH 29, 1943, at 11:15 P.M., the telephone rang at 3720 Grove Street, Oakland, California. Steve Nelson was not at home, but his wife took the call. Dr. Joseph W. Weinberg, a scientist working at the Radiation Laboratory in Berkeley, told her he was very anxious to see Nelson and that it had to be that night.

"He won't be home until late," Mrs. Nelson said, "but if it's important, you can come here and wait for him."

It was not until 1:30 A.M. that Steve Nelson arrived at his house. After a brief greeting, the two men got down to cases. "I have some information for you that may be very useful," Weinberg said. "I can't leave it here because it must be back at the Radiation Laboratory the first thing in the morning. It belongs to someone else, and it's in his handwriting." Then Weinberg proceeded to read aloud, while Nelson took it down—what security agents described as a "complicated formula dealing with the Radiation Laboratory's research into the military use of atomic energy."

Several days later, Nelson made his regular "contact" with Peter Ivanov, nominally the Soviet vice consul in San Francisco but actually one of the agents assigned to the atomic project by the Center in Moscow. The two agents agreed to meet at the "usual place." Late that night, the two men met briefly in the middle of an open field on the grounds of the St. Francis Hospital in San Francisco. Nelson handed Ivanov an envelope. On April 10, 1943, Vassili Zubilin, of the Soviet Embassy and the NKVD, visited Nelson's home. He gave Nelson ten bills of an unknown denomination—payment for an assignment well done. As he counted out the money, Nelson exclaimed: "Jesus, man, you count out money like a banker."

This series of events came at a midpoint in the successful drive by Soviet espionage agents to gather every possible fact, figure, and blueprint of the technical and theoretical process for building the atom bomb. The FBI (and subsequently the Counter-Intelligence Branch of the Ninth Corps area) was either physically present or electronically apprised of the meetings. One FBI agent had crouched behind a bush at the St. Francis Hospital grounds when Nelson handed the envelope to Ivanov. Surveillance of various Communist groups and individuals at Berkeley and in the Bay area had been carried out for some time. San Francisco was an important wartime port, and the Bureau knew that two very active underground groups—one at the University of California and the other in the Bay area—presented a danger. Rich patrons of the party served as hosts to high-ranking functionaries and to likely recruits. The Soviet Consulate in San Francisco served as a point of embarkation for espionage.

The catalogue of those who plunged into underground work—as well as of those who hung their clothes on a hickory limb but did little more than dip their toes in the water—is long, and the significant names will be listed in this account. The very numbers are significant—there was more activity in the Bay area than anywhere else in the United States with the exception of New York and Washington—for the apparatus could count on the temporary Communists and their fellow-traveling friends to supply the leads for professional agents. For the FBI, trying to cover all bases simultaneously, the numbers made countermeasures that much more difficult. When Steve Nelson met with a group of people, was he wearing his espionage or his party-organizer hat? Was it necessary to watch all those who attended? Perhaps more important: If espionage was on the agenda, was it directed to the atomic energy project?

When the MED began setting up its security defense, the FBI had long been on the scene. But the Bureau was under strict instruction not to impinge on the prerogatives of the MED. What MED leads it discovered through its watch on other spies, it was simply to pass on to the proper Army authorities. Before Weinberg paid his visit to Nelson, the FBI had been told by Major General G. V. Strong, head of G-2, to "keep out of our business." Only because of the Bureau's surveillance on the Bay area Communist Party in general— and Steve Nelson in particular—had it been able to "overhear" the conversations which took place at Steve Nelson's house.

For Ninth Corps Counter-Intelligence, the first "hard" indication that the Soviets were interested in the atomic project had come late in 1942. It was discovered then that one George Charles Eltenton, a chemical engineer doing secret research at the Shell Oil Laboratory in California, had been recruited by Vice Consul Peter Ivanov. Eltenton, Soviet-trained and dedicated to the ideology of his teachers, was a close friend of the rich Louise Bransten. Through her, he had been able to meet on a social basis (and to become friendly with) Communist and pro-Communist students and professors at the University of California, and to tap those designated by the Center for espionage work. It was Eltenton's assignment to evaluate them and then to put the question direct: Will you transmit data to us?

Early in 1943, Lieutenant James Sterling Murray, assigned to the MED by Ninth Corps G-2, learned from a confidential informant that a unidentified scientist had turned over secret information on the project to a member of the Communist party in San Francisco. This material was in turn given to Ivanov, taken to the Soviet Embassy in Washington, and sent out of the country by diplomatic pouch. The only name the investigators had as a start in running down the scientist was "Joe." But there were other clues.

"We had certain key things to go by in information from the confidential informant," Murray said. "The informant advised us that this particular scientist had a wife from Wisconsin, that he was very young and just shortly out of college, and that he was working solely in a certain physics field. We were able to go through the personnel records and, by examination, narrow the field down to two or three, one of which was Weinberg. Subsequently we were able to identify him as the man." This identification of "Joe" did not come quickly. The March episode, however, quickened apprehension. G-2 knew that the wall had been breached—and badly. By May 1943, a decision had been made to put a top-drawer man on the job of breaking what was known to be a spy ring. "Joe" had given Steve Nelson more than technical data: the MED timetable and the scope of its experiments.

The man called in was Lieutenant Colonel Boris T. Pash, chief of Counter-Intelligence for the Western Defense Command and the Fourth Army. Pash had been intensively trained in espionage and subversion procedures. The American-born son of the Metropolitan of the Greek Orthodox Catholic Church in this country, he spoke Russian and was not bound by any sentimental preconceptions of communism or the Soviet Union. By pulling together all the information gathered by his own and other security agencies, he discovered the existence at the Berkeley Radiation Laboratory of a tight Communist cell, strategically placed, and operating behind the front of the party-line Federation of Architects, Engineers, Chemists, and Technicians—a CIO "union" with members at all the atomic project installations from coast to coast.

At first it was believed that "Joe" might be a cover name, that behind this name was Giovanni Rossi Lomanitz. Why? Because of Lomanitz's past history. "We were able to procure that," says Pash. "Lomanitz was affiliated with some Communist-front organizations and actually was reported to be a Communist Party member." By the painstaking and systematic process of elimination, which is the only basis for good Counter-Intelligence, Colonel Pash and his men began nailing down the facts. "In our operational work," Pash reported, "we were able to procure a photograph of four men, and I had one of our men working on that photograph to determine the background of the personnel on that photograph." Three of the four men in the picture were Lomanitz, David Bohm, and Max Friedman, all scientists at Berkeley. The fourth was Joseph Weinberg. In the early part of June 1943, Pash was able to report to his superiors that he had succeeded in the first part of his assignment. But this was just the beginning.

"We found out," Pash has said, "that Lomanitz was a member of the Communist Party. From the conversations"—presumably taps had been placed on their telephones—"we had sufficient information to determine that both Weinberg and Bohm were members of the party." Though the evidence against Weinberg seemed the most damning, the consensus of those evaluating it was that Lomanitz was the most dangerous of the agents working with Steve Nelson, the ex-officio chief of the cell at the Radiation Laboratory. The question then was how to get rid of these men without creating a stir among the rest of the scientists. At both the laboratory and Los Alamos, security was anathema—and everything the military did was subject to deep suspicion. The simplest way out was to order cancellation of draft deferments. With General Groves's sanction, steps were taken to put Lomanitz in uniform. He had frequently proclaimed a passionate desire for combat duty, and it was thought that there would be very little kickback if his wish were granted.

As it happened, Groves and Pash miscalculated. Lomanitz had no taste, in the old British Army phrase, for cold steel. Instead of going off to war, Lomanitz set up a tremendous outcry that he was being "framed" for "union activities." He appealed to his draft board to continue his deferment, sought other jobs when the Radiation Laboratory would not intercede in his behalf, and delayed his induction by one month. More important, he wrote to Dr. Edward U. Condon, complaining that he was being railroaded into the Army. He also called on Dr. Oppenheimer at Los Alamos to come to his rescue. Condon wrote to Oppenheimer an "insulting" demand (Oppenheimer's word) that the atomic project fight to keep Lomanitz out of the Army. But Oppenheimer did not feel too insulted to fire off a telegram to an MED official stating that Lomanitz's work was "pre-eminently satisfactory." Though he knew why the induction had been ordered, he added: "Urge you support deferment of Lomanitz or insure by other means his continued availability to the project." (After Lomanitz had been drafted, Oppenheimer continued to seek his assignment to the atomic project.)

Between Lomanitz's notice of induction and his final entry into the Army, however, he found time to participate at least once more in the work of the Communist cell at the Radiation Laboratory. On August 12, 1943, Murray, now a captain and still continuing the physical surveillance of Joseph Weinberg, learned through that most reliable of "confidential informants"—the tapped telephone—that a meeting was to be held at Weinberg's house on Blake Street in Berkeley. Along with two MED investigators, he posted himself in the vicinity of the Weinberg house. His account, told under oath:

At approximately 9 o'clock I observed a man known to me to be Steve Nelson, and a woman known to me to be Bernadette Doyle [one of Nelson's most trusted assistants] approach the Weinberg home and enter therein. After their entry into the Weinberg home I, in the company of agents Harold Zindle and George Rathman, went to the roof of the apartment house which was immediately next door to the Weinberg home, and from an observation post on the roof I was able to look into the second-story apartment of Weinberg.

I noted Weinberg, Steve Nelson, and Bernadette Doyle, in company with at least five other members, some of whom were employed by the Radiation Laboratory, seated around a table in the dining room of the Weinberg apartment . . .

Q: Do you recall the other persons around the table in Weinberg's apartment at this meeting you are describing?

MURRAY: I don't recall all. I know Giovanni Rossi Lomanitz, David Bohm, Irving David Fox, Max Friedman . . . I believe the meeting broke up about 10:15 P.M. . . . I ran down to the street floor again and observed Nelson and Doyle leaving together. They turned east on Blake Street, and I turned east on Blake Street and was immediately in front of them. We proceeded up the street approximately 100 feet in that fashion, at which time I thought, for the purposes of the record, that I should make some face-to-face contact with Mr. Nelson, and so I swung on my heel and started west on Blake Street, and in so doing I touched the shoulder of Nelson. We both immediately pardoned each other, and I continued west on Blake Street.

Q: . . . Were there any FBI agents present, to your knowledge?

MURRAY: To my knowledge, the FBI was surveilling Steve Nelson and Bernadette Doyle until such time as they entered the Weinberg residence.

What the purpose of this meeting may have been is not a matter of public record. The assumption, from the investigative records, is that it was a council of war to determine why Lomanitz had suddenly lost his immunity, what might be done to restore him to the good graces of the MED authorities, and a review of security to protect the cell from further incursions by the FBI and the Army. Certainly no order was given to call a temporary halt to the activities of the cell. According to MED security officials, the flow of information to Steve Nelson and Peter Ivanov continued unabated. One theory holds that the members of the cell convinced Nelson, who, as a trained agent, would have folded the tents for a while, that a frontal attack would be the best strategy. It was no secret that General Groves was anxious to keep the scientists happy. He might agree to drastic action in individual cases, but he could not afford to slow down the work of the project. Though in this case Dr. Ernest Lawrence, head of the Radiation Laboratory, protested vigorously, Lomanitz's blatant Communist record and his zeal for proselytizing could explain the MED's concern. An organized protest was something else again.

On August 26, when Oppenheimer was on a visit to Berkeley from Los Alamos, Weinberg and Bohm decided to make another attempt to "save"

Lomanitz. From the nature of their conversation, it is clear that they were attempting to find out just how much Oppenheimer knew of their work with the apparatus. He brushed aside their accusations that Lomanitz had been "framed" and reassured them that their jobs were safe as long as they lived up to security regulations and desisted from political activity. But he was troubled by the meeting. For one thing, he was responsible for bringing Lomanitz into secret work. Beyond this, he had been in general charge of recruiting scientists, and he had for some time been aware of the ideological commitments of certain individuals at the Radiation Laboratory and at Los Alamos.

That day he dropped in to see Lieutenant Lyall Johnson, security officer at Berkeley, and told him he had some information to give, hinting at espionage. Johnson immediately reported to Colonel Pash, then busily at work trying to plug the information leaks at West Coast atomic installations. Pash knew that Eltenton had, through an intermediary, suggested to one or more people in the MED that they furnish data to the Soviet Union. He suspected that Oppenheimer had been one of those to whom feelers had been put out. Pash also had a surveillance report showing that Oppenheimer had spent the night with his mistress, Jean Tatlock, an on-again-off-again Communist who still maintained her associations with party functionaries. Pash, therefore, assumed that Oppenheimer had come to make a clean breast, and an appointment was arranged for the following day.

At the time, Pash was convinced that Oppenheimer was actively involved in espionage for the Soviets. In fact, on June 29, 1943, he had sent a memorandum to Colonel Lansdale, security officer for the Manhattan Engineer District, stationed at the Pentagon. The information he transmitted came in part from the FBI, in part from his own investigations. Subject of the memorandum was Julius Robert Oppenheimer. It read:

1. Information available to this office indicates that subject may still be connected with the Communist Party . . .

(a) Bernadette Doyle, organizer of the Communist Party in Alameda County, Calif., has referred to subject and his brother, Frank, as being regularly registered within the party.

(b) It is known that the Alameda County branch of the party was concerned over the Communist affiliation of subject and his brother, as it was not considered prudent for this connection to be known in view of the highly secret work on which both are engaged.

2. Result of surveillance on subject, upon arrival in San Francisco on 12 June 1943, indicate further possible Communist Party connections.

(a) Subject met and is alleged to have spent considerable time with one Jean Tatlock, the record of whom is attached.

(b) He attempted to contact by phone and was later thought to have visited a David Hawkins . . . a party member who has contacts with both Bernadette Doyle and Steve Nelson. [Hawkins, whose field was philosophy, was subsequently hired as historian of the Los Alamos project.]

. . . In view of the above there exists [the] possibility that while subject may not be furnishing information to the Communist Party direct, he may be making that information available to his other contacts, who, in turn, may be furnishing or will furnish such information, as it is made available to them by subject, to the Communist Party for transmission to the U.S.S.R.

The memorandum concluded with the recommendation that (1) Oppenheimer be separated from the atomic project or that (2) the Espionage—and riot—Act be read to him in order to let him know that the government would not tolerate any further leaks. It also suggested that Oppenheimer be told that there was a possibility of violence against his person at the hands of Axis agents—an excuse to assign him two bodyguards for the purpose of continuous surveillance.

This was the background of the Pash-Oppenheimer meeting on August 27, 1943. Pash had the office wired for sound, with an officer in the next room recording the conversation—something Oppenheimer was not aware of at the time nor years later, when he first challenged the supension of his security clearance. To Pash's surprise, Oppenheimer launched into a discussion of Lomanitz. The colonel cut him short. "Well, that is not the particular interest I have. It is something a little more—in my opinion, more serious." There was a pause, and Oppenheimer shifted without transition to the Eltenton affair.

(Later Colonel Pash recalled: "It was my definite feeling at the time that the interview Dr. Oppenheimer had with me was the result of Lomanitz's situation. I felt definitely at the time that Dr. Oppenheimer knew or had reason to know that we were investigating or making an investigation which was more thorough than a normal background investigation. It was my opinion that Dr. Oppenheimer wanted to present this information to us for the purpose of relieving any pressure that might be brought on him for further investigation of his personal situation.")

The story Oppenheimer told seemed straightforward. All it lacked was four important names. Three scientists on the atomic project, he said, had been approached by a Professor "X" with the suggestion that they transmit data to him. "X" in turn would pass it on to George Eltenton. It would then be microfilmed by a Soviet official at the consulate in San Francisco and sent to the U.S.S.R. "He told me," Pash testified in 1954, and this was borne out by the recordings, "that two of the men [approached] were down at 'Y,' as we called it, that was Los Alamos, and that one man had either gone or was to go to site 'X,' which, I believe, was Oak Ridge." But Oppenheimer refused flatly to identify the professor or the three scientists.*

Several months later, and only after he had received a flat order from General Groves, Oppenheimer disclosed that Professor Haakon Chevalier, known then only as a vociferous fellow traveler, had been the intermediary who carried Eltenton's message. But before he did, Counter-Intelligence had been feverishly attempting to identify the three scientists and the unidentified professor. A search through personnel records showed that a scientist was, in fact, about to be transferred from Los Alamos to Oak Ridge. On Pash's recommendation to General Groves, the transfer was canceled. This was based on

_____

*For a fuller account of Oppenheimer's disclosures and the extent of Communist infiltration of the atomic project, see Chapter V.

the security principle that though the espionage attempt had failed, the fact that it had been made was in itself suspicious. Obviously, there had been something in his past that made the Center believe he might be susceptible. Again on a security principle, it was important that his field of knowledge not be widened by allowing him to move to another atomic installation.

Identifying Professor "X" was another, and more difficult, matter. On November 22, Counter-Intelligence headquarters in San Francisco reported to Colonel Lansdale the result of their search:

... A record check of all professors and associates at the University of California was made with the Federal Bureau of Investigation and the results thereof contained in a progress report from the office dated 20 October 1943. A continued survey has been made and it is believed that it is entirely possible that the professor might be one of the following. ...

Nine names were listed, with descriptive material. They included Lomanitz, Friedman, Bohm, and Weinberg. After Weinberg's name there was the notation, "has been known to commit at least one espionage act." But Haakon Chevalier's name was not among them. By the time Oppenheimer had broken his vow of silence, the trail was cold. The only tangible result was a recommendation by Counter-Intelligence that "it is not believed that (Oppenheimer) should be taken into the confidence of the Army in matters pertaining to subversive investigations." Eltenton was outside the jurisdiction of the Army, since he worked for the Shell Oil laboratory and was a civilian. Chevalier remained untouched. Weinberg, who had been slated to go to Los Alamos at the recommendation of Oppenheimer, had his orders canceled and remained at the Radiation Laboratory.* When the war ended, Lomanitz returned to his old job at Berkeley. Bohm continued to work for the MED at the University of California until 1946. Only Robert R. Davis, who had joined the Communist Party out of curiosity and on the urging of Lomanitz, was asked to resign—even though his membership had been of very brief duration and probably meaningless.

If any sinister conclusions seem to be implied by this lack of action on the part of the government, they can be quickly dispelled. It was one of the overriding fears of General Groves that anything done to call attention to the atomic project would serve to alert the Nazis. The most public act would be a trial for violation of the Espionage Act—a trial which would have to be conducted under the rules of Anglo-Saxon jurisprudence. This would have broadcast far and wide the fact that the United States was working on the bomb. General Groves had trouble enough keeping the words "atomic energy" and "uranium" out of the papers. And to this extent, he was right: though the Nazis knew of American-British-Canadian interest in atomic research, seized German records show that they never suspected the magnitude of this effort or gave it serious consideration.

---

* On April 26, 1949, Weinberg testified in secret session before the House Un-American Activities Committee and denied all the charges against him. He was indicted for perjury, tried, and acquitted—in part because the committee refused to turn over to the prosecution the transcript of his testimony.

5 Oppenheimer: Room at the Top

AN ACCIDENT OF HISTORY made Dr. J. Robert Oppenheimer ("Oppy" and "Opje" to his friends) the "father" of the A-bomb. As director at Los Alamos, he guided the translation of scientific theory into an overwhelmingly devastating weapon. In another, quieter era, he would have been a kind of intellectual *flâneur*—charming, gently arrogant, quick at ideas, brilliant in conversation, whimsical in the exact sense of the word.* At Los Alamos, he demonstrated that though his scientific genius was definitely second to that of an Enrico Fermi or an Edward Teller, he had a great and extraordinary organizational capacity and the ability to ride herd on the prima donnas of research in nuclear energy.

It was his personal tragedy that this great achievement was compromised by an ideological conflict which went beyond his comprehension. He was charged with the responsibility of safeguarding the awesome contrivance that he created. That others were more lax or more bemused than he may condition the verdict of history. Oppenheimer, however, was the man on the scene. If he stumbled, as the record would seem to indicate, it may be because he allowed his heart to rule his mind and his past to determine his future. Certainly he remains an enigma in any account of the great plot to steal the atomic secret and its complex techniques.

It is not the purpose of this narrative to sit in judgment on his actions or to determine whether or not he was a part of the conspiracy. In a sense, this is an academic question for the keepers of dossiers to answer. By his own admission, he was contributing $150 a month to the party, handing his money to a notorious activist, Isaac Foldoff (Whittaker Chambers knew him as "Volkov"), until he was tapped for the atom-bomb project. That the party and the espionage apparatus in the United States considered him to be "nash" (one of ours) may or may not be significant. On the other hand, that the Atomic Energy Commission's Security Board cast doubt on his probity does not prove its members to be the Devil's kin.

The Center in Moscow could not have cared one way or another. A study of Oppenheimer's *zapiska* indicated that he was a target. Despite his distress over the Finnish war and the Hitler-Stalin Pact, he had remained on good terms with Communist friends and associates. His wife, Katherine, had drifted out of the party. But she still retained considerable affection for Steve Nelson, one of the party's most important functionaries.

Oppenheimer becomes important in any account of atomic espionage

---

* Time *described him as the "thin, angular man with the chill blue eyes."*

because of the men who surrounded him, because of the information he gave MED security officers, and because of the great interest which the apparatus showed in him. Beyond this, it is all conjecture. The facts speak for themselves, but they speak differently to different people.

This, then, is the record:

In any infiltration of the Los Alamos project, the Center knew Oppenheimer would be of prime importance. Counting on past experience in dealing with the scientific mind, it hoped to enlist him. Failing this, it was ready to settle for his benevolent neutrality. There were hands in plenty at the Radiation Laboratory and at other installations connected with the MED to supply the pieces which, when put together, form the jigsaw picture. But in espionage there is always room at the top—and only a laggard apparatus would have ignored so likely a prospect. The first step was to make the approach, direct or flank, which sounds out the prospect. In most cases, this is a delicate operation. The guiding mind of the Zubilin-Adams *apparat*, however, was certain that by using Steve Nelson the risk would be held to a minimum.

In the spring of 1942, Steve Nelson called Katherine Oppenheimer. She already knew that he was in the San Francisco area, this knowledge having come from a friend of hers who had worked in Albacete, headquarters of the International Brigades during the Spanish Civil War. According to Mrs. Oppenheimer, she invited the Nelsons and their baby to a picnic lunch at the Oppenheimer home. It is of some interest that Oppenheimer had not yet been appointed director of Los Alamos. But obviously the apparatus knew that he had from the very start been active in the preliminary work—serving on a committee of scientists under Arthur Compton, doing some of the necessary calculations, and consulting "more or less regularly with the staff of the Radiation Laboratory on the program for the electromagnetic separation of uranium isotopes."

In 1954, Oppenheimer described his meetings with Steve Nelson:

MR. ROBB: You knew he was a Communist Party functionary?

MR. OPPENHEIMER: I knew he was a Communist and an important Communist . . .

Q. At the time Steve Nelson was at your house you had some connection with this project, did you not?

A. Oh, yes.

Q. How many times did Steve Nelson come to your house?

A. I would say several, but I do not know precisely.

Q. Did you ever go to his house?

A. I am not clear. If so, it was only to call for him or something like that . . .

Q. Can you give us any idea how long these visits were?

A. A few hours . . .

Q. Was he a man of any education?

A. No.

Q. What did you talk about?

A. We didn't talk about much. Kitty and he reminisced . . .

Q. Did Nelson tell you what he was doing in California?
A. No. I knew he was connected with the Alameda County Organization (of the Communist Party).
Q. Did Nelson ever ask you what you were doing?
A. No . . . He knew I was a scientist.

The security files tell a different story. If accurate, they are evidence that Nelson carried out his apparatus assignment by asking Oppenheimer to turn over secret information to the Soviet Union. The approach was typical. There was talk about the heroic role of the Red Army and the fact that the Soviet Union was being shut out by the United States from receiving technical data which would help defeat the Nazis. Since the Soviets and the Americans were fighting the same enemies, Oppenheimer would be righting a wrong by giving help to those killing his country's enemies. What Oppenheimer is alleged to have answered is still classified information. But in the charges made against him by the Atomic Energy Commission there is the flat statement that "several years prior to 1945 you had told Steve Nelson that the Army was working on the atomic bomb."

Early in 1943, Oppenheimer was officially appointed director of the Los Alamos project—although it was not until July that, on categorical orders from General Groves, he was given clearance. But before he had taken up his duties, he was visited at his Eagle Hill house by Dr. Haakon Chevalier, a professor at the University of California. During the course of the evening, Chevalier followed Oppenheimer into the kitchen and discussed with him the possibility of turning over secret data to George Charles Eltenton. This information would, in turn, be transmitted to the Soviet Union. Oppenheimer, according to his account, rejected the idea violently. Since then he has given conflicting accounts of this conversation. But one fact he has never challenged—that months passed before he reported it to MED security officers, and this after it became obvious to him that they already knew something about the episode. When he finally talked, he also discussed a group of scientists at Los Alamos and at the Radiation Laboratory who were Communists. He attempted to explain why he had hired some of them and permitted others to be hired.

Oppenheimer had two long meetings with the MED's top security officers, Colonel Pash and Colonel Lansdale, in the course of which he discussed at great length not only the Chevalier-Eltenton incident but also his knowledge of the Communist affiliations of scientists working on the atom-bomb project. These conversations were recorded, and though Oppenheimer subsequently stated that he had been telling a "cock-and-bull story"—and that he had been an "idiot"—the transcripts are perhaps the most revealing documents on the lax security within MED. The *dramatis personae* of Oppenheimer's disclosures included Eltenton, Giovanni Rossi Lomanitz, Oppenheimer's brother Frank, and a number of others at Los Alamos and at the Radiation Laboratory who were Communists and, by Oppenheimer's own criterion, of "divided loyalty."*

---

* *It should be noted that in 1954, under oath, Oppenheimer denied any knowledge of the*

Since those for and against Oppenheimer have taken a passionate view of the events described, the best source seems to be the transcript of the critical conversations, as taken down from the recordings. (Here and there in the recordings, voices overlap or a speaker's words fade, but at no significant points. These breaks are denoted by asterisks in the transcript.) The first meeting, between Colonel Pash and Oppenheimer, took place in the New Classroom Building of the University of California at Berkeley on August 26, 1943. Present was Lieutenant Lyall Johnson, who had been informed the previous day by Oppenheimer of an espionage attempt on the atomic project made some six months earlier. After some preliminary remarks, the talk turned to Giovanni Rossi Lomanitz.

From the transcript:

MR. OPPENHEIMER: What I wanted to tell this fellow (Lomanitz) was that he had been indiscreet. *I know that that's right that he had revealed information.* I know that saying that much might in some cases embarrass him. It doesn't seem to have been capable of embarrassing him—to put it bluntly.

COLONEL PASH: Well, that's not the particular interest I have. It is something more, in my opinion, more serious. Mr. Johnson said there was a possibility that there may be some other groups interested.

O: I think that is true, but *I have no first-hand knowledge that may be, for that reason, useful,* but I think it is true that a man, whose name I never heard, who was attached to the Soviet consul, has indicated indirectly that he was in a position to transmit, without any danger of a leak, or scandal, or anything of that kind, information which they might supply . . . I have been particularly concerned about any indiscretions which took place in circles close enough to be in contact with it . . .

P: Could you give me a little more specific information as to exactly what information you have? You can realize that phase would be to me as interesting, pretty near, as the whole project is to you.

O: Well, I might say that the approaches were always to other people who were troubled by them, and sometimes came and discussed them with me; and that the approaches were always quite indirect so I feel that to give more, perhaps, than one name, would be to implicate people whose attitude was one of bewilderment rather than one of cooperation. I know of no case, and I am fairly sure that in all cases where I have heard of, these contacts would not have yielded a single thing.

That's as far as I can go on that. Now there is one man, whose name was mentioned to me a couple of times—I don't know of my own knowledge that he was involved as an intermediary. It seems, however, not impossible and if you wanted to watch him it might be the appropriate thing to do.

He spent quite a few years in the Soviet Union. He's an English * * * I think he's a chemical engineer. He was—he may not be here now—at the time I was with him here, employed by the Shell development. His name is

Communist affiliations of the people he had so freely discussed with Pash and Lansdale. It was these contradictions which led Thomas Murray, a liberal Democratic member of the Atomic Energy Commission, to file a minority report which held that Openheimer was "disloyal."

Eltenton . . . He has probably been asked to do what he can to provide information. Whether he is successful or not, I do not know. But he talked to a friend of his who is also an acquaintance of one of the men on the project, and that was one of the channels by which this thing went . . .

P: Anything that we may get which would eliminate a lot of research work on our part would necessarily bring to a closer conclusion anything that we are doing . . .

O: I don't know the name of the man attached to the consulate—I think I may have been told or I may not have been told and I have, at least not purposely, but actually forgotten. These incidents occurred of the order of about 5, 6, 7 months ago . . . I have known of two or three cases, and I think two of the men were with me at Los Alamos—they were men who were very closely associated with me.

P: Have they told you that they . . . were contacted for that purpose [divulging information]?

O: For that purpose . . . the form in which it came was that an interview be arranged with this man Eltenton, who had very good contacts with a man from the embassy attached to the consulate who was a very reliable guy (that's his story) and who had a lot of experience in microfilm work, or whatever the hell . . . [Emphasis added.]

Oppenheimer would not budge from his position that it was his "duty not to implicate" those of his colleagues who had been approached or the name of the man who had made the contact. He suggested that Colonel Pash investigate those in the project "who have been generally sympathetic to the Soviets and [are] somehow connected peripherally with the Communist movements in this country"—a designation which applied to him and to a dozen other scientists in the atomic-bomb project. He also informed Pash that the scientists who had been approached "were considering the step, which they would have regarded as thoroughly in line with the policy of this government, just making up for the fact that there were a couple of guys in the State Department who might block such communications." After all, the United States was sharing some of its atomic data with the British. Why not with the Soviet Union? "There is a great deal of feeling about that," Oppenheimer said, "and I don't think that the issues involved here seem to the people (on the project) very different."

Almost in the same breath, Oppenheimer stated that Eltenton might be "dangerous" to the country, yet argued with Pash that the intermediary —Chevalier, though he still did not give the name—was not in his "honest opinion" really involved. To Pash's point that, if three contacts had been made, there might be others that Oppenheimer did not know about, there was an assent—but still no co-operation. Instead, Oppenheimer brought the conversation around to Lomanitz, whose "indiscretions" were already known, and suggested that they might "very well be serious." He suggested that MED plant a man in the Federation of Architects, Engineers, Chemists and Technicians (CIO), of which Lomanitz was a hardworking organizer. And then he offered the usual justification for not worrying about Soviet espionage:

My view about this whole damn thing, of course, is that the information that we are working on is probably known to all the governments that care to find out. The information about what we are doing is probably of no use because it is so damn complicated . . . I do think that the intensity of our effort and our concern with the national investment involved—that is, information which might alter the course of the other governments and I don't think it would have any effect on Russia * * * it might very well have a very big effect on Germany . . . I think they don't need to know the technical details because if they were going to do it, they would do it in a different way. They wouldn't take our methods—they couldn't because of certain geographical differences, so I think the kind of thing that would do the greatest damage would just be the magnitude of the thing.

As it developed, the Soviet Union copied every part of the nuclear project that it was able to. After the Soviet tests of nuclear devices, the same scientists who had claimed that different methods would be used argued that the very similarity "proved" the existence of independent research. Pash, however, was not interested in these theories. Though the FBI was not allowed to aid in maintaining MED security, it had informed General Groves that Peter Ivanov, Soviet vice consul in San Francisco and an important cog in the Zubilin-Adams apparatus, was working closely with Steve Nelson and Eltenton. It had picked up information on the atomic project from these agents and knew that in mid-December 1942, Eltenton had been assigned to find a way to get through to the atomic scientists. Just how much MED security had been able to learn, either independently or from the FBI, becomes apparent from the meeting between Oppenheimer and Colonel Lansdale on September 12, 1943. Again, it was Lansdale's aim to pry loose some names, although his hopes were not high.

COLONEL LANSDALE: I want to say this—and without intent of flattery or complimenting or anything—that you're probably the most intelligent man I ever met and I'm not sold on myself that I kid you sometimes, see? . . . Since your discussion with Colonel Pash I think that the only sensible thing is to be as frank with you as I can . . . We have not been, I might say, asleep at the switch, to a dangerous extent. We did miss some things, but we have known since February that several people were transmitting information about this project to the Soviet government.

DR. OPPENHEIMER: I might say that I have not known that. I knew of this one attempt to obtain information, which was earlier . . .

L: Now, we have taken no action yet except with respect to Lomanitz.

O: Are they people who would be in a position to transmit substantial information?

L: Yes, I'm so informed . . .

O: Well, Lomanitz by virtue of being a theoretical physicist would probably have a rather broad knowledge of the things he is working on . . .

L: All right. Now I'll tell you this: They know, we know they know, about Tennessee [Oak Ridge], about Los Alamos, and Chicago [the Metallurgical Laboratory at the University].

O: And the connection of all that?

L: And the connection. We know that they know that the method, I may state it wrong, that the spectographic method, is being used at Berkeley. They know, of course, the method involved. They know that you would be in a position to start practical production in about six months from, say, February, and that perhaps six months thereafter you would be in a position to go into mass production. Now, you and I know, of course, how accurate these figures are . . . We, of course, have acted. The people who are responsible for this thing have been willing to take some risks in the hope of some return. It is essential that we know the channels of communication. We never had any way of knowing whether we have—whether the ones we know about are—

O: Are the main ones . . .

L: All we know is that [secret data has] gone through several hands to the Soviet government, some through consular channels. And of course they have many means of transmitting information, perhaps you know. The fact that it goes to the consulate today doesn't mean that it's going to the consulate tomorrow. The fact that it goes through Joe Doakes today doesn't mean it's going through him tomorrow. Of course, that's our problem.

O: No, the only thing that it does mean is that an effort is being made to get it . . .

L: We know, for instance, that it is the policy of the Communist Party at this time that when a man goes into the Army his official connections with the party are thereupon *ipso facto* severed.

O: Well, I was told—I was told by a man who came from my * * * a very prominent man who was a member of the Communist Party in the Middle West, that it was the policy of the party there that when a man entered confidential war work he was not supposed to remain a member of the party . . .

L: That severance is not a severance in fact. It's merely to enable the person to state without lying, without perjuring himself, that he is not a member . . .

O: I'm quite clear about—not to pull any punches, my brother has made a severance in fact.

L: Well, we know that he has been a member.

O: Yes . . .

L: I'm quite confident that your brother Frank has no connection with Communists. I'm not so sure about his wife.

O: I'm not sure, either . . . The thing that worried me is that their friends were very left wing, and I think it is not always necessary to call a unit meeting for it to be a pretty good contact.

Then, apologizing for the direct and pertinent questions he was going to ask, Lansdale edged over to the case of the three scientists who had been asked to give information—and to the name of the intermediary for Eltenton.

L: I think we know now who the man that you referred to as approaching the other college project was. I wonder if you feel that you're in a position to tell me.

O: I think it would be wrong . . .

L: How do you know that he hasn't contacted others?

O: I don't. I can't know that. It would seem obvious that he would have . . .

L: When the trail is cold it's stopped, when you have no reason not to suppose . . . that another attempt was made which you didn't hear about because it was successful.

O: Possibly. I am very, very inclined to doubt that it would have gone through this channel.

L: Why?

O: Because I had the feeling that this was a cocktail-party channel . . .

L: Well, people don't usually do things like that at cocktail parties. I know. All the stuff that we've picked up has certainly not been at cocktail parties . . . Now, while I would like to have [the names of the three scientists who were contacted] very much, it's not as essential as that we know the contact. Because . . . we don't know that channel. Now we've got no way of knowing whether the ones that we've picked up or the names that I know of are identical with that man. Now, that's a simple reason why I want that name, and I want to ask you pointblank if you'll give it to me. If you won't, well, no hard feelings.

This request for the name of the intermediary was a recurring theme in the conversation. Lansdale had determined to play it gently with Oppenheimer. He was, after all, responsible to General Groves, who had placed the Los Alamos director in a special kind of category. Lansdale, moreover, was aware that an antagonized Oppenheimer could do the project serious harm. He served as a buffer between the temperamental scientists and the military, yet continued to hold the loyalty of both. Lansdale's technique was to lead Oppenheimer by small steps to a reassessment of his obduracy, and he did so by pointing out that though he could understand a refusal based on "personal loyalty," the intermediary was not a close friend. Oppenheimer conceded this and added, "I'm worried about it a lot," but he still balked. Lansdale pursued the point. Under what circumstances would Oppenheimer talk?

O: If I had any evidence or anything that came to my attention which was indicative that something was transmitted * * *

L: Well, I'm telling you it is. Right today, I can't tell you the last time anything was passed, but I think it was about a week ago.

O: I mean something that there is a reasonable chance is the man whose name I don't want to give you.

Lansdale changed tack:

L: Who do you know on the project in Berkeley who are now . . . or have been members of the Communist Party?

O: I will try to answer that question. The answer will, however, be incomplete. I know for a fact, I know, I learned on my last visit to Berkeley that both Lomanitz and Weinberg were members. I suspected that before, but was not sure. I never had any way of knowing. I will think a minute, there were other people. There was a—I don't know whether she is still employed or was at one time a secretary who was a member.

L: Do you recall her name?

O: Yes. Her name was Jane Muir. I am, of course, not sure she was a member, but I think she was. In the case of my brother it is obvious that I know. In the case of the others, it's just things that pile up, that I look at that way. I'm not saying that I couldn't think of other people. You can raise some names.

Lansdale did: Joseph Weinberg and David Bohm. The two scientists had, not long before, visited Oppenheimer to protest the induction of Rossi Lomanitz by the Army and to determine how deeply they themselves were in trouble. "Did they tell you at this recent meeting that they were members?" Lansdale asked.

O: No. What they told me was the following: That they were afraid that Lomanitz was forced out because he was a member of the union and that their history was also somewhat Red.

L: By "their" you mean the union or Weinberg and Lomanitz?

O: Weinberg and Lomanitz. That they felt that they, as they put it, would also be framed, and they asked my advice as to whether they should leave the project. That is what they came to discuss. I said in my opinion Lomanitz was not being framed, that if they were fulfilling three conditions I thought that they should stay on the project. The conditions were first, that they abided in all strictness to all the security regulations; second, that they had no political activity or contacts of any kind; and third, that they—

L: Now why isn't that—can you tell me the names of anyone at Los Alamos that have been or are now party members?

O: I can't tell you the names of any who are now, but I know that at least Mrs. Serber was a member.* She comes from the Leof family in—

L: The Leof family in Philadelphia.

O: And I know that my wife was a member.

L: That was a long time ago.† Now, do you know? Was Mr. Serber a member

---

*Mr. Robb questioning Dr. Oppenheimer before the Gray Board in 1954:
"Q: You mentioned Mr. and Mrs. Serber yesterday. Did you know them very well?
"A: I did . . .
"Q: Was Mrs. Serber's position one which would be described as highly sensitive?
"A: Yes.
"Q: She had access to a great deal of classified information?
"A: Yes.
"Q: What did you know of her background so far as Communist connections were concerned?
"A: I knew she came of a radical family, the Leof family. I was told and heard in the transcript of my interview with Lansdale that I said she had been a member of the Communist Party. I have no current belief that this is true . . .
"Q: Was Mr. Serber at Los Alamos?
"A: Yes. He certainly was . . . He was head of a group in the theoretical physics division.
"Q: Likewise, I assume, in possession of a great deal of classified information?
"A: Indeed.
"Q: Did you have anything to do with bringing them there?
"A: Oh, yes. I was responsible."

† Oppenheimer, in his formal answer to the Atomic Energy Commission's statement of charges (1954): "In 1943, when I was alleged to have stated that 'I knew several persons then at Los Alamos who had been members of the Communist Party' I knew of only one; she was my

of the party?

O: I think it possible, but I don't know . . .

L: Now, have you yourself ever been a member of the Communist Party?

O: No.

L: You've probably belonged to every front organization on the (West) Coast.

O: Just about.

Then Lansdale gave Oppenheimer another of his gentle prods:

L: Now I have reason to believe that you yourself were felt out, I don't say asked, but felt out to ascertain how you felt about it, passing information, to the party.

This was the crux of the matter, and Oppenheimer must have wondered: first, if Haakon Chevalier had talked to any MED security officers; second, just how much Lansdale knew. He briefly stalled for time. "You have reason?" he asked, seeking an answer to both questions. "I say I have reason to believe," Lansdale answered. "That's as near as I can come to stating it. Am I right or wrong?" Oppenheimer gave the easy, and false, answer. "If it was," he said, "it was so gentle I did not know it." Lansdale pressed. "Do you have anyone who is close to you—no, that's the wrong word—who is an acquaintance of yours, who may have perhaps been a guest in your house, whom you perhaps knew through friends or relatives, who is a member of the Communist Party?" Certainly, Oppenheimer told Lansdale, then offered one name—not Chevalier. At this point, he made what can only be described as an incredible mistake; he began covering up associations which he should have been aware were known to Lansdale. Asked if he knew "a fellow named Rudy Lambert"—Lansdale did not add that he was an important agent of the NKVD—Oppenheimer answered, "I don't know; what does he look like?"

Again, asked if he knew Hannah Peters, he admitted a close friendship and volunteered that her husband was on the project. "How about a fellow named Isaac Folkoff?" Again, Oppenheimer ducked: "I don't know. I knew a Richard Folkoff who was a member of considerable importance."* The prod once more: "How about Haakon Chevalier?" This must have come as a shock, and Oppenheimer said he knew him quite well. "I wouldn't be surprised if he were a member of the party. He is quite a Red," Oppenheimer said.

At the very end of the interview with Lansdale, Oppenheimer suddenly returned to the subject of Hannah and Bernard Peters:

L: Well, is there anything else that you believe you can tell me that could give us any assistance?

O: Let me walk around the room and think.

L: Sure, it's getting warm, isn't it?

---

wife . . . Later, in 1944 or 1945, my brother Frank, who had been cleared for work in Berkeley and at Oak Ridge, came to Los Alamos from Oak Ridge with official approval."
  * Oppenheimer's answer to the AEC statement of charges: "It was probably through Spanish relief efforts that I met Dr. Thomas Addis and Rudy Lambert. As to the latter, our association never became close . . . Addis introduced me to Isaac Folkoff, who was, as Addis indicated, in some way connected with the Communist Party, and told me that Folkoff would from then on get in touch with me when there was need for money. This he did . . ."*

O: I have been thinking about this . . . I should have told you before, but I
have told you since—no, I haven't—but I will tell you now. You said Mrs.
Peters was a member of the Party. I do not know whether her husband is
or not, but I know that he was, in Germany, and that he was actually in
prison there, and I know that he always expressed a very great interest in the
Communists, and I think whether he is a member or not would perhaps
partly depend on whether he was a citizen or whether he was working on a
war job.

Prior to this, however, Oppenheimer had made a statement which—had
it been known in later years—would have served to answer those who
minimized Soviet espionage efforts and argued that they merely resulted in the
collection of valueless gossip. Oppenheimer's views came in answer to this
question: "Let me ask you this. How in your opinion would the Communists
engaged in espionage on this project transmit their information . . . Would it
be necessary for them to pass it in writing?" And Oppenheimer's answer:

"To be effective; it depends," he said. "I mean gossip could be effective,
but it could only be effective on the first sort of thing we talked about, namely,
the extent and purpose and dates of the project and how many people were
involved, where they were involved, and if it were hopeful or not and stuff
something like that. But if it were going to be anything of a technical nature,
well, I won't say it would be impossible but it would be very difficult to find a
method of transmission which would preserve the technical details without
having some of it written down."

Lansdale knew that the Communists employed both methods. The Lans-
dale-Oppenheimer interview, running to more than fourteen thousand words,
merely scratched the surface. It did not deal with the *modus operandi* of the
espionage onslaught. In September 1943, the MED had discovered but a small
outcropping of the Soviet iceberg. The perfidy of Klaus Fuchs was not known.
Neither was the extent of the *apparat's* flank attack from Canada. Lansdale
and Pash were aware of the activities of Giovanni Rossi Lomanitz and Joseph
Weinberg. They had the first worrying intimations of the Arthur Adams apparatus—and of Dr. Clarence Hiskey's complicity at the Metallurgical Laboratory in Chicago. Despite the protestations of those entrusted with security,
however, very little was done. In 1954, Oppenheimer would sketch for the
record, with one telling example, the interlocking nature of the infiltration at
Los Alamos. Under questioning by Gray Board counsel Robb, he also demonstrated that the error was not solely his own:

Q: Doctor, you knew a man named David Hawkins, did you not?
A: Yes . . . I believe we met him and his wife at my brother's at Stanford . . .
Q: You say that you understood that Hawkins had left-wing associations?
A: Yes . . . I understood it in part from the conversations we had and in part
from my brother . . .
Q: When did you have the understanding first?
A: Prior to his coming to Los Alamos.
Q: What were the left-wing associations that you understood he had?

A: Well, my brother was a good enough example.

Q: What others?

A: He and the Morrisons were closely acquainted.

Q: Who are the Morrisons?

A: Phillip Morrison was a student of mine and very far left . . .

Q: Was he a Communist?

A: I think it probable.*

Q: Did you ever make known to anyone that you thought that Phillip Morrison was probably a Communist?

A: No. . . . When he came to Los Alamos, General Groves let me understand that he knew Morrison had what he called a background and I was satisfied that the truth was known about him. . . . He came late and he worked in what was called the bomb physics division. . . . Then after the war he built quite an ingenious new kind of reactor. . . .

Q: What else did you know about Hawkins's left-wing associations? . . .

A: I think he had a brother-in-law of whom I have heard it said that he was a Communist . . .

Q: Did you know that Hawkins was a friend of Louise Bransten?

A: No . . .

Q: Hawkins wrote the manual of security for Los Alamos?

A: I don't remember that, but it would have been likely. I discussed security with him many times. His views and mine were in agreement. . . .

Q: Wasn't Hawkins, in fact, whether he had the title or not, pretty much your administrative assistant?

A: On the matters I have discussed, yes.

Q: Did Hawkins have access to all the secret information on the project at Los Alamos?

A: Most of it, I should think, yes.

Oppenheimer was not certain whether or not he had ever informed General Groves of the Hawkins "background." But when he was asked if he had continued to see Dr. Morrison after the war, he had a direct answer. He and several other scientists had dined with Morrison at the Hotel Brevoort in New York. "This," said Oppenheimer—and there must have been a small glint in his eye—"was during the time when [Morrison] was on a committee appointed by General Groves . . . to consider the international control of atomic energy, and I was on a committee appointed by [Secretary of State] Byrnes to consider the international control of atomic energy. We were, with encouragement as well as approval, doing a little cross-talking to see what ideas there were in the technical group."

---

* Subsequent to his employment on the atomic project, Morrison admitted under oath that he had been a member of the party. So, too, did David Hawkins.

6 Arthur Adams at Work

WHILE THE Berkeley-Los Alamos apparatus was busily probing, recruiting, and stealing, the East Coast network was as assiduously seining the scientific world for the facts and figures of atomic energy. The two spy groups, however, were working in tandem—not independently, as the rule book dictates. Arthur Adams not only had direct contact with operatives such as Steve Nelson, but his own sources were being thoroughly developed. As the MED co-ordinated the work of the SAM laboratory at Columbia University with that of the Metallurgical Laboratory at the University of Chicago, Adams widened his scope. SAM had done the theoretical and preliminary research on the gaseous diffusion process for what became the K-25 plant at Oak Ridge. The Metallurgical Laboratory, later to be known as the Atomic Energy Commission Argonne installation, was the site of the first controlled chain reaction—the birthplace of the knowledge that led to the bomb.

Arthur Alexandrovitch Adams had a willing scientific helper at SAM and in Chicago. He was a brilliant young chemist named Clarence Francis Hiskey (Americanized from "Sczcechowski"), whose blatant Communist activities in his earlier years somehow failed to disturb MED security. Hiskey himself had the devoted assistance of his wife, Marcia Sands Hiskey, who served in an important, though less exalted, capacity. It was not until Hiskey had been off the atomic project for over a year that Army Military Intelligence reported fully on his background. A G-2 report, dated June 5, 1945, stated:

Hiskey was active in Communist movements while attending graduate school at the University [of Wisconsin] . . . Allegedly Marcia, subject's wife, was a Communist. It was reported Hiskey had stated that the present form of government is no good, the Russian government is a model, and that Russia can do no wrong . . . Also remarked that the United States government should look to Russia for leadership. Hiskey reportedly urged radical-minded young men to take ROTC training to provide for possible "penetration of the Communist Party in the armed forces of the United States." In various lectures he discussed communism . . . Investigations conducted in 1942 revealed Hiskey read the Communist publications *Daily Worker* and *In Fact*, and he had definite Communist leaning . . . Hiskey and his wife lived for approximately 2 years with——whose brother was later president of the Young Communist League [cited as subversive by the Attorney General] at the University of Wisconsin.*

---

* *This is, of course, merely an excerpt from the June 5, 1945, G-2 report. It is enough to indicate what MED security should have known when Hiskey was investigated at the time he was brought into the project.*

This bald and awkwardly stated resumé (written in the stilted jargon of Intelligence reports) was but a small part of Hiskey's background. Following his graduate studies at Wisconsin, he had gone to the University of Tennessee in Knoxville, where he was employed as an instructor of chemistry from September 1939 to June of 1941. During this period he was a member-at-large of the Communist Party—occasionally attending meetings of the sizable cell which had infiltrated the TVA. He was of sufficient importance to be invited to the convocations of the all-powerful Central Committee of the Communist Party held two or three times a year to receive political reports and the "line" from Earl Browder and other leaders. Following these meetings, there were a series of "seminars" headed by important party functionaries, in which specific areas of party work were discussed. Hiskey was assigned to the seminar headed by Marcel Scherer, national head of the party's activities among chemists, engineers, and scientists. (He was also the power-behind-throne of the FAECT, the CIO Communist-dominated union of which Lomanitz, Bohm, Hiskey, and others mentioned in this narrative were members.)

In July or August of 1941, Hiskey was a guest at the housewarming of Kenneth May, a party functionary in Berkeley, whose break over communism with his father, Dean Samuel May of the University of California, had brought notoriety to one and considerable embarrassment to the other. The "housewarming" was, in effect, a gathering of the clan, attended by many members of the party cell at Berkeley, officials of the FAECT, and congenial fellow travelers.

During the academic year 1941-42, Hiskey was teaching chemistry at Columbia University. There he became acquainted with Dr. Harold Urey, discoverer of heavy water and one of the nation's most prominent nuclear physicists, who asked him to take part in the highly important, highly secret research being done at the SAM laboratory. Urey would have had no interest, one way or another, in Hiskey's possible connection with the Communist Party. (A decade later, he would be among those defending the atom spies, Ethel and Julius Rosenberg.) But even a superficial check of Hiskey's past should have alerted security officials. It was not until much later that MED security became suspicious. Meanwhile, Hiskey was cleared for access to laboratory files and other secret information.

As a good Communist, Hiskey informed the party of his new assignment. This is standard operating procedure. No matter what the job, party members must let their superiors know of every move, every change in employment, every vacation trip. That he was now doing secret work at SAM was, of course, immediately relayed to Moscow. There is reason to believe that Hiskey had already begun supplying data to the Soviets when, at Knoxville, he had done research in the properties of rhenium. But with the switch to the atomic energy field, he came directly within the province of Arthur Adams. How many meetings between Adams and Hiskey took place is not known. However, in September 1943, when the personnel of SAM were transferred to the Metallurgical Laboratory in Chicago, Hiskey was already under suspicion.

As a result of some of the disclosures made by Dr. Oppenheimer in his various talks with security officials, it was discovered that Kenneth May's "housewarming" at Berkeley in 1941 had been more than social for some of the guests. On the agenda had been a small caucus, at which was held, according to an MED officer, a council of war "in connection with the party's organization of scientists on the campus, at Shell Oil (laboratories), and in other fields at Berkeley." A preliminary investigation by G-2 stated, in a report submitted to the MED on March 10, 1943, that Hiskey was "communistic," and it questioned his discretion and integrity. It was recommended at the time that Hiskey's reserve commission, which he held as a result of college ROTC, be revoked. He was retained at the Metallurgical Laboratory but put under surveillance.

That, in effect, was the end of the ball game for Hiskey. When Adams met him in Chicago's Lincoln Park, two Military Intelligence agents were tailing the scientist. They saw Hiskey give Adams an envelope, and the two men parted, each with a security agent behind him. Adams returned to his hotel room, where it was possible to identify him. Since the Army had no jurisdiction over civilians, the FBI was immediately notified and went into action. From that point on, Adams was the focus of intensive attention from the Bureau. He was "surveilled" to the Chicago-New York train, where one of the FBI men employed an old but effective trick—the briefcase switch. When Adams got off the train, he was carrying a briefcase stuffed with papers; the FBI had his briefcase in custody. The envelope from Hiskey was turned over to Manhattan Project scientists for examination of the contents.

"My God," said one of them, "this is part of the formula for the atom bomb."

"The question," in the words of an MED security officer, "was what to do with Hiskey. We had trouble with scientists when we tried to move one. Someone—I think it was Colonel Lansdale—found in Hiskey's record that he had a second lieutenancy in college in the ROTC. Providentially, he had not given [it] up, and we called the Adjutant General, and we had him call Hiskey to active duty amidst a great furor that we were doing it deliberately, and so on; and we transferred Hiskey, I think to the Canol project, I think, in Canada, where, in the Quartermaster Corps, he counted underwear until that went out of business. He was then transferred to an outfit in the South Pacific" —actually, to Scofield Barracks in Hawaii, where he ran an Army chemical plant and won several commendations for his work. "He was promoted under ordinary steps from lieutenant to captain with no interference from us, and he finally came out of the Army as a captain."

This, however, was only a small part of the story. For as soon as Hiskey learned that he was being called up for active service, he phoned Adams in New York. Adams rushed out to Chicago to get the facts firsthand. He advised Hiskey not to make an issue of his call to Army duty but ordered him to find a replacement who would continue to furnish information to the Zubilin-Adams apparatus. Hiskey agreed, and the following day found him in Cleveland, at the hotel of John Hitchcock Chapin, a chemical engineer and, like Hiskey, a group leader at the Metallurgical Laboratory. (His assignment in Cleveland was "secret even within the project.") Chapin had worked with Hiskey for about a year and a half, both as SAM and Chicago. They were friends, but not very close. According to Chapin, they hobnobbed on the project; that was all. The one interest in common, besides science, was "sympathy" for the Soviet Union. The meeting between Hiskey and Chapin can best be recounted in Chapin's words:

CHAPIN: I was told that Arthur Adams was a Russian agent, and told by Hiskey, that is—

Q: When did he tell you that?

A: . . . It must have been the spring of 1944. Yes.

Q: April 29 or 30, do you know?

A: It could have been . . .

Q: All right, what else did he tell you?

A: I have to think now. He asked me whether I would be willing to meet Arthur Adams at some future date.

Q: What was your reply?

A: After thinking about it awhile, I said, yes, I would be willing to meet him . . .

Q: Why did Hiskey want you to meet Arthur Adams? . . .

A: Well, to the best of my recollection, it would be to discuss whether or not I should hand out any information to Adams on my work.

Q: Was any arrangement made at that time between you and Hiskey for you to meet Adams?

A: No definite arrangement, that is—well, it was arranged that I would meet Adams sometime probably, no date or anything like that.

Q: Did you give Hiskey a key?

A: Yes. I did.

Q: Explain the circumstances. . . .

A: The key would be a means of my knowing if Adams ever did get in touch with me—would be a means for my knowing that that was Arthur Adams, or the man that Hiskey had spoken about. . . . It was an ordinary key. I think it was the key to the basement of our apartment or something else. It was an extra key I had.

Q: But the key was to serve as a so-called instrument of identity, is that right?

A: Yes.

Q: Did you ever see Arthur Adams?

A: . . . Yes. He phoned (in the fall of 1944), and then he came around to our apartment sometime after that, and he did not come into our apartment actually, he came downstairs, and I went out and answered the doorbell, and went down to meet him, and he gave me the key, and I believe I asked him whether he would come up or not, and he did not, and suggested that we meet in a hotel room or something like that . . .

Q: Did you go to the Stevens Hotel?

A: . . . Well, I went when Adams was there in the room that he told me he would be in, and he suggested that he would like to—this again, I am trying to give you the essence of it—I honestly do not remember the details—the essence of it was that he would like to have me give him information on my work.

Q: What did you tell him?

A: I did not agree . . .

Q: How long were you in his room?

A: Oh, I would guess about an hour or so . . .

Q: In declining to furnish him any information, what reason did you give? What was your attitude to him?

A: I do not know . . .

Q: Well, when you left the room of Arthur Adams . . . did you say you would meet him again?

A: I do not think I agreed to meet him again, although he gave me his address . . .

Q: Did you report your conversation with Arthur Adams to any of your superiors or anyone in the project?

A: No. I did not . . .

Q: What happened to the key?

A: The FBI has it, so far as I know . . .

Q: Did you know that Clarence Hiskey was coming to see you in Cleveland?

A: No. I did not.

On one point, Chapin could give no logical answer: Why had he agreed to meet a Soviet agent who was seeking classified information on the atomic bomb? The closest he came to any kind of explanation was in stating that he "must have considered the possibility of co-operating with Adams—at least thought about it." The thought stayed with him for some time. He had agreed with Hiskey that when he went to Chicago, he would write a letter to him, addressed to Marcia Sands Hiskey in New York (Clarence had divorced her and remarried) for forwarding. This letter was to be the signal that he was ready to talk to Arthur Adams. There was one more mystery. Chapin was not a member of the Communist Party, although he had always been outspoken in his praise of the Soviet Union. Yet Hiskey had made a blunt proposal that he meet a Soviet agent and supply him with information. Chapin was sure that Hiskey was simply taking "a terrifically long chance."

Q: Did you meet with Adams in the belief that Russia was our ally at the time?

A: Oh, certainly.

Q: And that you had in the back of your mind that it was not too great a breach of the confidence that was placed in you to divulge information to an ally?

A: That must have been in the back of my mind . . .

Q: Have you had the feeling that the secret of the atom bomb should be internationally shared?

A: Oh, I have made no secret of that. Yes, I have always felt that probably it should.*

---

* *Chapin's explanation that he had pulled away from Adams because he got "cold feet" sounds eminently sensible. But his error in agreeing to see Adams lived to plague him. In 1946,*

Between the time that Hiskey asked Chapin to join the espionage apparatus and the first approach from Adams, G-2 had been busy on its own. On his way to Mineral Wells, Alaska, Hiskey stayed overnight at a United States post in Edmonton, Canada. While he was away from his room, a CIC agent, Charles Clark, searched his gear. Among Hiskey's clothes, Clark found a notebook full of data which General Groves later described as "top secret." From the FBI, G-2 learned that Hiskey was to have met a Soviet courier in Alaska who would pick up the notebook and deliver it to Arthur Adams.

The FBI had also begun to move in on Adams. He was put under a twenty-four-hour surveillance. An agent with technical equipment was stationed in a room next to Adams's at the Peter Cooper Hotel. About a half block away, at another hotel, the FBI set up a headquarters for a sixty-watt broadcasting station to direct the radio cars which maintained surveillance on Adams and his contacts. These contacts were in turn put under surveillance. From this, a diagram of interlocking relationships and activities began to emerge.

Steve Nelson arrived in New York. He was picked up by a Soviet consulate limousine which proceeded to Forty-fifth Street and Eighth Avenue. Adams was waiting at the corner. The two drove around for some thirty minutes, winding along the Central Park driveway and turning and twisting at random through New York City traffic. Then the limousine dropped Nelson and picked up Soviet Vice Consul Pavel Mikhailov. Some time later, after more aimless driving, Adams got out of the car. When Mikhailov stepped out, in front of the Soviet Consulate, he was carrying the briefcase Nelson had brought with him from the West Coast.

As a result of the FBI surveillance, it was noted that Adams frequently visited the jewelry store of Victoria Stone at 510 Madison Avenue and that he spent "about half his time" at her apartment. Microphones were planted in her telephone and in the fireplace of her apartment. Across the street in still another hotel, an agent monitored all conversations. By October 1944, Adams and his associates realized that they were being followed, but it never occurred to them that their phones were tapped—or if it did, they were unable to discover it and therefore felt safe. The surveillance became a kind of private war between the FBI and Adams & Co. Once a man with training knows that he is under surveillance, it is virtually impossible to tail him unnoticed. The briefcase switch, right after the Adams-Hiskey meeting in a Chicago park, could have been interpreted as misadventure by Adams, but he had been too long in the business to accept it as such.

The chase, as one former FBI man on the Adams case has said, became "a personal issue." Within ten to twenty minutes, the tail was spotted. Adams and/or his confederates always took precautions to backtrack. They would step into high-speed elevators and get off on different floors, go down into the subway and back up again, dash from one subway to another—in order to identify anyone who was trailing them. The FBI had strict instructions not to

---

he was asked to give a statement to the FBI, and he did so. (The Bureau knew the story, but wanted it from his lips.) In 1948, he was discharged from a post with a private company doing classified government work when he was denied security clearance.

lose Adams or his confederates. Since it was impossible to take chances, the FBI men had to remain right at the heels of the subject they were following. Adams made the most of this, treating those who tailed him with contempt. Often in backtracking he would come face to face with an FBI agent, would say where he was going, at what time he meant to leave, and where he would go from there.

This heckling once caused Adams some embarrassment. He was on his way, in 1945, to an appointment with Steve Nelson. In order to shake his tail, he walked into the lobby of the Waldorf Astoria, turned a corner, and then doubled back—walking right into the man following him. His mouth open to make a sneering remark, he collided sharply with the FBI agent, lost his balance, and fell, his thick glasses skidding across the lobby. Peering and groping, Adams searched on his hands and knees for the glasses, while people glared at the FBI agent. From that time on, Adams stopped heckling his trailers. Very little was achieved by this surveillance in tracing new contacts. But it served to harass the espionage apparatus, to hamper its movements, and to make its work more difficult. The real leads came from the telephone taps and the hidden microphones in the rooms of Adams, Victoria Stone, and Eric Bernay.

One of the Adams contacts was Dr. Louis Miller, who practiced medicine during the winter on Manhattan's West End Avenue and in the summer from a bungalow in the Rockaways. Probably Miller was Adams's physician. But a check was made of his personal effects, and a number of cablegrams in code from Mrs. Adams in the Soviet Union were found. A search of the papers of another contact turned up the original Immigration and Naturalization file on Barney Josephson, brother of a onetime associate of spy and terrorist George Mink. Victoria Stone's jewelry shop, at which the FBI maintained a stake-out, was particularly rewarding to Bureau agents.

After the shop was closed for business, it would be visited by Julius Heiman—his daughter, Beatrice, worked at the Soviet Embassy in Washington and seemed to commute to New York—and others connected with Adams. Marcia Hiskey had a Post Office box in Brooklyn, at which she received mail addressed to her or simply to her number. At least once a week, and sometimes more frequently, Marcia Hiskey fulfilled her appointed task by delivering the mail to the jewelry shop. The contents of the letters she brought to Adams, it would not be unseemly to suggest, were known to the FBI.

In February of 1945, the special detail on twenty-four-hour surveillance duty realized that it was now a case of the hunter hunted. An FBI agent noticed that he himself was being followed. He stepped into a drugstore and phoned the Bureau's radio center which directed operations from the room near Adams's hotel. Except for the seriousness of the situation, there was something more than a little comic about what ensued. When agents were sent out to tail the newcomer, there was in effect a small procession—with subject under surveillance tailed by an FBI man, he in turn tailed by the mysterious third man who was himself being tailed by still another FBI agent. When the third man peeled off, he was followed to a building on Eighty-second Street off Fifth

Avenue—the school for the children of Soviet diplomatic personnel, from whose upper story Oksana Kasenkina, the little Russian teacher, would leap for freedom after days of imprisonment.

The events of the following early morning offered the explanation for the countersurveillance. At 1 A.M., Adams stepped out of the apartment house where Victoria Stone lived. He was not wearing a hat, and to all appearances was merely taking her dog for a post-midnight stroll. Two FBI agents, standing by their radio car, observed him and followed on foot. Fifth Avenue was deserted, the shops were closed, and there seemed little likelihood that Adams could elude them. Then Adams did what any trained operative would have done. He waited until a late-cruising taxicab had almost drawn up to him, stepped into the middle of the street to flag it down, dropped the dog's leash, and hopped in—a clean escape. Against a move such as this, there is no checkmate. By the time the two FBI agents had dashed to their car, the cab had turned a corner and was gone.

Had Adams slipped away to rendezvous with another *apparatchik?* On the face of it, this did not seem likely. It became clear then that the apparatus had set up the countersurveillance the day before to draw attention from Adams, that he had been ordered to submerge—probably to surface elsewhere in the country where he was not known. This was bad news for the FBI, and it sprang into immediate action. Four hundred agents were routed out of bed or pulled from other assignments in an hour's time. They were posted at his hotel, Victoria Stone's apartment and jewelry shop, every place he had visited in his espionage peregrinations. But he could not be found. At FBI offices throughout the country, the teletypes began to clatter with descriptions of Adams. Railroad stations and bus terminals in the major cities were watched.

The system worked. When Adams and his associate, Eric Bernay, got off the train in Chicago, they knew that once more their trail had been picked up. Two FBI agents were waiting at the gates, and the surveillance was re-established. Perhaps resignedly, Adams continued his westward trek, while Bernay returned to New York. His first act was to call Victoria Stone to tell her that the strategic retreat had failed. Bernay reported that Adams had phoned him a few minutes after eluding the FBI. In his own apartment, Bernay had a suitcase packed with Adams's belongings and had met him at Grand Central Station. In thirty minutes, they were on board a train.*

Anger in his voice, Bernay said to Victoria Stone, "The goddam FBI picked him up at the station."

Adams tried to break free in Denver, failed, and moved on to Portland, Oregon. It was apparent then that Adams would attempt to leave the country. Normal procedure would have been to arrest him for espionage. But the Bureau in Washington could not get approval from either the Attorney General or the State Department. The FBI was given strict orders not to let him get away, but arrest was forbidden unless he boarded a ship. (The FBI men working on the case secretly hoped that he would cross over into Canada.

Bernay has admitted his part in the night's adventure but maintained that he had no idea what Adams was up to or that he was an espionage agent.

There, the Royal Canadian Mounted Police would, they knew, act swiftly.) Even then, the charge was not to be espionage but violation of the immigration statutes or the Selective Service Act.

When Adams arrived in Portland, his welcoming committee consisted of practically the entire FBI contingent. He went directly from the station to the docks, where a Soviet freighter was tied up. Agents from the Portland office were there ahead of him, forming a cordon around the gangplank. Adams stepped out of the cab and approached to within ten feet of dockside. Then he spun on his heel, walking quickly away. Another cab took him uptown to a small movie house. He watched the film for about two hours and returned to the station. Back in New York, the cat-and-mouse game began all over again. Thousands of man hours and dollars were being spent, the Adams apparatus was fully alerted, and the Bureau knew that it was a matter of time before he eluded surveillance again. Urgent representations were made to the State Department for permission to make an arrest. But this was never forthcoming.

Eventually, Arthur Alexandrovitch Adams slipped away—this time with intent to flee the country. It required only a few minutes of headway for him to hide aboard a Soviet freighter in New York. He was never seen again in the free world—and it is rumored that for his successful theft of American military and scientific secrets, he was awarded a bullet in the back of the head. By Soviet standards, he had bungled. Like Hollywood, the Center judges its stars by their last picture.

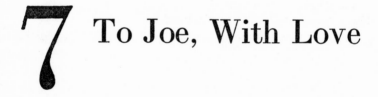

7 To Joe, With Love

IN THE SPRING OF 1949, a former Air Corps major heard a radio broadcast about a few grams of uranium which had disappeared from the Argonne Laboratory, an Atomic Energy Commission installation in Chicago. The United States Senate, in all its majesty, was embroiled in an investigation of what was either theft or carelessness. George Racey Jordan, the ex-major, contemplated the irony of this excitement. "If they're looking for uranium," he told a friend, "I can tell them about a thousand pounds that got away." As liaison officer, working closely with the Soviet Purchasing Commission at the air depot in Great Falls, Montana, he had seen far more than the passage to Russia of uranium during the years that Stalin was our "ally" and his every request tantamount to law. Major Jordan was not a professional soldier,

though he had served as a flier in World War I with Captain Eddie Ricken-
backer, but he followed orders.

His casual remark, however, set off a small war which filled newspaper
columns and involved the House Un-American Activities Committee before he
was vindicated. For it was repeated, along with his brief explanatory statements, to Senator Styles Bridges, a power in the Republican Party. Jordan was
invited to visit Senator Bridges. He told his story in greater detail. "Are you
certain you saw uranium?" Bridges asked. "Yes, sir," Jordan answered. "Could
you be certain enough to testify?" Bridges pressed. Jordan was. "I will think
it over for a few days and you will hear from me," Bridges told him.

Jordan heard instead from the radio commentator, Fulton Lewis, Jr. He
repeated his story to Lewis who immediately reported it to the FBI. Special
agents appeared at Jordan's house and at his office. They questioned him at
length and photostated his diary and all other corroborative evidence. When,
after many weeks, their investigation was concluded, Jordan appeared on the
Lewis nightly broadcast and once more, interrupted only by questions, told of
the wholesale movement of classified documents and war-precious materials to
the Soviet Union via the Army's United Nations Depot at Great Falls.

The reaction was immediate: Public clamor for a thorough investigation
and angry protests from Democrats still smarting from the Hiss case disclosures. Since at least one important New Deal figure had been mentioned, it
was charged that Jordan was "in the pay of the Republican Party," that he was
a publicity-seeker attempting to capitalize on the national concern over Communist espionage and subversion, and that he had invented his story out of
whole cloth. So, as it must to men who speak up on the Communist issue,
Major Jordan was subpoenaed by the House Un-American Activities Committee. When he took the witness stand on December 5, 1949, the mixture was not
as before. The Democratic members arranged to be the only ones present, and
their attitudes ranged from dubiety to the outright hostility of Representative
Francis E. Walter.

The thrust of the investigation went to two points in Jordan's account:
(1) Had shipments of uranium compounds been shipped to the Soviet Union
at a time when the Manhattan Engineer District was seeking desperately to
corner all supplies, and (2) had Harry Hopkins, the man closest to President
Roosevelt, helped to expedite these shipments? The committee's irritation at
Major Jordan should have been tempered by the witness who preceded him in
the hearings—senior investigator Louis J. Russell. Reading from a long statement prepared by the State Department, Russell verified the fact that several
shipments of uranium salts had indeed been shipped to the U.S.S.R., consigned to Colonel A. N. Kotikov, the Red Army officer who worked with
Jordan at Great Falls. Also consigned to Colonel Kotikov were one thousand
grams of heavy water, a rare and precious factor in early nuclear-fission experiments. Not immediately apparent was that at least two of these shipments had
been obtained by subterfuge. Had the committee rested there, the interest in
Jordan would have languished. It was only due to the earnest efforts of committee counsel Frank S. Tavenner to elicit the full story and the political

determination of the majority members to blow Jordan out of the water that a full disclosure followed.

From the start, it was clear that during his period of service as a World War II "retread," Jordan had harbored no ill will toward the Russians but had in fact enjoyed very friendly relations with them. What had disturbed him were the irregularities at Great Falls, the manner in which standard operating procedure was ignored, and the general lack of ordinary security measures.

Jordan told of his early assignment to an East Coast port of embarkation, expediting the movement of planes by ship to the Soviet Union. The attrition of submarine warfare, in which two-thirds of a Murmansk-bound convoy would often be sunk, forced the Lend-Lease Administration to seek other means of getting American planes to the Russian fighting fronts. A route was worked out by the Air Force to keep the planes moving. They were flown by USAAF pilots to Great Falls, winterized for operational use in sub-zero weather, and flown to Alaska where Soviet pilots took over for the long flight over Siberia to European Russia. Somewhere along the line, a decision was made to carry freight in the bombers—and this was where the trouble began.

It was Jordan's job to inspect the planes when they were ready to take off for Alaska and to give them clearance. At first, he kept notes of his observations on backs of old envelopes. From time to time, he copied these notes on sheets of paper. By 1944, his concern was such that he began to keep a detailed diary, including the names of all Soviet personnel who passed through Great Falls—incoming or outbound. His account of these experiences, as told to the committee, was the foundation from which Tavenner painstakingly drew a picture of Soviet deceit: *

"The air-freight movement was getting heavier, and in 1943 important Russian people used to go through with five or six suitcases," Jordan said. "I didn't stop them at that time because I thought maybe it was legitimate. But when they started sending the suitcases without people, I got interested, and sending fifty suitcases with armed couriers didn't seem proper and didn't have diplomatic immunity so far as I could see. I let the first two or three batches go through, and inquired of the State Department and the War Department whether the bags had diplomatic immunity. I couldn't get an answer from the State Department, but I did out of the War Department, and they said I was to be helpful to the Russians in every way."

Jordan also complained to his superior officer about this steady stream of suitcases—neither Lend-Lease nor diplomatic mail—which was being funneled through Great Falls. According to the notations in his diary, he also made a trip to Washington in order to get some clarification of his duties. As a result, he said, Lieutenant Colonel Robert S. Dahm of the Inspector General's office flew out to the Lend-Lease base on January 25, 1944 to determine what was going on. Jordan testified that on March 3, a team of ten inspectors arrived at Great Falls, spending two weeks gathering information. On April 7, Major

---

Jordan slipped on one point. Although most details of his story were eventually corroborated, he got his time sequence wrong and placed certain acts in 1944 when, in fact, they had occurred in 1943.

Fred A. Farrar, an air inspector, also came to see for himself. Major Jordan repeated his story, then took the inspector to see the hangars and to meet Colonel Kotikov, who was beginning to show signs of annoyance at this sudden interest. The military expressed concern, but, according to Jordan, the State Department showed open hostility to his "interference."

> I went to Washington on that trip and walked up and down the corridors of the State Department trying to find someone who would tell me they [the Soviet couriers] had diplomatic immunity. I was passed from one room to another. The impression I got from the State Department was that I was being too officious, and I would be better off if I helped expedite the movement . . . I saw a John Hazard and he told me everything was known in Washington and that they understood thoroughly what was going on, and there wasn't anything for me to worry about, that I should help the Russians all I could.

Q: Tell us your experience with the suitcases? . . .

A: A notation in my diary says Colonel Pavel Berizine and Colonel Yakiv came through with a large number (early in 1944) . . . I could always tell when suitcases were going to arrive because one of the cargo planes would be put on the line and left unloaded, and the mechanics would tell me the Russians had told them to leave a plane empty for a very special assignment.

Jordan was also alerted by a sudden burst of generosity on the part of the Soviet officers:

> The Russians are always very close with their money. They don't spend anything they don't have to. I used to have to pick up their checks at the Officers' Club where I ate with them.
>
> This night the Russians, much to my surprise, invited me to Great Falls for a chicken dinner. There was a lot of vodka . . . It happened I didn't drink. They suggested a toast to Stalin, Molotov, Roosevelt, and everybody else. I was suspicious, but I had left word at the control tower if a plane came in to call me at the restaurant, and a call came there. And I went to the field, and two armed Russian guards were standing over the suitcases. One of them tried to keep me out of the plane.
>
> The suitcases were black, cheap patent leather, with white rope sash cord tied around them and gobs of red sealing wax over the knots. They screamed diplomatic immunity, and I said, "That doesn't look diplomatic to me." I ripped the cords off and opened about one-third of them. I had one of our own guards stand with a rifle on his shoulder so they would know I had a little protection.

It was twenty degrees below zero—"cold enough for the fillings to drop out of your teeth"—as Jordan began to examine the contents of the suitcases by the plane's overhead lighting and with the aid of a flashlight. His inspection was fairly sketchy. Frequently he opened a suitcase, got a general idea of its contents, and made a brief notation on the back of an envelope. (When he later transcribed these to a sheet of paper, he included some additional observations that were still fresh in his memory.) Jordan worked as rapidly as he could, knowing that the Russian officers might arrive from the town and interrupt him.*

Jordan's documentary evidence was subjected to chemcial analysis and, by age tests of the ink and paper, proved to have been written at the time he claimed. In the notation of what he saw and read when searching the Soviet suitcases were technical terms used by atomic scientists and then still secret to all but a few Americans. These were convincing points, for those who sought to discount the Jordan story had hinted that his lists and diaries were forgeries. It is also doubtful that he would have been familiar with the names of unpublicized State Department officials like Alger Hiss and Assistant Secretary of State Francis Sayre. Here is what he set down:

> Always just 50 black suitcases each load with 2 or 3 couriers—usually 3 weeks apart. Papers always cut close . . . Tass folders—Amtorg—Panama Canal Commission maps—Oak Ridge—memos from Sayre & Hiss & others—State Dep't. letters—films—reports—"secret" cut off—large folders on machine tools, electric tools & concrete data—furnaces—White House memo from H.H. about "hell of a time getting these away from Groves"—bomb powder [the Soviet term for uranium salts]—Donets—Duban—Siberian development—oil machinery maps—blast furnaces—memos from State, Agriculture, Commerce —thousands of catalogues and dry-looking scientific data . . . tremendous folders of shipping data.
>
> Another load of suitcases—Aberdeen Proving Grounds—folders from Mexico City, Buenos Aires, Cuba—Sealed envelopes from Lomakin [a Soviet consul in New York who was later declared *persona non grata*]—Maps of U.S. auto companies marked strangely . . .
>
> Look up words on memos & maps labeled Oak Ridge—Manhattan Engineering Dep't or District I think it was—Uranium 92—neutron—proton and deuteron—isotope—energy produced by fission or splitting—look up cyclotron —Map of walls 5 feet thick of lead and water to control flying neutrons. Heavy water hydrogen or deuterons.

Q: Did you know who Groves was?

A: No sir. I do now . . .

Q: To whom was this note addressed?

A: I have been asked that question before, and it is very difficult for me to remember because I didn't really attach much importance to it; but I would like to tell you that something else happened that makes me think I know. I remember two or three days later asking Colonel Kotikov who a Mr. Mikoyan was . . . Colonel Kotikov told me he was one of the three most important men in Russia. I am sure I asked Colonel Kotikov who Mikoyan was because I had seen the name and was trying to be cagey with him. I had never heard the name before.

---

* *Among the contents of the suitcases were a good many catalogues. He examined some of them fairly closely. Years later, he was shown Soviet catalogues. They were, as well as he could remember, identical except that the American descriptions had been translated into Russian. Since then, expert comparisons have been made of United States and Soviet industrial*

Jordan recalled that in the suitcase with State Department papers, the folder marked "From Hiss" contained what seemed to be reports from the chief of the United States military mission in Moscow. "They had been sent through channels to Washington to the State Department, and somebody in the State Department had evidently photostated them and was sending them back," he said. "At the time, you must remember, I thought this material must be going through under authority, and I had no idea there was anything improper." But he also remembered that the thought ran through his mind: "This is something of a dirty trick to play on the chief of the military mission."

While Jordan was opening and examining suitcases, taking a hurried look at United States road maps on which the names of major industrial plants were written and puzzling over a very large blueprint marked "Oak Ridge," Colonel Kotikov stormed into the cabin of the plane demanding to know by what authority Jordan was perpetrating this outrage. "I will have you removed," he shouted. Jordan opened two or three more suitcases, explaining that he was doing his duty, that it was his job to inspect all cargo that went through the Lend-Lease base. Dismissing his rifle-at-the-ready guard, he walked to the barracks with Kotikov, who was now showing some nervousness, at his side asking whether the shipment would be held up and what Jordan intended to do. Where Kotikov had been threatening before, he was now placating. The shipment did go through, and if Kotikov reported the incident to the Embassy in Washington, no word was said either to the State Department, the War Department, or the Lend-Lease Administration.

The black suitcases, crammed with printed matter and documents, continued to go through. If planes were available, the shipment would go out immediately. From time to time, however, the suitcases were stored in a warehouse near the airfield. One courier would spread a blanket over them and sleep on it while another would stand guard. No such care was ever taken with ordinary shipments—in fact, the Soviet attitude was more cavalier than not about material shipped under Lend-Lease.

The majority members of the committee, particularly Representative Walter, seemed to have other fish to fry. Despite the testimony of their own investigator, they were out to prove that no uranium had been sent to the Soviet Union. They were further determined to show that the "H.H." who signed the White House note was not, and could not have been, Harry Hopkins. The two points were interlinked. For it was Jordan's testimony that whenever Colonel Kotikov wanted something done, he always threatened to take it to Hopkins, the Lend-Lease administrator in the early days of the war. At the Great Falls base, with many tons of equipment piling up for transshipment, there were always questions of priority. If there were any delays, Colonel Kotikov would call the Embassy in Washington and then put Jordan on the phone. Jordan would then get instructions from someone like General Piskounov or First Secretary Gromov, later discovered to be a high-ranking

catalogues. They simply reproduced drawings and photos of the equipment in the earlier American version, passing them off as Russian. This observation has since been fully documented by Lloyd Mallan and others who made an intensive study of this practice.

member of the NKVD. At one point, when there was a shortage of American fliers to pilot the planes to Alaska, Kotikov appealed to Hopkins, and almost immediately they began to pour in from air bases all around the United States.

"In one of the telephone calls," Jordan said, "Colonel Kotikov said that the Embassy had something very important to do with bomb powder, and would I expedite this particular shipment." Kotikov, whose desk was next to Jordan's, kept a zealously watched folder marked "Experimental Chemicals," and from it he had extracted a sheet of paper to which he referred in this conversation with the Embassy.

JORDAN: I saw the word "uranium," and what he called "bomb powder" was actually uranium. He had it marked "uranium." I did not know what uranium meant and had no inkling at the time it would ever be important. I just knew that that particular shipment I had to expedite. The first shipment of uranium that was expected came from Denver.

Q: What was the approximate date?

A: I can't tell you that. I remember 420 pounds came from a firm in Denver.

Q: Do you remember the name of the firm?

A: I would like to keep my memory and what I now know separate. I know now the name of the firm and everything else, but I didn't know it at the time.

At this point, Representative Walter began boring in:

Q: Did you make a note in your diary of the shipment of uranium?

A: No, because it was not important to me.

Q: Was the shipment made about the time you were making entries in your diary, that is sometime in 1944?

A: Undoubtedly. We made thirteen copies of everything. I am sure the War Department can find one of them.

Q: I am talking about this shipment of uranium. Was that made in 1944?

A: Sir, I don't know.

Q: The reason I say 1944 is because that was when you were making the entries in your diary.

A: I didn't put in my diary the reports to the War Department. We covered many, many details in our reports to the War Department . . .

Q: I am directing your attention to the shipment of uranium. Did you make a note of that in your diary?

A: No, I never made any such note.

It was the second shipment—one of one thousand pounds of uranium, seemingly involving Harry Hopkins—that upset the majority members.

JORDAN: We had a 1,200-pound shipment that went through from Canada. That is the one Mr. Hopkins mentioned to me and said to expedite it and not mention it to my superiors . . .

Q: You say you talked to Mr. Hopkins on the telephone about this particular shipment?

A: The Russian told me there was a special shipment being handled in a very special way . . . and I got on the phone. When I got on the phone, he said,

"Mr. Hopkins speaking" and asked if I had gotten the pilots I had asked for. I said I had. He said, "There is a certain shipment Colonel Kotikov will point out to you, and keep this very quiet."

Q: Mr. Hopkins said that?

A: Yes.

Q: When was that?

A: Two or three weeks before the shipment came through . . .

Q: How often did Mr. Hopkins call you?

A: That was the only time . . .

Q: How did you know it was Mr. Hopkins?

A: The Russian, Colonel Kotikov, told me it was Mr. Hopkins.

Q: But you personally did not know if it was Mr. Hopkins or not, did you?

A: Yes, I am pretty certain it was . . .

Q: What did he say?

A: I don't remember exactly what he said, but I knew from the conversation I had with him that I was to expedite this particular shipment, and this particular shipment came through and it was uranium. I don't think anybody but Mr. Hopkins would talk to me about uranium . . .

Q: And you also made the statement, which is a very serious one, that Mr. Hopkins told you "to keep quiet and say nothing about them, even to your superior officers, and not to leave any records of them."

A: That is correct.

Q: So far in answering our questions you haven't specifically testified you ever had a telephone conversation with Hopkins himself.

A: I said a moment ago I had a telephone conversation with Mr. Hopkins.

The Congressional Perry Masons went around and around, getting Jordan to repeat his story, putting words in his mouth which he had never uttered. With one breath they attempted to question the possibility of uranium shipments, but the next minute they cited the fact that export licenses for the uranium had been dated in 1943. Finally, Jordan snapped: "It is difficult for me to sit here and answer questions about minute details when I was working from five forty-five in the morning until eleven at night almost daily. We started in January 1943 and worked until September 1944, and much of this is telescoped in my mind together. It is difficult for me to tell you exactly when, but I know it was done, and I know it went through."

The hearing ended wih a promise from Jordan to supply the committee with the names of people who might corroborate his story and to furnish the staff with all the records he had kept. By the time the full story was in, there would be, in his phrase, "clouds of witnesses" to back him up on hundreds of details. He had barely stepped off the stand, however, before Representative Walter announced to the press that Jordan's account was "inherently incredible." Life magazine stated in its story on the Jordan testimony that both the FBI and G-2 had investigated and found that there was no truth to his testimony—a charge cut from the whole cloth. Newsweek also expressed doubt in its reportage:

According to Sidney Hyman, who organized Hopkins' papers for Robert Sherwood, author of "Roosevelt and Hopkins" [*Newsweek* stated], F. D. R.'s confidant didn't have the faintest understanding of the Manhattan project until he read about the A-bomb being dropped on Hiroshima. Hyman said: "He didn't know the difference between uranium and geranium." It wasn't until weeks later that Hopkins talked with several of the atomic scientists and learned about the 'engineering feat of production.' "

Sherwood, on the contrary, dealt in detail with Hopkins's very early involvement in atomic energy matters. Vannevar Bush wanted to enlist Hopkins's influence with President Roosevelt to get the atomic project moving. Bush's proposal, according to the Hopkins account, was embodied in a letter to be signed by Roosevelt, and Hopkins was the man who took it to the White House. In another passage, Sherwood stated: "It will be noted that Churchill was conducting this correspondence on the atomic project with Hopkins rather than with the President, and he continued to do so for many months thereafter." Few bothered to check, and a researcher's faulty memory was allowed to discredit Major Jordan.*

Two days later, on December 7, 1949, the majority members—still meeting without their Republican colleagues—were jolted by the testimony of General Groves. For though the matter of Harry Hopkins was never settled— nor can it ever be—the first glimmer of the truth behind Jordan's account became apparent. So, too, did the shenanigans of the Soviet Purchasing Commission in obtaining the uranium and the failures of civilian agencies of government to abide by the prohibitions against allowing uranium to be sold without the approval of the Manhattan Project. So well and carefully did the staff investigate that it was able to present documentary proof of facts which were not known to General Groves until the time they were developed by the committee.

The testimony of General Groves, corroborated in minute detail by former officials of the Lend-Lease Administration and the War Production Board—and backed up by intragovernmental correspondence, bills of lading, and other written records—is much too complex for a detailed recital. What it came to was this:

The Lend-Lease Administration received a request from the Soviet Purchasing Agency for two hundred pounds of uranium oxide and two hundred and twenty pounds of nitro-urano, a complex uranium salt. "There was a great deal of pressure being brought to bear on Lend-Lease, apparently, to give the Russians everything they could think of," Groves said. "There was a great deal of pressure brought to give them this uranium material." Before General Groves had learned of the request, it was granted and arrangements made for this shipment in 1943 to Kotikov at Great Falls. Groves was quite upset, but he felt that to revoke the permission would alert the Soviets to the significance of

---

* *This phase of the Jordan case is cited not to argue the complicity or gullibility of Hopkins but to show how easily those who deplore the discussion of past actions will leap to conclusions without abiding by their own strictures against "character assassination." Without comparing Jordan's testimony to the available records, his detractors had already sat in judgment.*

uranium to the United States. This might have been a somewhat naïve view, particularly since Groves knew at the time of Soviet espionage activities which had broken through to the secret knowledge that this country was working on the A-bomb. Nevertheless, he gave his approval.

The Soviet Purchasing Commission followed this by a request for eight tons of uranium oxide and eight tons of uranium chloride. This was turned down. The next request was for twenty-five pounds of pure uranium metal. The MED had not yet been able to purify uranium to the specifications sought by its own scientists, and the Soviets were given permission to purchase this uranium in the hope that they might find some metal refinery which had developed an adequate process. Finally, the Soviet Purchasing Agency was allowed to buy 2.2 pounds of impure uranium metal. (Groves believed that they would assume this to be what the United States was using in its experiments, thereby leading Soviet scientists astray.) Next, the Soviets asked for five hundred pounds of uranium nitrate and another five hundred pounds of urano-uranic oxide. This was turned down, but the Purchasing Commission set up a tremendous clamor that these salts were needed for medical purposes and for the hardening of gun barrels.

To quiet those within the federal government who insisted that the Soviet Union should have what it wanted, General Groves reversed himself, and a license for export was granted to an American supplier. Groves was certain that he had cut off all sources of supply and that the Russians would think that United States approval was based on a genuine desire to allow them this rare metal. The Soviets, however, instructed a dealer in metals to find it elsewhere. Without the knowledge or approval of General Groves, the export license was amended to allow the dealer to purchase the uranium in Canada— and it was shipped via Great Falls, as Jordan had testified. In June of 1944, another forty-five pounds of uranium nitrate was delivered to the Soviet Union —a fact that came as a considerable shock to some of the government witnesses testifying in 1949. It had been purchased for the Soviets by the Treasury Department. Among other gifts sent to Joseph Stalin were one thousand grams of heavy water—which, like graphite, was necessary in an atomic pile to slow down the fission process.

The sudden interest of the Soviets in uranium was the clearest indication that they were aware of American progress in nuclear physics. Prior to the request for 420 pounds of uranium salts, the Russians had never imported these compounds from the United States. Groves, of course, was aware of the significance of the continued Soviet demands for uranium. "From one month of the time I took over we never trusted [the Russians] one iota," he said. "Our whole security was based on not letting the Russians find out anthing. We were not worried about Germany or Japan. We were worried about Russia." How then was the Soviet Purchasing Commission able to override his orders that no critical materials be shipped to the U.S.S.R.? Groves never met Harry Hopkins. He was certain that there had been no direct approach by Hopkins to MED officials. But the wartime mood was pro-Soviet, and this was reflected in the actions and attitudes of most in the Administration.

After all, President Roosevelt had said of Stalin, "If I give him every-thing that I can and ask nothing of him in return, *noblesse oblige,* he won't try to annex anything and will work with me for a world of peace and democ-racy." And Hopkins, at a giant Madison Square Garden Rally for Russian War Relief had said, in an apostrophe to Stalin, "We are determined that nothing shall stop us from sharing with you all that we have." (Cheers.) It is no wonder, then, that there was pressure on Lend-Lease and from Lend-Lease to release to the Soviets strategic materials necessary for the atomic program. "Can you tell us who exerted the pressure?" General Groves was asked.

GROVES: No, I can't tell you who exerted the pressure on Lend-Lease. Of course, it could have been internal pressure. At any rate we saw every evidence of that pressure, and I believe your files of Lend-Lease will show how they repeatedly came back. It was evident from reading the [official records] that we didn't want this material shipped, yet they kept coming back and coming back.*

This anxiety to please the Soviet Union was such that no consideration was given to the possible effects on America's war effort. General Groves recalls one incident:

We were very anxious, in connection with the gaseous diffusion plant [then being built at Oak Ridge] to get certain equipment. If it had not been obtained, that plant would have been delayed in its completion. The Russians had a plant on the way. Of course, when I say they had it, you know who paid for it. That plant, some of it was boxed and on the dock when we got it, and I can still remember the difficulties we had getting it. One of the agreements we had to make was that we would replace that equipment and use all our priorities necessary to get it replaced quickly.

The Soviets, however, could not complain. They paid cash for the prod-ucts strategic to nuclear research so far mentioned, hoping thereby to avoid the attention of the Manhattan Project. But other materials, in short supply and necessary for that research, to the sum of more than sixteen million dollars, they received as part of Lend-Lease. The catalogue:

9,681 lbs. of beryllium metal
72,535 lbs. of cadmium alloys
834,989 lbs. of cadmium metals
33,600 lbs. of cobalt ore and concentrate
13,766,472 lbs. of aluminum tubing (vital in the construction of an atomic pile)
7,384,282 pounds of graphite
25,352 lbs. of thorium salts and compounds
228 lbs. of beryllium salts and compounds

---

* GROVES: *There are two kinds of pressure in Washington. One is the kind that comes from above, that you realize what it is. The other kind is constant hammering, repeating and repeating in the hope that you wear down or that something slips. Nobody has a thousand batting average. I believe that it was the hope of the people who kept pushing and pushing that they might catch me out of town, or that some day I would say to give it to them to shut them up.*

2,100 lbs. of cadmium oxide
18,995 lbs. of cadmium compounds
29,326 lbs. of cobalt compounds
806,941 lbs. of cobalt metal and scrap

It has been said that the uranium shipments would have been of little value to Soviet scientists, that the quantity was too small to matter. When asked about this, Groves stated: "Any amount would be of value in certain experimental work. That is, in anything to do with chemistry. After all, we designed and practically built the Hanford plant for separating plutonium and uranium when we had *one-millionth of a pound of plutonium*. The chemistry part could be very well handled." To activate an atomic pile, at least one ton of uranium would have been necessary. But at the time, the Soviets were not prepared to go into large-scale production. They wanted to know what the United States was doing and duplicate it in the laboratory. And this, with the help of enthusiastic Americans, they accomplished. When W. L. White was in Leningrad in 1944, he visited the bombed-out Kirov electrical plant and was shown what remained of Professor Joffe's famous laboratory. (Joffe was a nuclear physicist.) In the wreckage was a "curious contraption" described to him as a cyclotron, used by Joffe to split the atom. "Behind Urals, Professor Joffe has much newer, much better," White was told. "We have, like you call in America, Manhattan project." Like most Americans at the time, White had never heard of the MED. He thought the reference was to some industrial plant in New York.

If the Groves testimony was an eye-opener, there was more to come. When the House Un-American Activities Committee resumed hearings on January 24, 1950, the minority members, including Representative Richard Nixon, were present for the first time. In the interim, moreover, the committee staff had been delving into official papers and had come up with more evidence to corroborate the Jordan account of the happenings at Great Falls. Other military personnel were ready to come forward with statements of their own experiences, duplicating in kind what Major Jordan said in testimony.

Correspondence was put into the record from Lieutenant General L. G. Rudenko, chief of the Soviet Purchasing Commission, to Secretary of War Henry Stimson, insisting on the shipment of sixteen tons of uranium compounds. This had been followed by a memorandum to Groves from Colonel J. W. Boone, "acting for the Commanding General," for "information as to the supply of various forms of uranium" and asking for his recommendations "in order that materials can be made available." It was discovered that the earlier request for uranium compounds had been buried in long lists of desired chemicals, so as not to call attention to Soviet interest. Formal notification to the Lend-Lease Administration that the MED be "kept advised as to the progress" of negotiations for shipments of uranium was read into the record.*

A curious exchange took place during the testimony:
"COLONEL CRENSHAW: *General Groves' underlying philosophy was that the last thing in the world he wanted to do was to help the Russians in any way.*
"MR. WALTER: *Was he of that opinion, and did he take that attitude,* during the period when they were doing most of the fighting?" [*Emphasis added.*]

On March 3, committee investigator Donald T. Appell took the stand. After Jordan's original testimony, the charge had been made and reiterated that (1) his account of the thousands of pounds of papers and other documents passing through Great Falls was a myth and (2) that had he really broken into the black suitcases and seen what he later stated on the stand, he would certainly have reported it to higher authorities or at least commented on it in his diary at some length. Obviously, it was argued, no reports were made, otherwise some action would have been taken. *Ergo,* Jordan was a sensation-seeker. These attacks had done much to discredit Major Jordan in the public eye—to the point that documented corroboration was ignored by the press and public. As usual, by focusing attention on extraneous matters, the thrust of the major facts was blunted.

Appell's testimony was direct and reflected the excellence of his investigative procedures. He had obviously combed such files as the State Department and other federal agencies permitted him to enter—and he had come up with far more than a prima-facie case that Major Jordan had been telling the truth and that United States authorities had been incredibly naïve.

According to the documents presented by Appell, the Soviet Purchasing Commission had on January 19, 1944 attempted to formalize its practice of including large shipments of "diplomatic" cargo on Lend-Lease planes, and to increase the volume. In a letter to the International Section, War Department, the commission had requested that two C-47s a month be assigned to the transportation of "diplomatic mail." After a check with General Deane, head of the U. S. Military Mission in Moscow, the request was turned down on the ground that there was a shortage of cargo space. This refusal was subsequently reversed by General Bennett E. Meyers. The Soviets, however, had withdrawn their request before they had formal notice of General Meyers's action.

Nevertheless, the Soviets had shipped planeloads of so-called diplomatic mail—in violation of regulations—on January 28 (3,563 pounds), February 15 (4,180 pounds), February 17 (4,000 pounds), and February 28 (3,757 pounds). The G-2 report containing this information also noted that none of this had previously been known and added:

Major Jordan, who represents Air Staff at the ATC station at Great Falls, is reported to have examined one of the packages and found it contained blueprints of the A-20 plane, railroad guides showing long- and short-haul routes, and other technical data.

While the original request for special facilities was pending, however, the Soviet Purchasing Commission had made an end run—going to the Commanding General, Air Transport Command, asking for similar privileges. These had been granted. Subsequently, General Deane was once more notified. As he had in the first instance, Deane denied the Soviet request but was overruled by Averell Harriman, then ambassador to Moscow. But Jordan's complaints of Soviet irregularities were still echoing in Washington. On March 13, 1944 a special agent of Counter-Intelligence was sent to Ladd Field to interview Jordan. Here are significant excerpts of the CIC report:

. . . Major Jordan stated that he was desirous of conveying certain information to "Intelligence Authorities."

The following interesting information was supplied by Major Jordan:

The Soviet Union has made a practice of shipping freight to Moscow through the Alaskan Wing. This has been done for about two years. For the year 1943, the total freight shipped through Great Falls to the Russians was 768,254.2 pounds. This is to be compared with 433,112 pounds . . . from 1 January 1944 to 5 March 1944.

This material has been sent by members of the Consular Service, Russian Army Officers, Russian Engineers, and families of Russians who pass through here and others. The freight is diversified in nature . . . He added that, due to the shortage of personnel, the use of Russian-owned and operated aircraft, and the fact that a great deal of the freight is blanketed by diplomatic immunity, there is insufficient control over the material shipped to Russia. . . .

There is an incredible amount of diplomatic mail sent to Russia through Great Falls . . . All of this was protected from censorship by diplomatic immunity. It may be significant that it is not at all uncommon for the Russian mail or freight shipment to be accompanied by two men . . . One man sleeps while the other watches the parcels and vice versa . . .

This Agent observed that Major Jordan appeared to maintain accurate, detailed files and was very anxious to convey his information via Intelligence channels . . .

It is recommended that a prolonged interview be conducted with Major Jordan; that his records be scrutinized for information of an Intelligence nature; and that he be contacted regularly.

It is further recommended that the facts contained herein be given due consideration, with a view to contacting the State Department in order that they be made cognizant of the situation and that correcive measures be taken.

There is no record that the first recommendation was heeded. *Three months later,* however, the State Department "took cognizance." On June 16, Charles E. (Chip) Bohlen requested a copy of the CIC report. A State Department memorandum noted the irregularity of permitting large quantities of nondiplomatic mail to pass through Great Falls without proper censorship or customs inspection and suggested that the matter be adjusted in Washington, or by the American ambassador in Moscow. On July 6, the State Department conferred with representatives of the FBI, the Office of Censorship, Military Intelligence, the Air Transport Command, the Immigration and Naturalization Service, the Bureau of Customs, and the Foreign Economic Administration. All present expressed concern, and a decision was made that regulations be "explained" to the Soviet Embassy.

Twenty-two days later, the State Department forwarded to the Second Secretary of the Soviet Embassy detailed instructions on the procedure for handling nondiplomatic mail and non-Lend-Lease freight. The Second Secretary gracefully accepted the gentle admonition and promised that henceforth there would be no more violations. His name: Vassili Zubilin, chief of the atomic espionage ring in the United States. How seriously he took his instructions may be determined by this: In the files, there is a report stating that on September 20, 1944, another irregular shipment went through Great Falls.

Representative Nixon summed up for the committee:

NIXON: As I see it at present, the issues are five . . . and I want to see which of the charges are still at issue.

First of all, the charge was made that if the shipments were going through, Major Jordan should have made a report. In this regard, he did make a report of the charges at least on two occasions. Is that correct?

APPELL: Yes . . . that is correct . . .

NIXON: Another point that was made was whether or not he tore radar equipment out of C-47 planes. As I understand, this particular phase of his story was questioned in an article in *Life* magazine, in which they said that the report that Mr. Jordan (did so) was preposterous . . . and it was further said that as a matter of fact no C-47s were equipped with radar at the time mentioned by Major Jordan.

The investigation of the committee, in addition to your own, has shown (1) that C-47s equipped with radar and going to Russia did go through Great Falls, and (2) that Mr. Jordan specifically asked permission of Colonel Gitzinger in Dayton to tear the radar out of a specific plane on one occasion. [It was against regulations to divulge information on radar or to ship radar equipment to the U.S.S.R.]

APPELL: That is correct, and he received that permission from Colonel Gitzinger . . .

NIXON: Another point that Major Jordan made was that certain documents were going through Great Falls under diplomatic immunity; that he broke into the cases, examined the documents, and that some of the material in there which he examined consisted of plans, secret material, and so on . . . I think it is clear from your testimony that that phase of Major Jordan's testimony stands up. Is that correct?

At this point, Appell said that the committee had another witness who would offer corroboration. In fact, there were many ready to take the stand.

NIXON: On the point of the so-called shipments of uranium, as I understand the case, first, there is no question about the shipments going through. Is that correct?

APPELL: As to the shipments of uranium and heavy water, [they] have been completely documented to include even the number of the planes that flew [them] out of Great Falls.

NIXON: Isn't it true that these shipments were made with the knowledge and approval of our officials?

APPELL: Export declarations on these shipments were approved by Lend-Lease and later by its successor organization, Foreign Economic Administration.

NIXON: And in the case of one shipment . . . General Groves and members of the Atomic Energy Commission learned about it [only] when this committee began its investigation. Is that correct?

APPELL: Yes, sir.

Only on the role played by Harry Hopkins in expediting the uranium shipments—and whether or not the note in one of the black suitcases had been initialed "H. H."—was there no corroboration. As Nixon pointed out, carefully underlining the point, Major Jordan's story had been substantially documented on four of five points—the critical ones. When Major Jordan took the stand once more, the atmosphere in the hearing room was considerably more cordial. There was little for him to add. But the committee counsel, Frank Tavenner, laid the groundwork for what was to come when he asked Jordan, "Were you acquainted with a Russian by the name of Semen Vassilenko?" Jordan replied that he was, that Vassilenko and three aides had passed through Great Falls on February 17, 1944—as he had written in his diary—with a cargo of the now-famous black suitcases.

When Jordan concluded his testimony, Tavenner called Victor Kravchenko, a former member of the Soviet Purchasing Commission and author of *I Chose Freedom*. Kravchenko told the committee that one of the commission's assignments was espionage, that its members collected secret technical and military information, that this information was referred to as "super Lend-Lease," packed in suitcases, and shipped to Moscow. In February 1944, Kravchenko himself had helped Semen Vassilenko pack a suitcase with secret metallurgical information.

At this point, Jordan might have rested his case. But there was one more refinement—an affidavit not read into the record. It was written by Royall E. Norton, a former Chief Petty Officer in the Navy, then a GI Bill student at Clemson College in South Carolina. Before writing the affidavit, he had consulted with the president of Clemson and with former Supreme Court Justice (and former Secretary of State) James F. Byrnes. The affidavit bears repetition:

A PBM—a Catalina type [plane]—was being loaded [in Kodiak] for the take-off to Russia. I had finished checking the cargo against my inventory when I noticed three extra parachute bags that obviously were not filled with parachutes.

I started to inspect them, and in the first one found a wooden box . . . I lifted the top to see what was inside.

The Soviet pilot, who was making a final check in the cockpit, saw what I was doing and put on a terrific scene. He tried to make me stop, yelling in English: "Personal gear—personal!" I went on long enough to see what was in the box. It contained a solid stack of blueprints, all of about the same size and general appearance, as if they belonged to a set.

I unfolded the top one and examined it fairly carefully. I had had some little experience in reading blueprints. This was very unusual and different from anything I had ever seen. But I had studied enough chemistry in school to recognize it as a highly complicated pattern of atomic structures. Protons and neutrons were shown.

In the lower right hand corner was a group of words, which were probably an identification of the blueprint. I cannot remember the terms, but I do recall the figure "92." It meant nothing to me at the time, as I had never heard of atomic energy or atomic bombs . . . This was undoubtedly a blueprint of the atomic structure of the 92nd element, uranium.

8 Gouzenko: The Shock of Recognition

THERE IS a terrible sameness about the Soviet official face. The reporter in Moscow or Leningrad learns to recognize it almost immediately. It has nothing to do with features or racial type. It is an expression, not deadpan but withdrawn. It is the product of caution and training.¹

Eight years after Igor Gouzenko had walked out of the Soviet Embassy in Ottawa carrying the documents that would expose an espionage ring, he had not quite lost that official face. He stepped into the room at the Royal York in Toronto knowing the waiting reporter only by reputation and therefore warily, though the *bona fides* were reassuring. At that moment, he wore "the face." The reporter needed no introduction.

"I am Mr. Brown," said Gouzenko with the hint of a question in his inflection. The accent was Russian. The reporter wondered why members of the Soviet Intelligence *apparat* have such a fondness for the cover name of Brown. "Won't you sit down, Mr. Gouzenko," said the reporter. There was a smile of recognition at the name he no longer heard or could use—and the official face vanished. He was a pleasant-faced Russian, but the contours were firm and well-defined. A stocky man, he gave the impression of being short. More than anything he wanted to talk freely of his past, his present, his future. He wanted to discuss recent events in the Soviet Union, the position of the West, the failure of Americans and Canadians to understand the real nature of communism and the threat it posed. He wanted to tell of the novel he was finishing, *The Fall of the Titan*. (It was accepted by the Book-of-the-Month Club, and achieved both financial and critical success.)

It took no great intuition to realize that Igor Gouzenko was more than an entry in a secret police dossier, more than the flotsam of espionage. He was a man of character, stubborn as Russians can be, well read in politics and in literature, perceptive, and very talented. Fate, in catalysis with his needs and drives, had thrust on him his role as a protagonist in the never-ending drama of espionage and counterespionage. He took pride in the fact that his courage had projected him into the affairs of the world as the first to budge the rock of atomic perfidy and offer a brief glimpse at the underground world of spies and traitors. But he derived no pleasure from the notoriety and would have preferred to "surface" completely as Igor Gouzenko, the writer, the almost obsessive family man—as so many Russians are—the free citizen in a free society.

This, then, was the Gouzenko of 1953. What was the code clerk of 1945, recalled to Moscow for a more important assignment that might in turn lead to rank and power? He could be reconstructed only by extrapolation from known but two-dimensional facts. In effect, he had become the prisoner of his great exploit. And that exploit in turn was conditioned by the history of Soviet espionage, by the transcendent fascination of the atomic age, by his precise place in the unrolling story of Stalin's massive theft of the free world's nuclear secrets. In the unreality of the NKVD operation, he seemed slightly dwarfed, yet a pawn that acquired volition and direction. This diminution of the human species is common in the Soviet Union, where nothing is quite life-size except the State and its instruments of control. Yet the story of Gouzenko's exploit is an integral part of Gouzenko *qua* person and of his background.

Gouzenko was a student at the Moscow Institute of Architecture—one of the top five in his class and destined for a career of designing the wedding-cake palaces so dear to Stalin's heart—when he was tapped for training as a cipher clerk. He came from peasant stock, and his family shared the poverty that is normal to the vast majority in the Soviet Union. He had no *blat*, the Soviet equivalent of "pull." He was chosen to receive instruction in the Intelligence Administration of the Kuibishev Military Engineering Academy in Moscow—a coveted appointment. Having been a *Komsomol*, the Soviet equivalent of the Young Communist League, he was aware that from that moment on what little privacy he had been able to enjoy was ended. He was now part of the State, and a sensitive part at that.

It was no surprise to him that he was told to expect periodic investigations, special periods of unannounced twenty-four-hour surveillance, and continual scrutiny of his mind. Contact with foreigners was forbidden, and any new acquaintances were to be immediately reported. Association with girls was also forbidden without express permission from a superior. And it was made clear to him that the more trust was placed in him, the more suspect he would become.

"Each one who knows state secrets becomes an important and at the same time a dangerous person," Gouzenko was lectured. "The more an individual is trusted, the more closely he must be guarded. In your case, as a cipher clerk who will get to know the names and cover names of agents, and their secrets, there can be no relaxation ever—either on your part or on the part of the Special Section. Remember that at all times and watch your step."

When Gouzenko had completed his studies, he was assigned to Red Army Intelligence Headquarters. There he picked up the specialized vocabulary of Intelligence agents and became familiar with its table of organization. From a member of the *Otdel Spetsialnikh Zadanii*—the Special Tasks Branch —he learned the difference between "dry affairs" (regular espionage work) and "wet affairs" (the murder of an agent on whom suspicion had fallen). Telegrams from resident directors in other countries, calling for the "disposal" of once trusted men, passed through the cipher room and Gouzenko's hands. Intelligence Headquarters, housed in a large building at 19 Znamensky, processed the microfilm received from thousands of agents in the United States. Other thousands, according to Gouzenko, plied their trade in other countries of the world deemed important to the Kremlin. Agents spied on both the Yenan Communists and the Kuomintang in China. Microfilm was used whenever possible. Soviet scientists worked full time at adapting microphotographic techniques and equipment, stolen from Germany and the United States, to espionage purposes. A two-story white building, in the great courtyard of Intelligence Headquarters, was the processing laboratory, and it worked twenty-four hours a day.

After a time, Gouzenko carried a map of the world in his head as he followed the movements of agents through their reports to the Center. The same cover names would crop up repeatedly as he moved vicariously in faraway cities. The agent's reports on contacts, his fears of discovery, his request for instructions, his calls for money, the kind of codes he used—all of this built up a picture for the young lieutenant decoding the messages and encoding the Center's answers.

"It amazed me to note the psychological range employed in dealing with agents throughout the world," Gouzenko would write later. "Exhaustive files, compiled over a period of years at considerable cost, held histories on each agent, his motives, his habits, his weaknesses, his reason for being an agent. This knowledge was used to the best advantage when psychology was needed." These *zapiski*, making up the Great Index, were the source of leads on new agents when unexplored areas opened up to the Center:

People were bought, used and thrown over; many of them important personages in their own countries, being used wittingly and unwittingly by agents. Love, hate, resentment, anger, weakness of character and strength of character, courage and cowardice, were the tools used to get results by this monstrous, merciless and thoroughly efficient Soviet Intelligence machine.

If you . . . happen to be a person of some importance, or happen to be in a position whereby your knowledge might be useful, you are undoubtedly "intimately known" in the files in Moscow. This was clearly established by the varied approaches made on Soviet instruction when atomic bomb information was demanded. Astonishingly enough, it was shown there that when it comes to something really big, the money appeal isn't used. The appeal to "higher feelings" such as "the good of the world" proved most effective for Soviet Intelligence.

But the wide-eyed young Lieutenant Gouzenko quickly learned that these "higher feelings" were a carrot only for the dupes and outsiders. At the Center, the motivational force was fear. Good work was taken for granted. A small slip could lead to demotion and assignment to a penal battalion and front-line duty. A serious error usually meant death at the hands of a firing squad. At Intelligence Headquarters, there was a pervasive tension, a nervous strain which was never relaxed. Every man guarded his thoughts and watched his neighbor warily. For it was essential to carry out one's own assignments— and also to report the shortcomings of associates. Failure to do so made cipher clerks, lowly employees, and high-ranking officers subject to charges of laxness or ideological weakness. To turn in a friend was proof of loyalty, devotion to duty, and right thinking.

As the war progressed, the scope and importance of Soviet espionage increased. Stalin himself supervised its activities. Two tables of organization were set up—one for Tactical Intelligence, the other for Strategic Intelligence

—each with thousands of technicians, scientists, and experts. Within Strategic Intelligence, a new branch of Special Communications was organized, to which Gouzenko and others with a knowledge of languages were assigned. It was organized like a foreign office, with "desks" for each country. Political and economic information was handled by an Information Branch. Scientific and technical information went to the General Branch. There it was first screened by a "security reader" who would make certain that the identity of the agent and his area of operations was deleted. According to Gouzenko:

Everything was broken up into small sections so that only a very few of the top people had the complete picture. What the spies sent in was turned over to these security experts for analysis. Every reference to the source of the material was washed out first. When a scientist or an engineer got a blueprint to study, it was only a blueprint to him. It was his job to study it and to determine how it fitted in with whatever else he knew or had on the subject— and to see whether or not it was useful.

Men from every scientific and technical institute in the Soviet Union were recruited for work with Intelligence Headquarters. Every new batch of data passed through their hands. They not only evaluated but drafted queries for the agents, demanding further types of information needed to complete the data. As Soviet interest in atomic energy began to build, the Soviet system of mass production espionage came in good stead. Detailed instructions would go to twenty or more agents, asking for the same information. When the first flow from the laboratories at Berkeley, the University of Chicago, and Columbia began, agents in Canada and the United Kingdom were ordered to duplicate it—and also to add pertinent new data.

In June of 1943, Igor Gouzenko was given his overseas assignment. His work had been highly rated by his superiors, and the "Five"—a screening group made up of representatives of the Communist Party's Central Committee, the NKVD, Red Army Intelligence, the Ministry of External Affairs, and the Ministry of Foreign Trade—had attested to his efficiency and political reliability. He had been briefed on the ways of the iniquitous West and instructed to memorize a typewritten pamphlet marked "secret." The pamphlet was a guide to personal behavior. It warned:

Be careful . . . especially of women . . . There is something about the environment of a train and the leisurely hours spent thereon that provides opportunity for enemy agents to work their way into your confidence. The best rule in this regard is simply: Do not yield to cordial conversation with any foreigner . . .

Always wear a hat on the street . . .

Never overtip unless with a specific purpose in mind. That might make you conspicuous . . .

Never permit yourself to be more drunk than your guest or your host . . .

Keep your wives under reasonable control in shopping. Women lean toward excesses in purchasing . . .

Americans are particularly adept at entangling you under the mask of friendship. They like to employ a free and easy air in meeting you so that your natural caution is relaxed. They pretend to be telling you secrets as a friend and, especially in drinking, you might be inclined to fall in with the mood of the party . . . The supposedly friendly American . . . is the most dangerous type of foreigner.

The next step was to memorize his "legend." This was a false, detailed background on which the biographical data supplied to Canadian authorities was based. Gouzenko, for example, "learned" that he had been born in Gorky and that he had studied at the Economics Technical Institute there. No mention was made of his Red Army rank. His official position was that of translator and secretary employed by the Military Attaché. Even at the Embassy in Ottawa, only those with whom he worked directly were to know that he was the code clerk. The others, who would see him enter and leave the guarded wing on the second floor, might guess but never know. If "foreigners" questioned him about his duties, he was to say that he read newspapers for important stories and translated them for his superiors.

Gouzenko's assignment to Ottawa was in the nature of a plum. For this once neglected post was being built up. Knowledge of Canadian scientific and military activity had become important to the Center. The exchange of information between the United States and Canada resulting from the wartime alliance presented a new opportunity. The St. Lawrence was an important staging area for convoys, and the Center wanted detailed information on the number of ships, the size and nature of their cargoes, the facts and figures on the effectiveness of Nazi submarine warfare. Of significance to this account, there was also the matter of Canadian participation in nuclear and weapons research. Therefore, the Center drew up a new table of organization for its espionage activities in Canada, with Colonel Nicolai Zabotin at its head and some of its best men under him.

At the Embassy, Gouzenko was placed directly under one Ouspensky, who later moved onward and upward to Washington. Ouspensky showed him the elaborate precautionary method of entering the secret wing. A bell was hidden under the bannister on the first floor. This alerted the guards and gave them time to take their positions. Having climbed to the second floor, those seeking entry found a steel-covered door, hidden by a velvet curtain. There was a slit in the door to permit a guard to determine who was seeking entry. A second door, bigger and more heavily reinforced by steel, was then opened. It led to a carpeted corridor and a series of other steel doors. The windows in the secret wing were painted white so that no one could see in. They were protected by steel bars and steel shutters. A radio blared endlessly so as to make eavesdropping by those within the secret wing impossible. Two incinerators occupied separate rooms. The first, an ordinary model, was used by those in the wing to burn every scrap of paper not deemed necessary. The second incinerator—a large and powerful one, specially designed for the Embassy—was used for the almost ritual burning of codes. This ceremony was carefully witnessed by the top echelon of the apparatus and supervised by the NKVD chief. Its primary purpose, however, was to provide for speedy incineration of all incriminating documents in case of emergency.* ("It's big enough and powerful enough to consume a human body," an NKVD official told Gouzenko.)

The Zabotin network included Fred Rose, a member of the Canadian Parliament; a rich Canadian professor, Raymond Boyer, who stole the formula of RDX, a secret and powerful high-explosive; strategically placed Army and civilian personnel; an atomic scientist, Dr. Allan Nunn May; two members of the key National Research Council; two employees of the Munitions and Supply Department, and others fortunate enough not to be implicated by the documents taken out of the Embassy by Gouzenko. In addition, there were several important members of the network whose cover names shielded them. Their activities and peregrinations would occupy the attention of the Royal Canadian Mounted Police's investigations. But the plaguing knowledge would remain that Zabotin, by his own admission to Gouzenko, was one of ten spymasters in the Center's "pioneer" invasion of Canada. The other nine remained untouched. If there were any outcroppings, only the RCMP was aware of them and could never discover enough to permit the government to mount a prosecution. Also to plague Canadian and United States authorities: the names of Americans found in the documents, but with insufficient information for legal action.

This was all in the future of an Igor Gouzenko still gawking at the easy freedom enjoyed by his "capitalist" hosts, the abundance of food, the outgoing friendship extended by the "enemy"—and the differences between what he was seeing or experiencing and what he had been told about the "exploitation of workers" in Canada, the comparisons between life in Moscow and in Ottawa. These were reactions shared universally by those who are exposed to the West. The NKVD is, of course, cognizant of the erosion this works on the Communist will. As well as it can, it protects against the refusal of Soviet personnel abroad to return home by holding hostages—parents, children, brothers and sisters, a wife. In Gouzenko's case, however, there was a counter-pull: his young son, born in Canada. Neither ideological or idealistic principles were uppermost in the minds of the Gouzenkos when, in September 1944, he was told that he had been summoned to Moscow. How would they feed the child properly in the Soviet Union? Where would they get the fresh milk and vegetables, the other foods, which in Ottawa were as close as the nearest shop? Lend-Lease shipments of food went first to the important bureaucrats and then to the troops. The rest of the population was on low subsistence rations or worse.

Gouzenko asked Zabotin to query the Center. Could he remain at some other job? In a few days, the Center replied that for the time being Gouzenko might remain, continuing his duties as a code clerk. This was a sign that he had not been recalled for punishment or because there was doubt as to his devotion to the Kremlin. Had there been the slightest suspicion of him, he would never have been allowed to remain in so sensitive a spot. But he knew,

---

It should be noted that prior to the arrival of Colonel Zabotin and his staff the secret wing and the other espionage arrangements in Ottawa had been inspected by an official using the cover name "Molier." He was, in fact, Pavel Mikhailov, Soviet vice consul in New York City and the confederate of Arthur Alexandrovitch Adams.

before his wife Svetlana said it, that this was only a reprieve. At that point, after searching his conscience, he decided that his duty lay with his young son rather than with an aging mother then close to death. His decision came at a moment when the work of the secret section at the Embassy was almost on a three-shift basis. Two agents in the National Research Council were systematically delivering everything in the files to Colonel Zabotin. Every night, there would be another package for microfilming, to be returned to its proper place in the morning. So great was the volume that a second photographic studio was pressed into service.

All members of the Embassy staff were furnished with still and motion-picture cameras to photograph anything of interest or importance. Zabotin himself, when asked to go fishing on the Chalk River with a member of the Canadian Army General Staff, scored a coup. He returned to the Embassy in great excitement.

"This does not mean anything to you," said Zabotin, "but there is a very important plant on the Chalk River. Moscow has been asking me for a description." Gouzenko did not know that this was Canada's atomic installation. "I asked my Canadian friend if I might take some pictures for my album. He said yes and even rowed the boat in close so I could get a good picture with good light. Moscow will be very happy."

But for Gouzenko, the work of the Zabotin network began to assume a completely different aspect. He had come to develop an attachment to Canada and the Canadians. His decision to defect had heightened his sense of identity with the people to whom he now gave his loyalty. In June 1945, when his replacement arrived, Gouzenko knew that he would have to take the terrifying step. To ensure a welcome and to repay the Canadians for the asylum he expected, Gouzenko began selecting documents to take out with him. The papers he thought important he dog-eared slightly, leaving them in the files.

As he said to this writer, "You get convictions only with documents—never just with talk." He selected those documents which would prove conclusively that wholesale espionage was the Soviet order of the day. And he chose those papers which would condemn three men he considered most reprehensible: Dr. Allan Nunn May, Canadian MP Fred Rose, and Communist organizer Sam Carr. (When the Canadian authorities studied the documents, many were called and more than a few were chosen—for a prison cell.)

The story of Gouzenko's last, heart-pounding visit to the secret wing, the rapid stuffing of documents under his shirt, the shaken walk down the stairs past the NKVD guards, and the fruitless attempts to deliver his precious cargo to Ottawa newspapers have been frequently repeated. Simply walking out of the Embassy, weighed down as he was by the incriminating documents, took incredible courage. Had he been discovered, he would have been shot on the spot—his body dumped into the big incinerator and his family kidnaped and hurried off to the Soviet Union on a freighter.

He had taken only one precaution. Before making his raid on the network's files, he had pulled out two telegrams—one on the atomic bomb and the other concerning Fred Rose's activities—leaving copies. "If anything goes wrong, if they catch me," he told his wife, "you have these telegrams. Take them to the authorities, and they will give you protection." But this small bit of life insurance for his family made the exploit no less daring. He was one man against the NKVD. In his book, *The Iron Curtain,* Gouzenko summed up for himself:

I was born a very ordinary little man in Russia. I had never excelled in athletics. My triumphs seemed limited to the realm of studies. Dangerous living never appealed to me, and adventure always associated itself with un-romantic danger in my mind. But that night of September 5, 1945, I came as close to becoming a hero as I ever will.

What saved Gouzenko's life was the fear and shock at the Embassy when his act was discovered. Had Colonel Zabotin bided his time, he might have trapped Gouzenko. But he could not know that the code clerk and his wife had spent a day being turned away from newspapers and government offices. Nor could he know that Gouzenko had returned to his apartment in despair. He was closer to the end of the road than he thought. At 7:05 P.M., there was a knock at the door, and Zabotin's chauffeur called out to him. Gouzenko climbed out to a rear balcony and made arrangements with an RCAF sergeant to take care of his wife and children and to call the police. Members of the Embassy staff were still in Gouzenko's apartment, searching—the entrance door forced open—when the police arrived. From that point on, it was a matter for the highest levels of the Canadian government.

Gouzenko was spirited away to a safe hiding place. Meticulously, the Mounties questioned him, studied translations of the documents, and tracked down those implicated. Arrests were made, there were trials, and the guilty went to prison. The biggest catch, as Gouzenko had hoped, was Dr. Nunn May, the British physicist who was, he thought, safely out of it in London. A steadfast Communist to the bitter end, May confessed his own crimes but refused to implicate any of his confederates. Much of his story was either on the record or filed for reference in Gouzenko's mind. May and two others implicated by the Gouzenko papers were the first atomic spies in history to be apprehended.

Dr. Allan Nunn May had come to the attention of Colonel Zabotin not through any leads furnished by his agents or by the Canadian Communist Party. The order to contact the nuclear physicist came directly from the Direc-tor in Moscow. Early in 1943, Zabotin was told that May was a "very valuable source" and urged circumspection in the approach. "He is a *corporant,* and his cover name is Alek," the director informed Zabotin. "I consider it best to establish contact through Frank. Advise me immediately when you have estab-lished contact."

Gouzenko recalls that Zabotin was furious when he received the message. He had been working with secondary sources in gathering atomic bomb secrets, but the Center had failed until then to tell him that a member of the Com-munist Party (a *corporant*) was available through "Frank" (the high-ranking Communist functionary Sam Carr). So Zabotin went about it in his own way.

It was quickly determined that Dr. Nunn May was one of a team of British scientists working at the atomic energy laboratory in Montreal—a part of the National Research Council. As such, he had the confidence of the director of Canada's nuclear work, Dr. Cockcroft, and access to most of the results of the work being done there and at Chalk River.

Lieutenant Angelov, one of the men working with Gouzenko in the secret wing at the Embassy, was assigned to make the contact. Angelov (cover name, "Baxter") used no subtlety. He knew that Dr. May had worked for an apparatus in England and needed no more than a shove. In Montreal, Angelov looked up May in the telephone directory and, with no warning, went directly to the house. Dr. May, who is described by Gouzenko as "a scholarly, meekish man," answered the doorbell.

"Dr. Allan Nunn May?" Angelov asked.

"Yes," May answered.

"Best regards from Michael," Angelov said softly, using the identity greeting May had used in London. Nunn May's manner changed, as if he had been struck a blow. Angelov later told Gouzenko that he gave the appearance of "a man who was trapped." He almost dragged Angelov into the living room, shutting the door behind them. Then, almost tearfully, he said:

"I have cut off my old connection with Moscow."

Angelov laughed. "We have an assignment for you," he said. "If you refuse, that will be trouble for you, not for us." There was a long silence. Finally, May asked wearily: "What do you want?"

"Everything you can tell us about the atomic bomb project in the United States and Canada. We want it in a hurry." May agreed to meet "Baxter" the following week. "We can meet here then, but after that there must be some other place," May told Angelov. "The security people keep a very close watch, you know." Angelov nodded curtly. From his briefcase he took out two bottles of whiskey and two hundred dollars in cash which he offered with a sardonic smile.

A week later, the report—ten single-spaced pages—was in Gouzenko's hands for encoding. He read it through and told Colonel Zabotin that it would be a bad idea to transmit it through telegraphic channels. Though the Center wanted speed, the process of encoding and decoding could lead to serious errors. The material was too technical. Zabotin agreed to send it by diplomatic pouch. But he ordered Gouzenko to put in code a second report from May. This, Gouzenko told the RCMPs, was a full description of the Canadian project and the Manhattan Engineer District. It described the work being done at Los Alamos, at Oak Ridge, at the Hanford plutonium plant, and at the Metallurgical Laboratory in Chicago. A list of men working on the project was appended. It included General Groves, Dr. Oppenheimer, and others who were "in immediate contact." The Center had some of this information already—but May, Zabotin, and Gouzenko had no way of knowing this. The Center, however, was double-checking on the data it had received from the Zubilin-Adams *apparat*—and testing Dr. May.

Allan Nunn May continued to supply information throughout the spring and early summer of 1945. Nunn May was not "just another scientist," as some have said. In fact, he may have contributed more to the Soviet effort than Klaus Fuchs—who entered the picture a little later—or Bruno Pontecorvo. General Groves's evaluation is contradictory. On the one hand, he told Senator Bourke B. Hickenlooper in 1946 that "It is very doubtful if May (had) anything but a general knowledge of the construction of the atomic bomb." But almost in the same breath, Groves said, "May had spent more time and acquired more knowledge at the Argonne (Laboratory) than any other British physicist." And the Argonne Laboratory was perhaps the most important MED installation, since it provided the experimental base for most of what was done at Los Alamos and Hanford. In 1954, Groves would say of some of the material May handed over to Lieutenant Angelov that it was "all-important." Certainly the Center gave Dr. May high marks. Though notoriously stingy with money, it presented him with another five hundred dollars.

The significance of May's espionage work is suggested by the role he played in the Canadian and United States research.* He was the senior member of the British team which was headquartered in Montreal, and he represented his colleagues on several inter-Allied committees. In January of 1944, he made his first visit to the Metallurgical Laboratory (Argonne) in Chicago. He returned to the Argonne in April of 1944 for a two-week stint at a time of critical experiments in the use of graphite as a retarding agent in the atomic pile. Again, in August of that year, he developed plans for the Montreal pile with Argonne scientists. A fourth trip involved intensive work "in a highly secret and important new field," today still wrapped in a top-secret classification. By 1945, a somewhat worried Groves vetoed a suggestion that May return to the United States because "I did not like him to have such a wide knowledge of later developments."

There were, of course, others in the Zabotin apparatus attempting to penetrate the atomic project in Canada. This was communicated to the Director in a series of messages.

Item:
    Badeau [cover name for a member of the National Research Council] informs me that most secret work at present is on nuclear physics (bombardment of radioactive substances to produce energy). This is more hush-hush than radar and is being carried on at the University of Montreal and at McMaster University in Hamilton.

Item:
    . . . Ask Badeau whether he could obtain Uran. No. 235, let him be cautious.

Item:
    The Professor [Dr. Raymond Boyer] reported that the director of the National Chemical Research Committee, Stacey, told him about the new plant under construction: Pilot Plant . . . This plant will produce "Uranium." The

---

* *Said the Royal Commission report: "May would have access to practically every document in the [Montreal] lab."*

engineering personnel is being obtained from McGill University, and it is already moving into the district of the new plant. As a result of experiments carried out with Uranium, it has been found that Uranium may be used for filling bombs, which is already in fact being done.

The Americans have developed wide research work, having invested in this business 660 million dollars.

Item:

Badeau asks permission to change to work on uranium. There is a possibility either by being invited or by applying himself, but he warned that they are very careful in the selection of workers and that they are under strict observation.

Item:

Bacon [Professor Israel Halperin] is himself curious about the Chalk River Plant and the manufacture of uranium. He claims that there is a great deal of talk and speculation on the subject . . .

Item:

It has become very difficult to work with [Bacon], especially after my request for Ur 235 . . . Bacon explained to me the theory of nuclear energy, *which is probably known to you.* He refuses to put down in writing anything . . .

And this message from the Director in Moscow:

. . . Try to get from Alek [Dr. May] before departure detailed information on the progress of the work on uranium. Discuss with him: does he think it expedient for our undertaking to stay on the spot; will he be able to do that, or is it more useful for him and necessary to depart for London?

Colonel Zabotin answered the Director:

Facts given by Alek: (1) The test of the atomic bomb was conducted in New Mexico (with "49," "94-238"). The bomb dropped on Japan was made of uranium-235. It is known that the output of uranium-235 amounts to 400 grams daily at the magnetic separation plant at Clinton. The output of "49" is likely two times greater (some graphite units are planned for 250 mega watts, i.e., 250 grams each day). The scientific research work in this field is scheduled to be published, but without technical details. The Americans have already published a book on this subject.*

(2) Alek handed over to us a platinum with 162 micrograms of uranium 233 in the form of oxide in a thin lamina.

Item, Zabotin to the Director:

I beg you to inform me to what extent Alek's materials on the question of uranium satisfied you and our scientists . . . This is necessary for us to know in order that we may be able to set forth a number of tasks on this question to other clients [agents].

---

* *When this message was studied for the first time, it was assumed that this was a mistake. The message preceded publication of the Smyth Report on atomic energy by one day. However, the Smyth Report had already been written. At the very moment that Zabotin was reporting to the Center on this subject, President Truman, Secretary of State Byrnes, Secretary of War Stimson, and Fleet Admiral William D. Leahy—submitting to the strong pressure of the scientific community—decided to release the Smyth Report. The Zabotin apparatus in Canada knew before the American people what was going on at the White House.*

What the Director answered will probably never be known. If it was in the files of the Ottawa Embassy, Igor Gouzenko did not take it out with him. But Dr. Allan Nunn May had accomplished enough to merit a "well done" from his espionage superiors. Though the report of the Royal Commission in Canada did not so note, he also presented Stalin with a sample of enriched U-235. This was his most valuable contribution. An analysis by Soviet scientists opened to them that precious secret—the precise ingredients we were using in the bomb, extracted from nature at the cost of an untold number of scientific hours and hundreds of millions of dollars. This one gift was worth all the time, energy, money, and duplicated effort of the Soviet Intelligence service. The U-235 sample and a long scientific memorandum from May were considered so important that an NKVD colonel flew them to Moscow.

Nunn May left Canada two days before Gouzenko defected. But the manner of his going—and of his arrival in London—had been carefully planned by the Center, by Colonel Zabotin, and by Soviet agents in Great Britain. When it became known that Dr. May was scheduled to be transferred to King's College in London, the Director queried Zabotin, asking him to work out all arrangements for a meeting between May and his London "contact." Zabotin radioed back that the meetings with the contact would be on "October 7.1727"—that is, on any one of those three days—in front of the British Museum. This was standard procedure. If May could not keep the first appointment, or if he realized that he was being followed, he would attempt to complete the rendezvous on the 17th or the 27th. The time set was 11 P.M. "Identification sign: a newspaper under the left arm. Password: 'Best regards to Michael.'"

For reasons of his own, the resident Director in London insisted on modifying the arrangements, and the Center gave Zabotin new directions:

1. Place:
   In front of the British Museum in London, on Great Russell Street, at the opposite side of the street, about Museum Street, from the side of Tottenham Court Road, Alek walks from Tottenham Court Road, the contact man from the opposite side, Southampton Row.

2. Time:
   As indicated by you, however, it would be more expedient to carry out the meeting at 20 o'clock, if it should be convenient to Alek, as at 23 o'clock it is too dark. As for the time, agree about it with Alek and communicate the decision to me. In case the meeting should not take place in October, the time and day will be repeated in the following months.

3. Identification signs:
   Alek will have under his left arm the newspaper "Times," the contact man will have in his left hand the magazine "Picture Post."

4. The Password:
   The contact man: "What is the shortest way to the Strand?"
   Alek: "Well, come along. I am going that way."
   In the beginning of the business conversation Alek says: "Best regards from Michael."

Report on transmitting the conditions to Alek.

Allan Nunn May never kept the appointment. Gouzenko's defection put the entire Zabotin apparatus on ice. Immediate instructions were sent to all Soviet personnel, however remotely they might have been connected with Zabotin's depredations, to stop all activity. Zabotin was summoned back to Moscow. Without informing the Canadian gvernment of his departure, as protocol would dictate, he slipped across the border and departed the American continent on the Soviet ship S.S. "Suvarov." There are conflicting reports of his fate. According to some accounts, he died at sea. Press stories from Moscow reported that he suffered a heart attack on arrival. High-ranking Soviet agents who have since defected say that he was shot in the cellars of the NKVD's Lubianka Prison in the usual Communist manner—a bullet through the back of the head, a rubber ball in the mouth to absorb it, thereby preventing ricochet off the stone walls. Three other members of Zabotin's staff simply disappeared from Ottawa. The Soviet ambassador left for the Soviet Union "on a routine visit" but never returned.

Between October 1945 and February 1946, Scotland Yard's Special Branch kept a close surveillance on Dr. May. But having been told to desist, he was clearly grateful and made no attempt to make any contact with the British apparatus. On February 15, thirteen people were arrested in Canada. Simultaneously, the Special Branch picked up Nunn May for questioning. He showed no emotion—neither fear nor bravado. Asked if he knew of any leakage of atomic data in Canada, he professed complete ignorance. When he was confronted with the names of confederates, he blandly denied that they had any meaning to him. He was equally unmoved when it was suggested that he had given secret information to any unauthorized persons. Would he give the authorities any help? "Not," Nunn May answered quietly, "if it be counter-espionage." What did he mean by that? "I would not want to give any information that might implicate my friends," he answered.

Five days later, on February 20, May was questioned again. This time the Special Branch let him know that it was armed with more than suspicion. What broke Dr. May was a quiet recital of the arrangements for his meeting with a London contact. His guilty mind convinced him that the Special Branch knew all. "I did not keep that appointment," he said composedly. "When I returned I decided to wash my hands of the whole business." But he showed no sign of anguish or repentance and refused to identify any of the people he had spied for—either before or during his work on the atomic project. His confession was as spare of details, and as self-serving, as he could possibly make it:

About a year ago, whilst in Canada, I was contacted by an individual whose identity I decline to divulge . . . He apparently knew I was employed by the Montreal laboratory and he sought information from me concerning atomic research.

I gave and had given very careful consideration to the correctness of making sure that development of atomic energy was not confined to U.S.A. I

took the very painful decision that it was necessary to convey general information on atomic energy and make sure it was taken seriously . . .

After this preliminary meeting I met the individual on several subsequent occasions whilst in Canada. He made specific requests for information
which were just nonsense to me . . . But he did request samples of uranium
from me and information generally on atomic energy.

May then described the two kinds of uranium he had delivered to Lieutenant Angelov—though not naming him—and stated that he had also written
a report on atomic research. "This information," he said, "was mostly of a
character which has since been published or is about to be published"—the
"explanation" the Center had prescribed. May volunteered the fact that he
had given "very little" information on the proximity fuse, noted that he had
received two hundred dollars "against my will" and a bottle of whisky—but
made no mention of the five hundred dollars he had subsequently accepted.
And he insisted that he had not kept the appointment with his London contact because "this clandestine procedure was no longer appropriate in view of
the official release of information."

The whole affair was extremely painful to me and I only embarked on it
because I felt this was a contribution I could make to the safety of mankind. I
certainly did not do it for gain.

Nowhere did he say that the information had gone to the Soviet Union.

Not that it would have mattered. He never said another blinking word,
leaving it to his counsel at the trial. The Old Bailey, which had heard so much
of Britain's routine evil, did not tremble when the defense told the court that,
after all, Alan May's only crime had been to save foreign scientists some of the
drudgery and some of the time required to develop their own atomic bombs.
The Attorney General, Sir Hartley Shawcross, broke in eagerly to reassure the
court. "My Lord, I think I ought to make it abundantly clear that there is no
kind of suggestion that the Russians are enemies . . . The offense consists in the
communication of information to unauthorized persons—it might be to your
lordship, it might be to me or to anyone." On this warm note, the defense
concluded: "He had nothing to gain, except what we all have to gain by doing
what we believe to be right."

"Ten years of penal servitude," said My Lord.

But even before Dr. May stood in the dock of the Old Bailey, Solomon
Lozovski, Deputy Commissar of Foreign Affairs, had reassured the Canadian
government that no harm had been intended, that the Soviets had gotten
nothing of value—and did not want it in the first place. His words are historic:

Soviet organizations have become aware that in the latter periods of the
war certain members of the staff of the Soviet Military Attaché in Canada
received, from Canadian nationals with whom they were acquainted, certain
information of a secret character which did not, however, present great interest
for the Soviet organizations. It has transpired that this information referred to
technical data of which the Soviet organizations had no need in view of the
advanced technical attainment in the U.S.S.R.: the information could be

found in the well-known brochure of the American, H. D. Smyth, *Atomic Energy*.

It would therefore be ridiculous to affirm that delivery of insignificant secret data of this kind could create any threat to the security of Canada . . .

To take any other view, Lozovski warned, would be to succumb to the sensationalism of the corrupt Western press. In short, America's atomic secrets had been thrust upon a reluctant Soviet Union—bored, but unwilling to offend its faithful friends. This must have been cold comfort for Allan Nunn May or the thirteen arrested in Canada. That Lozovski's statement was in every particular a lie did not really matter.

9 The Case of the Sad-Eyed Spy

HE LOOKED INCONGRUOUS in his old double-breasted, peak-lapelled, blue pin-stripe suit. The trousers were too long, and the fit was bad, as if he had taken it hastily from the hanger of a cheap ready-to-wear shop and put it on without bothering to wait for alterations. He would have looked far more appropriate in a druggist's smock, standing behind the counter of a lower East Side store—selling pacifiers to frantic mothers, making out prescriptions for cough syrup, and forgetting to charge the poorer neighborhood kids for their ice cream cones.

There was nothing distinctive about his round face and blurred Jewish features. Only his eyes spoke out with the kind of sadness that no single life could have accumulated—a sadness that is there at birth, the legacy of ghettos and constant flight, and the unfulfilled dreams that are older than Christianity. The eyes said, "How can you hurt me unless I let you?" They also said, "You caught me because arrest and conviction were the only honor left to me, the only bringers of rest."

Harry Gold stood in the doorway of a small room in the Old Senate Office Building. He was flanked by two guards who towered over him, but their presence was unnecessary. To Robert Morris and William A. Rusher, counsel for the Senate Internal Security Subcommittee, he said, "When we're through you can put a postage stamp on me and mail me back to Lewisburg prison. I wouldn't *want* to run away." The penitentiary had become home, and its laboratory, where he was pioneering in research on blood diseases, was the refuge. The guards watched stolidly as Morris and Rusher briefly discussed the manner in which he would be questioned. But Harry Gold neither wanted nor objected to the hours ahead on the stand. Once he began to speak, it was clear that he got a certain enjoyment from it; the years in the underground, followed by the years in prison, had never given him a chance to talk freely.

Gold's appearance before the Senate Internal Security Subcommittee, noted only by the slapdash immortalization in headlines of its more sensational aspects, was in a sense the first revelation of the man. Up to that time, he had been a series of notations in the files of the Center and of the FBI, an object of curiosity, and a witness constricted by the laws of evidence to disclose only what was precisely germane to the trial of Ethel and Julius Rosenberg. The man in the rumpled suit was at best two-dimensional as he faced an impassive jury and a hostile press. In the more relaxed atmosphere of a Senate hearing room, Harry Gold could speak in a soft monotone of the events and motives which led him to his crucial association with Klaus Fuchs and David Greenglass—both, like himself, confessed spies, though for far different reasons.

Harry Gold was never a member of the Communist Party and "never had any desire to be one." He did not consider espionage an exciting vocation and disliked most of the people he worked for in the apparatus. What small sums of money he was given by the Soviets came nowhere near compensating him for the time and effort he gave in carrying out his assignments. In fact, they did not even repay what he took out of his own pocket. Why, then, did he spy? His tangential explanations are but a small part of the story. Belief in the Soviet Union's noble experiment, a vague commitment to socialism, the bitter taste of anti-Semitism, gratitude to a friend who had helped him and then recruited him—were these enough to overcome the immigrant boy's devotion to science, his compunctions against betrayal, his love of family? Some deeper alienation must have been the compulsive factor, but certainly it is not easily apparent to the armchair analyst.

Certainly it has never been clear to Harry Gold.

When he was asked: "You never had much happiness in your life?" Gold answered emphatically, perhaps too emphatically, "I have been very happy." Then, with considerable irritation, he added: "There has been an incredible mountain, or a whole mountain range, of trash that has appeared—anywhere from saying that I got into this because I was disappointed in love . . . through reasons that I felt inferior, and I wanted the adulation of people . . . It is sheer balderdash . . . I was cocksure. That was my only trouble. I was always sure I was doing the right thing. I did have qualms. I knew this much: I was committing a crime. I was fully aware that I was committing a crime. I knew that. And where we lived in South Philadelphia, it was, as I said, a poor neighborhood, but criminal deeds were looked down upon."

It was almost as if he were talking to himself.

"I couldn't kid myself. I was stealing. And to add to that I was stealing from Dr. Gustav T. Reich, who was research director for the Pennsylvania Sugar Company. And Doc Reich, well, so to speak, he sort of raised me from a pup. I started to work in the lab, cleaning spittoons, and when I finally left . . .

I think I was a capable chemist. Reich taught me a lot and made a lot available to me. I was violating that man's confidence . . . I wasn't happy about it. But it seemed to me that the greater over-all good of the objective merited the means, or justified the means that I was using."

Perhaps the answer was in his life.

He was born in Bern, Switzerland, before the lights had gone out in Europe. The year was 1912, and his parents were in slow transit to the golden streets of the New World. At the age of two, he became part of the hopeful, grinding atmosphere of Jewish immigrant existence—which lives in poverty but does not admit of it. The Golds settled in Philadelphia, away from the protection of numbers shared by those who found their way to New York's Jewish slums, though with a ghetto of its own. The anti-Semitism he faced had nothing to do with not being admitted to the right clubs or fraternities. It was physical and violent—beatings at the hands of other children and the terror of what he later called the "brick-throwing, window-smashing forays" of raiders from the Neck, "a marshy section south of the city dump," whose inhabitants lived "under extremely primitive conditions and, amid the mosquitoes and filth, raised hogs and did a desultory sort of produce farming." This he could learn to take. But his father's experiences, described by Harry Gold in a long biographical sketch he prepared in 1950, cut much deeper:

When Pop first began to work for the Victor Talking Machine Company in 1915, the job was one which at that time had the designation of "lifetime." The company was run on a benevolently philanthropic basis, with a high wage rate, assistance if needed in buying a home, and gifts . . . at Thanksgiving and Christmas. The workmen were of a good, solid substantial type and their main criterion for judging the respect of a fellow employee was his ability at his job.

But, in 1920, things began to change. There was a mass influx of immigrant Italian workers, such as were needed in the changeover from the old craftsman technique to large-scale production. These newcomers were crudely anti-Semitic, and made Pop, one of the few Jewish workers, the object of their humor. They stole his chisels, put glue on his tools and good clothes, and in general made life intolerable for him. There was no point in protesting to the foreman, because that worthy was also full of hatred for the Jews . . .

Beginning about 1926, my father came under an Irish foreman at RCA, a man who was more bitterly intolerant than anyone Pop had yet encountered. He told Pop, "You Jew son-of-a-bitch I'm going to make you quit," and so put him on a specially speeded-up production line where my father was the only one handsanding cabinets. Then Sam Gold would come home at night, with his fingertips raw and bleeding . . . And Mom would bathe the wounded members and would put ointment on them, and Pop would go back to work the next morning. But he never quit, not my Pop. Nor did he ever utter a word of complaint to us boys, in fact he always tried to conceal his fingers from us.

Much has been made of Gold's sentimental attachment to socialism in his high school days and early manhood. Among his heroes was Eugene Victor Debs, Socialist Party candidate for President and a champion of labor rights, but there were many in the country who shared this kind of admiration for a man who put his cause above himself. In Gold's home, there was much talk of

Freiheit und Brüderlichkeit, much reading of the *Jewish Daily Forward,* much admiration for Norman Thomas. But this was anti-Communist, or at least non-Communist, socialism. What Gold read in the crusading socialist press, moreover, affected him because it seemed much closer to life than "a dreary subject called civics" taught to him at school, which bore no relationship to "the actualities of Thirty-ninth Ward politics as practiced in South Philadelphia in the days of the Vare regime." But as a thin, frail boy, Harry Gold had only revulsion when an older friend joined the Communist Party. "Bolshevism," Gold would write, "was just a name for a wild and vaguely defined phenomenon going on in an eighteenth-century land thousands of miles away."

Gold was graduated from a Philadelphia public high school in 1928, at the age of sixteen. It was not until two years later that he had saved enough money to go to college. But after two years at the University of Pennsylvania, majoring in chemistry and chemical engineering, he was forced to drop out. It was not until 1940 that he was able to complete his undergraduate education and earn a degree of bachelor of science. The need to help his family during the depression years—and the hours and days he devoted to doing the underground's bidding—slowed him up. Much of what he learned—knowledge which might have made him pre-eminent in the scientific world—he picked up at the various jobs he held. Dr. Reich, his mentor at the Pennsylvania Sugar Company laboratory, was as much responsible for this as any man. But the depression cut like a knife across this association, and in December 1932, "just ten days before Christmas," Gold was laid off:

Then it was that Ferdinand (Fred) Heller, a research chemist in the main lab, suggested that I should take my family to the Birobidjan area of Soviet Russia. He was serious, too. This was to me nonsense of course, because as bad as things were, I still considered this my home . . . But here was also the disgraceful specter and the deep ignominy of charity. And the first thing that followed my firing from work was the necessity for returning our new parlor suite (the first in sixteen years, and which was Mom's joy).

For five weeks, Gold searched for work. Then Fred Heller came bearing glad tidings. A friend of his, Tom Black, was leaving his job with a soap-manufacturing company in Jersey City for a better position. And Heller had arranged that Gold should get Black's old job. Gold's mother packed a worn cardboard suitcase for him, and with six dollars in borrowed money and a jacket lent to him by a friend, Gold boarded a Greyhound bus for Jersey City. He arrived at Black's apartment in the very early morning, at 1 A.M.

Tom was waiting for me in the hall downstairs; I can still see the huge, friendly grin in that freckled face crowned with those untamed reddish curls and the bearlike grip of his hand. We ate and then stayed up until 6 A.M. while Tom briefed me on soap chemistry and, in particular, on the "complicating circumstances" [that Gold was to say his mother was Christian and his father converted].

During those hours of anticipation, Black said to Gold: "You are a socialist. Fred Heller has told me that. And that's why I brought you here for the job. I am a Communist, and I am going to make a Communist out of you, too." Gold got the job the next day, at thirty dollars a week, nineteen of which he sent home to keep his family off relief. But with the job went the steady pressure of Tom Black and his friends. Gold was taken to party meetings, sent to the Workers' School in New York, where he picked up a few pamphlets but did not enroll, and taken into a social group in Greenwich Village which salted its Communist persuasiveness with talk of the arts and of literature. Gold tried hard to find some interest in the Communist Party, if only out of gratitude to Tom Black and to Vera Kane, whose get-togethers at her Village apartment enriched his life. She was a "graceful" woman of thirty, warm and gay, who gave Gold a feeling of belonging. His description of the party, how-ever, is caustic and true:

> I met such assorted characters as Joe McKenzie, the seaman, a young man with gaps in his teeth (due to his penchant, when drunk, for slugging it out with Jersey City's outsize uniformed police); an earnest old Pole who was an ex-anarchist; and a volatile Greek barber who once, in petulance at a meeting which had drearily degenerated into a discussion of Marxian dialectics, de-clared, "The hell with this stuff—give me five good men, and I'll take Journal Square by storm."
> These were at least sincere, but there were others, people who frankly were in it only for the purpose of gratifying some ulterior motives: a whole host of despicable bohemians who prattled of free love; others who were ob-viously lazy bums, and would never ever work, under any economic system, depression or no depression; and finally, a certain type . . . to whom no one but this weird conglomeration of individuals would listen, if even they did . . . In spite of Tom's unrestrained enthusiasm, the whole dreary crew seemed to be a very futile threat to even the admittedly unsteady economy of the United States in early 1933.

It may not be reaching too far to suggest that this sordid view of the American Communist Party may have contributed to Gold's acceptance of an espionage assignment. For, given the argument that the Soviet Union was striving to build a new society, that she needed help, contemplation of the misfits and outcasts who seemed her only allies in the United States may have convinced Gold that it was up to him—singlehandedly and in heroic pose—to lend a helping hand. But this was to come later—and much later than that he was to realize what a small cog he was in the apparatus. In September 1933, however, Gold was thinking in terms of the NRA, which had revitalized the Pennsylvania Sugar Company and brought him an offer from Dr. Reich to return to his job in the research laboratory. He accepted readily for two reasons: he would be reunited with his family, and he would escape the pres-sure to join a Communist movement he abhorred.

But this was not to be the case. Tom Black continued to visit him, still mingling humor and dialectics in his efforts to recruit Harry Gold. Then, in April 1934, he suddenly stopped propagandizing. During one of his visits to the Gold home, Tom Black took his friend aside.

"Harry," he said. "You've been stalling me. You've been trying to get out of joining the Communist Party. And possibly I don't blame you. You know, we are scientific men, and maybe we don't belong in." For Gold, there was an immediate sense of relief. He did not know that Black had been taken into the underground apparatus. Black immediately made this clear.

"But there is something you can do," he said. "There is something that would be very helpful to the Soviet Union and something in which you can take pride. The Pennsylvania Sugar Company has processes, processes on industrial solvents. There are materials of the type which are used in various finishes and lacquers. The people of the Soviet Union need these processes. If you will obtain as many of them as you can in complete detail and give them to me, I will see to it that those processes are turned over to the Soviet Union and that they will be utilized."

"And that," says Harry Gold, "is how I began it."

He was grateful to Tom Black for getting him a job. He had a "genuine sympathy for the people of the Soviet Union." But most of all, Gold had that attitude noted by Colonel Lansdale in his dealings with the MED scientists. "I got so that I could ignore authority if I thought I was right," Gold tesified. "I have seen it repeated in other people, particularly those in the scientific fields . . . We get to know our own job, and most of us get to know it fairly well. And so we think that, 'Well, if we are right in this, we are right in all our other decisions.' . . . It seemed to me that I had the perfect right to take this authority into my hands to give information which the Soviet Union had no right to. I simply arrogated this right to myself."

And so, in his own words, the "stealing" began.

At this point, the case of the sad-eyed spy was also the case of the naïve spy. The formulas and blueprints which he took from the Pennsylvania Sugar Company's files were not turned over to a courier for microfilming—the usual procedure. Instead, Gold would copy them himself, working hours of the night at the drudging work, never realizing that there was an easier method. After about a year, as the laboratory branched out into other industrial fields, the mass of material became too great. Black and Gold turned to their Greenwich Village friend, Vera Kane, "in desperation"—and she seemed to be as naïve as they. She suggested that they have copies made by a commercial firm in downtown New York.

"The matter again arose," Gold recalled, "of how we were going to pay for this copying. The blueprints were very large. The blueprints for a chemical plant can be very detailed. And there were reports, and they were thick—fifty or sixty pages apiece—and to pay for that—I was making a little over thirty dollars a week and Black about fifty—we just didn't have the funds." It never occurred to any of them that the Soviets would be willing, in fact delighted, to do the copy work. Black took the problem to his Soviet contact and returned jubilantly with a solution.

"Hurry," he said to Gold, "all our troubles are over. Now we can get all the information we want copied. I've got a wonderful setup. Furthermore, we have got some very good news about some of the processes you sent to the Soviet Union. They are very happy about them, and they've got them in operation. And there is a Russian who works for Amtorg who is very anxious to meet you. He is also the person who is going to arrange for the photocopy-ing of any amount of material you want. And he can photocopy it and return it to you very quickly."

The man from Amtorg, first of a series of Russians Gold worked with, went under the cover name of "Paul" or "Paul Smith." Gold knew nothing else about him except that he was the organizer of an industrial espionage apparatus in the United States. The meeting took place near Pennsylvania Station in New York. Gold and Black were instructed to stroll along the west side of Seventh Avenue. "Paul" unobtrusively joined them and ". . . then the man mentioned very peremptorily to Black—he just sort of shoved him off with his hand and said something to the effect that Black could leave now, and Black left." This show of authority from the short, stocky man—blond, oval-faced, and with "a nose that flared somewhat at the bottom"—seemed to impress Gold.

As they walked along the dark, quiet streets, Gold was given his first orientation in espionage methods. He was asked for a detailed account of his life and his background, as well as those of his mother and father. He was told very precisely what kind of information the apparatus wanted. And he was given the routine arrangements for further meetings, providing for all contin-gencies. From that moment on, Gold was no longer a *novator* but a full fledged agent. Thinking back at those early days, Gold said:

At this particular phase, the beginning, the question of doing it against the United States had not arisen. It was more a question of strengthening the Soviet Union. You see, this is also part of the pattern. I realized much later that these people operated with me in the very manner that a virtuoso would play the violin. They did a superb job on me . . . They knew what would appeal to me and what would repel me.

For instance, as we went along, I was not a paid agent, but I paid other people for their efforts, and they would continually commend me in very indirect fashion, of course, and would sort of low-rate the people who were accepting money from us. You see, they knew that I would feel good if I were told that I was doing this merely because I had a genuine desire to do it. They knew that money in itself would not appeal to me at all.

The agents assigned to work with Gold were not interested in theoretical formulas or in research that was still in the development stage. "I found," Gold noted, "that they were very, very slavishly addicted to processes as they worked, as they were in actual operation. In fact, they told me, 'If a process is good enough to make a profit in competition in the United States, then that is what we want.' " On several occasions, Gold learned of work being done which promised to lead to methods far superior to those then in existence. But his offer to procure the basic research was always brushed aside. "We would much rather have a process that works at 80 per-cent efficiency, but which makes a profit for the man who runs it, than one which works at 99 per-cent efficiency but which is merely in the theoretical stage," Gold was instructed. "We want things that work."

Harry Gold had run through "Steve"—a hulking dandy who wore spats

—and "Fred"—a martinet who did not ask for material but demanded it—
when the well began to run dry at the Pennsylvania Sugar Company. The
choice of "Fred," who rubbed Gold the wrong way, was deliberate. The apparatus was preparing Gold for the major leagues, and it was necessary to know if
he would take discipline. He was also being tested in another way. The apparatus took him off the job of stealing chemical data and assigned him to a
make-work project: routine and unimportant spying on followers of Leon
Trotsky. What Gold had to do was not significant. What counted, simply, was
this: He was told that the spying was preparatory to an attempt on Trosky's
life. Gold accepted this and passed the test. By accepting a part, no matter how
minor, in something that would lead to murder, Gold had demonstrated that
he was fully committed to any assignment he was ordered to carry out. He was
probably aware of this at the time, as he later explained:

> Well, here is what happened over a period of a year. I got sick. I think it
was part of the over-all pattern . . . We started off in a very innocuous fashion.
What, after all, are chemical solvents? But then, step by step, they advanced
the tempo. They advanced the level on which we worked, or rather, they
degraded the level on which we worked . . . And you got used to it. It got to be
a way of life with me.
> It was a dreary, monotonous drudgery. If anyone has any idea that there
is something glamorous or exciting about this, let them be disabused of it right
now . . . You work for years trying to get information. Sometimes you are
unsuccessful. You spend long hours waiting on street corners . . . And what
became even more important, I was gradually losing my identity and my desire
to be an individual. I was becoming someone who could be told what to do
and who would do it . . . I didn't want to back out. Even if I wanted, I was set
in this way.

But for a man of such deep alienation as Harry Gold, there were com-
pensations in the work. The world of science was impersonal, antiseptic. In the
apparatus, for all of the loss of identity, he was somebody. And he was able to
develop a warm and deep friendship with one of the Russians who received the
data he gathered from other agents or stole himself. The Russian went under
the cover name of "Sam" (the name on his passport was Semen Markovich
Semenov) and like Gold, he was a Jew. He was built more or less like Gold,
though where the American ran to fat, the Russian was solidly built. Gold was
struck by his black, dancing eyes and warm smile.

"Semenov was the only one of the Soviets who could have passed for an
American," Gold has said, "in the manner in which he spoke, dressed, and
acted—and especially in the way he wore his hat. For some reason or other,
foreigners never put hats on their heads as Americans do." But "Sam" com-
mended himself to Harry Gold in more important ways. He was erudite in the
arts and in science, a mathematician and a mechanical engineer, with a master's degree from M.I.T. "He had read widely in English literature and was
thoroughly familiar with the works of Charles Dickens, Fenimore Cooper,
Somerset Maugham, Sinclair Lewis, and Thomas Wolfe—and the poets
Wordsworth, Browning, Sandburg, Frost and Edgar Lee Masters." In mo-

ments of fatigue or exhilaration, he would recite long passages from his favorite writers.

Basically, Semenov was an ebullient man, as so many Russians are, given to the boisterous joke and the personal anecdote. Again like many Russians, he had moody periods in which he deplored the kind of life he was leading—standing on street corners waiting for his "contacts" and dodging the FBI. During these times, he would talk nostalgically of his boyhood in Russia and his love of skiing, of his homesickness. He also worried about Gold and urged him not to overwork. Once, after Gold had to report an unsuccessful mission, Semenov exploded:

"Look at you," he said violently. "You not only look like a ghost, but you are one. You're positively dead on your feet and exhausted. What must your mother think? You goddam fool, I don't want to hear another word about coming to New York tomorrow"—Gold was still commuting from Philadelphia to make his contacts—"or for several weeks. Go home and spend some time with your family. This is an order. I'll bet you that son-of-a-bitch Brothman hasn't even started his report. The hell with this Buna-S and everything—even if it means Moscow will fall tomorrow."

Then, according to Gold, "Sam" calmed down. "Come," he said, "we'll go to the Ferris Wheel Bar and have a few double Canadian Clubs and some food, and then I'll put you in a cab personally and see that you get on the train to Philadelphia. I'll buy you a parlor-car seat and a couple of Corona-Coronas." Semenov was also concerned because espionage work prevented Gold from marrying and raising a family: "Don't think that our people fail to recognize the sacrifice you are making. You can't go on in this lousy business indefinitely. You have to get out and forget it completely. And then you can go ahead and run around with girls every night and pick out a nice one and get married and have children."

Perhaps this was part of the virtuoso performance that Gold would later mention, but he still believes it was sincere—and others who knew Semenov in the underground attest to this. Perhaps he really believed it when he told Gold, "The obtaining of information in this underhanded way will not always be necessary. You'll see. After the war is won, there will come a time of great co-operation between all nations. You will come freely to Moscow and will meet all of your friends, and we'll have a wonderful party, and I'll show you around the city. Oh, we'll have a great time." Gold was not the best judge of men, and he responded openly to those who showed signs of friendship or affection, and this eventually led to his downfall. But certainly the relationship with Semenov compensated for much that was barren in his life.

Before Harry Gold came to his strange and fatal interview with Klaus Fuchs, he had three major experiences in the underground. The first was with one Ben Smilg, who was described as "an important government official" to Gold. Smilg was connected with the air-development center at Wright Field near Dayton. Over the years, he had been carefully prepared for espionage work by the apparatus, which even helped pay his tuition at the Massachusetts Institute of Technology. But for two years, he refused to give Gold any information. When persuasion failed, Gold was instructed by the apparatus to attempt blackmail. The Center in Moscow forwarded to Gold photocopies of the receipts Smilg had signed during his college years—receipts for sums of three hundred and four hundred dollars which the apparatus had given him for his M.I.T. education. But this did not budge Smilg, and Gold was told to leave him alone.

The second experience was with Alfred Dean Slack. Like Gold, he had never joined the Communist Party and felt considerable antipathy to communism. The depression years, his struggle to put himself through college, and an unhappy first marriage, however, left him bitter and lost. His brother-in-law, a fellow worker at the Eastman Kodak Laboratories, began indoctrinating him on the evils of capitalism and the brave new world of the Soviets. When Gold was assigned to courier work with Slack, he was being paid as much as two hundred dollars for each report—a very big sum for the apparatus. Oddly enough, Semenov, who despised paid agents, had considerable respect for Slack and defended him. Slack's reports required a considerable amount of work to prepare, he said. Toward the end of his association with Gold, Slack began to show extreme reluctance. Contact was lost when Slack was transferred from a chemical plant in Kingsport, Tennessee, to Oak Ridge. But before then, he had given Gold the formula for the secret explosive RDX (which Professor Raymond Boyer had already passed to Colonel Zabotin's spy ring in Canada), for nylon, and for the manufacture of Kodachrome film and developers.*

The third experience was with Abe Brothman, an expert chemist but a braggart, liar, and highly unreliable agent. In the meticulous notes which Gold prepared for the FBI, he wrote this of Brothman's contribution:

(1) Data on design of mixing equipment—essentially all Brothman's design. Obtained while Brothman worked for the Hendrick Co.
(2) Data on production of Buna-S, synthetic rubber. The information was probably given to the Hendrick Co. by either the United States Rubber Co. or Standard Oil of New Jersey.

It is interesting that Gold considered the theft of this Kodachrome process, used for detecting camouflage, the most important to the Soviets:

"The material could not be duplicated anywhere else but in the files of Eastman Kodak . . . But the plant . . . that manufactured the emulsion for color photography was run in a different way from [that] in which other chemical plants are ordinarily run . . . The man conducting the process merely carried it out in mechanical fashion and never knew what he was actually doing.

"The people who carried out the research on the various sensitizers and developers used in the production of these various types of color film, particularly the groups of film that are used in aerial photography for detecting camouflage, these people worked in separate departments . . . from the men who actually carried out the work. Usually people take out patents . . . But in this case, on certain critical materials, vital to these processes, I don't believe that Eastman took out patents.

"They tried to keep them as industrial secrets. This material was not available anywhere else in the world, and there was no way that the Soviet Union could duplicate this material except in one of two fashions: Either they had to steal it from Eastman Kodak or start an organization fully as large, if not larger, than Eastman's with any number of superbly trained organic chemists . . .

"This is something where there was no theory. It was just a matter of know-how—a matter of very, very specialized know-how on minutiae, very, very little things, but things which might take two or three years to find out. It might take a man two or three years to develop a particular sensitizer. Some of these photographic emulsions had six or seven layers . . ."

(3) Data on manufacture of magnesium powder for flares and Aerosol spray and containers for insects. Both of these were developed while Abe was a partner at Chemurgy Design Corp.; the Aerosol spray composition, however, was a Department of Agriculture idea. Neither of these projects was ever turned over to Sam as he did not want them, because of his contempt for any of Brothman's own work.

Brothman, however, was not new to espionage. In 1940, he had met with Elizabeth Bentley and her superior, Jacob Golos—"John" to Brothman—in a Chinese restaurant on New York's West Thirty-third Street. During Brothman's trial, Betty Bentley was to testify in her almost prim manner: "Mr. Golos said in Mr. Brothman's presence that I was to be the representative of the Communist Party from whom he was to take directives." As a party member, he was expected to pay his dues to her, and to receive in turn a disquisition on the shifting party line. He was also to give her blueprints and technical data which she was told to take down in shorthand. Some of his data was industrial, some military. But Betty Bentley and Abe Brothman did not get along well. For one thing, he repeatedly violated one of the prime rules of espionage: he was not punctual. Sometimes he would be an hour late to a meeting with her—or he might not show up at all. He did not perform his "tasks" or was late with them. He also asked too many questions. Brothman, in turn, complained about Miss Bentley. She did not show the proper gratitude, he said. And she was unable to take down his formulas correctly. He demanded another contact.

Because he was a chemist, Gold was assigned to take over. At 10 P.M. on a Monday in September of 1941, he waited on a New York side street for a car with the license number 2N9088. Brothman, as usual, was fifteen minutes late. Gold slipped into the front seat alongside Brothman and said, "Hello, Abe, I bring regards from Helen." This was the identification signal. From that point on there were meetings at various cafeterias and automats, but Brothman continued to be late or to violate security. He also tended to be touchy.

His instructions were to gather any and all information on the manufacture of high-octane gasoline, on techniques for the manufacture of natural and synthetic rubber, organic chemicals, synthetic alcohol, colloidal graphite, and lubricants. Brothman resented being given orders and boasted that his services were of great value to the Soviet Union. He had given "Helen"—Miss Bentley —complete plans for the turbine airplane engine and for the Jeep, then new and one of the wonders of the war. He made very large promises about giving Gold "complete plans plus all the descriptive material for a military explosive plant" being constructed in Tennessee. This may have had something to do with Oak Ridge, but Brothman never delivered.

Nevertheless, Brothman and Gold got along reasonably well, to the point where the "contact's" persistent questioning forced Gold, who used the name "Frank Kessler," to invent a story of a wife and two children, who were twins, of his married life, of the children's illnesses, and of his "wife's" infidelities. To keep Brothman happy and to feed his vanity, Gold arranged a meeting with a "very important Soviet official who wants to meet you"—with Semenov playing the part, flattering Brothman, and regaling him with descriptions of Moscow life. And Brothman had his good side, too. He knew that Gold was paying for the trips between New York and Philadelphia. Without making an issue of it, he would pick up dinner tabs or press a ten-dollar bill into Gold's hand from time to time.

But all of this was, in a sense, part of Gold's salad days in the *apparat*. Late in 1943, Semenov told him to drop Brothman and Slack. Gravely "Sam" said: "Forget them. Forget everything you ever knew about them. You are never to see them or to meet them or have anything to do with them again." (Had Gold followed these instructions, he would never have been caught.) And Semenov went on: "Something has come up, and it is so tremendous that you have got to exert your complete efforts to carry it through successfully. You've got to concentrate on it completely. Before you make a single move in connection with this, you are to think, think twice, think three times. You cannot make any mistakes. It must be carried through."

Then, to Gold's surprise, he was asked: "Do you wish to accept this assignment? It will be extremely dangerous." This was the first time he had ever been given a choice. "Yes," he said proudly, "I'll accept this assignment."

. . . [Semenov] told me there was a man recently come to this country from England. He said he was going to work with a group of American scientists in the New York City area, that this man would have information on the construction of a new type of weapon. I don't think he called it an atom bomb, but he did say it was a new type of weapon and that I would meet with this man and would obtain information from him.

In late January or early February of 1944, Harry Gold received his instructions. He was to walk on an East Side street, near the Henry Street Settlement. He was to carry an extra pair of gloves in his hand and a book with a green binding. The man he was to meet would carry a tennis ball in his left hand. On a deserted street, alongside an excavation, Gold saw a slim, boyish-looking man, wearing horn-rimmed glasses. In his left hand, as he sauntered toward Gold, the man held a tennis ball. He was Klaus Fuchs.

10 Fuchs: The Compulsive Traitor

IT IS AN ATTRIBUTE of the psychologically successful spy to be able to turn his moral judgments against himself into moral judgments against society. In the case of Klaus Fuchs, this was an absolute necessity, for his entire political life, starting with his student days in Germany, was morally repugnant. A colleague on the British atomic project once described Fuchs as "a colorless, disembodied, methodical brain"—but this was a superficial diagnosis. Once having divorced himself from the moral imperatives which motivate most men, Fuchs divorced himself as well from the social preoccupations of men. He was methodical, but in a compulsive sense. In fact, compulsion was the most eminent factor in his life. His dedication to science was compulsive, for he would work all day, then withdraw to his room and work late into the night. He drank only on occasion and socially, but at such times, he felt compelled to down great quantities of liquor.

At first glance, the boyish, absent-minded look was deceptive. But behind the thick, horn-rimmed glasses, his eyes had a hard, unwavering fixity which should have been a clue to more than determination. From a very early age, he had decided that the tolerant humanism of his father—a minister of varying faiths—was a form of weakness. The eyes said that Klaus Fuchs had made his decision according to his own lights. It was no longer necessary to debate the point. He knew what was right, whatever the world might argue. Women found him appealing, and he made use of them. But he was bound by no laws of society, of brotherhood, or of love. Yet, though he prided himself on the rigor of his logic, spinning a rationale for every act, none of his explanations could survive the acid bath of examination. In short, he was a nihilist who used constructive achievement for destructive ends. It may be that like most nihilists he was a little mad.

In his student days in Germany, Klaus Fuchs was a Communist. But in the feverish activities of the pre-Hitler youth movements, he did not belong to that group of misty-eyed idealists who took up the hammer and sickle in the belief that it was their time's crucifix. From the very start he subscribed to the ruthless Nechaevist doctrine that evil was a weapon of the Revolution and must triumph before communism could succeed. Fuchs held, with the tougher and more sophisticated of his fellow conspirators, that a precondition to the defeat of Nazism was the destruction of all Social Democratic and liberal forces within the country. And so, like the Stalinized leadership, he was not only willing to, but actually did work with Nazi students against democratic and socialist elements. His first betrayals came when he headed a student group,

106

presumably a "united front" of anti-Nazis, whose primary purpose was to suck in Social Democrats and expose them to Nazi vengeance. His later rationalizations for his espionage had a hollow ring, for he included among them the fact that the Nazis had beaten him and thrown him into the river on the day Hitler became *Reichschancellor*.

The Fuchs family remained in Germany, fighting Hitler, but Klaus escaped to France and then went on to England. There is some controversy as to whether he told the British immigration authorities that he was a Communist. Rebecca West, a careful journalist, insists that he did. His counsel, when he was tried for violation of the Official Secrets Act, stated that "in England, Fuchs never pretended to be anything but a Communist." The British government, Scotland Yard, and MI-5, which had motives for obscuring the facts, have always argued that the only evidence to any Communist associations was the allegation of the German Foreign Office, based on a suspect Gestapo report. This report was kicked back and forth, admittedly, by the British bureaucracy, but it was never called to the attention of General Groves or the Manhattan District security officers. Given the Groves hypothesis that once a scientist was involved in secret atomic work it was safer to keep him on than to fire him, the chances are that the accusations of the Gestapo would not have barred Fuchs from Los Alamos.

There is no record of any contacts between Fuchs and the open Communist Party in Great Britain. He was a refugee, poor and obligated to friends for food, shelter, and the cost of his education. However, those who provided for his physical and economic needs in his early days as a student of mathematical physics were far to the left of "liberalism." During his brief stay in Paris, en route to Great Britain, Fuchs had been fed and clothed by the French Communist underground, many of whose agents later joined General Charles de Gaulle's hegira out of France. It is far more than any extrapolation from known facts to assert that Fuchs was under careful party observation from the moment that he began to demonstrate his scientific brilliance.

When "enemy aliens" were transported to Canada, in part to protect them from the consequences of a possible Nazi invasion, Fuchs was sent with them. It is a matter of record that his closest associate at the Sherbrooke internment camp near Quebec was one Hans Kahle, a long-time Communist trained at the Lenin School of revolution and subversion in Moscow, commander of a unit in the International Brigades during the Spanish Civil War, and an agent of the NKVD. When some of the refugees were recalled to England for special service, Fuchs and Kahle were among them. Kahle, a member of the central committee of the German Communist Party in exile, was attached to Professor J. B. S. Haldane at the Admiralty—a post which rejoiced his NKVD masters in Moscow. Fuchs returned to his research in mathematical physics at Edinburgh University. Kahle and Fuchs met several times in Great Britain after January 1941. It is a mattter of record that they were seen together once at a Communist meeting in London.

At the time of this meeting, Fuchs was already working on the atomic bomb. He had been chosen for this by Professor Rudolf Peierls, an outstanding physicist who had read some of Fuch's papers in scientific journals, who desperately needed someone who could do the elaborate calculations needed in nuclear research, and who had discovered that in wartime Britain a native physicist was hard to find. The security services took cognizance of the Gestapo report but advised that there was little else to go on in determining the reliability of Fuchs. They also noted that if he had espionage in his heart, he would unburden himself to the Soviets rather than to the Nazis. The atomic project, moreover, was under the Ministry of Aircraft Production, whose considered policy was that anyone who could help win the war should be called into service, no matter what his politics.

In May 1941, Klaus Fuchs began work on the atomic project. In October, British scientists had sufficiently advanced in their work on the gaseous diffusion method of separating uranium isotopes that they were given the dignity of a special organization with its secret code name, "Tube Alloys." In typical British fashion, "Tube Alloys" set up no elaborate front. It worked out of inconspicuous headquarters on Old Queen Street, Westminister, with a small staff which processed the reports from British universities engaged in atomic research. Of all those reporting, Fuchs was the most punctual, methodical, and quick to learn. As a result, he rose in the scientific hierarchy—and he was known for his ability to take on any problem, to solve it, and then to explain the results with unusual clarity.

Unfortunately, he was doing this explaining to others besides his colleagues and superiors at "Tube Alloys." Shortly after he began his secret work, Fuchs made contact with "Alexander"—secretary to the Military Attaché at the Soviet Embassy. "Alexander"—in his official duties—was Simon Davidovich Kremer. In his confession, Fuchs seems to indicate that the first step down the espionage road was his. He stated that he made the overture to "another member of the Communist Party," who in turn bore the glad tidings to the underground. But if Fuchs had approached Kahle, the "other member," and volunteered to supply information, the Center would have been more than somewhat leery. The chronology of events and the known facts clearly establish that Fuchs, who had been somewhat perturbed by the Hitler-Stalin Pact and the Soviet invasion of Finland, found all his doubts resolved when the Nazis broke the Kremlin's heart by invading Russian soil.

That this Hitlerian infamy coincided with Fuchs's involvement in atomic research was a fortuitous circumstance. From his confession, it is clear that he expressed consternation to Kahle over Soviet military difficulties, that he discussed his secret work, that this information was submitted to the Center, and that Fuchs was given his marching orders. In his confession, a document that is short on espionage background but redundant in rationalization, Fuchs said:

I have had continuous contact with persons who were completely unknown to me, except that I knew they would hand over whatever information I gave them to the Russian authorities. At this time, I had complete confidence in Russian policy, and I believed that the Western Allies deliberately allowed Russia and Germany to fight each other to the death, I therefore had no hesitation in giving all the information I had, even though occasionally I tried to concentrate mainly on giving information about the results of my own work.

This last clause is, of course, nonsense, for in any kind of complicated research it is often impossible to tell where one man's work ends and the next man's begins. But it had not taken Klaus Fuchs very long to realize that he was an important man on the project, a very important man, and from this point on it was easy enough to convince himself that the mathematical computations he made for Peierls were really his own. It became clear to those who interrogated him after his arrest that Fuchs believed that the secrets of atomic energy were peculiarly his, to bestow as and to whom he wished.

In 1941 and 1942, Fuchs met repeatedly with "Alexander" in London. This meant that to deliver the carbon copies of his own highly detailed reports to "Tube Alloys"—as well as manuscript material on the work of others— Fuchs had to travel several hours by train from Birmingham, where he was working with Professor Peierls. Accustomed to the double and triple betrayals of the German underground, Fuchs remained uncertain after his first meeting with "Alexander" as to his *bona fides*. Perhaps, he thought, it might be a plot. He therefore marched into the Soviet Embassy to find out for himself. The reaction of the Soviet officials with whom he spoke was one of absolute shock. An agent never visits an embassy or speaks openly of his work. Frantic inquiries immediately went to the Center in Moscow—and normally Fuchs would have been quietly told to "go private"—meaning, to cease and desist. But his *zapiska* in the Great Index was sufficiently detailed to indicate that he was the kind of man to violate the rules so blatantly.

"Alexander" left England before the arrest of Fuchs, which explains why the description of him in the confession was good enough to enable MI-5 to make an identification. The next agent assigned to Fuchs was a woman who met him in Banbury, a town some forty miles from Birmingham. Usually they met on a country lane, though once they risked being seen in a pub opposite the Banbury railroad station. Of her, Fuchs had little to say. She was British and would have been apprehended had he given MI-5 any kind of lead. But Fuchs was subject to frequent lapses of memory, even after he was professing an eagerness to co-operate with British authorities. Given Fuchs's fondness of women, there may have been other reasons for his reluctance to involve her. Whoever she was, she served as a courier for less than a year. Then Fuchs informed her that he was being transferred to the United States. At their next meeting, she brought precise instructions for a meeting with "Raymond," who would meet him on New York's lower East Side.

Had the politics of Klaus Fuchs suffered a sea change en route to the United States, the apparatus would still have owed him much. There have been some who minimize the information Fuchs gave to the Soviets. But Dr. Karl Cohen of Columbia University has unequivocally shown that even before Fuchs was exposed to the work being done on this side of the Atlantic, he was in a position to enrich vastly the Soviet store of knowledge:

Fuchs's name appeared on theoretical papers on the gaseous diffusion process to my certain knowledge in 1942, and I believe as early as 1941. Because of visits to this country of Peierls and others in 1942, when the relative merits of the Birmingham and Columbia versions of the diffusion process were discussed at length, and the . . . Anglo-American interchange of technical information, it is clear that before Fuchs' arrival he had good knowledge of the American plans for the gaseous diffusion plant. It is important to bear in mind that because of Fuchs' grasp of the theoretical principles involved, which interrelate the process variables so that the choice of a few determines the remainder within narrow limits, *he would be able to reconstitute our whole program from only scattered pieces of information.* [Emphasis added.]

Work on the control problem [of the gaseous diffusion method] was being carried out by the SAM laboratory under my direction and by a section of the Kellex Corporation . . . The future operating company [at Oak Ridge], the Carbide and Carbon Chemicals Corp., was also interested. Fuchs arrived in New York . . . and a series of meetings were set up, to be held at the Kellex Corporation and at the SAM laboratory wherein the two American groups and the British group [which included Fuchs] could compare results. After several meetings in December, a division of work was adopted, Fuchs' part of which was to calculate numerically for the [Oak Ridge plant] the effects of fluctuations on production rates.

All phases of the control problem depend on the intimate details of plant construction, and in the course of his assigned task, Fuchs obtained from the Kellex Corporation complete knowledge of the process design of the K-25 plant [at Oak Ridge].

At the first meeting between Fuchs and Harry Gold, there was little transfer of information. Fuchs simply discussed the general organization of the Manhattan Project work in New York and made arrangements for future meetings. Gold would later recall six or seven such in various parts of New York City and its environs. Sometimes the meetings would last but a minute—just long enough for Fuchs to hand Gold a bulky envelope. At others, they would walk together for long periods of time while Fuchs gave Gold an oral report. The written reports were on legal-size yellow pages, sometimes up to a hundred of them, in Fuchs's tiny, crabbed handwriting. The Joint Atomic Energy Committee has classified substantial portions of the Fuchs confession, but according to the British security officers who questioned Fuchs, he supplied careful plans for the design of the uranium bomb and almost everything about the gaseous diffusion process for separating U-235. This latter information gave the Soviets a vital shortcut, bypassing other, less effective, processes.

Harry Gold, who had sufficient scientific knowledge to grasp some of the importance of the data he got, said: "They contained everything, from what I could see by looking at it. They not only contained a tremendous amount of theoretical mathematics, but the practical setup. I think that as much as any one man knew about the progress of the atom bomb, except possibly those at the very top of the project, Fuchs knew, and was in a position to give. Possibly he knew even more than the top people, because he was in intimate contact with it, in daily contact with it, you see."

When Gold was assigned to serve as the go-between for Fuchs, the Center cut him off from Semen Semenov. The bomb was too important to entrust the delivery of data to a "legal" agent who might be under suspicion. A new agent, Anatoli A. Yakovlev, known to Gold as "John," took over. He was far more efficient, far more precise, than Semenov—and he timed a rendezvous so carefully that Gold would leave Fuchs, turn a corner, and find "John" waiting for him.

Then, in July of 1944, Fuchs suddenly disappeared. A series of alternate meeting places and times had been devised by Gold, but Fuchs was never there. Finally, in desperation, and at the prompting of Yakovlev, Gold went to Fuchs's apartment at 128 West Seventy-seventh Street in Manhattan. Neither the doorman nor the janitor could tell him anything more than that Fuchs had moved. The apparatus was aware that he might have been transferred suddenly, with no way of leaving word of his whereabouts. There was no real fear that he had defected. But by this time, the Center was pressing its agents everywhere to supply data on the atomic bomb, and Fuchs was a prime source. Violating all the rules, Yakovlev gave Gold the address of Fuchs's sister, Kristel, married and living in Cambridge.*

On a warm afternoon, Gold presented himself at Kristel's house, introduced himself as a close friend of Fuchs, and said that he had urgent business to transact with her brother. But Kristel knew nothing definite about his whereabouts, just that he was "somewhere in the Southwest." He had, however, said that he would spend a few days with her during the Christmas season. Gold gave Kristel a phone number in New York and departed. But before he did, he made one serious mistake. In an effort to ingratiate himself with Kristel, he talked about his two nonexistent children, Davie and Essie, repeating the story he had manufactured for Abe Brothman. (Years later, when the FBI visited Kristel, she remembered it. This small detail helped confirm a suspicion, for Brothman had casually mentioned the same two children to the FBI when, following Elizabeth Bentley's confession, they had visited him.)

When Fuchs arrived in Cambridge for the Christmas holidays, he was given Gold's message and dutifully phoned New York. Gold was hastily summoned from Philadelphia and sent packing once more to Kristel's house. There he was spirited into Fuchs's bedroom. The mathematical physicist seemed a little less eager to supply information, but he obediently agreed to put

---

* How Yakovlev came to know of Fuchs's sister offers an interesting insight into the discipline of the underground. Gold described it in his testimony before the Senate Internal Security Subcommittee:

"Yakovlev obtained for me the name of Fuchs's sister. She had come into the matter once before—Mrs. Heinemann, Mrs. Kristel Heinemann.

"Q: How had she come into the matter?

"A: . . . As part of the general pattern of which I spoke. On one occasion, Fuchs spoke to me, after we had met several times, and he told me that his sister was also living in the United States, in Cambridge, with her husband, and that there was a possibility that these two might separate, and he asked for permission, or rather asked me to ask for permission for him—that if his sister came to New York City that they could live together, that is, so that he could be with his sister. He was very fond of her . . . He had to obtain permission . . . from a Russian, Yakovlev."

In fact, Yakovlev did not have the authority to grant that permission. It came, after due deliberation, from the Center in Moscow.

what he knew in writing. Several days later, on a Boston street corner, Fuchs presented Gold with a lengthy document. Again according to British sources—the Joint Atomic Energy Committee is still fearful that the Soviets may not know the value of what Fuchs gave them—it was treasure-trove. For now Fuchs could give, in his carefully annotated way, the details of MED work on the plutonium bomb, including the design and method of construction, on implosion and the implosion lens, and on the atomic piles for the manufacture of plutonium at Hanford, Washington. For this information, Gold offered Fuchs $1,500 in cash—a gift from Yakovlev and "the Soviet people." It was haughtily refused—a gesture which should not have impressed Gold, since he had already spent well over four thousand dollars of his own money, saved from a fifty-dollars-a-week salary, in expenses directly attributable to his espionage work.

The meeting in Cambridge had one other consequence. The apparatus once more had Fuchs firmly between thumb and forefinger, and Gold insisted on arranging a rendezvous somewhere near Los Alamos. The date was set for 4 P.M. of June 2, 1945—some five months ahead—in Santa Fe at the Castillo Bridge. Fuchs agreed with some reluctance, for his months at Los Alamos, undogged by *apparatchiks,* had convinced him that he was free. Without the need for the very careful lying necessary to the working agent, Fuchs had for the first time since his student days in Germany shown signs of social adjustment. He bought a second-hand Buick which he drove with some abandon, he went to parties, and he suddenly seemed aware that people existed for purposes other than sex or intellectual drudgery.

Late in May, just before Harry Gold departed for Santa Fe, he was given new instructions by Yakovlev. The normally submissive Gold was tired and irritable from days of around-the-clock work at the Pennsylvania Sugar Company laboratory—work made necessary in order to get him the free time to take the long train trip to the Southwest. When he was told that after seeing Fuchs he was to travel to Albuquerque to receive information from another espionage contact, Gold objected strenuously.

"I protested very bitterly about this additional task," he was to recall. "I complained that I was jeopardizing the whole matter of the information I was getting from Fuchs. It represented an additional delay, an additional period or interval in which something could happen, and I just for once got up on my hindlegs and almost flatly refused to go to Albuquerque. But I was told that this was very important, extremely vital, that I had to get this information. There was no nonsense about it." Gold, however, was right. The side trip brought him into contact with David Greenglass, and in time, this would be the link to Ethel and Julius Rosenberg. For this breach of *apparat* security the Rosenbergs would pay with their lives.

Weary from the long train ride, Gold appeared on the Castillo Bridge in Santa Fe punctually at 4 P.M. As a precautionary measure, so that he would not have to ask directions, he had bought a street map. On time as usual, Fuchs met him in his Buick, and the two drove off. Fuchs silently handed Gold a thick sheaf of papers and then launched into his oral report. The work on actual construction of the atomic bomb was going along at a rapid rate, he said, and a bomb would be tested perhaps in a month at a desert site near Alamogordo. Fuchs expressed his surprise at the success of the MED in building the bomb. He had always felt that the war would long be over before all the problems were solved. But, he told Gold, he had not counted on American ingenuity and industrial potential. "I sadly underestimated it." he added. The next rendezvous was set for September 19, at 6 P.M., near a church on a road leading into Sante Fe.

And that was it. Gold took a bus to Albuquerque, where he met Greenglass—then boarded a train for the journey back to New York. On a deserted road near a cemetery in Queens, he handed Yakovlev two folders—one marked "Doctor" and the second marked "Other." The exchange between the two agents was very brief, and Gold returned to Philadelphia, glad that he would not be required to travel cross-country until September.

Then, once more, he was aboard a train, Santa Fe-bound, unaware that this would be his last espionage assignment. Between the two meetings, however, much had happened. The bomb had been tested at Alamogordo with Fuchs as a witness on July 16, 1945. On August 6, the bomb fell on Hiroshima, ushering in the era of the Great Mushroom, and on August 9, Nagasaki was devastated. On August 15 the war in the Pacific ended as suddenly as it had begun. Immediately, General Groves began arranging what he had all along desired—a bill of divorcement between the nuclear research of the United States and its British Empire allies. British scientists were almost abruptly edged out and began making preparations for their return to universities in England and Scotland.

On September 19, Fuchs volunteered to drive into Santa Fe in order to pick up the liquor for a farewell party the scientists and technicians at Los Alamos were planning. The meeting with Gold, scheduled for that evening, was one of the longest he had ever had. His written report was highly detailed and very important. For he not only delivered to the Soviets the dimensions of the bomb, he also included the sizes of the parts, how they were put together, what the bomb was made of and how, and what triggered the explosion. He also reported to Gold that the British and the Americans were coming to "a parting of the ways" and that he would be returning to his post at Birmingham. Neither Gold nor Fuchs knew that just two weeks before, Igor Gouzenko had defected with his incriminating documents, or that the Canadian government was in the process of translating cover names to real names in preparation for the highly secret investigation of a Royal Commission.

Fuchs had other problems to discuss, far more personal in nature, which he felt would make it difficult to continue his espionage work. This is how Gold recounts the conversation:

Fuchs told me that his father [who knew of his underground Communist activities in Germany] was getting a little foolish, and that was just what he was afraid of. He said:
"The British, in an effort to reward me and compensate me, have told me they are going to bring my father to England so that I can be with the old

man in his remaining years." He said, "But if they do, he is bound to prattle about my activities in the student Communist Party." He said, "And then people will begin to wonder about my background, and once they begin to pry, you know what will happen." He said, "So how in the world am I going to keep them from doing this presumed kindness to me without arousing suspicion?"

It was a bit of a quandary.

Nevertheless, Fuchs was still willing to maintain contact with the apparatus. Since there was no way to receive instructions from Yakovlev (and, of course, the Center), Fuchs himself worked out a plan for resuming his association once he returned to England. He would, he said, be at the entrance to one of London's underground stations on the first Saturday of every month. In one hand, he would be carrying five books held together by a string. In the other hand, he would carry two books. Whoever was to contact him would identify himself by holding a copy of Bennet Cerf's *Try and Stop Me*. Neither man knew that orders had already gone out to all resident directors—and to "legal" and "illegal" agents—putting espionage apparatuses in the United States and in Europe on ice until the Gouzenko investigation had been terminated and the Center knew just what men had been implicated.

Fuchs remained at Los Alamos, the last of the British scientists to go, until June 1946. He handled all the housekeeping details, wrote his final reports. In November 1945, he made an official trip to Montreal, where he was offered and accepted the position of chief of the Theoretical Physics Division at the Harwell Research Establishment, Britain's new nuclear-energy center. On June 28, 1946, he boarded a plane for England—the warm praise for his essential work and keen sense of security still echoing in his mind. At Harwell, he plunged into the work of building its massive atomic pile. From the £278 a year he had received as a professor at Birmingham, he was jumped in pay to £1,200—and this was quickly increased to £1,500. For a time, he made no effort to keep the appointments with Soviet agents at the Mornington Crescent Station, but lived a normal and quiet life. Then, in 1947, after a visit to his Communist brother Gerhardt in Switzerland, Klaus Fuchs reached out for the espionage apron strings once more. Simon Kremer had gone to the Soviet Zone of Germany, but Fuchs was able to give his message to a woman Communist. The meetings with the elaborate recognition signals began once more for him. Though his old rationalization, hatred of Nazism, no longer prompted him, the old compulsion and the old arrogance had not been appeased.

After his arrest, Fuchs told security officers that he had met with his new Soviet contact eight times between 1947 and 1949. At the first encounter, he accepted £100, the first money he had not loftily brushed aside. What he might have told the apparatus is not really known. The British were building a plutonium pile at Windscale and another at Cumberland. Odds and ends of information about his activities in the United States crept into his reports. But the Soviets were now no longer passively listening and reading. They began urging him to divulge specific details of the hydrogen fusion bomb. They suspected that he was holding back and tried to force him to visit Paris, where he could discuss the British project with a scientist as highly placed as himself—presumably Joiliot-Curie. But Fuchs refused.

Meanwhile at Harwell, the British had finally and with great diffidence decided to set up some kind of security system—in part impelled by the reluctance of the United States to share further data as a result of the Gouzenko disclosures. Wing Commander Henry Arnold was appointed Special Security Officer and began sifting the spotty files maintained at the time by the British government. He reported to MI-5 the scant details of Fuchs's past, relying mostly on the discredited Gestapo report. But there was no other evidence, and Fuchs remained in the clear. In the United States, however, atomic security had been turned over to the FBI with the passage of the Atomic Energy Act of 1946. Material which the Bureau had been unable to use against MED personnel was joined to Counter-Intelligence files and correlated with new information which the FBI began to unearth.

In the summer of 1949, the FBI made its first major breakthrough, identifying Fuchs as a Soviet agent. It has been said that the lead came from an address book, taken from Professor Israel Halperin by the Royal Canadian Mounted Police, which listed Fuchs's name. This is not so. It was a far more significant discovery, one of such importance that it is still highly classified.* The very bad news sped to England and to Wing Commander Arnold. He had the facts, but no evidence that would stand up in court. To confront Fuchs would be risky. The British plan, characteristically, was to seduce him into a confession.

As an alternative, security officials suggested that Fuchs be induced to resign. Obviously, they could no longer allow him to continue passing on the data of nuclear experimentation. But this was also difficult of achievement. With his usual conceit, Fuchs made no secret of the fact that he considered himself the most important man at Harwell (he was actually third-most-important) and of his conviction that the research center would shut down if he left for an academic post. Two events made matters easy for MI-5. The first was what may or may not have been a random shot at the windshield of a car in which Fuchs was being driven back to Harwell from a committee meeting at Wembley. A visibly panicked Fuchs slid to the floor of the car and would not proceed until he had protection. To him, this was a warning from his Soviet masters who he felt might be preparing to liquidate him to prevent any confession. Fuchs was wise enough in the ways of the apparatus to know that only by talking could he save his life if the Center had made a decision to end it.

The second event was a letter from his father telling him that he was accepting a post at the University of Leipzig in East Germany. This, Fuchs knew, would raise eyebrows among the security officers and lead to a more stringent investigation of his past than had so far been conducted. He therefore volunteered the information to Wing Commander Arnold and suggested

---

* *Though the author knows the nature of this break-through, he must limit himself to this explanation: A highly secret intelligence group penetrated the communications system of an Iron Curtain country and discovered the names of Fuchs and other traitors. The group made its findings known to the FBI.*

that it might be wise for him to leave Harwell since the Communists might attempt to put pressure on him by arresting his father. In the course of subsequent discussion, he adroitly mentioned a casual association with the Communists in his student days. When he had finished a full recital of his years in England and America—even mentioning the Communist he had known in the internment camp in Canada—he was asked by William J. Skardon, who had been selected to handle the Fuchs case:

"Were you not in touch with a Soviet official while you were in New York? Did you not pass on information to a Soviet representative about your work?"

"I don't think so," Fuchs answered, smiling at the preposterous notion.

"I am in possession of precise information that you have been guilty of espionage for the Soviet Union," Skardon insisted. Again Fuchs demurred, but in a manner which led Skardon to remark that the answer was hardly a categorical one.

"I don't understand," said Fuchs. "Perhaps you will tell me what evidence you have. I have done no such thing." But he suggested that though he was innocent, he should resign from Harwell if he were under suspicion.

This was on December 21, 1949. On January 10, 1950, Sir John Cock-Croft, the director of Harwell, informed Fuchs that his father's presence in East Germany made it necessary for him to submit his resignation. There were other meetings with Skardon during which gentle pressures were put on Fuchs to speak. He began to feel that the authorities recognized his indispensability at Harwell and that, if he confessed, all would be forgiven. By a series of elaborate mental contortions, he convinced himself that having done wrong, he could wipe the slate clean by promising never again to sin. It would be a transaction between his conscience and Skardon.

On January 22, Fuchs told Arnold he would like to see Skardon again. Two days later, Skardon visited Fuchs at his small prefabricated house on the Harwell base. It should be noted that Skardon was still not fully convinced of Fuchs's guilt. At worst, he believed, the scientist had committed some minor indiscretions which had been magnified by the FBI into a serious crime. If he could shake Fuchs loose of the facts, that would end the matter—though MI-5 might take some convincing.

"You wanted to see me?" Skardon asked.

"Yes," said Fuchs, "it's rather up to me now."

But for several hours, he rambled on about his youth in Germany, his heroic battles against the Nazis, and his passion for science. Finally, he announced that, though he had a clear conscience, he was prepared to confess.

"When did it start?" Skardon asked—and got the jolt of his life.

"About the middle of 1942," Fuchs said quietly, "and it continued until about a year ago." And then, in a compulsive stream, he told the story of his treason, speaking rapidly but calmly. When Skardon left the Fuchs house, he had made no arrest. The case had now become one of high policy involving possible diplomatic repercussions. Fuchs, however, was in what bordered on a state of euphoria. He had confessed, and he fully expected that he would be allowed to remain at Harwell—in fact, that a more important post which had just opened up would be offered to him. The following day, Fuchs visited Arnold and urged speed in settling the business with Skardon. A meeting of British and American nuclear scientists was scheduled, Fuchs said, and it was important that he represent Harwell so that suspicions damaging to the British project would not be raised.

Punctilious to the end, the British did not bring Fuchs under guard to the War Office in London. He was invited to be present and eagerly made his appearance. "I ought to tell you," Skardon said, "that you are not obliged to make a statement, and you must not be induced to do so by any promise or threat which has been held out to you."

"I understand," Fuchs answered. "Carry on."

It was at this time that he dictated the famous statement, as revealing a document as any in criminal history, full of vanity and condescension and third-rate armchair analysis. It read, Rebecca West wrote, "like the ramblings of an exceptionally silly boy of sixteen." Its single contribution was the phrase "controlled schizophrenia" by which Fuchs explained his ability to live a double life. It had more meaning than he suspected, for Fuchs's schizophrenia consisted in being god and man simultaneously. His major concern was that Skardon get on with it, so that he would be able to get back to his work. But he had to return the following day because, by some perverted logic, he would not disclose to Skardon the technical details of the information he had stolen for the Soviets. He would speak of this only to someone cleared for secret information.

On February 10, 1950, Klaus Fuchs sat behind a cast-iron grille in the ancient Bow Street police court, calm, no paler than usual, and, as one observer remarked, "the most inconspicuous person in the room." His arraignment was brief and consisted mostly of Skardon's testimony. It was established that the information supplied by Fuchs had been "of the greatest possible value to a potential enemy." The trial, on March 1, 1950, was almost as brief, lasting one hour and twenty-seven minutes. Fuchs's face was blank when he heard his sentence, the maximum—fourteen years.

But though his defense counsel elicited from the prosecution that Fuchs had been completely co-operative, Fuchs remained tight-lipped when he was visited by two FBI agents who sought from him a description of the man he had known as "Raymond"—Harry Gold. Repeatedly, he was shown photographs of his former confederate, but Fuchs persisted in a denial that he could recognize him. Only after Gold had confessed did Fuchs find himself able to make an identification. After his release from prison, moreover, Klaus Fuchs forgot his long protestations of love for England and the democratic world. He slipped behind the Iron Curtain to East Germany to continue his nuclear research.

Much, however, had happened to Gold between the moment that he gave a last backward look at Klaus Fuchs and the day that he decided to confess.

For some fifteen months after his last trip to Santa Fe, the apparatus left

Gold alone. There were several abortive stabs at meetings, but the summons always arrived too late for Gold to keep the appointment—until he felt that Yakovlev had dropped him. There had been no repercussions from the Gouzenko case, and Gold began to feel that he had escaped detection and could "go private." He had even gone into partnership with one of his former sources, Abe Brothman.

In December 1946, he received a phone call from Yakovlev. "This is John," the agent said. "Have you been well?" This was a code question. It meant: Was Gold under surveillance? Gold conceded that he was well. By code, Yakovlev set a time and a place for a meeting the following evening—at a theater in the Bronx. But it was not Yakovlev who appeared. Instead a "quite large and rather tough-looking character" approached him. "I am Paul," he said. "Give me what you have from the doctor." Gold had nothing and said so, and the large and "tigerish" man furiously directed him to Third Avenue and Forty-second Street, where Yakovlev was waiting. Gold was asked for news of Fuchs or for any papers from him he might not have delivered. The two men sat in a Third Avenue bar and chatted until Gold mentioned that he was in partnership with Brothman. Yakovlev jumped to his feet, threw some bills on the table and said, "You fool, you have spoiled eleven years of preparation"— and he dashed out.

Yakovlev was right. For the association with Brothman was the major cause of Gold's downfall. Brothman had spied for Elizabeth Bentley and Jacob Golos. He also knew Gold's real name—Gold had told him when they became partners—and that he lived in Philadelphia (though he still believed the stories about Gold's two mythical children and unfaithful wife). On May 29, 1947, two FBI agents visited Brothman. They showed him a photo of Jacob Golos, the Soviet spy who had recruited him years before. "Never saw him," Brothman said. Then they showed him a photo of Elizabeth Bentley. Brothman, who was never very fast on his feet, suddenly reversed himself. Somewhat shaken, he said he knew Miss Bentley as "Helen"—the secretary of the man he had not been able to identify. And he quickly explained that he had lied about Golos because he thought the FBI was investigating an espionage matter and "I didn't want to get involved." All he wanted was to be protected from unfavorable publicity.

Brothman could have limited himself to a story about legitimate business dealings with Golos. But for some reason, perhaps because he resented Gold's ability, he deliberately and unnecessarily dragged him in.

"This man with the Russian name," he said disingenuously, "he came to my office some time in 1938 and told me he had some connection with the Russian government. He said he might be able to get me some business with the Russian government . . . I first loaned him blueprints for a vat or some machinery for a chemical process. We became quite friendly. I used to have dinner with Helen and him. Sometimes Helen came to my office for blueprints or plans. Then another party came instead of her, Harry Gold. I got to like Harry Gold. He was a good man in chemistry. Finally I asked him to come to work with me." Brothman admitted that he had once been a member of the

Young Communist League—but that had been a long time ago, and now he had little time for politics. No, he had never gotten any contracts from the Russians or from Amtorg, but he had bid for them.

Having implicated Gold, Brothman called him in desperation to think of some kind of story that would get them both off the hook. He swore that he had mentioned Gold because the FBI had a picture of the two them together— which was a lie. "Help me, Harry," he pleaded. Gold had no alternative. And so, when the FBI questioned him, he admitted readily that the man in the photo was a "Golush or Golish," a "real phoney-baloney" who had represented himself as a legitimate businessman. This "character" had asked him to deal with Abe Brothman on some chemical processes, since Gold was a chemist. Gold had been promised the world for his co-operation in this business deal, but nothing had ever come of it. Who had introduced him to Golos? One Carter Hoodless, a young man of some social standing (and, fortunately, for Gold, dead) had brought them together at a meeting of the American Chemical Society.

It was a good story, for Golos had misrepresented himself to loyal Americans in his work for the apparatus—and this the FBI knew. Gold and Brothman refined the story, coached each other thoroughly, and gave a good accounting of themselves when they appeared in 1947 before a federal grand jury investigating the Bentley charges. There is a wide gap between suspicion and knowledge, between knowledge and evidence, and so no indictments were handed up. Continued questioning by the Justice Department attorneys might have broken down the Brothman-Gold story. But suddenly, on orders from the White House, the espionage investigation at New York's Federal Courthouse was brusquely called off—among those questioned had been Alger Hiss and Harry Dexter White—and the government switched abruptly to the Smith Act cases of the twelve Communist Party leaders. Brothman breathed a sigh of relief, and Gold fervently prayed that he would have no more to do with the apparatus. (He was mistaken. A Soviet agent made a final contact with him to learn what he had told the grand jury.)

By this time, Gold had had his fill of Brothman. The two men did not get along, the business was not doing well—and Gold could not forget the gratuitous betrayal. He left New York and found a post as senior biochemist at the Heart Laboratory of the Philadelphia General Hospital.* For a while, it seemed that perhaps he might once again live a normal life. But from the moment that he read of Fuchs's arrest, he was certain that his days as a free man were done. He considered going to the FBI, but rejected the idea. He simply waited.

He had three months of waiting. For the FBI had very little to go on. Fuchs had described Gold as a man of about forty, five feet eight inches tall and weighing about 180 pounds,† with a round face and a Slavic look, possibly a scientist. The description given by Fuchs's sister was even less helpful, although she seemed to remember the name Davidson. The FBI found a New

---

* At the time of his arrest, he was chief research chemist.
† Gold was in fact five feet six inches tall and weighed 163 pounds.

Yorker with the name who roughly fitted the description. When a photo was shown to Fuchs, he "identified" him immediately. Fuchs's sister was certain that the FBI had the wrong man. Carefully and methodically, the FBI gathered together a list of 1,500 suspects. One by one they were eliminated until there were one hundred, fifty, ten. Gold was among the ten. And then, two pieces fit together. Brothman's assistant, Miss Moskowitz, part of the apparatus, had casually mentioned that Gold had two children. Essie and David—the two mythical nonidentical twins. And Mrs. Heinemann, Fuchs's sister, recalled that the man who had visited Fuchs at Cambridge also had chatted of his children, Essie and David.

This, however, was hardly evidence to take into a court of law. The FBI decided that its one hope, unless Gold made a major slip, was to get a confession. The best account of what followed is Gold's, written down in a massive autobiography for the use of his lawyer, John Hamilton. The day was May 15, 1950, a Monday:

When Special Agents Miller and Brennan first walked into the Heart Station lab at three that afternoon, even before they showed me their indentification, I knew who they were. And when Miller said they would like to speak to me "about Abe Brothman—and some other matters," that last phrase sent a disturbing tremor through me . . . That night in the Bureau's offices in the Widener Building, for five hours I stubbornly repeated the story Abe and I had concocted in 1947 . . . I tried desperately to create the illusion that I was genuinely doing all in my power to cooperate . . . Questions such as "Were you west of the Mississippi" were, to put it mildly, very upsetting . . .

For the next few days, the FBI let Gold realize that he was under surveillance. Now and then a special agent would drop in casually at his place of work to ask a few innocuous questions. It was all very friendly, with no pressure of any kind except the psychological squeeze:

On Friday came further blows that jolted and badly shook me up . . . The special agents and I were together for nine hours, until 2 A.M., during which I submitted page after page of my handwriting and printing, calmly agreed to have motion pictures taken—"Sure, go ahead"—and went over and over the Brothman story. Then, about a half hour before we broke up, came the sharp stab of this question by Dick Brennan, "Did you ever tell Abe Brothman or Miriam Moskowitz that you were married and had two children?" And when I stoutly answered in the negative, "But Miss Moskowitz said you had. Why do you deny it? Why lie about something like this?"

I knew why, all right, because this was the story I had also told Mrs. Heinemann. So I kept desperately trying to veer the conversation away from this deadly reef. Then followed the pictures: "Do you know him? Him? Her? Ever see this person before?" . . . And then the shocker: "Do you know who he is?" The white, staring and somehow dully expressionless face, with those huge glasses—Klaus Fuchs.

"I do not know him," Gold said, but his voice was reedy. "I recognize him as Dr. Emil Fuchs, the Briton who got in trouble over there, but I don't know him. I've never been in England."

And the terrifying answer: "Oh, yes. You know him. You met him in Cambridge."

And the too casual answer: "Never been there in my life."

The two special agents gave up before Gold did, and they agreed to meet the following day. But Gold was busy until the evening with a heart patient— and then there was a half-hour session at FBI headquarters. Miller and Brennan were even more weary than Gold, for the adrenalin which kept the suspect alert was not shooting into their veins, and they called it a day. On Sunday, Gold was back at the hospital, doing an experimental gastrectomy on a dog, and then back to the Widener Building. The strangest aspect of these days of questioning and surveillance was Gold's inertia. He knew that in his cellar were blueprints from Brothman, notes and directions from his Soviet superiors —a kitchen middens of incriminating evidence which so many spies collect in violation of the rules and with no logic other than the subconscious wish to get caught. During the Sunday questioning, Gold reminded himself that he must destroy this material. But as he describes it, his attitude toward the FBI was wonderfully ambivalent:

I was literally walking on eggs. But somehow, as it seemed that Miller and Brennan began to droop with defeat, I strangely enough began to feel sorry for them; they had given it such a good try. Yes, I was almost in the clear. However, instead of going directly home and frenziedly cleaning out all those terribly damaging bits of evidence which I knew were there (though even I had no conception as to the prodigious extent of this bonanza), I went to see . . . the dog at the med school . . . I did not actually begin the search for the accusatory items until 5 A.M. on Monday . . . I had a dully fatalistic and apathetic approach toward the impending search; what would be would happen, and that was all. Possibly it was the sheer and utter exhaustion of that past week which had produced this reaction in me.

But when I started to look, in the depressing gray of the early morning, I was horrified: Good Lord, here was a letter from Slack dated February 1945; a stub of a plane ticket from Albuquerque to Kansas City; a rough draft of a report on a visit to Cambridge; a street map of Dayton, Ohio; a card containing instructions from Sam relating to a procedure for approaching Ben Smilg; all this was here and more—I tore it all up and flushed it down the toilet (some I shoved down near the bottom of our rubbish can in the cellar). Yes, I had taken care of everything.

On Monday morning, Miller and Brennan arrived to search Gold's room, with his permission and almost at his request. They went through school notes and laboratory notations and chemical literature references. They examined every book, including mathematical textbooks and a large collection of paperbacks. Then, as Gold wrote, it began:

First, a copy of Paul de Kruif's *Microbe Hunters* in a pocketbook edition turned up—and in the lower right-hand corner was a tiny tag: "Sibley, Lindsay, and Carr."

"What's this?" said Dick [Brennan].

"Oh, I don't know," I replied. "Must have picked it up on a used-book

counter somewhere. Lord knows where they get them." But I did know; it was
the name of the Rochester department store where I had purchased the book
on one of my visits to Slack.

Then Scott [Miller] found a Pennsylvania Railroad train schedule:
"Washington—Philadelphia—New York—Boston—Montreal," and dated 1945.
"How about this?"

"Goodness knows. I probably picked it up when I went (on a trip) to
New York." Again, the truth was that I had used the schedule on my trip to
see Mrs. Heinemann.

None of this was evidence. None of it proved anything at all except to
Gold's guilt-ridden mind. The FBI men were asking questions, but only by
Gold's overelaborate casualness could they get a clue—and they knew far
better than he that their subjective reactions were just that. No federal prose-
cutor would put any reliance on their value. But they continued to look,
hoping to find something which would shatter Gold's defenses. Like all well-
trained interrogators, they knew that what Gold feared and what he knew
would be of far greater importance in breaking him down than legal evidence.
They were right. It is not the bullet but the crack of the rifle which frightens.
Sound Jamesian psychology was on their side. What broke Gold was Gold
himself, though he described it as "the stunning blow."

From in back of my bulky, worn copy of . . . Principles of Chemical
Engineering, Dick pulled a sickeningly familiar tan-colored street map of
Sante Fe. Oh, God. This I had overlooked. I knew that it existed, but, in my
hasty scrutiny that morning, could not find it, and so had assumed that at
some previous time it must have been destroyed.

"So you were never west of the Mississippi," Brennan said. "How about
this, Harry?" There could have been a thousand explanations, but Gold saw
the blood on his hands.

"Give me a minute," he said, slumping down in his chair. One of the
FBI men gave him a cigarette. He smoked it and then spoke the words: "Yes, I
am the man to whom Klaus Fuchs gave the information on atomic energy." He
had reached the end of the line. It was now a matter of police routine. At first,
Gold was determined to speak merely of Fuchs and to cover up for all the
others. But once the "fatal words" had been uttered, there was no stopping the
confession. Unlike Fuchs, who remained riveted to his compulsion, Gold found
liberation by speaking out, by making his perfidy plain. Some have called this
"informing," but psychologically it is far more complex than that.

The map of Santa Fe had been the needle's eye of truth through which
he could not clamber. And so he entered the gray world of courtrooms, of
testimony against Abe Brothman and Miriam Moskowitz, against David
Greenglass and the Rosenbergs. But more than anything else, he was a witness
against himself. The gates of Lewisburg Penitentiary closed behind him finally, and he was safe in his laboratory. The evil he had done remained
outside the prison walls.

11 The Rosenbergs, Greenglass, and a Will to Treason

ON THE DAY that the Supreme Court, in all its majesty, met to consider for the seventh time the case of Ethel and Julius Rosenberg, one Willi Goettling, an unemployed laborer in East Berlin, was tried and summarily shot for committing a "disturbance." For seven years, the Rosenbergs had the benefit of every legal maneuver, every opportunity offered to the innocent and the guilty by American law and tradition. Yet Willi Goettling, executed for a misdemeanor and forgotten before his body had been tossed into an unmarked grave, caused no anguish to the world's conscience. But every device of propaganda and implication was employed in the defense of the Rosenbergs though their will to treason and their stony lack of humanity were apparent for all who would see.

The character of Ethel and Julius Rosenberg can best be exemplified by anticipating the unfolding of their story and offering up three pieces of evidence:

Item: "I decided a long while ago," Julius Rosenberg told Max Ellitcher, an engineer he tried to "develop" into an espionage agent, "that this was what I wanted to do. I made a point of getting close to one person after another until I reached a Russian who would listen to my proposition about getting information to the Soviet Union."

Item: At a time when Rosenberg was attempting to get his brother-in-law David Greenglass to flee, he suddenly asked: "Do you think we will beat the FBI?"

Greenglass answered, "I don't know."

"Well," Rosenberg said, "you know, if I get word that it is too hot, we'll just have to take off and leave the children and the women behind."

"We are going to leave them and go?" a startled Greenglass asked.

"Maybe yes, may no," Rosenberg said.

"How can you think that way?"

Rosenberg gave him a disgusted look. "The Russians will send in division after division against a position, and they will all be killed, and they won't bat an eyelash," Rosenberg answered, "as long as something is being done to gain their end."

Item: When Mrs. Tessie Greenglass, mother of David and of Ethel Rosenberg, visited her daughter at Sing Sing's Death Row to plead for a confession which would spare the lives of the convicted spies, she said: "Ethel,

David is not lying. He is telling the truth. Why do you go on this way? If you don't believe in capitalism or free enterprise or anything else, if you believe in the Russians and feel they are right, think of your children. Think of what you are going to do to them."

"You are not my mother," Ethel said harshly. "Leave. I don't want to have anything more to do with you." And that night, she was singing arias in the voice she thought was made for grand opera.

This is the world that Ethel and Julius Rosenberg made for themselves —a world into which they dragged David Greenglass and his protesting wife Ruth, and many others whose names were part of the index to the case or remain in the FBI files, the doom they subscribed to neatly ticketed. A defecting Soviet engineer, who worked on data supplied by the Center, has described to American security officers the "thousands" of Signal Corps blueprints and documents his section handled. A good part of this data we know today, from confessions, partial confessions, and incriminating attempts to cover up, came from men and women recruited by the zealous Julius Rosenberg before, during, and after he had been admitted to the elite of atomic spies.*

The wreckage of lives—the bright young men from poor families, whose hard-won educations came to nothing as a result of Rosenberg's blandishments —makes a long catalogue. But Julius Rosenberg cozily offered the apple of espionage to his own family, and this ultimate perfidy led to his downfall. From the moment that Julius—a dark, bespectacled student with that drive and verbal assurance which are a product of New York's municipally owned City College—substituted for the placid faith of his fathers the combative Communist dogma, he was out to proselytize. At CCNY, he was not a leader of the Young Communist League, but an active member who gathered around him a group of young engineering students, later to be brought into his apparatus. He was also courting Ethel Greenglass, three years his senior, who shared Julius's Communist passion. Mrs. Tessie Greenglass had little use for Julius— "all that communism he talks about"—but David, Ethel's younger brother, was fair game. By a combination of lofty lectures on the merits of the Soviet system, by the pressure of derision for lacking the guts to accept "conversion," and by the skillful use of David's hero-worship for him—"he was my mentor," Greenglass would later testify—Julius was able to bring the sixteen-year-old boy into the YCL.

But David Greenglass was not made for the solemn mumbo jumbo of communism's Junior Achievement. As he later put it, "It bored me. It held no interest for my type of personality. I couldn't subject myself to the discipline that was required. I would rather lie in bed on Sunday morning than be up at six o'clock shoving *Daily Workers* under people's doors. And so I tapered off and stopped going." In 1940, when he was eighteen, he had simply dropped out. "But unwilling to subject myself to the discipline of the Young Communist League, I was not unwilling to believe in the principles behind it." What those principles were, Greenglass had only the vaguest idea. If asked to discuss

---

* *The details of Rosenberg's activities in other areas of Soviet espionage are not germane to this account. But the record is there, though few outside the FBI and Army Counter-Intelligence have bothered to examine it or correlate the information.*

the Marxist theories of surplus value or the mystical concept of dialectical materialism, he would have laughed, or as typically made a sarcastic remark.

Greenglass has said that "philosophically," he was a Communist. "Everything they stood for, I identified myself with. But my idea of what communism was, wasn't the actuality of communism. It was an idealized version of communism." But everything he knew, idealized or not, came from Julius Rosenberg. "He was the one who taught me about what communism was. It was his own version. Probably he lied to me, or maybe he even believed what he told me. I don't know. But in that way, he was my mentor."

Psychologically, this is of considerable importance. The young Greenglass not only respected a brother-in-law with a college education (David went to college for one semester, then was forced to drop out in order to go to work) and his intellectual conversation; he was also dominated by and to a degree afraid of him. Repeatedly in his conversation about Julius Rosenberg, Greenglass described his "persuasiveness." Rosenberg was a "salesman" who could "sell iceboxes to Eskimos"—a persistent phrase. (Greenglass has always tended to be a cliché expert, though, like many self-taught people, he often brought unconscious humor to these hackneyed expressions by misusing them.)

It was not until Greenglass was out of the Army and out of the apparatus that he developed the courage to stand up in opposition to the Rosenbergs. But it is also true that his lazy communism served a deeper purpose. Though on the surface he seemed the complete extrovert, ready always for the loud and inconsequential argument, he nourished a deep persecution feeling. This coupled to his ambivalence about Rosenberg—later transferred to the scientists he worked with on the Los Alamos project—demanded that in some way he strike back at those superior to him intellectually or in the scientific hierarchy. One of the people who observed him closely during the period between his arrest and trial had this to say of him:

From the outset of the investigation, Greenglass exhibited a friendly, easygoing, self-assured manner. He was extremely garrulous and expounded at great length on inconsequential matters. He was sometimes impatient and sarcastic, but usually was able to control his emotions. Greenglass appeared both courageous and honest. He was loyal to his family and friends [which explains why his first confession, though accurate about his own deeds, glossed over or evaded those of his co-conspirators] and was generous to the point of improvidence. Having a sense of humor and enjoying a joke, he took pleasure in attempting to startle others by his unexpected knowledge of facts and situations. He dressed in a sloppy manner and in rather poor taste, possibly because of color blindness. He did not like to shave regularly and had his hair cut infrequently.

Greenglass, who was a moderate cigarette smoker and did not care for alcoholic beverages, was extremely fond of food and tended to obesity. He enjoyed movies, chess, conversation, tampering with gadgets, and being better informed than his scholastic achievements would seem to indicate.

Had circumstances—financial difficulties and the tight-knit relations of the Greenglass family—not prevented it, David Greenglass would have shucked off his minimal Communist involvement and would by now be a well-paid research worker in an industrial laboratory. Many young men, far more committed to communism, were able during their military service to cut the social and political umbilical cord which held them to communism. When Greenglass married the girl he had known since early boyhood, Ruth Printz, he was only twenty. She might have tugged him away from the Rosenberg influence. But though she had no sympathy with communism, she felt that as an "obedient wife" she should go along with him, sharing his views and being in turn subject to the domineering of Ethel and Julius Rosenberg. This influence on the Greenglasses proved its value when the Rosenbergs plunged feet first into the espionage pit.

But this plunge was well prepared by the Center in Moscow. Julius firmly believed that he had by his own persistence brought himself to the attention of the apparatus. The contrary was true. For it was not until the Center decided that his connections could be of value that he was given the accolade he sought. At the beginning, he and Ethel were merely two hard-working members of the Communist Party. She was active, in an unimportant way, in the work of the Communist-controlled Local 65, United Retail and Wholesale Employees. (She also made repeated efforts to break into the fields of professional singing and acting, but she had more ambition than ability, and her small size, pinched features, and plump appearance did not exactly thrust her forward. It simply added to her sense of frustration, but oddly enough gave her that sense of importance so common among would-be performers.)

The Rosenbergs lived at Knickerbocker Village, a housing development in the lower East Side which streamlined slum-living by adding modern plumbing but reduced the organic community life of the tenements and the family shops to an antiseptic level. When, in September 1940, Rosenberg rose like the phoenix from a piddling private job to the position of junior civilian engineer with a Signal Corps Depot in Brooklyn, the Communist Party rewarded him by making him federal civil-service chief of the Federation of Architects, Engineers, Chemists, and Technicians—the same union of scientific workers which was employed to such good advantage in the infiltration of the Radiation Laboratory at the University of California in Berkeley and the SAM laboratory at Columbia. His Communist classmate of the City College days, Joel Barr—a talented engineer with a rich musical background—was part of the FAECT cell. So, too, was Mike Sidorovich, whose wife, along with Vivian Glassman (also in FAECT), became couriers for what eventually grew into the Rosenberg espionage apparatus.

Julius Rosenberg was very proud of his work with the FAECT and tried very hard to get David Greenglass to join. Once he insisted on taking Greenglass to a meeting, which was no more interesting to the young technician than attending the Young Communist League.

"While I was there [at FAECT headquarters] and going there and coming back," Greenglass would later recall, "he told me a little bit about the union. He said that most of the members were Communists or sympathizers, and that in the course of a jurisdictional dispute with the UAW over the engineers who were working in the Brewster Aeronautical Corporation that was in existence at the time in New York City, that he felt that the UAW was not being very fair, and they should have been, because at the time the UAW leadership was communistic. This is his words."

Just when Rosenberg was switched from party activity to spying is not clear. In the latter part of 1942, and until November 1943, he was reporting to Jacob Golos, spymaster of an apparatus in government which ranged from Assistant Treasury Secretary Harry Dexter White to William Remington—with way stations in every sensitive agency, including the Office of Strategic Services. Rosenberg would arrange a rendezvous with Golos by calling Elizabeth Bentley in the very early hours of the morning. His greeting would be, "This is Julius." She would get dressed and from a pay station relay the message to Golos. On one occasion, she drove with Golos to Knickerbocker Village—he was to meet "Julius, an engineer"—where he got out of the car and conferred in the shadows with Rosenberg.

As late as February 1944, Julius Rosenberg was not yet a full-fledged member of the apparatus. Party records introduced by the prosecution at his trial showed that during that month he was shifted from Branch 16-B of the Industrial Division of the Communist party to the Eastern Branch of the First Assembly District under Transfer No. 12179. Had he already been in the apparatus, he would have severed all formal connection with the party. By June 1944, he was already active as an espionage agent. The Center in Moscow had tested his reliability and his willingness. If his probity is today questioned, it can only be said that he made one slip in making use of David Greenglass. But there is reason to believe that his relationship with Greenglass was the single most important factor in the Center's decision to allow Rosenberg his great desire to be a spy.

The June 1944 date can be set because of his visit to Max Ellitcher, a former City College classmate, shortly after D-day, the invasion of France by Allied troops. Rosenberg had risen in the civilian Signal Corps ranks to the post of inspector—which gave him free entry to industrial plants doing classified work as well as to military installations. He was on some kind of official business in Washington and took the opportunity to call on a college acquaintance. Ellitcher had never been particularly active in left-wing politics at City College. But he had with some reluctance allowed himself to be recruited into the Communist Party by his good friend Morton Sobell, already funneling classified information to Rosenberg. What recommended him most to the Center's attention was the fact that he worked for Navy Ordnance on fire control devices for ground-to-air rockets and other antiaircraft devices. His special field was computers.

Rosenberg exchanged some reminiscences and expressed his elation at the opening of the second front and then, rather importantly, asked Ellitcher if he could get his wife to leave the room. In 1951, Ellitcher testified of their conversation:

He talked to me first about the job that the Soviet Union was doing in the war effort and how at present a good deal of military information was

being denied them by some 'interests' in the United States, and because of that
their effort was being impeded. He said that there were many people imple-
menting aid to the Soviet Union by providing classified information about
military equipment and so forth, and asked whether in my capacity at the
Bureau of Ordnance would I have access to, and would I be able to get, such
information and would I turn it over to him . . .

Well, he asked about any plans or blueprints or anything that might be
of value, and that all these things are needed, and that the choice would not
be mine. If I had some such information, it should be turned over, and someone would evaluate it.

"If you agree to give me this information," Rosenberg said to Ellitcher,
"I'll take it to New York myself and have it processed photographically and
the material will be returned. It can all be done very safely in one night so
that you can return everything before it is missed. There's really no danger.
The microfilm will be carried in containers to protect it, and if anyone should
tamper with it, any unauthorized person, the film will be exposed. It's very
safe."

The normal reaction to a proposal of this kind would be to throw the
seducer out of the house and to call the FBI. But in relatively few instances
does it happen that way. Rosenberg was a very bad judge of people, but the
apparatus has always made an evaluation of the "prospect" and knows that he
will be thrilled, flattered, or frightened. In Ellitcher's case, moreover, he was a
civilian employee of the Navy, and exposure of his Communist membership
might mean dismissal or worse. It would not have been necessary to make the
threat. A casual word dropped would be sufficient reminder. Ellitcher, however, showed no disposition to sound the alarm, though he was clearly not
ready to submit himself to the apparatus. He said he would think it over.
Rosenberg could report neither success nor failure—and for the next years he
continued to try to lure Ellitcher a step at a time into the apparatus. He did
not succeed and, in fact, chalked up one more witness against himself.

At a subsequent meeting in New York that summer, Rosenberg again
tried to win over Ellitcher. This time, to grease the skids, he argued that their
mutual friend Morton Sobell was in espionage for the Soviet Union. When
Ellitcher repeated this to Sobell, there was an angry scene. "He should not have
mentioned my name," Sobell shouted. "He should not have told you that."
Ellitcher tried to explain that Rosenberg knew about their close friendship
and therefore felt that it would not be dangerous, but Sobell would not be
mollified: "It makes no difference," he said. "He should not have done it."
This, however, did not prevent Sobell from adding Uncle-Joe-Needs-You arguments to those of Rosenberg—nor from asking Ellitcher to suggest likely prospects for the apparatus.

The relationship between Ellitcher and Rosenberg, however, was a see-
saw. At some meetings, Rosenberg would press hard for information and urge
Ellitcher not to leave the Navy Department for civilian employ. At other
meetings, such as the one which took place in 1947, when Ellitcher seemed to
be weakening, Rosenberg held him off by saying, "There's a leak somewhere,

and I've got to take precautions. You better not see me again until this blows over—or until you are contacted." At this time, of course, the apparatus had become jittery over Elizabeth Bentley's defection and was waiting to discover just how much she had told the FBI, what people were under suspicion, how much could be proved.

The last significant episode involving Julius Rosenberg occurred in early August 1948. At that time, the newspapers were full of Elizabeth Bentley's testimony before Senate and House investigating committees. Ellitcher had finally quit his job with the Navy, packed his family in the car and driven to the Sobell home in Queens—planning, as they had agreed, to stay there until he found a place of his own.

When I got there [Ellitcher testified at the Rosenberg trial] we put [our one] child to bed. I called Sobell aside and told him that I thought we had been followed by one or two cars from Washington to New York. At this point he became very angry and said I should not have come to the house under those circumstances. I told him that . . . whoever was following me would probably know about it. In any case it was our only destination. He was still angry and concerned. However, he didn't seem to believe that I had been followed. He told me to leave the house . . . I told him that it was not possible. I didn't know where to go . . .

He finally agreed that I would stay. However, a short time later he came over to me and said he had some . . . information he should have given Julius Rosenberg some time ago . . . It was too valuable to be destroyed and yet too dangerous to keep around. He said he wanted to deliver it to Rosenberg that night.

Ellitcher argued that, under the circumstances, it was dangerous and silly to venture out. But Sobell insisted that it had to be done and asked Ellitcher to accompany him. As they left, Ellitcher noticed that Sobell had a small 35-millimeter film can in his pocket which he carefully locked in the glove compartment of his car. The two men drove to the lower East Side and parked a few blocks away from Knickerbocker Village. Sobell disappeared with the 35-millimeter film. Half an hour later, he returned, and he was in a more relaxed mood.

"Well, what does Julie think about this, my being followed?" Ellitcher asked.

"It's all right," Sobell said. "Don't be concerned about it. It's O.K. Julie says he once talked to Elizabeth Bentley on the phone, but he's pretty sure she didn't know who he was. Everything is all right."

Everything, obviously, was not all right. For there was more building up against Julius Rosenberg than those after-midnight calls to signal a meeting with Jacob Golos. Harry Gold had already appeared before a federal grand jury, weaving the tangled web which later ensnared him. There was a road ahead for all of them, and a spoor on the path behind them. Ironically, had Yakovlev and Rosenberg and Gold strictly observed the etiquette of espionage, they might never have been discovered. It was a kind of tragic daisy chain. Elizabeth Bentley led to Abe Brothman, and he involved Harry Gold. Klaus

Fuchs was tied to Harry Gold and Yakovlev—and Yakovlev had brought Gold and David Greenglass together. Greenglass was tied to Ethel and Julius Rosenberg—and they in turn completed the circle with Elizabeth Bentley. It was all very bad form.

Rosenberg could have had no premonition of this in the fall of 1944, when he and Ethel invited Ruth Greenglass to dinner. His Soviet contact had told him that David Greenglass, now in the Army, was working at Los Alamos on something called an atomic bomb, that the Soviet Union was very interested in any facts it could ascertain about this new device, and that David was to be recruited. The Center had all the facts about the relationship between Julius and David, the hold the older man had on his brother-in-law. It knew that David loved his wife and would be rashly tempted to do what Rosenberg asked if it meant that there would be enough money to allow Ruth to live in Albuquerque—close enough to Los Alamos so that he could spend the weekends with her. In similar circumstances, very many servicemen would have, with Greenglass, let heaven wait for this temporal and temporary joy.

Greenglass had sought military service, but his color blindness led to several rejections by the Navy. In April of 1943, he had been drafted into the Army. After a smattering of basic training, he was assigned to duty at the Aberdeen Proving Ground in Maryland. Then had begun for him that life of military gypsy which became the lot of soldiers who remained stateside. In November 1943, Ruth Greenglass joined the army of peripatetic wives who crowded trains and buses, joining David at the Pomona Air Force Base in California. But what had been planned as a first wedding anniversary reunion became a little more permanent when she got a job at a hemp factory as a file clerk. When David was transferred again, she returned to New York. But the couple planned to be with each other again, if only during their second anniversary, on November 29, 1944. Meanwhile, however, David was pulled out of routine machinist duty and assigned to Oak Ridge, the Manhattan Engineer District.

For two weeks, Greenglass was given a thorough indoctrination in security, told he was now part of a highly secret project but given no idea what he would be doing. Then he was sent out to Los Alamos, to work in the "E" shop, machining highly secret parts for the nuclear experiments and the atomic bomb. He worked then under Dr. George Kistiakowsky of Harvard, later to become President Eisenhower's special assistant on scientific matters. The "E" shop was working on the high-explosive aspects of the bomb and on the special lens which turned the shattering force of the atom inward. By the time Greenglass was discharged from the service in February 1946, he had become foreman of the shop and wore a sergeant's stripes.

The dinner invitation which brought Ruth Greenglass to the Rosenberg apartment at 10 Monroe Street in mid-November 1944 could not have seemed significant when she rang the doorbell. Perhaps, she thought, Ethel and Julius planned to commiserate with her because the wedding anniversary trip would have to be called off; Ruth didn't have the money for it. The account of that

dinner has been thoroughly dramatized in a number of accounts, but this is
how Ruth gave it on the witness stand:

> Julius said that I might have noticed that for some time he and Ethel
> had not been actively pursuing any Communist Party activities, that they
> didn't buy the *Daily Worker* at the usual newsstand; that for two years he
> had been trying to get in touch with people who would assist him to help
> the Russian people more directly . . . and he went on to tell me that David
> was working on the atomic bomb and I asked him how he knew because I
> had received an affidavit from the War Department telling me—

MR. E. H. BLOCH [counsel for the Rosenbergs]: I move to strike out the "because."

THE COURT: All right, strike out "because."

Q: Just tell us what went on in the conversation.

A: I said that I had received an affidavit from the War Department telling me
that my mail to David would be censored and his to me because he was
working on a top secret project.

THE COURT: Madam, could you sit back?

THE WITNESS: Yes, I am sorry.

THE COURT: And just speak a little slower, please.

THE WITNESS: Yes.

A: [continued] And he said—I wanted to know how he knew what David was
doing. He said that his friends had told him that David was working on the
atomic bomb, and he went on to tell me that the bomb was the most destruc-
tive weapon used so far, that it had dangerous radiation effects, that the
United States and Britain were working on this project jointly, and that
he felt that the information should be shared with Russia, who was our ally
at the time, because if all nations had the information then one nation
wouldn't use the bomb as a threat against another.

> He said that he wanted me to tell my husband David that he should
> give information to Julius to be passed to the Russians. And at first I ob-
> jected to this. I didn't think it was right. I said that the people who are in
> charge of the work on the bomb were in a better position to know whether
> the information should be shared or not.

> Ethel Rosenberg said that I should at least tell it to David, that she
> felt that this was right for David, that he would want it, that I should
> give him the message and let him decide for himself . . . Julius and Ethel
> persuaded me to give my husband the message and they told me the
> information—

MR. E. H. BLOCH: I move to strike it out.

THE COURT: All right, strike out the word "persuaded." As a result of this
conversation you decided to give your husband—

THE WITNESS: I decided to give my husband the message and Julius Rosenberg
told me the things he wanted me to ask my husband.

Following routine practice, Rosenberg did not ask for any information
that would have shocked Greenglass. It was of minor importance—the kind of

thing that could be rationalized easily as not damaging to anyone: a description of the physical layout at Los Alamos, the names of the important scientists there (this, of course, was a closely guarded secret, since knowledge of their presence and their specialty would give away the nature of the work), what the security measures were, whether Los Alamos was camouflaged. Rosenberg also warned Ruth to tell David to be very circumspect, not to indulge in political conversation, not to remove any blueprints or sketches, and not to be obvious in asking questions. (The last point was a waste of breath. Before he had even considered espionage, Greenglass had irritated the scientists who came into the "E" or Theta shop by asking too many questions—simply out of unregenerate curiosity.) To clinch Ruth's participation in this first step, Rosenberg gave her the $150 she needed to make the trip to Albuquerque.

Ruth Greenglass arrived in Albuquerque and registered at the Hotel Franciscan just before her wedding anniversary. David was able to get what she recalls as a "five-day" pass—probably three days and a weekend. She mentioned nothing to him until the third day, when they were walking along Route 66 on the outskirts of the city. At first, his reaction to Rosenberg's request was as negative as Ruth's. Then he learned that Julius had given her $150 and, past an initial anger that she had accepted it, Greenglass began to change his mind. The following morning, to Ruth's surprise and chagrin, he told her he would co-operate with the Rosenbergs. And so they were caught.

When Ruth Greenglass returned to New York, she brought back with her the answers to Rosenberg's questions, all carefully memorized. He was delighted and asked her to write it all down for him. He was even more pleased when she told him that David would be in New York on furlough in about a month. "How would you like to go to Albuquerque to live?" he said, offering the reward.

"I'd be very happy to be near David," Ruth answered.

"You are going to go there," he said. "You'll probably be able to find a job, but if you can't, just don't worry about the money. It will be taken care of." For those who experienced years of separation during the war, it is easy to understand—though not to condone—the effect of this declaration. When David Greenglass arrived in New York, Ruth was able to give him the news that, due to the generosity of Rosenberg's "friends," they would be able to be together in Albuquerque—at least on weekends, when David could leave Los Alamos. The bill was presented a few days later. Julius Rosenberg appeared one morning at 266 Stanton Street, where the Greenglasses lived.

"He asked me what I was doing out there, and I told him I was working on lenses. H.E. lens molds," Greenglass testified. This was an unexpected bonanza, though Rosenberg may not have known it. The apparatus had been prodding its agents for information on the implosion lens—Yakovlev had expressed considerable eagerness to get at least a schematic drawing of it from Harry Gold—and Greenglass could diagram it for Rosenberg, which he did.*

---

* During the trial, the Rosenberg defense conceded that Greenglass could have made this and other drawings. But it argued that they were neither important nor secret. This contention was torpedoed by the prosecution, which put on the stand Dr. Walter Koski of Johns

That day, he also wrote a full report on everything he had picked up, either by questioning his associates or overhearing their shop talk. Because his handwriting was not good, Ethel Rosenberg dutifully typed the material for Julius.

Several nights later, the Greenglasses were invited to dinner at the Rosenbergs'. Present that evening was Ann Sidorovich, whose husband Greenglass had known. The Sidoroviches had moved to Cleveland, but Ann had made a special trip to New York in order to be present. Before dinner, Mrs. Sidorovich left. It was at this point that Julius told the Greenglasses that "this woman" would be the courier who would receive information from him about the atomic bomb. During the dinner, Rosenberg outlined a plan for meeting with her. Either "this woman" or someone else would go to Denver. She would meet with Ruth in a motion-picture theater, and they would exchange pocketbooks in the dark. Ruth's pocketbook would contain David's data for the apparatus. Rosenberg said that Ann Sidorovich had been present "so that we would know what she looked like." Then the question was asked: Supposing the apparatus decided to send someone else?

"So Julius said to my wife," Greenglass testified, " 'Well, I'll give you something so that you will be able to identify the person that does come.' "

Well, Rosenberg and my wife and Ethel went into the kitchen, and I was in the living room. And then a little while later, after they had been there for about five minutes or so, they came out and my wife had in her hand a Jello box side . . . And it had been cut, and Julius had the other part of it.

This recognition symbol was to cause much hilarity among those who professed to believe that Rosenberg was innocent. It was, however, one of the oldest devices—and perhaps the most reliable—in espionage work. For the side of the Jello box had been cut in a jagged pattern. When the courier presented

---

Hopkins, who had done some of the implosion research at Los Alamos and taken his diagrams for translation into finished products to the Theta shop. Here is his testimony:

"Q: Do you recognize that exhibit [a copy made by Greenglass of the drawing he had given Rosenberg] as . . . a substantially accurate replica of a sketch that you made at or about the time which you have testified to at Los Alamos in connection with your experimentation?

"A: I do.

"Q: Is it a reasonably accurate portrayal of a sketch of a type of lens mold or lens that you required in the course of your experimental work at the time?

"A: It is . . .

"Q: What does it portray to you? [Another Greenglass drawing.]

"A: It is essentially—it is a sketch, a rough sketch of our experimental setup for studying cylindrical implosion . . .

"Q: Did you know [in 1944 and 1945] that the experiments which you were conducting and the effects as they were observed by you could have been of advantage to a foreign nation?

"A: To the best of my knowledge and all of my colleagues who were involved in this field, there was no information in text books or technical journals on this patricular subject.

"Q: In other words, you were engaged in a new and original field?

"A: Correct.

"Q: And up to that point and continuing right up until this trial, has the information relating to the lens mold and the lens and the experimentation to which you have testified continued to be secret information?

"A: It still is.

"Q: . . . Is it not a fact that one expert could ascertain at that time, if shown Exhibits 2, 6, and 7, the nature and the object of the activity that was under way at Los Alamos in relation to the production of the atom bomb?

"A: He could."

This colloquy not only demonstrates the importance of Greenglass' contribution to the Soviet atomic bomb effort but, since an official of the Atomic Energy Commission sat in the courtroom declassifying documents needed in the trial (though not shown to the press) and then immediately classified them again, it destroys the later contention of the Rosenberg defense that Greenglass was coached by the FBI. The FBI had no access to the sketches for the implosion lens.

his half to Ruth Greenglass, she could match it against her own. There was no possibility for a slip-up—although more sophisticated agents like Hede Massing had once objected to so "old-fashioned" a method for making an "identity." David Greenglass, however, was impressed.

"That's very clever," he said.

"The simplest things are the cleverest," Rosenberg told him, as Ruth put her half in her wallet.

Before the Greenglasses left that night, Rosenberg told David that the apparatus wanted very much to discuss the implosion lens with him before he left New York. A rendezvous was arranged several nights later, to take place somewhere between Forty-second Street and Fifty-ninth Street on First Avenue, a grim neighborhood of warehouses and abattoirs before they were torn down for the United Nations, completely deserted after dark. Julius introduced David to a Russian. Greenglass and the Russian drove through empty streets, while the Russian, muffled in an overcoat, his hat pulled down over his eyes, asked searching questions about the lens, the formula for its curvature, the high-explosive used, and the means of detonation. He was obviously a man with scientific knowledge, which would indicate that he might have been Semen Semenov—but Greenglass was never able to identify him. The questions extended beyond what Greenglass then knew, so he was instructed to get more information to supply to the courier who visited him in Albuquerque or made contact with his wife in Denver.

Julius Rosenberg had made the introduction. When the Russian finished pumping Greenglass, the two returned to the corner where they had left Rosenberg. The Russian got out of the car, and Julius said to David: "Go home now. I'll stay with him." And Rosenberg and his Russian disappeared dramatically into the darkness.

It was early on a June 1945 Sunday that the doorbell rang at the small apartment the Greenglasses had taken in Albuquerque. "Mr. Greenglass?" asked a sad-eyed man. "I bring regards from Julius." He seemed startled and apprehensive that the man who let him in was a soldier. Greenglass walked to his wife's purse, took out the wallet, and produced her half of the Jello box. Harry Gold, his visitor, presented the other half, and they matched them. The fit was perfect.

"Do you have anything for me?" Gold asked.

"Yes," said Greenglass, "but I've got to write it up. If you come back in the afternoon, I'll give it to you." And he started to tell Gold about a number of people at Los Alamos who were, he believed, ready to be recruited. Gold, the professional, was horrified. He brushed aside Greenglass' explanation that he was only following Julius's orders. "I don't want to know about it," Gold said and departed hastily, refusing an offer of breakfast. This overlapping of espionage rings was a violation of the rules, but Yakovlev had insisted on it. Recruitment of agents by Greenglass would have been against the rules, too, but also a senseless risk.

When Gold returned that afternoon, Greenglass had filled several sheets of paper with more advanced designs of the lens mold as well as a description of the progress of the research in cylindrical implosion—the material which had been demanded of him by the Russian.* Gold accepted it and gave Greenglass an envelope with five hundred dollars. He departed with considerable misgivings, as well he might have. The trip to Albuquerque cost Ethel and Julius Rosenberg their lives and sent Greenglass to prison under a fifteen-year sentence, for Gold was the link in the investigative chain. "Will it be enough?" Gold asked when he gave Greenglass the money. "Well, it will be enough for the present," Greenglass answered him.

In September 1945, Greenglass and his wife were back in New York on another furlough—and they had even bigger news. In January 1945, Julius had given him a very general description of the atomic bomb in order to brief him on what to look for. "There is fissionable material at one end of a tube," Rosenberg had said, "and at the other end of the tube there is a sliding member that is also fissionable, and when they are brought together under great pressure, a nuclear reaction takes place." This, in elementary terms, was the Hiroshima bomb. But Greenglass, during the September visit, had in his possession details of the more advanced Nagasaki bomb. Rosenberg asked him to "write it up" immediately and gave him two hundred dollars. That night, at the Rosenberg apartment, David handed his brother-in-law twelve pages of text and diagram. "This is very good," Rosenberg said. "We ought to have it typed up immediately." And Ruth Greenglass added, "We'll probably have to correct the grammar." Ethel Rosenberg set up a bridge table, put her typewriter on it, and the three clustered around her as she typed. That night, too, Rosenberg boasted that, as a Signal Corps inspector, he had seen a proximity fuse at a plant manufacturing it and had put it in his briefcase and walked out.

When the typing had been completed, Julius asked David what he intended to do, now that the war was over. "Get out of the Army," said Greenglass. Rosenberg argued that he should stay at Los Alamos, in a civilian capacity, in order to continue his espionage work. But though Greenglass was not yet ready to defy his brother-in-law, he wanted to break loose from the apparatus. He had gotten into it out of mixed motives—to impress Julius and to provide his wife with the means to be near him. Now the war was over. He wanted to earn a living, to continue his education. He had heard enough from Rosenberg to disillusion him thoroughly on the "idealism" of the Communist cause. He no longer needed the money the apparatus provided. It was almost a symbolic act when the originals of notes which Ethel Rosenberg had typed were burned in a frying pan and dumped down the drain.

When Greenglass was honorably discharged from the Army in February

---

* "I showed," Greenglass testified, "a high-explosive lens mold. I showed the way it would look with this high-explosive in it with the detonators on, and I showed the steel tube in the middle which would be exploded by this lens mold." And describing this sketch to the jury, he said:

"'A' is the light source which projects a light through this tube 'E,' which shows a camera set up to take a picture of this light source. Around the tube is a cross-section of the high-explosive lens 'C' and a detonator 'B' showing where it is detonated, and the course is that when the lens is detonated, it collapses the tube, implodes the tube, and the camera, through the lens 'B' and the film 'D,' shows a picture of the implosion."

All of this was corroborated by Dr. Koski.

1946, he had already been involved by his brother in a business partnership with Julius Rosenberg. At first, they bought and sold war surplus goods, then they set up a machine shop. But there was increasing friction between the two. David insisted that his brother-in-law treated him like an employee and that he did not attend to business. Rosenberg was still trying to woo David back into the apparatus, and the two argued about politics incessantly. Julius also held out what we have come to know as a prime lure. He urged Greenglass to return to school, particularly to one of those universities where he had friends from Los Alamos. It was his duty to maintain his relationship with these scientists and technicians, some of them still doing secret work.

"Well, how am I going to do all this?" Greenglass would say. He had a wife to support, and the GI Bill of Rights could hardly cover his expenses.

"So the Russians will send you to school," was Rosenberg's answer. "I do it all the time. I have a number of people that I send to school. I am the paymaster." When Greenglass refused, Rosenberg would show his annoyance, but he did not drop the subject.

During the postwar period, Rosenberg did not give up espionage activities. But he had a need to boast of his achievements, and the only person with whom he could speak frankly, other than his wife, was Greenglass. There was safety in this, for as a former co-conspirator, Greenglass was bound to silence. Late in 1947, Rosenberg told him that he had gotten information from "one of my boys" on a new scientific development—a "sky platform."*

In a courtroom which thought he was talking in science-fiction terms, this exchange took place:

Q: Did he tell you just what information had been given to him by one of the boys concerning the sky platform project? Did he describe it to you at all?
A: Yes, he did. He described it in front of my brother, too.
Q: How did he describe it?
A: He said that it was some large vessel which would be suspended at a point of gravity between the moon and the earth and as a satellite it would spin around the earth . . .
Q: Let me ask you this. Did he mention any other projects, government projects, concerning which he had obtained information?
A: He once stated to me in the presence of a worker of ours that they had solved the problem of atomic energy for airplanes, and later on I asked him if this was true, and he said that he had gotten the mathematics of it, the mathematics was solved on this.
Q: Did he say where he had gotten this?
A: He said he got it from one of his contacts . . . meaning scientists in this country.

In 1949, the partnership between Greenglass and Rosenberg broke up. Julius owed David four thousand dollars at the time and attempted strenu-

---

* When Greenglass testified to this before the Senate Internal Security Subcommittee on April 27, 1956, he was accused by The New York Times and other newspapers of trying to capitalize on the American reaction to the Soviet sputnik by adding new spice to his story. The fact: He described the "sky platform" on March 12, 1951, during the Rosenberg trial, long before the Soviets had sent their first sputnik aloft—and long before United States scientists had the vaguest inkling of this Soviet project.

ously to evade the debt, causing still more dissension—and the two drifted apart. Occasionally they met at a Friday-night dinner, the command performances exacted by Mrs. Tessie Greenglass, but they were distant with each other. Then, on a morning in February 1950, Rosenberg went to Greenglass's apartment and awakened him. (Greenglass was working nights and slept late.) With no explanation, Rosenberg insisted that Greenglass get dressed and go for a walk, and the urgency in his voice was such that he got no argument. Walking along the East Side streets, Rosenberg said:

"You remember the man who came to see you in Albuquerque? Well, Klaus Fuchs was also one of his contacts." The Fuchs story had been on page one for several days. "The man who came to see you will undoubtedly be arrested now. You'll have to leave the country. Think it over, and we'll make plans."

Greenglass did not like the idea. He said he needed money to pay his debts, an arguemtnt which did not impress Rosenberg particularly, though he agreed to help him. "Why doesn't this other guy leave—the one who came to me in Albuquerque?" Greenglass asked. "That's something else again," Rosenberg answered cryptically. Greenglass, however, made no move to leave, and perhaps Rosenberg was given reassurances that Harry Gold would not talk. In any case, he did not press for immediate flight until May 22 or 23—shortly after Ruth Greenglass had left the hospital after giving birth to their first child. Rosenberg was now really excited, and he brandished a copy of the *New York Herald Tribune,* which carried a picture of Harry Gold and the story of his arrest.

"This is the man who saw you in Albuquerque," Rosenberg said. Greenglass was not quite sure, but Rosenberg insisted. "Don't worry, I'm telling you this is the man, and you'll have to leave the country." He had one thousand dollars for Greenglass and a promise of six thousand. Then he gave instructions: David was to go to the Mexican border and apply for a tourist card. In Mexico City, he was to write a letter to the Soviet ambassador on some innocuous matter, signing it "I. Jackson." Three days later, he was to stand on the Plaza Colon, at 5 P.M., holding a guidebook with his middle finger between the pages. He would be approached by a man and was to say, "That is a magnificent statue." The answering signal would be, "Oh, there are much more beautiful statues in Paris." The man would give him a passport to Sweden, where a similar rendezvous was arranged with an eventual destination of Czechoslovakia.

Rosenberg also said that he would probably have to leave the country. "I knew Jacob Golos and maybe Elizabeth Bentley knows me," he said. As a precaution, he advised Greenglass to get a lawyer and said that he was already in touch with his own. For Rosenberg, the pressure was building. He knew that with Greenglass out of the country, he would be relatively safe—at least from the charge of atomic espionage. But Greenglass continued to stall. Early in June, Rosenberg brought him four thousand dollars in a brown paper wrapper—the get-away money. (Ironically he used it to retain a lawyer when he was arrested.) Rosenberg had one question:

"Are you being followed?"

"Yes, I am," Greenglass said.

"What are you going to do now?" Rosenberg asked.

"I'm not going to do anything," Greenglass said. "I'm going to stay right here." Rosenberg left in a state of great agitation, ready now to make his own escape. But it was too late. Harry Gold had already tentatively identified a photo of Greenglass and, after searching his memory, recalled his name. On June 15, at 1:45 P.M., two FBI agents visited him at his apartment in Rivington Street. They advised him of his right not to make a statement and suggested that he might want a lawyer. Then they questioned him "regarding material which had been lost, strayed, or stolen from the Los Alamos atom-bomb project."

At 1:57, Greenglass, who was pleasant throughout his questioning, signed a waiver of search. In a footlocker, the FBI found some old photos of David and Ruth Greenglass taken in Albuquerque. These were rushed to Philadelphia for Harry Gold to examine. Meanwhile, Greenglass agreed voluntarily to accompany the FBI agents to the Federal Courthouse on Foley Square. He was questioned in Conference Room U on the 29th Floor where the Bureau is headquartered. At 8:30 P.M., word was received that Gold had made a positive identification. Greenglass was confronted with this and told of Gold's visit to Albuquerque on June 3, 1945 and of the transfer of classified information. He promptly confessed that he was guilty, signing a statement to that effect. But he insisted that he did not know who might have asked his wife to suggest espionage.

The Bureau, however, already knew of Rosenberg's involvement with Elizabeth Bentley. From Rosenberg's behavior, they also knew that his association with Greenglass was more than familial. Like Harry Gold, Greenglass attempted to shield his confederates. Like Gold, he finally began his long and earnest confession. That night, he slept at FBI headquarters. The following day, he was taken to a barber shop for a shave and a haircut he badly needed. Then, at 1:50 P.M., he was arraigned, his lawyer O. John Rogge at his side.

Julius Rosenberg should have known that the string had been played out. But he continued to go about his business. Ethel Rosenberg questioned Ruth Greenglass closely following David's arrest: Had he talked? she asked. Ruth said, "David is innocent. We're going to fight it." Sustained by the incredible conviction that they would remain untouched and that they could outsmart the FBI, the Rosenbergs began to relax. Then, on July 17, three FBI agents presented themselves at the Rosenberg apartment at 10 Monroe Street. Ethel was brash, almost flippant. She demanded a warrant before allowing the FBI to search the apartment—which was her right. The FBI men were startled by the manner in which the two Rosenberg children addressed their parents, using first names. The children—particularly the older boy, Michael, who was under the care of a psychiatrist—were completely undisciplined. (The Rosenbergs believed that a child should never be punished or restrained.) "Are you going to hang my daddy?" Michael asked gaily. So obstreperous did the children become that Ethel was asked to take them to the home of their grandpar-ents, of course accompanied by an FBI agent. Julius was arrested that day, though he denied any complicity. On August 11, Ethel was taken into custody.

The trial of the Rosenbergs has been rehearsed in books and articles *ad infinitum*. But certain facts are of significance. The prosecution, expecting a long defense, had 102 witnesses ready to take the stand—most of them held back for rebuttal. But the entire Rosenberg defense consisted of a denial of the charges by Ethel and Julius when they took the stand. And even those denials were compromised by the frequent resort to the Fifth Amendment. (Morton Sobell, a co-defendant, did not even testify in his own defense.) Neither of the Rosenbergs showed any emotion as the government unveiled its evidence. Given the Rosenberg defense strategy, only a fraction of the prosecution wit-nesses were called. When the sentence of death was pronounced, Ethel and Julius Rosenberg were impassive, almost lethargic.

In the months that followed, as the case dragged through appeal after appeal, a vast propaganda campaign was mounted to prove that the Rosen-bergs had not been given a fair trial, that Judge Irving Kaufman had shown bias, that anti-Semitism was the motive behind the arrest and prosecution, that it was all another Dreyfus or Sacco-Vanzetti case, and that the issue was "peace." The Rosenberg children were used as pawns to pump up sympathy for the condemned and exhibited at mass meetings. Pickets paraded in front of the White House, and there were riots in Europe. Eminent citizens proclaimed the innocence of the Rosenbergs and made unconscionable charges against the FBI, only to admit that they had never even read the trial record. Millions of dollars were collected, though where they went has never been determined. It was a Roman holiday for the Communists, for their dupes, and for the unin-formed—and generous men who conceded the guilt but sought a commutation of the death sentence found themselves involved in a hysteria of which they wanted no part.

During the period of mass insanity, few remembered that at the conclu-sion of the trial, after Judge Kaufman had pronounced sentence, both defense lawyers had risen to their feet to thank the Court for its fairness and its courtesies, to praise the FBI for the co-operation it had given them. A study of the record shows no mystery. It is conclusive in its proof of guilt. But one question has plagued many who have not chased a legal or emotion will o' the wisp: Why did the Rosenbergs accept death rather than confess? At the very moment that they faced the electric chair, a word would have saved their lives. At Sing Sing prison, a line was kept open to the White House, just in case they decided to talk. But to the end, the Rosenbergs remained silent—sending back the last meal because it was not precisely what they had ordered, complaining that the execution should be postponed because they had "unfinished busi-ness." Julius Rosenberg showed fear only once, on the last day of his life, when he learned that the last possible appeal had been rejected.

A psychiatrist who followed the case had this answer to the enigma:

"Julius Rosenberg was an unimportant man until he became an espio-nage agent. Then in his own eyes—and to use a word he knew—he became a

Mensch, a man, a significant part of a great cause. His ego was nourished by the importance of his treason. And the Soviets flattered and manipulated him. They gave him motivation. They made him feel that he was walking the stage of history. The great demonstrations, the appeals to the President, the request for clemency from the Pope—all these fed that feeling. And the same applied to Ethel Rosenberg. If she could not sing at the Metropolitan Opera House, she could speak to the world. To confess would have destroyed this. To themselves, they would have become two more defectors, two more informers. They would no longer be heroic. From their behavior after the trial, it is clear that they had lost all sense of reality. They were shielded by a mystical belief that somehow the power they worshiped would liberate them. By stealing America's atomic secrets, they had made America tremble. How could they die?"

This could be the answer. A simpler answer would be that they were Communists.

12 "Peking Joan" and the House on Harvard Street

THE STORY OF Joan Chase Hinton, a brilliant atomic scientist who defected to Red China, made little stir in the United States. The Atomic Energy Commission did its utmost to suppress the simple fact that she had gone over to the Communists and exacted a pledge from the veteran newsman, Walter Trohan of the *Chicago Tribune,* not to publish any hint of what he had learned to be true. It was not until three years after Joan Hinton had defected—and two years after Trohan sought confirmation from the AEC—that reluctant admissions were made. By that time, Joan Hinton was filling the airwaves with violent anti-American propaganda, spreading the lie that the United States was conducting germ warfare in Korea, giving aid and comfort to an enemy engaged in killing American soldiers, and urging scientists to give up all atomic research.

This was in 1951. In 1954 and 1956, there was a mild flurry of interest when Joan's brother William Howard Hinton, who had remained in Communist China throughout most of the Korean War, was questioned by the Senate Internal Security Subcommittee. Bill Hinton was an unstable young man with too much "progressive" schooling, a conscientious objector during World War II until the "gallantry" of the Red Army and the boredom of a Quaker work farm had become too much for him. Then he volunteered for military service, was turned down, and landed on his feet as a propaganda analyst in China for the Office of War Information. Given his political predilections, he fell in easily with a group of State Department Foreign Service officers and Institute of Pacific Relations "researchers" in the Far East who could see no good in the anti-Communist Nationalist forces and all virtue in the Yenan Communists.

After a period with the United Nations Relief and Rehabilitation Administration (UNRRA), presumably administering aid to the Chinese people, he went on the Red Chinese payroll as an agricultural expert. His views of the world were expressed in a letter to Joan and their sister Jean, written from behind the Bamboo Curtain. "That great beast America," he said, "looks down upon the world and licks its lips . . . So far I have seen no evidence of the anti-American feeling that is supposed to be rampant here. This worries me a little, since it indicates the people have not yet learned who their enemies are." Having served the Communists during the Korean war, he returned to the United States to preach the glories of Red China and the iniquities of his own country. His journey back to the "great beast" was facilitated by a benevolent Soviet Union which paid his expenses, briefed him in Moscow, and sent him back to the West via Czechoslovakia.

But what of Joan Chase Hinton? No Congressional committee has given her any particular scrutiny. The AEC remains silent, except for a brief resumé of her activities at Los Alamos and the Argonne National Laboratories. The FBI, by law, cannot speak out. And yet she was an integral part of the great plot to loot America of its atomic secrets, to give Communist countries information they were economically incapable of developing, and of feeding the vast propaganda machine which the Communist world has employed to discredit her native country. Yet enough psychological and actual evidence is available to construct the story of her role.

It is important to go back to her mother, Carmelita Hinton and the Putney School which she founded and directed in that Vermont town, to the ambiance which created her character and guided her actions. For Putney was one of those special communities which spring up in the midst of New England's flinty conservatism. The school was "progressive" and "experimental." Its faculty was rabidly left-wing, including at times notorious Communists. On its board of trustees was Owen Lattimore, the nation's foremost apologist for the Chinese Communists and an expert political casuist. Among Carmelita Hinton's close friends were Nathan Gregory Silvermaster and his wife Helen. Silvermaster was busy then colonizing the Washington bureaucracy with Communist Party members and was a ranking member of Elizabeth Bentley's espionage apparatus. Around the Putney School, moreover, a group of interesting and persuasive people of Communist or fellow-traveling orientation had gathered. Among them were Alger and Priscilla Hiss and Harry Dexter White, the Assistant Secretary of the Treasury who doubled in brass as a Soviet agent.

It was in this atmosphere that Joan Chase Hinton grew up, a precocious and in-turned child surrounded by people who saw fascists under every bed and smelled reaction in every breeze. Her sister, Jean, was more openly political. Joan was interested in science from the time that she could turn the pages of a book and read its print. Under healthier circumstances, this love of the beauty, truth, and order in mathematics, physics, and chemistry might have been an integrated part of her life. But from the "progressive" acres of Putney, she was sent to Bennington College in Vermont. There Joan was an oddball, whereas at Radcliffe she would have been considered a talented and studious girl. Joan Hinton at Bennington had no interest in dates or in trips to New York to learn about "life" and the great world. Though her politics were acceptable, even unnoticed, her attitude toward education did not conform to the superficial concerns of her classmates. While they were out dancing and necking, she was building a Wilson cloud-chamber and studying advanced texts in nuclear physics. The only impression she left was of a girl who did not wear lipstick and confined her beauty treatments to running a comb through her hair.

When she moved on to Cornell, for work at its cyclotron, she often forgot to do even that. A skinny, tall, unkempt girl, she deplored all the visible and emotional aspects of femininity. She was simply interested in research—as if science were not a means but an end in itself. What had once been considered talent in the abstruse field she chose for herself was now being assessed as genius—although this was an overstatement from male students who were startled and somewhat overcome by so intense a female. Since the world of science is, like the world of any specialized art or craft, a small one, her reputation began to grow in academic circles. When she transferred to the University of Wisconsin for advanced studies, she was already known to her peers and superiors.

It was then that Joan Chase Hinton decided that she wanted to take part in the accelerating researches of the Manhattan Engineer District at Los Alamos. That she knew what this work was about is an index to the lax security of the scientific community. That she applied directly at Los Alamos should have raised a few eyebrows. That she was hired is even more astonishing. No records exist which give a clue to her assault on the MED's bastion. It is possible that Dr. J. Robert Oppenheimer raised the portcullis. He was a close enough friend of Carmelita Hinton to lend her his ranch, Perro Caliente, in the Upper Pecos for the summer of 1945—and Joan visited her there briefly. All that is known to date is that she "pulled strings"—and this comes without further documentation from a former Intelligence officer.

However it was done, Joan Hinton found herself at Los Alamos in one of its most sensitive laboratories and wearing the "white badge" assigned to those who had access to all information. Her title was "research assistant," but she was highly enough regarded to be one of those present and participating when the first atomic bomb was assembled. (As she would say dramatically in one of her "Peking Joan" broadcasts from Red China, "I held the bomb in my hands.")

Those entrusted with the security of Los Alamos and the entire MED project have never disclosed how she passed her investigation. Though her own life may have been bare of political activities, associations are of great importance in determining the risk involved in hiring a given person. And Joan Hinton was not only Carmelita's daughter; she was also Jean's sister, and very close to her. While Joan was preparing herself for a significant role in nuclear research, Jean had gone on to overt pro-Communist activity. Married to William Greene, a nonpolitical and somewhat bewildered businessman who eventually divorced her, Jean had moved to Washington and was deep in Communist works.

Her mother's friend, Silvermaster, got her a government job. She was extremely active in the affairs of the United Federal Workers Union, under strong Red domination. And the Greene home on Harvard Street was a meeting ground for a wide variety of fellow-travelers, Communists, espionage agents, and Soviet personnel. Rear Admiral Ellis M. Zacharias, once deputy chief of the Office of Naval Intelligence, describes the visitors to the House on Harvard Street—his information based on the reports of an ONI agent who was assigned to live next door to the Greenes and to report on their activities:

The people who visited them in that house represented a strange assortment of callers—Americans, Britons, Chinese—as well as Russians. Among the Americans were agitators of the most leftwing trade unions which have since been expelled from the CIO; young scientists and designers engaged in secret war work; a famous senator from New England who was especially loquacious with what appeared to us as classified information; the daughter of one of our top-ranking admirals in a key position of the Pacific war; and people who seemed to be engaged in recruiting members for the apparatus. Most of the Russian visitors were employees of the Soviet Purchasing Mission.

The members of the Soviet Purchasing Commission, as this account has already noted, had the double mission of prying loose as much Lend-Lease as possible and of serving as cover for espionage. But the two Soviet officials who most frequently were seen at the House on Harvard Street were Major General Ilya M. Sarayev, head of Red Army Intelligence's American division, and Colonel Pavel E. Berezin, a specialist on aircraft with NKVD status. General Sarayev's title, Assistant Military Attaché, did not hide the fact that he was one of the most important Soviet agents working out of the Embassy in Washington. The names of both men figure prominently in security reports on Soviet espionage in the United States.

From the vantage point of the house next door, agents of ONI and the FBI were able to observe Sarayev and Berezin as they entered and left. Peering through powerful binoculars, they were able to see, but not hear, Jean Hinton Greene and the two Soviet officers in earnest conversation. There seemed to be considerable traffic between the living room and the basement when Sarayev and Berezin were visiting—and it was discovered that the House on Harvard Street had an elaborate shop and darkroom, though Jean Hinton was not a photography enthusiast. Other frequent visitors were Silvermaster and William Ullmann, both members of the Bentley apparatus in Washington. In short, the House on Harvard Street was a magnet for every security agency in the United States, for it included in its polarity individuals known to Counter-Intelligence in a variety of guises. Only the MED's security group seemed to have neither knowledge of nor interest in the comings and goings of Joan Chase Hinton's sister.

The FBI and ONI were both restraind by Presidential directive from any interference in the atomic project. From time to time, as one Soviet apparatus overlapped the functions of another, the FBI would become privy to certain facts and submit them, from Director J. Edgar Hoover to General Groves, in the belief that action would be taken. (Both MED security and the FBI kept an eye on Steve Nelson, to cite an example, since he was supervising both atomic spies and their cousins in less spectacular areas of espionage endeavor.) And so it was with utter frustration that the ONI watched the postman deliver fat envelopes to Jean Hinton Greene, the return address corner inscribed "JCH/Box 1663/Sante Fe, Mexico." This was the Post Office box used by everyone at Los Alamos, whether of high rank or lowly, so that there would be no hint to mail handlers of the nature of the work being done there.

What Joan Hinton wrote to her sister—or how unconsciously or wittingly she was indiscreet—will never be known. Though the MED was warned of Joan Hinton's close relationship to a sister so surrounded by suspect characters, there is no record that any action was taken to investigate or to intercept the mail. Certainly when the Gray Board sifted through the security files of the Manhattan project, seeking evidence both favorable and unfavorable in the case of J. Robert Oppenheimer, there was not even a hint that he had been at any time linked with the Hintons. From Jean Hinton Greene's mysterious remarks to the ONI man who had insinuated himself into the Greene household, if only on a neighborly basis, it is clear that she was well aware of the work her sister was doing at Los Alamos—in itself a breach of security. And on the same day that the bomb was dropped on Hiroshima, Jean Greene burst out proudly that her sister was one of those who had manufactured the atomic weapon. She also boasted that one of her house guests had been a British atomic scientist working on the project. Admiral Zacharias has summarized the reaction of Naval Intelligence to these events:

> The revelation shocked us. Here was a house frequented by two of Russia's secret agents in the United States, in which the untold secrets of the atomic weapon might be fully disclosed. We could not ascertain how much of this data was conveyed to General Sarayev and Colonel Berezin, or how much of it they could pick up themselves. But the mere connection between these two groups of people—the one group which had access to the information which the other group was most anxious to obtain—virtually scared the daylights out of us.

Naval Intelligence did not know that Joan Chase Hinton was particularly valuable as a source. Most of the Soviet espionage success at the MED had been in areas other than the physical manufacture of the bomb, though David Greenglass was important here. But ONI was sufficiently overwrought to violate the Presidential directive. A Navy representative was sent to Dr. Richard Tolman, one of the atomic scientists working with General Groves. Dr. Tolman, by coincidence, was in Washington and easily available—and ONI informed him of Joan Chase Hinton, her associations, and of the goings on at the

House on Harvard Street. Presumably Dr. Tolman reported this conversation to General Groves. If he did, it made little impression, since Groves made no mention of Joan Hinton in discussing security problems in his book *Now It Can Be Told*.

With the fighting over, the staff at Los Alamos was reduced, and Joan Hinton, instead of going back to Putney, moved in with her sister Jean at Harvard Street. She claimed that she had resigned in shame and anger over the dropping of the bomb on Hiroshima and Nagasaki. And she vowed that she would devote herself to "peace" and to the outlawing of the bomb—in other words, to unilateral American nuclear disarmament. Once quiet and unaggressive, she became a crusader. But her zeal to change United States policy was frustrated by the stubborn and unreasonable men charged with the nation's safety—and her feelings were hurt. In almost childish terms, she described her experiences years later for *People's China*, a magazine published by the Communist government:

After Hiroshima, I first joined the Association of Los Alamos Scientists and then participated in their mass migration to Washington. I spent some six weeks there working for the Federation of American Scientists [then attempting to frighten the American people and government into ceasing all nuclear research]. I was both enthusiastic and inexperienced. I will never forget my chagrin when I went to a certain senator's office to get some information and the secretary condescendingly looked up at me, asking: "Is this in connection with your school work?" Me, an atomic scientist, coming to Washington to fight for scientific freedom and world peace, the very nerve of her! Well, my heart was in the right place anyway.

And so, having been mistaken for a student by an overworked secretary, her importance not recognized at sight, Joan Hinton railed against the American system. At the Putney School or at Bennington College, the fact that she asked a question, that she "showed interest," would have won her praise and understanding, but in the "corrupt" United States Senate she was not overwhelmed with attention. Joan Hinton swore that she would never again work for the atomic project. Her Communist friends, however, had different ideas. Just as the apparatus had urged David Greenglass to remain at Los Alamos or to complete his education so that he would be more valuable to the Center in Moscow, Joan Hinton was told that it was her duty to return to the project and to rise with it. She sought out Dr. Enrico Fermi, one of the great nuclear physicists then assembling a staff for the Institute of Nuclear Studies at the University of Chicago, and asked that he accept her. Dr. Fermi agreed, and Joan Hinton happily told her friends at Harvard Street that she was to be his scientific secretary.

At the University of Chicago, she was given a fellowship in nuclear physics. Her major work was with the "heavy-water boilers"—declassified in 1951—but she was given access, according to the Atomic Energy Commission's belated admission, to secret data of considerable value to any nation seeking to develop its own atomic energy installations. "In the room where I studied," she later said in a letter to the Federation of American Scientists and in her propaganda writings, "there was only a little space in the corner for a desk. The rest of the room was piled high with cases of heavy water right up to the ceiling—for Argonne." And it was made known to her and to others that she was on the way up in the hierarchy of nuclear researchers.

Had she remained, it is probable that she would have risen very high. For some reason, two detailed reports on her by ONI and other security agencies were ignored by the Atomic Energy Commission, which blithely allowed her to continue at the Institute. She remained in constant touch with the Argonne scientists who were not inhibited by the fact that she no longer had top-security clearance.

But other forces were at work. Passage of the Atomic Energy Act, late in 1946, placed AEC security in the hands of the FBI. Methodically, it began to put together information about those who had been permitted to operate unmolested in the palmier days of the MED. Elizabeth Bentley had told her story to the Bureau, and in 1947 a grand jury began to hear evidence in New York of Soviet espionage. The Center in Moscow had pushed the panic button, and the implicated members of its "legal" apparatus were recalled. Harry Gold and Abe Brothman had been called before the federal grand jury. Though they talked their way out of an indictment, the professional espionage agents knew that it was a matter of time. One after another, Americans in the apparatus were being advised to leave the country. With the FBI methodically closing in, there was no course left to them except flight or exposure.

Joan Hinton's brother was in China, working for the Communist regime, so the pull for her was to him. Late in 1947, she received credentials from the China Welfare Fund, since cited by the Attorney General as subversive, to go to the mainland as a relief worker. In her application for a passport, she stated as her reason for leaving the United States: "I am going to China to work in welfare and to get married. My fiancé is waiting for me in Shanghai"—then still in Nationalist hands. On December 12, 1947, she was issued a passport. Among her effects when she sailed was a suitcase full of notes and other data on her work at Los Alamos and at the Argonne National Laboratories. In Shanghai, she married an American dairy-cattle expert. Then, with her new husband, her brother Bill, and his wife Bertha, she slipped behind the Bamboo Curtain.*

Joan Hinton's first destination in the Communist-controlled area of the mainland was a secret scientific installation in the Shensi Mountains. Counter-Intelligence lost track of her movements until she turned up near the Mongolian border, where the Chinese Communists and the Soviet Union were at work on a joint atomic energy project. In 1951, an escapee from behind the Iron Curtain who was interviewed in Austria stated that he had attended a meeting of atomic scientists in the Soviet Union. Among those present, he said,

---

* It is of some significance that while Joan Hinton was preparing to defect to Red China, Carmelita Hinton and her daughter-in-law Bertha were attending a Communist "peace conference" in Prague and then voyaging to Moscow. It is also ironic that at the time Walter Trohan of the Chicago Tribune was being told by the AEC that to print the story of Joan's defection might endanger her life, Carmelita Hinton was sponsoring the so-called Waldorf Peace Conference in New York, described by Secretary of State Dean Acheson as a major Soviet propaganda effort.

were "Bruno Pontecorvo and a woman named Hinton." Then, in Spetember 1951, she appeared at a "peace" conference in Red China to deliver an impassioned speech against her fellow Americans in Korea and against her country. A series of propaganda broadcasts, which led Admiral Zacharias to call her "Peking Joan," followed. And in a letter to the Federation of American Scientists in the United States, she pleaded:

> Use your strength, use whatever you can, to work for peace and against war . . . The American government drives for war abroad and attacks the democratic rights of American people at home . . . The Chinese people have a will so strong that nothing America can do will ever stop them. The Chinese people are not afraid of America. If she must fight, China will show that she is made of steel.

Joan Hinton has gone a long way from the studious girl at Bennington, building a cloud-chamber. She is in an alien land, helping the enemy create the weapons to destroy her own country. On the witness stand, her brother Bill attempted to evade questions concerning her present activities. Finally he insisted that she was working on an "animal farm"—though he would not say what she was doing there. If he spoke the truth, he must have meant George Orwell's "animal farm," in which all pigs are equal, but some pigs are more equal than others. Her feed grain is treason, for she is nourishing the Behemoth. Or perhaps she has changed her field of endeavor on this "animal farm" and is developing cultures for the germ warfare she so cynically accused her countrymen of waging.

13 Pontecorvo, Burgess, and MacLean

FROM THE SAME highly classified source that gave the FBI its lead to Klaus Fuchs in 1949, there came an equally disturbing piece of information. A nuclear physicist of considerable status was also supplying information to the Soviet Union. Neither his name nor his nationality was known, though there were indications that he was foreign born and possibly connected in some way with the British. This was all United States security agencies and MI-5 in Great Britain had to go on—so frustratingly little that it could be of no help. In the Gold case, the FBI had a rough description from Fuchs and his sister. They had a vague idea of his background. With this as a start, method and persistence could help them sift through 1,500 suspects. But here they had nothing more than the category "nuclear physicist." Was he theoretical or experimental? Did he work at Los Alamos or Chalk River or Harwell?

When it was too late, when the mysterious scientist was out of their reach, the FBI and MI-5 learned who he was. In effect, Dr. Bruno Pontecorvo told them himself by disappearing behind the Iron Curtain. And again, the British, who had uttered a *mea culpa* over the laxity of their check on Klaus Fuchs, struck palm to brow and said, "But of course. We should have known." Following which they argued, as they had in the Fuchs case, "Even knowing, we could have done nothing." The fact is that their suspicions had been aroused, on the basis of other information, before Bruno Pontecorvo fled, but they had "sat like patience on a monument," convinced that he would act like a pukka sahib. This, perhaps, is what makes England great.

Having let Pontecorvo slip through their fingers, they then allowed Guy Burgess and Donald MacLean to take the road to Moscow. Pontecorvo, Burgess, and MacLean were involved in atomic espionage. Pontecorvo, however, took far more with him to the Soviet Union than Western nuclear knowledge —his own brilliant and questing mind. Burgess and MacLean were not simply repositories of information—although what they told the Soviets did incalculable political harm. They too had the capacity for continuing treason. That the lives of the Burgess-MacLean duo and Pontecorvo had touched was probably as coincidental as any chain of events can be in the Communist conspiracy. The paths of the three men crossed on both personal and espionage terms, if the hints and less-than-candid utterances of British authorities are to be believed. But how brief or how crucial these tenuous contacts may have been, the world will not know until Pontecorvo, Burgess, and/or MacLean redefect—or MI-5 turns garrulous.

Here, then, are their stories:

It has been said that Pontecorvo's soul, like that of Klaus Fuchs, was bruised by World War I and the trauma of fascism. This, however, is far from the reality. Bruno Pontecorvo, one of eight children, was born to a prosperous family in Pisa. In the interbellum years, his Jewish origin did not bring him any religious or political discrimination. Until the late 1930s—and then reluctantly, under pressure from Hitler—Benito Mussolini had neither preached nor practiced anti-Semitism. Jews were part of the Fascist regime, and those in private life carried on their businesses without a hint of molestation. The number of Italian Jews who supported Mussolini—or who simply lived under his rule without giving too much thought to politics—was overwhelmingly in excess of those who joined the Socialist or Communist opposition. For the most part, Italians of all religions who were militantly against Mussolini fought him from the safety of France. It was not until 1938, when anti-Semitism became a Fascist policy, that Pontecorvo had cause to complain of the treatment accorded his family by the Mussolini regime. For it was not until then that his father's business began suffering, and by that time Bruno had been out of Italy for two years.

Like his seven brothers and sisters, Bruno was a brilliant student. After attending the *Ginnasio* and the *Liceo classico,* he entered the University of Pisa, getting his doctorate in physics with honors at the University of Rome in 1934. He was then twenty-one years old. Continuing at the University of Rome as teacher and researcher, Pontecorvo was part of a group of advanced physicists working under one of the great men in the field, Dr. Enrico Fermi. This group, under Fermi's tutelage, developed a process for creating radioactive elements by bombarding them with slow neutrons—a step in nuclear theory which led toward the atomic bomb. A patent for the process was the legal basis for a suit against the United States government by those responsible for it. They claimed one million dollars, but settled for $300,000. Pontecorvo's share was fifteen thousand dollars—but he never collected it. He was already behind the Iron Curtain when the litigation ended.

As a result of his reputation and achievement, Pontecorvo was awarded a national fellowship by the Italian government for further study in Paris at the Collège de France. He took with him to France, in February 1936, a predilection for bohemianism and communism. The two may have been of a common origin, for the party encourages social and sexual nonconformism among its intellectuals. And if Bruno Pontecorvo at that time did not hold a party card, he had certainly received a thorough indoctrination from other members of his family. His brother Gilberto had from his student days been actively involved in party activities. In 1939, he was forced to flee to France, where he was a leader in Communist youth movements, and he plunged into underground work as a courier. (In the postwar period, he returned to Italy as a party functionary. On November 19, 1950, he was of sufficient importance in the party to be tried and acquitted of sedition. This past did not prevent him from becoming one of Italy's most famous movie directors. In 1961, he won the Italian equivalent of the "Oscar.")

Bruno's sister Giuliana married Duccio Tabet, also a functionary of the Italian Communist Party. After the war, she was assigned by the party to work closely with, and encircle, Pietro Nenni, leader of the left-wing Socialist Party, which joined in a "united front" with the Communists. Pontecorvo's first cousin, Emilio Sereni, had the distinction of rising to one of the highest positions in the Italian Communist Party—member of the powerful Central Committee. In the confused days after liberation, Sereni held several ministries in the government and today represents a Communist constituency in the Chamber of Deputies.

The bohemianism took another form. During his Paris days, Bruno Pontecorvo worked with the Communist physicist, Joliot-Curie, at the Institute of Radium. At night, he frequented the Café de Floré on the Left Bank, and it was here—among the artists, eccentrics, and homosexuals—that, according to the Deuxième Bureau, he met Donald MacLean. It was here, too, that he met Helene Marianne Nordblom, a tall, slender platinum-blonde from Stockholm. Probably, she was already a Communist. She moved into Pontecorvo's rooms at 17 Place du Panthéon, and on July 30, 1938, bore him a son. He was named Gilberto, after Bruno's Communist brother. It was not until January 9, 1940, that the two were married. The Communists and bohemians who made up the

Pontecorvo circle of friends accepted the irregular arrangement as a matter of course—and it did not hinder Pontecorvo's rise to the important post of research associate at the Laboratory of Nuclear Chemistry at the Collège de France. Espionage during that period was, of course, unnecessary. Joliot-Curie made certain that every scrap of knowledge in the nuclear field then residing in France was published.

Using Paris as a base, Pontecorvo traveled about Europe inspecting research centers and blowing his own horn. (Friends have since noted that he was an inveterate job-seeker, always on the hunt for better and more lucrative positions.) But the conflict between the West and the Axis powers kept inching up on him. Pontecorvo's only reaction to the Hitler-Stalin Pact seems to have been one of annoyance for the way in which it inhibited his movements and his possibilities for advance. He was not perturbed by the "phoney war" during which Germany and France faced each other across the Maginot Line. When the Nazi blitz made Paris untenable for an Italian of Jewish blood with Communist connections, Pontecorvo, his wife, and the child born out of wedlock but legitimatized, fled south from Paris. They joined his sister Giuliana and her husband, Duccio Tabet, in Lisbon. On August 9, 1940, the Pontecorvos and the Tabets boarded the Portuguese ship S.S. "Oranza" for the United States. The Pontecorvos were completely straightforward in the papers they signed, but the Tabets claimed first to be doctors and then business people.

In New York, Bruno Pontecorvo immediately called friends of friends in the academic field who knew him by reputation. His offers of service to the great universities were not accepted, but he was able to find a well-paying job with an Oklahoma firm as a consultant on radiographic oil-well logging. This was not precisely his field, but by applying himself he was able to work out new techniques for which he sought a patent. His presence in the United States was known, however, to the scientists who made up the first phalanx in the atomic energy project. His old mentor, Dr. Fermi, had been snatched from the jaws of the Axis by a careful and clever maneuver of a highly secret Intelligence group in this country. They had quietly pulled the strings in the scientific community to snatch a Nobel Prize for Dr. Fermi. The Mussolini regime had risen to the bait, allowing Fermi to leave Italy, where he was under guard, in order to accept the award. Once out, Fermi had refused to return to Rome, and his subtle liberators were able to bring him to the United States.

Fermi remembered Pontecorvo and the contribution he had made to nuclear physics in Rome. A recommendation to the British authorities led to an assignment with the Anglo-Canadian research group in Montreal. Neither the Atomic Energy Commission nor Scotland Yard has been prepared to name the scientist or scientists who suggested Pontecorvo—and there can be legitimate grounds for conjecture about this silence. Pontecorvo was still an Italian citizen, though he had filed first papers for United States naturalization. It would have been standard procedure, had the recommendation come from Fermi, for him to have gone to Los Alamos or to the Metallurgical Laboratory in Chicago. By one of those tantalizing coincidences, Pontecorvo arrived at the

Canadian atomic energy installation at just about the same time as Nunn May, who in turn was a friend of both Donald MacLean and Guy Burgess when all three had been students at Cambridge and in London. (British Intelligence records indicate that the Nunn May-Burgess-MacLean association in London between 1940 and 1943 was very close.)

At Chalk River, the Canadian heavy-water pile, Nunn May and Pontecorvo were so casually aloof to each other that it caused some comment, but their associates ascribed it to a difference in personalities. Nunn May was extremely reserved, whereas Pontecorvo plunged into his work with the kind of gay *élan* he showed on the tennis courts, where he was an outstanding amateur. But Pontecorvo's six years at Chalk River were not uninterrupted. He made at least one trip to Washington, where, it is reported but not confirmed, he visited the House on Harvard Street. Hindsight would indicate that he was one of those mentioned under a cover name in the Gouzenko papers. But of the whole "G" group* in the table of organization removed from the Soviet Embassy in Ottawa by the code clerk, no person was ever satisfactorily identified.

Hindsight, again, raises a question about Pontecorvo's behavior in Canada between 1943 and 1949. In an extremely politicalized atmosphere, Pontecorvo refused to discuss politics. His colleagues, with a few notable exceptions, spoke out with great vigor about the course of the war, the performance of the Red Army, the strong points and the shortcomings of the Anglo-American leadership, the "second front," and the "stuffiness" of the military which demanded a modicum of security. After the war, many of them were equally vocal in condemning the United States for using the atomic bomb against Hiroshima and Nagasaki, in their horror over what their nimble brains had wrought, and in their ambivalence toward further experimentation in nuclear weapons of destruction. Pontecorvo, however, made it a point never to enter into these political bull sessions or into the shop talk of the nuclear fraternity. He limited himself to cheerful chatter and to innocuous flirtation at social gatherings. That he should have so acted proves nothing, except in the light of his later defection, but at the time his behavior was a great relief to security officials who were hard put to sort out the normally disgruntled from the dangerous.

In 1949, Bruno Pontecorvo again demonstrated a departure from the norm by requesting that he be retained at Chalk River. The British, however, had other plans and offered him an important post at Harwell, their newly established nuclear research center near Birmingham. He accepted, and there was no trouble over the transfer. In 1948, he had applied for and received British naturalization after a long interview with security officers to whom he blandly failed to comment on his Communist relatives or associations. The only reservations of Harwell's directors concerned Pontecorvo's weakness for women (his wife Marianne had left him in 1947 after one of his escapades, then reluctantly returned), and the farflung net he was continually casting out

---

* *The cover names of each cluster of agents began with the same letter. The RCMP had to rely on internal evidence to break that cover.*

for employment in British, French, and American universities. But this was accepted as the mild instability of a genius. Since Pontecorvo loved money and was for sale to the highest academic bidder, however, it came as something of a surprise to his colleagues when he turned down tempting and highly lucrative offers from Cornell University and from the General Electric Company to accept a post at Harwell which, though important in the nuclear field, paid considerably less.

But whatever external force impelled Pontecorvo to go to Harwell—as we know today, it was the Soviet apparatus—he continued to seek the kind of income which he considered commensurate with his fame in scientific circles. He openly flirted with offers from the Anglo-Iranian Oil Company and from two Italian universities. But on arriving at Harwell, it was obvious that his personality had suffered a sea change. Pontecorvo seemed anxious to get out of the atomic energy program. He was no longer the life of the party. In fact, it was noted that something seemed to be preying on his mind, and his colleagues remarked that they saw signs of premature aging. Perhaps, very much like an addict, he was trying to kick the espionage habit. But the apparatus would not release him, and he was in no position to break loose. His Communist faith had always been osmotic, but he knew that his Soviet masters could destroy him simply by leaking a few bits of evidence which would incriminate him and destroy his career.

For Pontecorvo, the solution seemed simple. He would find some minor reason for losing his security clearance and accept a research and teaching post at Liverpool University. In this way, his reputation would remain unscathed— it might be given the added luster of martyrdom—and he would have a legitimate excuse to offer the apparatus for his departure from the green pastures of espionage at Harwell. When, early in 1950, the Fuchs confession had shaken England and the British Parliament, Pontecorvo thought he had found a way out. He suddenly appeared at the office of Wing Commander Arnold, the security officer who had handled the Fuchs case, with a "confession" of his own. In applying for British naturalization, Pontecorvo told Arnold, he had committed a sin of omission by not disclosing that his brother Gilberto was a Communist functionary. He did not mention his sister Giuliana, her husband Duccio Tabet, or his first cousin Emilio Sereni. Given the jittery state of British public opinion, this should have been enough to win him a polite request to resign from Harwell.

Arnold, like any good security officer, simply thanked Pontecorvo for his "frankness" and seemed to let the matter go. But two days later, he summoned Pontecorvo to ask him if it were not true that during a recent trip to a scientific meeting at Lake Como, he had conferred with Gilberto. Bruno admitted this, passing it off as a fraternal meeting, but his obvious agitation alerted Arnold. Nothing was said to Pontecorvo, but his conscience whispered that somehow he had betrayed himself. He did not know until some months later that he was under suspicion and that inquiries had been made to Stockholm by Scotland Yard. The information received was very damaging: The Swedish police reported that according to their record, both Bruno and Marianne Pontecorvo were members of the Communist Party.

The return in May 1950 of MacLean from a Cairo assignment which had been cut short after a riotous and scandalous drunken episode, brought the matter to a head. Technically, MacLean was back in England on sick leave, with no disciplinary implications. He therefore still maintained an easy social relationship with other Foreign Ministry officials, particularly those of the "Q," or security branch. And from them, he learned that his friend Pontecorvo was being watched. That much is known, though it has been suppressed by the British. It is also known that this information was conveyed to Pontecorvo, though there is no "hard" evidence that MacLean was the messenger of mercy. Since MacLean was in communication with the Soviet apparatus in England, it is conceivable that he did not himself warn Pontecorvo. A word to his superiors would have been transmitted to the Center in Moscow, which would have had no difficulty in relaying news of this dangerous state of affairs to Pontecorvo. It has been established that he knew and that he inavertently gave away this knowledge in a number of cryptic remarks he made to friends in June and July of 1950. They were of an *ave atque vale* nature: "I hope we will someday play again," to a tennis partner, as if in farewell; his wife's behavior at a party shortly before they departed on July 26, 1950 for a "vacation" in Europe (she burst into tears when saying what should have been a casual *au revoir* to their hosts). But this was nothing to cause Scotland Yard to appear on the double or to do more than puzzle friends.

Optimist and extrovert, Bruno Pontecorvo believed that once out of England, he would be safe. He counted for protection on his well-founded reputation as western Europe's leading experimental nuclear physicist and on the British propensity to avoid scandal wherever possible. Universities in France or Italy, he believed, would not be shocked or intimidated by rumors that he was a Communist, and the British government was in no position to make a public announcement that he was an atom spy—a charge that would lay it open to cries of McCarthyism from the opposition and from the back benches. And so Bruno and Marianne Pontecorvo, with their three children, set out on a camping trip on the Continent. Offers from his friends to lend him equipment were surprisingly turned down, although Pontecorvo was a great borrower. One friend had some francs in Paris, which he offered to trade Pontecorvo for British pounds, the transaction to be completed on his return. But Bruno insisted on paying cash then and there. Wing Commander Arnold knew of the Pontecorvos' departure, but he made no effort to stop them. Later, British security pleaded that it had no right to prevent a British subject from leaving the island—but as any police officer can attest, a thousand excuses could have been found. It was simply assumed that he would return. To do otherwise would not be cricket. The Pontecorvos contributed to that belief by leaving most of their possessions behind, including £165 in a British bank, £1,714 in Montreal, and no provisions for Bruno's share of the patent suit against the United States government.

Scotland Yard and its European counterparts have traced the erratic course of the Pontecorvos as they moved in Europe, southeast toward Italy. The details are of no real significance except to the dossier-makers. Of interest here are several observations. First, the family drove in Bruno's Vanguard

Standard (license number NVC 744), a car of which he was inordinately proud. Second, they traveled very light. Third, he carried with him a brown zipper briefcase which he kept at his side at all times, with a zealousness noted by porters and by those few friends who have come forward to describe his actions. The Pontecorvos stopped briefly at Ladispoli, a resort town near Rome where Giuliana Tabet had taken a house for the summer, leaving their youngest child with her. Then they proceeded to Circeo, a coastal town south of Anzio, where Bruno intended to spend some time skin-diving among the submerged Roman ruins.

It was at Circeo, named after Circe, that Bruno Pontecorvo heard the siren call. On his thirty-seventh birthday, August 22, 1950, he was visited by Gilberto, his Communist functionary brother. The two men conferred long and seriously in what has been described as a "council of war." During this meeting Bruno Pontecorvo was either convinced or coerced into believing that the finger of exposure was about to be pointed at him, that he would not be safe anywhere in western Europe, and that his only recourse was to flee behind the Iron Curtain, where he would be welcomed, praised, and given an important post in the Soviet Union's nuclear research project. Those who have delved long and minutely into the events of those days are certain that the threat of Communist blackmail was waved delicately before his eyes should he decide to bluff it out by remaining in France or Italy.

Whether he was induced by the carrot or beaten by the stick, Pontecorvo agreed on that day to the plans the Center had made for him. That he was not happy about them is a matter of record. The evidence shows that from this point on, he seemed preoccupied and worried. His easygoing manner disappeared, and he became curt and irritable. The following day, he had a minor accident with his car and insisted on driving to Rome to have it repaired. The excuse was a thin one; the work on the car could have been done by any mechanic in a few hours. But Pontecorvo was needed in Rome for further planning of his flight. He returned to Circeo, gathered up his family and drove to Ladispoli to pick up his youngest child. Giuliana cut short her escape from the heat of Rome to return with him, and there were further conferences at her house on Via Gabi. Gilberto, too, was present at this gathering of the Communist side of the Pontecorvo clan.

Bruno had promised to meet his parents at Chamonix, in France, on his return trip—a visit which would combine pleasure with the business of inspecting a scientific laboratory with which Harwell was exchanging information on cosmic rays. But this side trip was abruptly, almost rudely, canceled in a letter to the elder Pontecorvos, whch flatly stated that the children were not well. "It is not possible to come to Chamonix," he wrote "as we shall have no time, and it would tire the children." On August 29, he appeared with Marianne at the Rome office of the Scandinavian Airways System to book a one-way passage for himself (under his own name) and for his wife and three children (under the name of Nordblom-Pontecorvo). While he was talking to the airlines clerk, Marianne, thoroughly distraught and haggard, dragged him away from the counter, and the two were observed in a heated discussion. When he returned to the clerk, he asked that his own ticket be changed to include a return trip.

The transaction completed, Pontecorvo was unable to pay for the tickets in cash and asked that he be permitted to return the next day. But there was another hitch. The airline would not accept Italian currency. An angry Pontecorvo returned a few hours later with ten crisp one-hundred-dollar bills, somewhat startling the clerk, with which to pay the required $602. A careful investigation by British and Italian authorities shows that he neither cashed a check for that sum nor converted lire for American bills. On August 31, he wrote to his superiors in Harwell complaining of "plenty of car trouble," promising to be back in England by September 7, apologizing for his failure to make an appearance at Chamonix, and ending, "Good-by, everybody."

From the scene at the SAS office, it is reasonable to assume that Pontecorvo had not at that time told his wife that he was planning to defect. Obviously, he had said only that he was leaving her and the children with the Nordbloms in Stockholm and returning to Rome on business. On September 1, the Pontecorvos boarded a plane in Rome. When they put down in Munich, they remained on board. They arrived in Stockholm at 8:50 P.M., and Bruno made inquiries about hotel accommodations. The apparatus was, however, taking no chances that Marianne Nordblom-Pontecorvo might call family or friends. That night, the family was held virtually incommunicado at one of the party's "halfway houses," where agents in transit can hide out. On September 2, the Pontecorvo family flew from Stockholm to Helsinki. Since they had no visas, their passports were impounded. Bruno was asked to fill out routine forms in which he stated that the purpose of the trip was "tourism," that they expected to remain in Finland for one week, and that their passports could be returned to them at a local hotel. He refused coach service from the airport to the city, and the family luggage, eleven valises, were piled into a large black Buick sedan with diplomatic license plates. It was shortly after 3 P.M. that Bruno Pontecorvo, still clutching the bulging brown briefcase, helped his family into the car and climbed in.

The Buick took off in the direction of Porkkala, a Soviet enclave near Helsinki, which has its own landing strip for military planes. And that was the last time that Bruno Pontecorvo was seen west of the Iron Curtain. Later, passengers on the Stockholm-Helsinki flight told British Intelligence that the youngest Pontecorvo boy had loudly announced that he was on the way to see the Soviet Union and had repeatedly asked, "Is that Russia down there?" A British report quotes Pontecorvo as having blurted out to a friend, shortly before his disappearance, "I dare not go back." Every effort, however, was made to keep the defection quiet as long as possible and to confuse efforts to determine where and how Bruno Pontecorvo had gone. Though Pontecorvo had been expected at Harwell on the seventh, it was not until September 21 that the British authorities began to investigate his disappearance. Giuliana Tabet, when questioned, stated that the Pontecorvos had been living with her until September 6,—or five days after they had boarded the plane for Stockholm. She added that on leaving Bruno told her he was driving back through France at a leisurely pace. But she contradicted her story by adding that she had later received a letter from him asking her to pay for the garaging of his Vanguard Standard and also to arrange for its shipment to England. (The car was later found by police in a Rome garage, stripped of its license plates and other identifying marks.)

It was not until October 20, 1950, that the British authorities finally made public a terse account of Pontecorvo's disappearance. The Soviet minister in Helsinki, Lieutenant General G. M. Savenenkov, immediately warned the Finnish government that any publicity about Pontecorvo would be "very unwelcome" to his government. By that time, Scotland Yard and MI-5, working with the police forces of Europe, had traced the movements of Bruno and his family to Malino airport in Helsinki and to the Buick which took them in the direction of Porkkala. But the government continued to argue that it had no idea of Pontecorvo's whereabouts, nor even that he had gone to the Soviet Union. Reports that he was behind the Iron Curtain gathering together a staff of nuclear scientists from the captive nations, that he was working on an atomic project in Sinkiang, and that he was seen at scientific gatherings in Moscow were brushed aside as rumor by British authorities determined to minimize their failure to keep a watch on Pontecorvo after he was under suspicion.

It was Bruno Pontecorvo, looking grim and emotionally weary, who eventually announced to the world from Moscow that he had defected to the Communists "because of Horoshima." He did not explain why he would continue his nuclear researches in the Soviet Union or, on December 13, 1958, accept from his masters the Lenin Prize for constructing a ten-billion electron volt synchrophastron—an atomic particle accelerator. Nor would he comment on the information he bequeathed to the Communists—his highly expert knowledge of the Chalk River atomic installations, the solution to problems encountered by the United States in the construction of its plutonium pile at Hanford, or the theory and practice he had picked up at Harwell.

In a way, what he gave to the apparatus during his years in Canada and Great Britain, or what he put down on paper when he reached Moscow, was secondary to the gift of his brilliant and inventive mind. He was, according to his former colleagues, one of the greatest experimental physicists—and Dr. Fermi would note, in a devastating understatement, that Pontecorvo "might be very valuable to Russia" for "his general scientific competence."

But though the Pontecorvo defection, coming hard on the heels of the Fuchs confession, disturbed the British, they were to be truly rocked by what followed. The impact was so great that, for a few weeks, they ceased their barrage of sardonic remarks about America's fear of Communist treason. The cause of this traumatic experience was the disappearance behind the Iron Curtain of two young men, British-born and educated at the best schools, not tainted by the accident of foreign birth, and of good family. That subconscious disdain and suspicion of all those not born British had cushioned the shock of Fuchs and Pontecorvo. Nunn May had been bad enough, but he had taken his medicine and remained in England. The case of Guy Burgess and Donald

MacLean opened for England, if only briefly, a view of the nature of Communist perfidy.

Guy Burgess figures in this account only tangentially. He was a spy, but there is no evidence that he ever had access to atomic secrets. He is mentioned only because of his political, personal, and sexual association with Donald MacLean. Beyond this, he is one more skeleton that the British regret did not remain in the closet. For he is living proof of the conviction among English intellectuals that the most conclusive evidence of a man's non-communism is his confession that he is a Communist. Cyril Connolly, the British author and critic, recounts that, in the days before World War II, a very close friend of Burgess was startled by an almost incredible conversation. "Guy had confided to him," Connolly wrote blandly, "that he was not only a member but a secret agent of the Communist Party, and he had then invited him to join this work." Nevertheless, when the war broke out, he was given a sensitive position in MI-6—the British equivalent of the Office of Strategic Services. After the war, he was posted to the United States as Second Secretary to the British Embassy. This appointment came after a severe reprimand for divulging "secret matters about which he had official knowledge." His cardinal sin, however, was in lending himself to anti-British talk. But before any action could be taken against him, he had disappeared with MacLean. To the very last, he was talking about "Those horrible American purges."*

Donald MacLean had a somewhat similar, though more devastating, record. His father, Sir Donald MacLean, had been a distinguished statesman, respected by King George V and the Parliament until the day of his death. His son, therefore, could trade on that patrimony of honor. And to the very end, after his treason had been established, there were British leaders who sought ways to exculpate him—and themselves for tolerating his behavior. Despite his aggressive Communist activities at Cambridge—and his professed need for what he called an occasional drinking "orgy"—he was considered the "golden boy" of the Foreign Service. His very first assignment in 1938, to Paris, was a plum. He gravitated quickly to the Left Bank and to the Café de Flore, Bruno Pontecorvo's hangout, where the two became friends. It was at this emporium of liquor and phony art that he met Melinda Marling, an American heiress who was willing to marry and support him—and eventually to give up everything in order to join him in his Muscovite captivity. In 1944, he was assigned to the United States as First Secretary to the British Embassy.

Despite his heavy drinking and homosexuality—traits he shared with Burgess—and the irregularity of his family life (Melinda lived with her family in New York while he maintained "bachelor" quarters in Washington) he was given one of the most important and sensitive posts available to a British diplomat in wartime Washington—secretary of the Combined Policy Committee on Atomic Development, with a top-priority pass admitting him to all nuclear installations at any hour of the day or night. In this post, he was fully

_____

* The poet W. H. Auden, who knew Burgess for years, told a London Daily Express reporter after the defection: "Burgess was an open Communist in the 1930's . . . While he was at the Embassy in Washington he was still pro-Communist." Obviously, like a betrayed wife, Scotland Yard was the last to know.

informed on all exchanges of atomic data between the United States and Great
Britain. He happily forwarded what he knew to the Zubilin apparatus working out of the Soviet Embassy. What scientific data he was able to absorb is
still being debated. But he was able to tell the Soviets, in the years after the
Horoshima explosion, how many atomic bombs the United States had in its
arsenal, what the production rate and schedule of these bombs were, and how
much uranium had been stockpiled—all matters of acute interest to the Center
in Moscow.*

In 1948, MacLean was transferred to Cairo with a promotion to Coun-
selor of the Embassy. The Egyptian police complained that he associated with
known Soviet espionage agents, but nothing was done. Then, in 1950, on one
of his periodic "orgies," he assaulted an armed watchman and broke the leg of
a fellow British diplomat. Two months later, he broke into the apartment of a
friend, drank up all the available liquor, smashed the furniture, and wrecked
the bathtub. For this bit of fun, he was sent home on sick leave, and punished
by being ordered to consult a psychiatrist. When he returned to the Foreign
Office, after a week's drinking, he was immediately appointed head of the
American Department. One day a friend called Cyril Connolly, the unmoved
repository of this kind of confidence, to say that, in his cups, MacLean had
blurted out, "What would you do if I told you I was a Communist agent?
Well, I am. Go on, report me." The friend and Connolly agreed that the idea
was "preposterous."

Again, in April 1951, MacLean pummeled an associate who had spoken
against Alger Hiss. "I'm the English Hiss," MacLean said before he stalked off.
The Foreign Office, which was then seeking to discover who in its midst was
giving the Soviets secret information, did nothing. Even after it had narrowed
the suspects down to three men, including Burgess and MacLean, it refused to
act. On May 26, 1951, the two men disappeared. When the story of their
defection leaked to the British press, the stock excuse was given: The British
government had no right to detain either man. As more than one irate member of Parliament remarked: Two atom spies, MacLean and Pontecorvo, were
allowed to escape to the Soviet Union because a handful of civil servants had
been too timid to do their duty.

---

* The Daily Express *stated, after MacLean's defection, that he was "head of Chancery
in Washington, the man who decides who sees the telegrams: and head of the American desk
in London, the man who sees and drafts the telegrams as they go." No wonder, the* Daily Express *commented, that Secretary of State Dean Acheson exclaimed, "My God, he knew everything."*

14 The AEC's Early War Against Security

AT THE END of World War II, the United States had the most powerful Army, Navy and Air Force in history. No other country could match America in what came to be known as "conventional" weapons. In its military arsenal, moreover, was the atomic bomb. And on the drawing board, there were plans for the far more powerful hydrogen or "super" bomb. An arrogant or imperialist nation could have, with this tremendous power at its disposal, dictated the terms of victory. A wise nation would have imposed the kind of durable peace which could not be threatened by the Soviet Union. It is no twenty-twenty hindsight to note that had the nation's leaders bothered to read the signs, they would have known Stalin was already preparing to parlay the defeat of the Axis powers into the first steps toward Soviet hegemony.*

But the United States, succumbing to pressure from those who wanted a quick "return to normalcy," began immediately to scrap its Armed Forces. A small but vocal group sought to panic President Truman into making all nuclear secrets public, taking the world's most powerful weapon out of the hands that fashioned it. Simultaneously, there was a loud demand for "internationalization" of atomic energy by the delivery of American know-how and the Manhattan Project installations to the United Nations. President Truman was never fully convinced that the United States should divest itself of the advantage it held by a monopoly in atomic bombs. But the campaign was so persistent—and it reached up so high into his Administration—that Mr. Truman's freedom of action was inhibited and his thinking, for a time, confused.

As late as 1949, Representative Chet Holifield, vice chairman of the Joint Congressional Atomic Energy Committee, was still railing against "trigger-happy admirals and generals" who, he deplored, "want to take over the bomb, both as to production and custody." His cry of "wolf" was unnecessary, for the Atomic Energy Act had codified the surrender to civilians of Los Alamos, the Argonne National Laboratory, Hanford, and other former MED installations. The wisdom of this move can be endlessly debated. But on one aspect of the act, there can be general agreement. By taking Atomic Energy Commission security from Army bureaucrats who failed to understand the problem and turning it over to the Federal Bureau of Investigation, the nation had raised its guard appreciably. The voluminous security files of the MED were taken from the AEC, and the FBI was empowered to make a check on all the

---

* *Professor Philip E. Mosely, who served in the State Department and was an adviser at both the Moscow Conference in 1943 and the Potsdam Conference, has written of "the reversal of the Soviet 'party line' that had already been put into effect in November 1944. From that time on, Soviet propaganda . . . returned to the harsh insistence that while one enemy, Hitler, had been beaten, the main enemy, capitalism, had yet to be destroyed."*

personnel who transferred from the older organization to the newly created civilian body.*

Due process and due deliberation were to be exercised in evaluating derogatory evidence concerning the AEC personnel. At the same time, the Atomic Energy Act firmly stated that no nuclear information was to be divulged until Congress had approved some adequate system of international control. In short, the House and Senate were seeking to lock the stable door before any new horses were stolen. Key members had been quietly informed by Bernard Baruch—America's representative on atomic matters at the United Nations—of a report he had made to President Truman: The Soviet Purchasing Commission had ordered $1.5 million worth of special equipment in this country, using blueprints and specifications which the experts recognized immediately as coming unmistakably from the MED. Some months after this disclosure, Isaac Don Levine, writing for *Plain Talk,* asserted: "It is no longer a secret that Mr. Baruch used his influence to stop the execution of this order, which made him the special target of the Soviet diplomats [at the U.N.] as well as of the pro-Soviet elements in our midst."†

(Baruch's discovery of the Soviet Union's wholesale pillaging of American atomic secrets confirmed the evidence adduced by Western scientists from their discussions with Soviet counterparts. As noted earlier in this account, Soviet nuclear science even employed the same technical neologisms that the men of Los Alamos, Oak Ridge, and Chalk River had invented and thought secret.)

Locking the stable door at this time was, of course, essential. Nuclear physics as applied to bomb technology was still an infant science. It was more than regrettable that the atomic scientists, overriding common sense and seized by a kind of hysteria, had been able to catch President Truman off-balance and get his assent to the immediate release of the Smyth Report, *Atomic Energy for Military Purposes.* Why it was necessary to publish anything, before the world and the nation had recovered from its astonishment over the Hiroshima bombing, has never been fully explained. At the time—just four days after the advent of the Atomic Age—many scientists argued that this detailed and invaluable guidebook to the military uses of nuclear power told nothing that any physicist did not know. If this was so, then why the hurry? But it was not so. As David Lilienthal, one of the strongest "no-secrecy" advocates testified, the Smyth Report was "the principal breach of security since the beginning of the atomic energy enterprise." And the *Bulletin of the Atomic Scientists,* which propagandized for the elimination of secrecy, was constrained to

---

* *Review of security cases was mandatory where derogatory information was found in the files. This, rather than any baleful influences, was responsible for the Oppenheimer hearings. The FBI presented to the AEC what it had gathered together after a study of Oppenheimer's file and a full field investigation. At this point, it would have been a clear violation of the Congressional intent to ignore the charges against Oppenheimer. The first moves, therefore, were inaugurated by a Democratic Administration and came to a culmination in 1954, when the wheels could no longer be stopped. Even had Dr. Oppenheimer been among the stoutest proponents of the H-bomb—and he was just the opposite—it would have been impossible to avoid confronting him with what the files showed and then coming to a determination as to his fitness to retain a "Q" clearance.*

† *Levine, who has probably had more close contacts with former Soviet espionage agents than any other American journalist, estimates that during the MED period the NKVD had some one hundred agents scattered throughout the American-Canadian atomic project.*

admit that the "revelation that plutonium can be and was fabricated in large plants, that it can be and was used for filling bombs, was in no way urgent, and an invitation to engineers abroad to try to duplicate processes which they know to be successful." The Smyth Report did far more than that—as the Soviets themselves publicly acknowledged after the arrest of Allan Nunn May.

The Atomic Energy Act as finally written was designed to prevent repetitions of this sorry haste as the United States, now divorced from its British and Canadian junior partners, looked ahead. But no law is any better than the men who administer it. The first chairman of the Atomic Energy Commission was Lilienthal, recommended to that post by Undersecretary of State Dean Acheson and appointed without the knowledge (and to the consternation) of both Secretary James F. Byrnes and Bernard Baruch. Lilienthal was an excellent administrator and a most persuasive man. (Harold Ickes once described him as "the busiest propagandist the United States has ever produced.") But he was given to strong views and an inflexibility of mind. As coauthor with Acheson of a report on the international control of atomic energy, he had run head-on into Baruch, who demanded safeguards before the United States surrendered its monopoly in atomic weapons. The Baruch view prevailed with President Truman, but not before Lilienthal had delivered himself of this involuted piece of logic:

When the [Acheson-Lilienthal] plan is in full operation there will no longer be secrets about atomic energy. We believe that this is the firmest basis of security; for in the long term there can be no international control and no international cooperation which does not presuppose international community of knowledge.

Yet Lilienthal was chosen to administer law which in its language and intent insisted on continued secrecy and set up machinery for preserving it. If the United States was to maintain its lead and to checkmate Soviet espionage efforts to keep pace with new American discoveries and technologies—and if the FBI's countermeasures were to be successful—a man less antagonistic to these purposes should have been selected.

Much had already been accomplished simply by announcing that henceforward the FBI would be entrusted with the task of surveillance. The Center in Moscow, whose opinion of the Bureau has always been high, immediately called a temporary halt to the activities of its various apparatuses in this country. Soviet "diplomatic" officials, who had been doubling in brass as "legal" *apparatchiks,* were suddenly recalled, and the "illegals" were ordered to "go private" until the Center had surveyed the situation and regrouped its forces. Though there have been, since the passage of the Atomic Energy Act, several hundred minor infractions of security regulations and a number of major attempts at espionage, the FBI was able to prevent depredations on the previous scale. In 1951, the Joint Congressional Atomic Energy Committee reported:

Since mid-1946, when the law creating the joint committee and the Atomic Energy Commission was enacted, American espionage defenses, so far as is known, have not been breached. The Federal Bureau of Investigation and other interested agencies have reported no successful act of atomic espionage committed against the United States from mid-1946 onward.

It was not for want of trying. For the Center in Moscow, which presumably "knew everything"—making further espionage unnecessary—devoted endless time and buckets of money (and incurred considerable risk) to penetrate the FBI shield. As of May 1, 1960, there were six hundred Soviet and Soviet-bloc officials in the United States, with 890 "dependents" to act as auxiliaries. A host of defectors from the Communist empire have documented their agreement that between 70 and 80 per cent of these "diplomats" had full or part-time Intelligence assignments. Since 1952, moreover, the Center in Moscow increasingly stressed the use of "illegals"—agents without diplomatic immunity—in conducting its "deep-cover" espionage affairs. Not all of them, of course, were assigned to nuclear work. But an FBI study of Soviet espionage, prepared early in 1960 to be used by Ambassador Henry Cabot Lodge in countering Soviet breast-beating over the U-2 incident, lifted the curtain briefly on the Center's continued onslaught:

For example, the prosecution of Judith Coplon, an employee of the Department of Justice in early 1950, was followed in October 1950 by a Soviet assignment to Boris Morros, an American motion-picture producer who was cooperating with the FBI, to revive his acquaintance with a member of the United States Atomic Energy Commission to obtain compromising information concerning this individual; and to carefully explore the possibility of placing a secretary in his office who could furnish information of the Russians . . .

From July 1955 through May 1956, [Assistant Soviet Military Attaché Ivan Aleksandrovich] Bubchikov maintained contact with a naturalized American citizen of Russian origin who was employed as a sales engineer. In July 1955, [Bubchikov] appeared at the sales engineer's residence late in the evening and sought his cooperation in securing data concerning jet fuel, atomic submarines, and aeronautical developments . . . This operation . . . was featured by clandestine meetings, complex recognition signals, and a variety of "drop areas" in which the source deposited [seemingly important material prepared by the FBI] for the Soviet . . .

In August of 1955, [Assistant Soviet Military Attaché Yuri Pavlovich] Krylov contacted an employee of the Atomic Energy Commission and attempted to obtain from him information concerning the technical aspects of nuclear power. In December 1955, he contacted a former commissioner of the Atomic Energy Commission in an effort to develop information concerning atomic energy for space heating. In February 1956, he attempted to purchase 26 unclassified films on peace-time atomic energy.*

The FBI's job was to protect the Atomic Energy Commission and its installations from spies. In the days of Lilienthal's hegemony, the Bureau's work was hardly facilitated by an attitude of aloofness amounting almost to hostility at the AEC. The administrators and many of the scientists took an

---

* The FBI could divulge this information because Morros had "surfaced" to become a government witness in several espionage trials. Krylov and Bubchikov had been declared persona non grata by the State Department for violation of their diplomatic status. Other, and similar, cases remain secret. It is preferable to keep a known agent under surveillance so that he may lead the FBI to his contacts and thereby expose them.

even dimmer view of the FBI than they had of military security agencies. The AEC, moreover, by its curious reading of the Atomic Energy Act, suspended security procedures, took it upon itself to broadcast the products of nuclear research, and in general sought to act as a law unto itself. Lilienthal, appearing before the Joint Congressional Committee, defended these practices as in the national interest. And it might well be argued that behind these actions was nothing more than the stubborn belief on the part of Chairman Lilienthal that all secrets must be internationalized—but they hardly made the FBI's work easier.

In security matters, Lilienthal shared the views of many scientists that he knew better than the FBI—and in brushing aside one derogatory report, he resorted to the old chestnut that it was based on information furnished by a "nine-year-old." (Though pressed, he never gave chapter-and-verse.) Lilienthal testified under oath in 1948, moreover, that the AEC in effect frequently bypassed the required FBI check of personnel by authorizing "emergency" clearances. In other instances, scientists and technicians were assigned to secret projects before the FBI check was completed. In practice, this AEC policy was no favor, and it worked real hardship on many of those concerned. They sold their homes, moved their families, and took up jobs which they considered permanent only to be told that clearance had been refused. If the accounts later published by the *Bulletin of Atomic Scientists* are to be believed, the AEC under Lilienthal refused to give them any explanation or the detailed statement of charges to which they were entitled. Blame was vaguely placed on the shoulders of the FBI, further increasing the antisecurity bias of the scientific community.

Though by 1947 the nature of the Communist conspiracy and its assault on United States atomic secrets had been well publicized and thoroughly documented by the Gouzenko documents, the Atomic Energy Commission, at Lilienthal's behest and according to his later testimony, gave clearance to Dr. Edward U. Condon (whose associations have been described in this narrative) and to Dr. Frank P. Graham, despite the adverse recommendation of the AEC's own director of security. Dr. Graham's file probably shows nothing more than several "front" associations and an embattled ignorance of the Communist threat. This determination on his part to think no ill of Communists was demonstrated in a speech he delivered in 1949, reported by the International News Service:

Senator Frank P. Graham declared today that it has not been proven that American Communists are disloyal to the United States. The former North Carolina University president explained that so-called liberal thinkers in this nation are not convinced that a Communist is necessarily un-American. He said the nation's "liberal" element is "groping" to discover if United States Communists really take direct and unquestioned orders from Moscow. As one of the gropers, Graham mentioned Atomic Energy Commission chairman David Lilienthal.

This antagonistic attitude toward counterespionage on Lilienthal's part was earlier demonstrated when, for the first eight months of his tenure as AEC chairman, he failed to appoint any director of security. The post was finally filled by a man who had no background in security matters or procedures, whatever his other merits. In evaluating AEC research fellows, the official in charge, when asked if he had passed on the Communist background of some of the applicants—a relevant factor in making any determination—stated: "I have no competence in that field."

In those critical and formative years, there was very little check of the truth of statements made on the standard Personnel Security Questionnaire. The employee in charge of the U-235 vault, it was later discovered, had been arrested for grand larceny but had failed to state this fact—a punishable offense. Instead of being summarily fired or disciplined, he was simply transferred to other duties. The general laxity was demonstrated by a May 10, 1949, AEC memorandum to all guards at the Argonne National Laboratory. Subject: "Persons allowed unlimited access to property." The memorandum stated:

The following persons *and their guests* will be allowed *unlimited access to all areas of the property at all times* upon identification of themselves. [Emphasis added.]

When security procedures were set up for the AEC, they were so cumbersome and complex that it required a Navy cartographer to put them into chart form. They were still incomprehensible—at least to Chairman Brien McMahon of the Joint Atomic Energy Committee—and required the attention of some twenty to thirty different offices, with no clear indication of final authority on the granting of clearances. As one senator, who studied the chart, said, "Well, you can figure that after going through the maze, if you're entitled to clearance, you'll come out. But if you're not entitled, you can keep going around in circles forever." Given this situation, it is a tribute to the FBI that no major espionage took place under the Lilienthal stewardship. When the Joint Atomic Energy Committee investigated charges by Senator Bourke Hickenlooper of "incredible mismanagement" of the AEC, it was also discovered that physical security at atomic installations was almost a joke.

Special investigators were sent to the various AEC sites. They wandered about, put machined parts and other classified materials in their pockets, and wandered out again with no search or check. One investigator carried out two uranium slugs in his pocket. When these facts were broadcast to the public, Merle E. Smith, president of the Guards' Union, Local 21, at Hanford, wrote in defense of his fellow guards, giving a startling picture of physical security procedures:

Various news items have accented the fact that two uranium slugs were carried by an individual through three guard posts with guards on duty. As a result, in the minds of many people, the Hanford guards are pictured as inefficient and guilty of failure in performance of their duty . . .

I do not believe that there is a single patrolman or patrol officer on the Hanford works guard who has not been appalled at the security laxness which has existed for some time and still exists. Unfortunately, patrol supervision is allowed little or no voice in the policies laid down for the security of this plant. These policies are drawn up by the Security Department . . .

How could a man walk through three guard posts carrying two slugs of uranium? At two of these posts, there are no orders calling for a search of persons entering or leaving. At only one of these posts may a superficial spot search be made. By superficial, I mean a pat search. Spot searching means the searching of perhaps one out of five individuals. For the past year, even this type of search has been practically discontinued . . .

Some weeks ago some 20 per cent of the Hanford patrol force was terminated by order of the security departments. As a consequence of these terminations, we are very short-handed and, of necessity, posts have been undermanned or not manned at all. Suggestions both verbal and written have been offered by both patrolmen and patrol officers, pointing out security weaknesses . . .*

But the biggest gap between the intent of Congress in setting up the Atomic Energy Commission and the performance under Lilienthal was found to be in the exchange of atomic information and the shipment of radioactive isotopes to foreign countries. It had been made legally clear in the Atomic Energy Act that there was to be "no exchange of information with other nations for industrial purposes." No radioactive isotopes were to be released by the AEC except for clearly determined medical purposes such as research and therapy. The AEC chairman, following his own personal beliefs, decided that there was no secrecy about isotopes and that nothing could be gained by not shipping them to other countries, even if the purpose was not the saving of human life. This became established policy, so that on April 28, 1949, a shipment of isotopes went to the Norwegian Defense Research Establishment, to be used for a study of steel and iron under high temperatures in jets, rockets, and artillery. (Prior to this, the AEC had allocated isotopes to Frédéric Joliot-Curie, the Communist physicist in France.)

This shipment to the Norwegian Defense Research Establishment, significantly enough, had been strongly opposed by the General Advisory Council of the AEC, a special group made up of Doctors Oppenheimer, Isadore Rabi, Conant, Fermi, and others with experience in the atomic energy project dating back to the pre-MED days. Lilienthal, when confronted with the facts, argued at first that isotopes had only been shipped for medical research and then insisted that the Norwegians could have gotten them from European cyclotrons. His climaxing argument: a refusal to release the radio-active isotopes would have caused scientists overseas to "become disaffected in their attitude toward the United States." It was further noted that four of the five AEC commissioners voted for the shipment, with Lewis L. Strauss failing to concur on the ground that it "oversteps its (AEC's) statutory provisions."

But it was Dr. Oppenheimer who destroyed Lilienthal's argument that the isotopes for military purposes were as easily available from European cyclo-

---

Among the suggestions made by the patrol officers to the Security Department: a request that the men at guard posts be given some sort of briefing in order to know what they should search for. It was found that none of the guards had ever seen a uranium slug or had one described to him.

trons. He pointed out that more than two hundred millicuries of Carbon 14 had been produced at Oak Ridge, or millions of times more than the amount available prior to that time. This Carbon 14 had cost the United States only ten thousand dollars, but it would take, Oppenheimer said, one thousand cyclotrons to equal this output—and the cost would be one hundred million dollars. Not noted in the debate was the danger of broadening the target area for Soviet agents. It was subsequently discovered that the Norwegian official who requested the isotopes had been forced to resign because he was a Communist agent.

The "why-take-precautions" attitude rampant among those entrusted with the husbanding of America's atomic resources—aided and abetted by the systematic campaign of those who simultaneously believed that the world's safety depended on sharing all nuclear data with the Soviet Union though there were no secrets left to share—may have accounted for the almost jaunty manner in which the still unsolved "Mystery of the Missing Uranium" was handled. The history of the world was not deflected from its course by the theft, loss, or problematical recovery of some forty-two grams of enriched uranium oxide. But the case posed some very serious questions which have yet to be answered. There are men in the United States Senate who hold to the view that the AEC'c explanation offered by a platoon of officials, was more ingenious than convincing. And if the AEC's tortured account was, in fact, accurate, it opened the lid to a Pandora's box of new charges which were never answered. The facts, as stated by Senator Hickenlooper, were these:

1. A container of about 9 or 10 ounces of uranium oxide enriched with 32 grams of uranium 235 was discovered missing at the Argonne National Laboratory, Chicago, on February 8, 1949.*

The AEC chairman, David E. Lilienthal, has attempted to minimize this quantity. He has sneered at the nation's "four-gram jitters." The truth is that for research in the field of weapon development, this is a vast quantity of this precious material. Dr. Allan Nunn May, the British scientist, drew a ten-year prison sentence for stealing one one-thousandth of a gram of U-235; and we began building Hanford before we had as much as is still missing.

2. The AEC, in direct violation of its duty, did not notify the Federal Bureau of Investigation of this loss until March 28, 1949.

Mr. Lilienthal has declared that there was no suspicion of theft or espionage. This is completely untrue. The FBI was called in *only* because there was suspicion of theft and espionage; and though the trail was completely cold, the FBI made its investigation on the assumption of theft and espionage.

3. The AEC did not notify the chairman of the (Joint) Congressional Committee until April 27, 1949, though the law requires that such notification be made immediately.

4. When this loss was reported publicly on May 17, 1949, by the New

---

* The AEC, in announcing the loss, stated that the uranium had been contained in "a brown bottle." Subsequently, it announced that the "brown bottle" had been found. But in its full report to the Joint Atomic Energy Committee, the AEC presented a clear Mason jar as the receptacle in question. Despite an FBI report that a majority of those questioned had stated that the container had been "a brown bottle," the AEC insisted that this was an error based on the fallible recollections of "eyewitnesses." This is one of the many puzzling aspects of the controversy.

York *Daily News,* Mr. Lilienthal replied that the loss was trivial and that it was being partially recovered from "waste." . . . But there is no satisfactory evidence that what is now being reclaimed is, indeed, from the missing parcel.

We have no conclusive evidence that a theft has been committed; but neither do we have conclusive evidence that a theft has not been committed.

The AEC's explanation, somewhat elusively stated by Dr. Walter Zinn, director of the Argonne Laboratory, presented a different picture. Dr. Zinn said that the bottle—whether brown or clear—had been locked in a storage vault. When orders were given to ship all uranium to a central deposit, an inventory was made of the materials in the vault. The inventory showed that the bottle of missing uranium was included and had been shipped. Zinn insisted that is was "fairly certain" that, despite the written evidence, the bottle had remained behind, but he could account for this lapse only by adding that "the young man who did the packing clearly was not capable at the time of understanding the figures well enough to know that he had left something out." It is a matter of record that no discrepancy was discovered at the receiving end. Zinn called this "a hole in the inventory system." He argued that no check had been made when the material was stored in the central deposit. He conceded that it had always been customary to make an inventory at the sending and receiving ends of other shipments—but not in this case.

The "transfer" from the original vault took place on September 16, 1948. The loss was not discovered until February 7, 1949, when a careful check of the contents of the central deposit was made. "Very thorough searches showed that the bottle itself, so to speak, did not seem to exist," Zinn said. "No bottle carrying the right label or any type of description did exist anywhere." It was recalled, however, that twelve galvanized iron cans, holding the waste of uranium machining operations, were awaiting shipment to a special plant which recovers the pure metal from the debris. It was "surmised" that the contents of the missing bottle had been inadvertently dumped into the waste receptacles. By a highly technical process, samplings from the twelve cans were analyzed. It was then learned that one of the cans had four times the amount of U-235 the AEC considered "normal." By dissolving all the material in this can, the Oak Ridge Laboratory was able to "recover" 27.31 grams of U-235. No explanation was offered for the inability to recover the other four-plus grams—a sizable amount of U-235.

Zinn's account of "what might have happened" was accepted as proof of "what did happen." The AEC assured the committee and the public that these lax procedures for the handling and inventory of U-235 and other uranium products had been tightened so that it could not happen again. But this left the Atomic Energy Commission planted firmly on the horns of a dilemma. If the uranium was not stolen by a spy but simply mislaid due to carelessness, the AEC stood self-condemned of the "incredible mismanagement" that Senator Hickenlooper charged.

In the shipment of radioactive isotopes to the Norwegian Military Research Establishment, the committee majority shared Dr. Oppenheimer's view that "you could use a bottle of beer for atomic energy—in fact, you do," and that the AEC had not violated the letter or spirit of the law. In the case of the missing uranium, the committee majority accepted the AEC's account but did not condemn the carelessness it laid bare. The majority report found much to praise, almost nothing to criticize in the management of the AEC under Lilienthal. The minority report, signed by six Republicans, was moderately critical. It cited the abuses in security—highlighted some months later when, on August 22, 1950, a former Los Alamos scientist was arrested for stealing a glass vial of plutonium "as a souvenir," which he buried beneath his house. (The theft had occurred years earlier, but was discovered due to FBI vigilance.)

But the crux of the minority report was in two brief paragraphs touching on matters which would occupy the nation's attention and lead to the controversy over Dr. Oppenheimer and the aversion he shared with some of his scientific colleagues for continued advances in nuclear weaponry:

Since the establishment of the Commission, almost three years ago, it has been aware, through authoritative recommendations, of the pressing urgency of putting into action certain programs that will strengthen our reserve of atomic materials and aid the objective of capturing and having available for effective use the largest practicable degree of the power of those atomic materials for weapons and other purposes.

The Commission's approach to this supreme task has been leisurely, has been characterized by indecision, and a number of the most important of these recommended projects have not developed into operating plants.

Among those projects was the development of the hydrogen bomb. The "why" of the AEC's indecision in time divided Americans, stirred up the scientific community, and led to serious charges against Dr. Oppenheimer. Much of the debate on both sides was complex, technical, and given to red-herring techniques. The missing factor in any understanding of the issues, however, remained as always the inability of many people to grasp a series of propositions:

(1) The Soviet onslaught on the American monoply of the atomic bomb was two-pronged—first to steal the secret and second to immobilize further development by the United States—in the latter instances employing Pavlovian techniques.

(2) By the very nature of the secondary onslaught, the Soviet Union's most effective troops would be men and women whose dedication to American principles and abhorrence of tyranny could not be questioned.

15 Phase Two: Soviet Atomic Judo

ON JULY 16, 1945—the day the first atomic device was tested at Alamogordo —"a group of nuclear scientists met around a conference table in a small, hushed room in the Metallurgy Building of the University of Chicago." So begins a horror tale told months afterward by Dr. Robert M. Hutchins, later to win fortune and fame of a sort as head of the Fund for the Republic. The purpose of this meeting, according to Dr. Hutchins, was to organize politically, to suppress knowledge of the atomic bomb, and to urge that it never be used against the Japanese. "These men knew that once the bomb was dropped, once the world learned that fission chain reaction could be accomplished, atomic bombs could be produced by any reasonably advanced nation on earth, and that the end result could be annihilation of all life on this planet."

This apocryphal tale fits none of the known facts. The record shows that the atomic scientists exhibited exhilaration at their success, congratulating themselves that they had probably saved the lives of American boys preparing to storm the beaches of the Japanese homeland.* From the moment that they knew the bomb experiment would be successful, moreover, they itched to tell the world about it. In fact, five weeks before the "meeting" described by Hutchins, a group of seven scientists from the same laboratory had stated to Secretary of War Henry Stimson that "it would be foolish to retain our leadership in nucleonics by secrecy." While Nazi Germany was still fighting, the atomic scientists had grudgingly tolerated what security General Groves and the MED were able to impose. Once the Hitler regime had collapsed, the attitude at Los Alamos was exemplified by the words of a leading physicist to his approving colleagues: "We will say the opposite of what General Groves says, no matter what it is."

Much earlier, Dr. Leo Szilard—one of those who urged the development of the bomb and sought Albert Einstein to intercede with Franklin D. Roosevelt in aid of this purpose—had shifted to the position later adopted by many in the scientific community. In March 1945, according to the *Bulletin of the Atomic Scientists,* Szilard wrote to President Roosevelt making two somewhat curious points: (1) the atomic bomb would weaken the United States in its relations with the Soviet Union, and (2) the fear among scientists was not what the Germans might have done with the bomb but "what the government of the United States might do to other countries."

It is always dangerous to suggest that men of high principle have been

---

* Dr. Kistiakowsky, according to one account, "threw his arms around Dr. Oppenheimer and embraced him with shouts of glee" after the Alamogordo test.

169

manipulated. It is even more dangerous to point out that the manipulators were conscious instruments of a conspiracy, for by a kind of perverse reasoning this is taken to mean that the men of high principle were Communists. It is precisely because so many of the eminent scientists were *not* Communists—and in an untutored way opposed to communism—that the manipulators could operate.* In the middle and lower ranks of the scientific world, as this account has demonstrated, were men who ranged from dedicated party members to intellectually unco-ordinated fellow-travelers. They served as the Typhoid Marys among scientists unconsciously susceptible to the virus. Phase One of the Kremlin's strategy was to steal all the atomic secrets it could. Phase Two was to make use of the "confusion potential" among scientists to turn America's atomic strength against it by applying the techniques of judo. This is what happened, according to plans carefully made and excellently executed by the Kremlin.

This atomic judo was described by Henry A. Kissinger in *Nuclear Weapons and Foreign Policy*, written well after the Soviet Union had exploded its own devices and had shifted to an attempted strategy of atomic blackmail:

The Communist campaign, finely attuned to prevailing fears, almost imperceptibly shifted the primary concern away from Soviet aggression—the real security problem—to the immorality of the use of nuclear weapons, which happened to represent the most effective means of resisting it. Because of its skill in exploiting the inhibitions of the non-Soviet world, the Soviet Union has discovered two forms of "atomic blackmail": The threat of its growing nuclear arsenal and an appeal to the West's moral inhibitions. In either case the consequence is a lowered will to resist.

Phase Two, in its early stages, consisted of a vast campaign to convince America and the world that Hiroshima and Nagasaki had been a crime against humanity (as opposed, of course, to Stalin's planned liquidation of millions of peasants—which was "social engineering"), that further development of more powerful nuclear weapons must be stopped, and that all the data thus far amassed must be turned over to the United Nations for dissemination to the world. This was a time in which the scientists who had so eagerly contemplated the first bombs toured the country describing the terrors of atomic war, expressed horror over the fate of "unborn generations," organized themselves into a semi-hysterical lobby which descended on Washington, became the self-elected guardians of American conscience, and posed as the ultimate authorities on Soviet intentions and geopolitical strategy.

Since many of these scientists had world-wide reputations and visitors' cards to the highest government circles, their influence was pervasive. According to notes kept by Secretary of Commerce Henry A. Wallace of the September 21, 1945, meeting of the Truman Cabinet, Secretary of War Stimson reported then that scientists were urging:

---

* *Since no one likes to be called a dupe, the scientists involved have taken umbrage at this analysis and charge those who make it of questioning their loyalty.*

... the free interchange of scientific information between different members of the United Nations. [Stimson] said that the scientists told him . . . that future bombs would be infinitely more destructive . . . He said some were afraid they would be so powerful as to ignite the atmosphere and put an end to the world.

The Walter Millis summary of the James Forrestal diaries states:

According to Forrestal's notes, (Wallace) was "completely, everlastingly and wholeheartedly in favor of giving [all atomic secrets] to the Russians . . . Failure to give them our knowledge would make an embittered and sour people."

In the Senate, the battle was continued by Senator Claude Pepper, fresh from his triumphs before Communist-front audiences, who called on the United States to "destroy every atomic bomb we have" and to plow under all American atomic installations. One of the few in high government circles at that time who took Stalin at his word and who pointed out that the Soviets still believed that "the capitalistic and communistic concepts could not live together in the same world" were Secretary Forrestal. His suspicion of Soviet intentions and his insistence that the atomic bomb "belongs to the American people" and should not be given away without national consent brought him the unrelenting attacks of political gossip columnists like Drew Pearson, the scientific community, and the dupes of Soviet manipulation. Forrestal subscribed to General Eisenhower's formulation, uttered at high-level Administration meetings, that "any agreement about atomic weapons without enforceable methods of inspection would be most dangerous for the United States."

Those who sided with Forrestal were not acting out of paranoid fear of the Soviet Union. They were fully aware of Stalin's intentions in regard to the atomic bomb which, at that time, Soviet scientists were feverishly working to build. The Millis summary of the Forrestal diaries spelled it out clearly:

Forrestal entered in his diary the gist of an Intelligence report on Soviet atomic strategy. This represented Soviet policy as one of pressing for disarmament and outlawry of atomic weapons on the world stage while refusing to allow any inspection of Russia's own atomic activities. The result would be to create a world opinion that would force the Western powers to disarm and drop their atomic development, permitting the Soviet Union to continue its own atomic operations while the West slept.

On one level, there was the open conspiracy as exemplified by obviously Soviet-motivated propaganda efforts. The Scientific and Cultural Conference, held at the Waldorf Astoria Hotel in New York in 1949, was clearly in this category. It was part and parcel of a well-financed drive which included the Stockholm "Peace" Appeal, presumably signed by millions of people—though most of them were behind the Iron Curtain—the Partisans for Peace which sprang up in France and Italy, the organized pickets who paraded before American embassies, the riots and demonstrations against the atomic bomb, and the Belgrade Conference of recent memory which roasted the United States for not agreeing to "atomic disarmament" on Soviet terms (in the interests of mankind's future) but hardly murmured when the Communists resumed massive atomic tests in the atmosphere.

On another level, there was the unscientific chatter of men with access to mass communications. Modern man, it suddenly developed, was obsolete because he still clung to the primitive notion that aggression must not go unanswered—or because he refused to forget the lesson of the Rhineland and Munich that appeasement is the surest road to war. Men superlatively trained in the disciplines of science cast them aside for an emotionalism easy to comprehend but somewhat harder to forgive. An atomic scientist told a correspondent for one of the news magazines, when they were on their way to the first (and by today's standards small) tests on Bikini Atoll: "This nuclear explosion, or one like it, can split the earth into two parts which will then orbit independently." Warnings of a runaway chain reaction which would obliterate the entire solar system appeared *ad infinitum* in the popular press. Science-fiction writers turned out scare novels by the dozens. One of these, written by a fellow-traveler, described the end of the world in 1960, as a result of American nuclear tests. Though the scientists then—and now—had little more than guesswork to back their predictions of a deformed population, the fear of "fallout"—that detritus of nuclear blasts—was everywhere expressed.

The first victory of Phase Two was the defeat of the May-Johnson bill—a demonstration of the validity of Senator Brien McMahon's rueful remark that "the scientists participated in the formation of our international policy." In this case, the participation was negative. The bill—proposed by President Truman and drafted with the aid of such scientists and experts as Vannevar Bush, Karl T. Compton, James B. Conant, Enrico Fermi, Ernest O. Lawrence, and J. Robert Oppenheimer (though he later withdrew his support)—called for the orderly and expeditious development of military and peaceful uses of atomic energy by a joint Pentagon-civilian body. It was Dr. Szilard who sounded the tocsin against the measure. Scientists at atomic installations were suddenly reported to be in a state of "near revolt" over the May-Johnson bill. They denounced a "military conspiracy" and charged that they had been "forbidden to speak"—though they had done little else since Hiroshima. Secrecy, said four hundred of Los Alamos' finest, "will lead to an unending war, more savage than the last." *The Nation* criticized the bill because it considered atomic energy in the "narrow terms of national security."

The May-Johnson bill, once it had been garroted, was followed by S.1717, the product of Senator McMahon. S.1717 completely excluded the military from even the remotest association with any nuclear projects. It further stated that "basic scientific information" in the atomic energy field be "freely disseminated." And it gave a proposed Atomic Energy Commission the right to determine what information could be disclosed without violation of the Espionage Act, adding that in cases where no determination was made against disclosure, the punitive provisions of the act would be automatically suspended. In other words, all the wraps were off unless the AEC specifically laid down a prohibition.

When Senator Arthur Vandenberg introduced an amendment, eventually passed by the Congress, establishing a Military Liaison Committee to be kept informed of the work of the Atomic Energy Commission, the tocsin sounded again. McMahon charged that the Vandenberg amendment would allow the Pentagon to "look into every single phone call, every single file, every single action . . . anything from the hiring of janitors at atomic energy installations to the construction of atomic plants." Eighteen organizations immediately protested the amendment, and one propagandist left an indignant letter at the White House. In his diary, a somewhat puzzled Vandenberg wrote:

There is a perfectly legitimate demand in the country (especially among scientists and educators) that final peacetime control of atomic energy should rest in civilian hands . . . But! I do not agree that in the present state of world affairs the Army and the Navy should be totally excluded from consultation when they see the national security to be involved . . .

The trouble with those who have been most violently urging civilian control is that they all but ignore the national security factor. Of course, they are supported in this viewpoint by every Communist and every fellow-traveler and every parlor-pink in the country, because these latter groups would like to make the national security as insecure as possible.

The *Daily Worker* had its own response: "Atomic Fascism."

The House of Representatives, undaunted, amended the Atomic Energy Act to require at least a modicum of secrecy and security—though this was to a degree ignored by those who first administered it. But the real battle was joined over the hydrogen or fusion bomb, for which most of the theoretical work had been done by Dr. Edward Teller at the instigation of Oppenheimer before the Hiroshima bomb was exploded. According to John J. McCloy, the H-bomb could have been an actuality by 1947—except for the remarkable gyrations, feet-dragging, and general obstructionism of Oppenheimer and others of his colleagues who had been most zealous in beating the Nazis to the atomic, or fission, bomb.

In discussing Oppenheimer's role, there are great obstacles to any definitive statement of his position. He himself stated in 1954, and not facetiously, that "in the nine years we have been talking about these things, I have said almost everything on almost every side of every question." Oppenheimer was under oath and facing the loss of his security clearance, so this may have been a legal maneuver. But taking hyperbole into account, it was a fair statement of fact. What is significant in this context is not what he said at various occasions but the net effect of his personality and his sentiments on the scientific community. In its statement of charges, the Atomic Energy Commission attempted to synthesize what this effect had been. Disassociating the charge from its loyalty-security implications and evaluating it simply as a summary of Oppenheimer's point of view, it makes interesting reading:

It was reported that in 1945 you expressed the view that "there is a reasonable possibility that it [the hydrogen bomb] can be made," but that the feasibility of the hydrogen bomb did not appear, on theoretical grounds, as certain as the fission bomb appeared certain, on theoretical grounds, when the Los Alamos Laboratory was started; and that in the autumn of 1949 the General Advisory Committee expressed the view that "an imaginative and concerted attack on the problem has a better than even chance of producing the weapon within five years." It was further reported that in the autumn of 1949, and subsequently, you strongly opposed the development of the hydrogen bomb: (1) on moral grounds, (2) by claiming that it was not feasible, (3) by claiming that there were insufficient facilities and scientific personnel to carry on the development, and (4) that it was not politically desirable. It was further reported that even after it was determined, as a matter of national policy, to proceed with the development of a hydrogen bomb, you continued to oppose the project and declined to cooperate fully in the project. It was further reported that you departed from your proper role as an adviser to the Commission by causing the distribution separately and in private to top personnel at Los Alamos of the majority and minority reports of the General Advisory Committee on the development of the hydrogen bomb, for the purpose of trying to turn such top personnel against the development of the hydrogen bomb. It was further reported that you were instrumental in persuading other outstanding scientists not to work on the hydrogen-bomb project, and that the opposition to the hydrogen bomb, of which you are the most experienced, most powerful, and most effective member, has definitely slowed down its development.

In view of the emotions and the controversy aroused by the Oppenheimer hearings—inflamed partly by his leaking to *The New York Times* of the bare charges and his written answer, without the evidence which might have allowed a dispassionate evaluation—it is necessary to note that it was certainly within Oppenheimer's right to oppose the hydrogen bomb. But it must also be added that this right did not include a corollary privilege of attempting to veto high government policy while he maintained his position as a member of the General Advisory Committee. Of the four reasons for his opposition, as ascribed to him by the AEC, only one was proper: that the facilities and the personnel to make the bomb were inadequate. Holding the other three, he should have resigned from the GAC and openly taken his case to the public and to the scientific community. As an adviser, his role was limited to the scientific and the technical; it did not extend to the moral and political. He himself stated that in the postwar years "our principal duty was to make our technical experience and judgment available . . . in a context and against a background of the official views of the government."

Of considerable importance is the next question: Were the AEC's charges well founded? Had they been in a political debate rather than as the basis for a formal hearing, would Oppenheimer have denied them? And is there documentary evidence to sustain the AEC? On some aspects of the AEC's contention, there is sharply divided testimony. There are some who asserted that even after the hydrogen bomb had been ordered by President Truman, Oppenheimer and his colleagues carried on a campaign against participation by other scientists in the project. There is equally firm testimony that he did not. Oppenheimer's own testimony is hardly categorical, one way or another. In considering the subtle brainwashing which was a major end of Phase Two, the facts as they can be ascertained are of value to this account. They can be broken down into several categories.

1. *Did Dr. Oppenheimer believe in 1949 that the hydrogen, or the thermonuclear, or super bomb was not feasible? Or did he use that argument because he believed that the hydrogen bomb should not be made for moral reasons?*

On September 20, 1944—and after he had been informed by MED security officials that the Soviets had penetrated to an unspecified degree the secret of the atomic bomb—Oppenheimer wrote to Dr. Richard Tolman, urgently pressing for work on the super bomb:*

I should like, therefore, to put in writing at an early date the recommendation that the subject of *initiating violent thermonuclear reactions be pursued with vigor and diligence, and promptly.* In this connection I should like to point out that gadgets of reasonable efficiency and suitable design can almost certainly induct significant thermonuclear reaction in deuterium . . . [Emphasis added.]

It is not at all clear whether we shall actually make this development during the present project, but it is of great importance that such (deletion) gadgets form an experimentally possible transition from a simple gadget to the super and thus open the possibility of a not purely theoretical approach to the latter. . . .

At the present time, site Y [Los Alamos] does not contemplate undertaking this, but I believe that with a somewhat longer time scale than our present one, this line of investigation might prove profitable.

In general, not only for the scientific but for the political evaluation of the possibilities of our project, the critical, prompt, and effective exploration of the extent to which energy can be released by thermonuclear reactions is clearly of profound importance. Several members of this laboratory, notably Teller, Bethe, von Neumann, Rabi, and Fermi have expressed great interest in the problems outlined above . . .

This was Oppenheimer in 1944, when the pressure of the scientific community—and the emotional drive—was to pile up armaments against the Nazis. Yet on October 29, 1949, as chairman of the General Advisory Committee, in a climate of opinion conditioned by a new kind of pressure against "warmongering" or exacerbating the Kremlin's sensibilities, Oppenheimer would write:

We believe a super bomb should never be produced. Mankind would be far better off not to have a demonstration of the feasibility of such a weapon until the present climate of world opinion changes.

2. *Did the argument that superiority in nuclear weapons would be a liability to the United States stem from scientific considerations, as Oppen-*

---

* *The parts of this letter dealing with technical aspects are still classified.*

*heimer and the politicalized atomic scientists argued, or was it casuistry based
on the change in the world situation?*

Writing to Dr. Tolman on October 4, 1944, Oppenheimer stated a view
sharply at variance with the "logic" of 1949:

In transmitting to you the recommendations of workers at site Y on the
technical and scientific developments which should be supported in the postwar period, it would seem unnecessary to provide a summary of our opinions.
I should like, however, to emphasize a general point of view which I believe is
shared by *most of the responsible members of this project*. [Emphasis added.]

Urging experimentation and development of the super bomb in a postwar era's more "scientifically sound manner," Oppenheimer argued:

The above considerations are all intended to focus attention to one
point. Such technical hegemony as this country now possesses in the scientific
and technical aspects of the problem of using nuclear reactors for explosive
weapons is the result of a few years of intensive but inevitably poorly planned
work. This hegemony can presumably be maintained only by continued development both on the technical and on the fundamental scientific aspects of the
problem, for which the availability of the active materials and the participation of qualified scientists and engineers are equally indispensable. *No government can adequately fulfill its responsibilities as custodian if it rests upon the
wartime achievements of this project, however great they may temporarily
seem, to insure future mastery in this field.* [Emphasis added.]

Within two years, although the scientific facts had not changed, Oppenheimer would be taking a diametrically opposed line. All that had changed
was the politics of the situation. No longer did Oppenheimer argue for steps to
"insure the future mastery" of this country in nuclear weapons. Like the
sponge he had always been in political matters, he absorbed and made his own
the arguments of some of his colleagues, attempted to persuade men like Dr.
Edward Teller to resign from the project, wisecracked that as far as he was
concerned "you can give Los Alamos back to the Indians," and used his persuasive powers to argue against the very "hegemony" he had once sought. As
those who have engaged in converstaion with Dr. Oppenheimer will attest, he
was a most persuasive man.

*3. Did Oppenheimer attempt to dissuade his fellow scientists from en-
gaging in research on the super bomb?*

Oppenheimer has conceded that his lack of enthusiasm for continuing
and accelerating work on the hydrogen bomb, even after the Soviets exploded
their first atomic device in 1949, helped to discourage other scientists and
militated against their participation in the vital work. (In point of fact, progress of the work at Los Alamos and the other atomic installations began grinding to a halt right after Hiroshima and did not move into gear until President
Truman ordered a crash program on the super bomb.) Whether he actively
campaigned against the new project is difficult to determine. The testimony of

his friends contradicts that of other scientists—and Oppenheimer's self-admitted fallibility of memory does not aid in arriving at any conclusions.

It is not to impugn motives but to demonstrate the amazing success of Phase Two that the sole documentary evidence—a diary kept by Dr. Luis Alvarez and the testimony of Dr. Teller, "father" of the H-bomb—are presented here. Alvarez began to keep this diary shortly after the Soviets had exploded their device in September of 1949, and he elaborated on its brief references in testimony before the Gray Board:

October 5, 1949. Latimer and I thought independently that the Russians could be working hard on the super and might get there ahead of us. The only thing to do seems to get there first . . .

October 8, 1949. Arrived Washington after lunch. Went to AEC and talked with Pitzer, Gen. McCormack, Latimer, and Paul Fine. Told them what we planned to do and got good response.

October 10, 1949 . . . Went to Capitol and had lunch with Senator McMahon and Representative Hinshaw. Told them of our plans and got good reactions.

(Testimony: "They said, 'We hope you can get something going.' ")

Back to AEC—saw Lilienthal. He was only lukewarm to proposition.

(Testimony: "I must confess that I was somewhat shocked by his behavior. He did not even seem to want to talk about the program. He turned his chair around and looked out the window and indicated that he did not want to even discuss the matter. He did not like the idea of thermonuclear weapons.")

October 11, 1949. In New York . . . we went to see Rabi and found him happy about our plans. He is worried, too.

(Testimony: "He agreed with us that the hydrogen bomb program was a very good program, and he was happy we were doing something to get it reactivated.")

October 16, 1949 . . . Drew Pearson's first mention of "H-bomb."

October 17, 1949. Talked with Hafstad, Zinn, and Pitzer this afternoon on phone. Things are going as well as possible . . . Zinn says he has ideas about how to do the job . . .

October 24, 1949. . . . Hafstad (at Oak Ridge Conference) says nothing has happened in the last week about our program. This is very disappointing in view of Hafstad's enthusiasm last week when he left . . . Apparently Zinn has thrown a lot of doubts in people's mind about the wisdom of our program . . . Talked with Teller . . . [I] felt Oppie was lukewarm to our project and Conant was definitely opposed.

Chicago meeting—then on to Washington—talked with all GAC and most of AEC Commissioners. Particularly interesting talk with Oppie after he briefed Bradbury and Norstad at GAC meeting. Pretty foggy thinking.

(Testimony: "He [Oppenheimer] said that he did not think the United States should build the hydrogen bomb, and the main reason that he gave for this if my memory serves me correctly, and I think it does, was that if we built a hydrogen bomb, then the Russians would build a hydrogen bomb, whereas if we did not build a hydrogen bomb, then the Russians would not build a hydrogen bomb. I found this such an odd point of view that I don't understand it to this day. I told Dr. Oppenheimer that he might find that a reassuring point of view . . . Dr. Serber* was present and agreed with Dr. Oppenheimer and this surprised me greatly in view of the fact that two or three days before he had gone to see Dr. Oppenheimer telling me that he would try to convert Dr. Oppenheimer's lukewarmness into some enthusiasm for our project.")

After the conversation with Oppenheimer, Alvarez felt that "the program was dead." It remained at least moribund, except for some lonely work still being done by Dr. Teller at Los Alamos, until the President revived it by ordering construction of the super bomb in January of 1950. Alvarez noted that though some experts had said the fission bomb was impossible, it had been built. "The technology [for the A-bomb] was developed because of the climate at Los Alamos, enthusiastic people [including Oppenheimer], who said we don't care what the experts say, we will make it work. This was the thing that was missing in the hydrogen-bomb program after the war, and the thing which came into being some while after the Presidential directive," Alvarez said. Then, in December 1950, almost a year after the President had ordered all-out work on the super, Alvarez was told by Oppenheimer: "We all agree that the hydrogen-bomb program should be stopped, but if we were to stop it or to suggest that it be stopped, this would cause so much disruption at Los Alamos and in other laboratories where they are doing instrumentation work that I feel we should let it go on, and it will die a natural death with the coming test when those tests fail. That will be the natural time to chop the hydrogen-bomb program off."†

Edward Teller's account of Oppenheimer's activities—and of his influence on other scientists in support of his opposition to the hydrogen bomb—bolstered the Alvarez testimony and diary. Teller characterized Oppenheimer's effect on the program as one of "hindrance" which hurt the morale at Los Alamos until President Truman's directive. After that time, Oppenheimer was, in general, cold to the project—with one exception, in June 1951, when he warmly supported a new approach in research. And Teller added:

Prior to the [President's] announcement, preceding it perhaps by two or

---

* See testimony concerning Dr. Serber on pp. 74-75.

† Alvarez testified that he was a member of a long-range planning committee on the hydrogen bomb to which he and Dr. C. C. Lauritsen were appointed by Oppenheimer. At the end of 1950, Alvarez was given evidence of the feelings of some of the scientists:

"I do know that Dr. Lauritsen apparently had strong reasons, probably some of a moral nature, for not wanting the hydrogen bomb. I do know that Dr. Lauritsen's closest associate, Dr. William Fowler, had been giving lectures on the radio against the hydrogen bomb. I was in Pasadena staying with Dr. Bacher one night when I was giving a lecture at Cal. Tech., and at a dinner party that night all I heard was stories about why you should not have hydrogen bombs, and the fact that the members of the staff at Cal. Tech. were giving public lectures and talking on the radio against the hydrogen bomb."

Alvarez also had the following colloquy with Roger Robb, counsel for the Gray Board:

"Q: You testified as others did that Dr. Oppenheimer did a splendid job at Los Alamos. Did it strike you as peculiar that one who had done such a splendid job at Los Alamos [on the atomic bomb] could entertain opinions which you considered so wrong in respect to the hydrogen bomb?

"A: I was very surprised when I found that he had these opinions since he had used the super as the primary incentive to get me to join the Manhattan District [during the war] . . . He had spent almost a solid afternoon telling me about the exciting possibilities of the super, and asked me to join and help with the building of such a device. So I was therefore very surprised when I found he had these objections [in 1949]."

three days, I saw Dr. Oppenheimer at an atomic energy conference concerning another matter, and during this meeting it became clear to me that in Dr. Oppenheimer's opinion a decision was impending and this would be a go-ahead decision.

At that time I asked Oppenheimer, if this is now the decision, would he then please really help us to work, recalling the very effective work during the war. Oppenheimer's answer to this was in the negative . . . This negative reply gave me the feeling that I should not look to Oppenheimer for help under any circumstances.

A few months later, during the spring, I nevertheless called up Oppenheimer and I asked him not for direct help but for his support in recruiting people. Dr. Oppenheimer said then, "You know, in this matter, I am neutral. I would be glad, however, to recommend to you some very good people who are working here at the Institute" [of Advanced Studies in Princeton, headed by Oppenheimer] and he mentioned a few. I wrote to all of them and tried to persuade them to come to Los Alamos. None of them came.

Fortunately for the United States and the free world, Dr. Teller was able to recruit a group of scientists and to infuse them with his own drive to build the super. On November 1, 1952, the first fusion bomb was exploded at Eniwetok, and the United States maintained a lead which the Soviets were desperately trying to eliminate. It is now known that the Soviets, having gathered from their various apparatuses the know-how of the atomic bomb and the theoretical aspects of the hydrogen bomb, began work on both simultaneously. Given a more advanced technology and a firmer industrial base, they might have been able to explode their own fusion device before the Eniwetok test. Given its limitations, the Soviet Union's "success" can be explained in terms used by Jerome Wiesner: "All science and technology, in doing something the first time, is extremely difficult and takes a few strokes of genius and brilliance. Doing it the second time, once it has been demonstrated and the general outlines are there, is a good deal simpler."

The bemused attitude of many American scientists, and the two-way stretch of their political thinking, did not end with the explosion of the Soviet bomb or the increasingly apparent knowledge that the Communists would use such nuclear weapons as they had to bluff and blackmail the free world. Scientists and scholars remained convinced that any agreement between East and West was a step forward—no matter who benefited by it. Men of otherwise reasonable judgment subscribed to the call of a series of meetings which brought together Soviet and Western scientists in what was to be a marriage of true minds. "Political disagreements should not influence men of science in estimating what is probable," Bertrand Russell declared in launching the Pugwash Conferences financed by the multimillionaire apologist for the Soviet Union, Cyrus Eaton. "We have not yet found that the views of experts on this question depend in any degree upon their politics or prejudices . . . The abolition of war will demand distasteful limitations of national sovereignty . . . Remember humanity and forget the rest."

The Pugwash Conferences helped to maintain the same kind of blind optimism and blind fear that caused the delay in the work on the hydrogen bomb. Lord Russell emerged from the first thinking precisely what the secret conspirators wanted him to believe—that the Communist countries would be "gradually improved by public opinion from within if the fear of alien hostility were removed." This hoary argument was garnished by Eaton's statement to Chairman J. William Fulbright of the Senate Foreign Relations Committee that he was "convinced that agreement can be reached between East and West" and by his article in the *Foreign Policy Bulletin* painting a cozy picture of Soviet integrity:

> Each scientist there believed what the other scientists were saying . . . All of us were convinced that the Russians were being completely honest, completely frank. Therefore, it made for a remarkable community where the cards were all on the table, where everyone was aboveboard with everyone else.

This description by Eaton—and even by others whose motives cannot be questioned—has lived on in the attitude of those who to this day insist that Soviet scientists are scientists first and only incidentally tools of the Kremlin. But it was the Western scientists who placed their cards on the table. The Soviet scientists, whose commissar was Aleksandr Vasilevich Topchiev, simply repeated the Communist propaganda line on cessation of atomic testing and repeated *Pravda's* charges against the United States. They were further bound by Topchiev's strictures on the uses of science:

> Our scientists cannot and must not stand aside from ideological struggle between communism and capitalism. Some scientific workers try mechanically to extend to the field of ideology the slogan of peaceful coexistence of states with different social and economic systems. A time has come, they say, when we can permit ourselves this coexistence of two ideologies. This is a profoundly mistaken conclusion . . . Any indefiniteness, neutrality, or an a-political stand, which V. I. Lenin constantly opposed, is now more than ever intolerable in our midst.*

Topchiev was, and is, the First Secretary of the Soviet Academy of Science, which Dr. Eugene Rabinowitch, editor of the *Bulletin of Atomic Scientists*—after his initial belief that Soviet scientists "share a common language [with those of the West] and approach problems in the same way"—described as "the general staff" of a "highly organized scientific army" utilizing "propaganda slogans." Topchiev clearly outmatched the scientists with whom he met and even convinced one Cornell professor that the answer to the problem of atomic testing and inspection would be a proviso in the treaty "making it a citizen's legal duty to report knowledge of secret testing to the International Control Commission."

It was by a combination of propaganda and confusion, of tugs at the heartstrings and punches at the terror zone, of fantasies and appeals to "reason," that the Center in Moscow and its masters in the Kremlin muddied the

---

* *It is interesting to note that at these "cards-on-the-table" conferences, one of the Soviet delegates accompanying Topchiev was a Professor N. A. Talensky. Talensky, however, is a major general, Soviet Army General Staff, and is described in the Biographical Dictionary of the U.S.S.R. as "one of the most . . . influential military theoreticians on the general staff."*

waters of American policy and weakened the will to resist. Among those from the West present at these conferences were members of the apparatus, one of whom defected to the Soviet Union. Were the open conspiracy and the manipulation of sincere and decent men more dangerous than the theft of atomic secrets? The history of Western wishful thinking during the past two decades may offer an answer.

16 The Unfinished Chapter

HISTORY is a jigsaw puzzle. From time to time, the impertinent researcher fits in a new piece, making the configuration clearer. But in the attrition of time, some pieces are lost. Others are willfully destroyed by those who have something to hide or something to gain. The puzzle is never completed. Yet each piece, as it is fitted into place, generates its own fascination. Take, for example, the conversation between veteran correspondent Frank Conniff and Marshal Zhukov, then the Soviet Union's most influential military man, in 1955. Conniff, with William Randolph Hearst Jr. and Bob Considine, was making a Pulitzer-Prize-winning investigation of the new men in the Kremlin—and of their hot-and-cold aggressions.

"If our intentions were to conquer the world," Zhukov stated, "we would have marched to the Channel in 1946 when your country had demobilized."

"But, marshal," Conniff answered, "it is generally believed that the reason you didn't march was because we had the atom bomb."

"Ah, yes," Zhukov said. *"But you only had five."*

In the context of this account, that remark assumes importance simply because Zhukov could so casually allude to what was considered in the early postwar era the free world's most strategic secret. For three American newspapermen to ask him how he knew would have been both futile and impolitic. Hearst, Conniff, and Considine, moreover, could have made some educated guesses. This single disclosure fits in neatly with two other pieces of the historical jigsaw—the first now forgotten, the second never generally known.

Piece 1. In December 1946, Dr. Robert Bacher, who had headed the bomb physics division of the MED, made an inspection of Los Alamos. By that time, production of atomic bombs had slowed down almost to a halt. Many scientists had departed from Los Alamos, trailing moral indignation, for lucrative positions and the luxury of demanding that the United States share the

new and more sophisticated secrets of nuclear research with the Soviet Union.*
Walter Lippmann was excoriating Bernard Baruch for failing to trust the
Kremlin. And David Lilienthal was proposing that this country build atomic
energy plants in the Soviet Union as a token of good faith. Only the more
dedicated scientists continued to work in the depleted laboratories of Los
Alamos. Testifying with some horror in 1949 to the crumbling state of America's defenses apparent three years earlier, Bacher said:

> I spent two days as a representative of the [Atomic Energy] Commission
> going over what we had. I was very deeply shocked to find out how few atomic
> weapons we had at that time. This came as rather a considerable surprise to
> me in spite of the fact that I had been rather intimately associated with work of
> the Los Alamos project—roughly a year before. Judging by the consternation
> which appeared on some of the faces around there, I concluded that this must
> have been the first detailed inventory that had been made.

Piece 2. Though the American people were told in 1949 by the Joint
Atomic Energy Committee's majority members that David Lilienthal had
found a shambles at Los Alamos but brought order and efficiency to the bomb
project—and again in 1954 by Dr. Oppenheimer that he had opposed the
hydrogen bomb because he wanted all effort to be focused on perfecting the
fission bomb—the facts were somewhat at variance. For in 1948, shortly before
the Soviet blockade of Berlin, another inventory was made at Los Alamos by
the AEC. A check of A-bomb components showed that most, if not all, of
America's nuclear arsenal was probably worthless. An essential ingredient of
the stored bombs, it was discovered, had deteriorated and could not be
counted on to bring about the necessary chain reaction.

President Truman has been roundly criticized for resorting to an airlift
when the Red Army interposed its forces between West Germany and Berlin
by closing the corridor. But knowing that America's major deterrent had been
tragically compromised—and suspecting that the Kremlin risked war because
it knew of America's impotence—he could not do otherwise. Hasty demobiliza-
tion and the policies of Defense Secretary Louis Johnson had left United States
Armed Forces a shell, as the world discovered when the North Koreans
marched across the 38th Parallel in 1950. In the light of that knowledge, the
President made do with what he had, and only the healthy respect for America's ability to rearm rapidly prevented the Soviet Union from embarking on a
new military adventure in 1948.

This view of the atomic project—decimated by scientists whose tragic
flaw was an arrogant belief that they knew better than "ordinary men" and
could therefore impose their will on the body politic—contrasts sadly with J.
Robert Oppenheimer's description of Los Alamos when Nazism was the
enemy. "There was a community of aim and effort that's very hard to repro-

---

*Those who argued that there could be no such thing as a "scientific secret" changed
their approach after the Fuchs disclosures. "Why bother hiding what the Soviet Union already
knows?" they argued. In 1953, Medford Evans, a former official of the AEC, answered them in
The Secret War for the A-Bomb: "The case of Klaus Fuchs dramatized the lie that there was
no secret of the atomic bomb. There were many secrets, and there still are. A complex scientific
and industrial project generates new secrets daily."

duce," he told John Dos Passos in 1952. "The work went on in an atmosphere of intellectual cordiality. People took pleasure in fitting their minds into other people's minds. That's what made it a community." It was the purpose of Phase Two, in the Kremlin's assault on America's nuclear defenses, to destroy that community—and in the crucial years, it succeeded.

But Phase One, or espionage, and Phase Two are interrelated. Therefore, it is still asked by those who consider the random political pronouncements of scientists as more valid than those of experts trained in cold war strategy: "Did the Soviets really steal the secrets of nuclear energy and its military application?" The question has been exhaustively answered, but it continues to be repeated because what it really asks is something else again: "Do spies and traitors exist?" Protesting the purity of their craft and the brotherhood of the test-tube, the scientists in effect denied this. In the West, it is almost an article of faith that a scientist is by definition a free soul seeking data unadulterated by political bias. Is Bertrand Russell's *Materia Mathematica* less valid because he would rather be Red than dead?

To those who shun logic's assessment in favor of a curbstone opinion, it is possible to reject the Center's vast researches in Western nuclear strongboxes as an aberrative manifestation of the time's plague. For them no consequence impinges on this "truth." Science, like love, conquers all. Hence the next—and already answered—question: "Wouldn't Soviet science have eventually arrived at the theoretical, experimental, and technological data of portable nuclear fission independently of the Center's efforts?" At this point, science and observable phenomena part company. For a fact, to have meaning, must lie snugly in its context. What Soviet science might have done begs the question. Far more important is what Soviet science did do, given the state of postwar technology and Russia's shattered industrial plant.

Knowing that controlled fission in a small package had been achieved by the United States, Soviet scientists could, once the state allocated money and materials, have duplicated the theoretical labors which preceded the development of American nuclear weapons and, in time, have also repeated the preliminary laboratory experiments of Fermi, Teller, Bacher, and their colleagues. But this work would simply deposit them at the locked door of the Atomic Age. Even the Smyth Report, which according to Senator McMahon "brought other countries from one and a-half to two years closer to their achievement of our own knowledge of atomic secrets," would not have sufficed to unlock that door—for all of the book's wealth of detail.

Without the aid of the Center's spies and its far-ranging apparatus—and at a cost which might have thoroughly disrupted the shaky Soviet economy— the Kremlin's scientists would probably have built the nuclear devices now in their possession. But there is more than a possibility that without the certainty of success—a certainty which could come only from categorical knowledge that the blueprint was theirs and could not fail to be made three-dimensional— Stalin would have delayed while he took stock of the wreckage about him. He was a cautious and dubious man, and it was in his nature to look suspiciously at what had not been, in our contemporary gobbledygook, "concretized." Imagination and the venture spirit entered the Kremlin with Nikita Khrushchev.

In 1951, the Joint Congressional Atomic Energy Committee was ready to concede that had the Soviets started from scratch, it might have extended the "nuclear gap" by up to ten years. Other experts have set the figure higher. It took four years for the massed industrial might and accumulated efficiency of such industrial giants as du Pont, General Electric, Tennessee Eastman, the Bell System, and a host of other corporations—working with the greatest convention in history of scientific minds and mobilizing existent resources of trained labor and raw materials—to produce the primitive bomb which fell on Hiroshima.

Even with the mass of data supplied by Fuchs, Nunn May, Hiskey, and other agents to ease the Soviet way (and the millions of dollars in scarce metals and strategic supplies, specifically designed for atomic development and graciously donated by the Lend-Lease Administration), the U.S.S.R. took four years to explode its first atomic device. It will never be known whether this was, in fact, a bomb—but we have President Truman's word that it was not. We have no one's word that it was. Whether the fissionable materials used in the Soviet test of 1949 were manufactured behind the Iron Curtain or stolen from the United States is also a moot point. Medford Evans has made a convincing case for the possibility of theft, and his argument is bolstered by the admission of Dr. Bacher, head of the Los Alamos bomb physics division, that no inventory of America's uranium stockpile was made until July 1950.

Certainly, the Soviets continued to reach out for the product of the decadent United States right up until the zero hour of their test. Hardly noticed among the piled-up sensations of the Judith Coplon espionage trial was the testimony of FBI Special Agent Robert Lamphere on June 7, 1949. Lamphere was called to identify a report he had written which had found its way into Miss Coplon's hands. It disclosed that the Atomic Energy Commission, presumably standing guard over all materials and equipment pertaining to nuclear energy, had allowed Amtorg, a cover for Soviet espionage, to thwart the clearly stated intent of the McMahon Act—by means as yet unexplained. According to *The New York Times*, Lamphere's report stated that:

. . . no export license had been issued for the shipment of atomic equipment that reached Soviet Russia aboard the steamship Mikhail Kutuzov in August 1947. It said a shipment of similar secret instruments was found aboard the steamship Murmansk in New York harbor Sept. 2, 1948, but American authorities removed the shipment because it had not been authorized. Then a third shipment was found on a dock in Claremont, N. J., Jan. 14, 1949, and this was also confiscated.

To understand the greatness of America's contribution to the Soviet atomic project, it is necessary simply to recapitulate in brief some of the facts, figures, and problems solved by Western inventive and engineering genius under the driving leadership of General Groves. The major point is not that the atomic bombs which ended the Pacific war cost x billions of dollars,* but rather how those bombs were made. The scientists and engineers had no guidelines, no technological precedents. They took raw theory, sometimes imperfect or tentative, and almost by trial and error began to construct the tremendously complex plants at Hanford, Oak Ridge, and Los Alamos. No one really knew what would work and what would not. Everything was tried. Since time was an essential factor, Groves and his associates could not afford to worry about duplication or waste motion if this would advance the work. There was no certain knowledge that one process might be superior to another—the scientists often differed—so different methods were simultaneously employed, at a justifiable cost in money and man-hours.

No other country in the world could have sustained this push.

Yet it took the United States, Britain, and Canada four years.

It took the Soviet Union four years.

Q.E.D.

Before the bomb could be built, means had to be found for the mass separation of fissionable U-235 from U-238 which contained it in very small quantities. To this end, the green light was given to three different methods: the gaseous diffusion process, the electromagnetic process, and the thermal diffusion process. Eventually, the gaseous diffusion process proved to be the most effective. And it was this process, which Klaus Fuch helped develop, to which the Soviets became heir. Had the U.S.S.R. been compelled by sound security at the MED to duplicate this three-pronged assault, the story of the last decade would have been differently written. The bad quality of Soviet workmanship, to which any visitor to the U.S.S.R. can attest, would have led to serious failures. But with the knowledge that they were moving down an already blazed trail, Soviet scientists proceeded with confidence.

The electromagnetic process plant cost close to four hundred million dollars. Electric power, of which the Soviet Union had a drastic shortage, alone counted for ten million dollars. Earmarked by the Treasury for the MED's industrial use were 86,000 tons of silver. General Groves has written of the "fabulous" amounts of special equipment needed—"the enormous oval-shaped electromagnets, the process bins and the units enclosed in them, the control cubicles, motor generator sets, vacuum systems, chemical recovery equipment and thousands of smaller parts." To give a small idea of these requirements, Groves notes that 128 carloads of electrical equipment arrived at Oak Ridge in one two-week period. (It was the severe shortages in the Soviet Union of the materials to manufacture this equipment during the postwar years that led President Truman and others to conclude that the atomic explosions detected after 1949 were caused by laboratory-created devices rather than production-line bombs.) In building the plant and beginning operations, 24,000 skilled men were needed—and the MED was compelled to send many of them to school to learn their new and unprecedented tasks. The electromagnets, 20'x20'x20', had to be rebuilt because of unforeseen bugs. One building in

---

* *Even the AEC cannot estimate with any degree of certainty an approximate cost.*

the complex of structures was put out of action when a bird perched on a high-tension wire and shorted it.

Groves drove ahead at a breakneck pace, refusing to allow the perversity of inanimate objects or a more nagging human obtuseness to deter him. "The task of whipping the bugs out of equipment, overcoming failures, low efficiencies and losses, with untrained personnel, while surrounded by the dirt and din of construction work, was a prodigious one," he has stated—and this was an understatement. Often equipment would be installed at one end of a plant while construction work was still going on at the other—and this in handling equipment where tolerances were microscopic. Yet by mid-July 1944, the electromagnetic plant at Oak Ridge was delivering required amounts of fissionable materials to Los Alamos. Could this "miracle of the MED" have been repeated in the chaos of postwar Russia without precise blueprints?

The gaseous diffusion process, according to General Groves's statement, was "completely novel."* It was one, moreover, which required the ultimate in engineering and technological sophistication. Its purpose was to separate U-235 from U-328. The method, Groves wrote in *Now It Can Be Told:*

was based on the theory that if uranium gas was pumped against a porous barrier, the lighter molecules of the gas, containing U-235, would pass through more rapidly than the heavier U-238 molecules. The heart of the process was, therefore, the barrier, a porous thin metal sheet or membrane with millions of submicroscopic openings per square inch . . . However, there is so little difference in mass between the hexaflourides of U-235 and U-238 that it was impossible to gain much separation in a single diffusion step. This is why there had to be several thousand successive stages.

Despite a crash program to develop the necessary barriers, it was not until the entire K-25 plant at Oak Ridge had been constructed (at a cost of two hundred million dollars and covering close to forty-five acres of space) that the problem was solved. Then came a new problem: how to mass-produce the barriers. Union Carbide found the answer. Special gas pumps to propel the uranium gas were devised by Allis Chalmers. In designing the plant, the engineers suggested that solid nickel be used for the hundreds of miles of piping, in order to prevent corrosion—an excellent idea except that it would have required more than the world's total nickel output. A revolutionary new method of nickel-plating had to be devised—and was. New instruments, new methods of welding (and men sent to school to learn it), means of keeping equipment clinically clean—these were the order of the day. Another 25,000 skilled workers and technicians had to be found for K-25.

It is not necessary to describe the construction of the thermal diffusion plant or the plutonium installation at Hanford to make the point. Every inch

---

* *The Groves characterization is somewhat overenthusiastic. Some years prior to the launching of the great American experiment in 1939, Dr. Gustav Ludwig Hertz of the N. V. Philips Gloeilampenfabrieken company in Holland had discovered the basic theoretical principles of the gaseous diffusion process. Dr. Hertz, a winner of the Nobel Prize in Physics, had also begun the practical application of his theories. Using his work as a starting point, MED scientists perfected it and took the long leap forward to its application on a mass production basis. The Philips Laboratories, which had ties with Dr. Fermi and collaborated in planning his escape from Italy, successfully hid its patents from the invading Nazis.*

of the road which led to the Alamogordo test was dangerous and uncharted. Like the pioneers, the scientists and engineers had to cut through virgin forests, blunder into impassable terrain and retrace their steps, forge new implements in the wilderness. All the massed scientific and technological might of three nations had to be mobilized. A whole new world was created at Hanford, Oak Ridge, and Los Alamos. Yet such is the nature of science that Dr. Walter Zinn, director of the Argonne National Laboratory, would remark that these new discoveries could sometimes be reduced, for transmission to a hostile nation, to "just a number."

The Soviet Union received far more than a number from the traitors, the dupes, and the professional agents. Thousands of words in the precise handwriting of Klaus Fuchs, sketches from David Greenglass, applied theory from the Communist cell at Berkeley, data from Clarence Hiskey, experimental techniques from Pontecorvo, bomb technology from Joan Hinton, invaluable materials from Nunn May, blueprints that funneled through Great Falls—this was the ball game. Every piece of information which reached the Center in Moscow for distribution to teams of Soviet and German scientists saved Stalin and his successors thousands of man-hours in laboratories and over drawing boards. Every piece of information sped the Soviet traveler down the road hacked out by Western scientific genius. Given this help, the wonder is not that the Soviet Union developed a nuclear device of its own in four years but that it took so long.

And what of the super bomb, which Oppenheimer had in 1944 urged as essential to America's postwar arsenal? What of the "community of aim and effort" which abruptly ended with World War II, when the Soviet Union, rather than Nazi Germany, became the potential enemy? This, too, has been discussed. But armchair analysis aside, the flat and incontrovertible fact has been stated by Joseph Alsop and the scientist Ralph Lapp: "Between July 1945 and January 1950, there was no serious or concerted American effort to make the hydrogen bomb." Neither the scientific community (as a whole) nor the Atomic Energy Commission was really willing or ready to push ahead in a manner of comparable to the earlier Los Alamos effort.

This, then, is the unfinished chapter. For the full story will not be closed by history. All the pieces of the jigsaw puzzle will never be fitted into place. But most of the blank places can be filled when those who now refuse to observe the emerging pattern cease to deny the facts of Soviet espionage, to belabor those who expose it, and to hamper those who must detect it. The spies, when discovered, flee the country or go to prison. But the spies do not act alone. They are aided and abetted by an underground conspiracy which gives them cover and supplies them with a constant stream of new recruits. Phase One of the greatest plot in history would not have succeeded had communism been understood and rejected by all honorable men in the 1930s and 1940s. It would not have succeeded had the scientific community not been poisoned in its thinking by *apparatchiks* and friends of *apparatchiks* who convinced it that security, FBI vigilance, and a concern over subversion were an abomination.

Phase Two would have failed had not the intellectual community absorbed, almost with the air it breathed, the notion that the world's most vicious tyranny was an occasionally misguided but essentially idealistic experiment in social engineering. It would have failed had it realized that the uncertain verities of science do not apply to a battlefield where secret armies clash. Scientists construct, but the Communists, in Harold Laski's phrase, are dedicated to "the organization of catastrophe." Science and communism are mutually antagonistic.

Until the Communists have told their last lie, betrayed their last friend, and conquered their last enemy, Phase Two will continue. Voices will continue to plead that the Kremlin be given still another chance to demonstrate its good intentions. Only when Communist perfidy has been forever ground into the dust can this chapter be ended.

WHAT YOU SHOULD KNOW ABOUT INFLATION

**NEW
AND REVISED
EDITION**

by Henry Hazlitt

Preface to the New Edition

THIS BOOK was first published in 1960. For the present edition, the main statistical comparisons and tables have been brought up to date. Where older figures and comparisons illustrate the particular principle or contention involved fully as well as more recent figures would, however, they have been allowed to stand.

HENRY HAZLITT

July, 1964.

Preface

OVER the years in which I have been writing the weekly "Business Tides" column for *Newsweek,* I have received frequent inquiries from readers asking where they could obtain a brief and simple exposition of the causes and cure of inflation. Others have asked for advice concerning what course they could follow personally to prevent further erosion in the purchasing power of their savings. This book is designed to answer these needs.

Most of the material in it has appeared in my *Newsweek* articles during recent years; but all of the statistics and references have been brought up to date, and new material has been added to complete and round out the exposition.

The book has been deliberately kept short. But readers who are not interested in some of the collateral problems, but wish only a brief over-all view, may find what they are looking for either in the first six chapters or in the final chapter, "The ABC of Inflation," which attempts to summarize what is most important in the preceding discussion.

There are some repetitions in the book, but I offer no apology for them. When, as in this subject, basic causes are persistently ignored and basic principles persistently forgotten, it is necessary that they be patiently reiterated until they are at last understood and acted upon.

HENRY HAZLITT

July, 1960.

Contents

1 What Inflation Is

No SUBJECT is so much discussed today—or so little understood—as inflation. The politicians in Washington talk of it as if it were some horrible visitation from without, over which they had no control—like a flood, a foreign invasion, or a plague. It is something they are always promising to "fight"—if Congress or the people will only give them the "weapons" or "a strong law" to do the job.

Yet the plain truth is that our political leaders have brought on inflation by their own money and fiscal policies. They are promising to fight with their right hand the conditions brought on with their left.

Inflation, always and everywhere, is primarily caused by an increase in the supply of money and credit. In fact, inflation *is* the increase in the supply of money and credit. If you turn to the *American College Dictionary,* for example, you will find the first definition of inflation given as follows: "Undue *expansion* or increase of the *currency* of a country, esp. by issuing of paper money not redeemable in specie."

In recent years, however, the term has come to be used in a radically different sense. This is recognized in the second definition given by the *American College Dictionary:* "A substantial *rise of prices* caused by an undue expansion in paper money or bank credit." Now obviously a rise of prices *caused* by an expansion of the money supply is not the same thing as the expansion of the money supply itself. A cause or condition is clearly not identical with one of its consequences. The use of the word "inflation" with these two quite different meanings leads to endless confusion.

The word "inflation" originally applied solely to the quantity of money. It meant that the volume of money was *inflated,* blown up, overextended. It is not mere pedantry to insist that the word should be used only in its original meaning. To use it to mean "a rise in prices" is to deflect attention away from the real cause of inflation and the real cure for it.

Let us see what happens under inflation, and why it happens. When the supply of money is increased, people have more money to offer for goods. If the supply of goods does not increase—or does not increase as much as the supply of money—then the prices of goods will go up. Each individual dollar becomes less valuable because there are more dollars. Therefore more of them will be offered against, say, a pair of shoes or a hundred bushels of wheat than before. A "price" is an *exchange ratio* between a dollar and a unit of goods. When people have more dollars, they value each dollar less. Goods then rise in price, not because goods are scarcer than before, but because dollars are more abundant.

In the old days, governments inflated by clipping and debasing the coinage. Then they found they could inflate cheaper and faster simply by grinding out paper money on a printing press. This is what happened with the French assignats in 1789, and with our own currency during the Revolutionary War. Today the method is a little more indirect. Our government sells its bonds or other IOU's to the banks. In payment, the banks create "deposits" on their books against which the government can draw. A bank in turn may sell its government IOU's to the Federal Reserve Bank, which pays for them either by creating a deposit credit or having more Federal Reserve notes printed and paying them out. This is how money is manufactured.

The greater part of the "money supply" of this country is represented not by hand-to-hand currency but by bank deposits which are drawn against by checks. Hence when most economists measure our money supply they add demand deposits (and now frequently, also, time deposits) to currency outside of banks to get the total. The total of money and credit so measured (including time deposits) was $63.3 billion at the end of December 1939, and $308.8 billion at the end of December, 1963. This increase of 388 per cent in the supply of money is overwhelmingly the reason why wholesale prices rose 138 per cent in the same period.

2 Some Qualifications

IT IS OFTEN ARGUED that to attribute inflation solely to an increase in the volume of money is "oversimplification." This is true. Many qualifications have to be kept in mind.

For example, the "money supply" must be thought of as including not only the supply of hand-to-hand currency, but the supply of bank credit—especially in the United States, where most payments are made by check.

It is also an oversimplification to say that the value of an individual dollar depends simply on the *present* supply of dollars outstanding. It depends also on the *expected future* supply of dollars. If most people fear, for example, that the supply of dollars is going to be even greater a year from now than at present, then the present value of the dollar (as measured by its purchasing power) will be lower than the present quantity of dollars would otherwise warrant.

Again, the value of any monetary unit, such as the dollar, depends not merely on the *quantity* of dollars but on their *quality*. When a country goes off the gold standard, for example, it means in effect that gold, or the right to get gold, has suddenly turned into mere paper. The value of the monetary unit therefore usually falls immediately, even if there has not yet been any increase in the quantity of money. This is because the people have more faith in gold than they have in the promises or judgment of the government's monetary managers. There is hardly a case on record, in fact, in which departure from the gold standard has not soon been followed by a further increase in bank credit and in printing-press money.

In short, the value of money varies for basically the same reasons as the value of any commodity. Just as the value of a bushel of wheat depends not only on the total present supply of wheat but on the expected future supply and on the quality of the wheat, so the value of a dollar depends on a similar variety of considerations. The value of money, like the value of goods, is not determined by merely mechanical or physical relationships, but primarily by psychological factors which may often be complicated.

In dealing with the causes and cure of inflation, it is one thing to keep in mind real complications; it is quite another to be confused or misled by needless or nonexistent complications.

For example, it is frequently said that the value of the dollar depends not merely on the quantity of dollars but on their "velocity of circulation." Increased "velocity of circulation, however, is not a cause of a further fall in the value of the dollar; it is itself one of the consequences of the fear that the value of the dollar is going to fall (or, to put it the other way round, of the belief that the price of goods is going to rise). It is this belief that makes people more eager to exchange dollars for goods. The emphasis by some writers on "velocity of circulation" is just another example of the error of substituting dubious mechanical for real psychological reasons.

Another blind alley: in answer to those who point out that inflation is primarily caused by an increase in money and credit, it is contended that the increase in commodity prices often occurs *before* the increase in the money supply. This is true. This is what happened immediately after the outbreak of war in Korea. Strategic raw materials began to go up in price on the fear that they were going to be scarce. Speculators and manufacturers began to buy them to hold for profit or protective inventories. *But to do this they had to borrow more money from the banks.* The rise in prices was accompanied by an equally marked rise in bank loans and deposits. From May 31, 1950, to May 30, 1951, the loans of the country's banks increased by $12 billion. If these increased loans had not been made, and new money (some $6 billion by the end of January 1951) had not been issued against the loans, the rise in prices could not have been sustained. The price rise was made possible, in short, only by an increased supply of money.

3 Some Popular Fallacies

ONE OF THE most stubborn fallacies about inflation is the assumption that it is caused, not by an increase in the quantity of money, but by a "shortage of goods."

It is true that a *rise in prices* (which, as we have seen, should not be identified with inflation) can be caused *either* by an increase in the quantity of money *or* by a shortage of goods—or partly by both. Wheat, for example, may rise in price either because there is an increase in the supply of money or a failure of the wheat crop. But we seldom find, even in conditions of total war, a *general* rise of prices caused by a *general* shortage of goods. Yet so stubborn is the fallacy that inflation is caused by a "shortage of goods," that even in the Germany of 1923, after prices had soared hundreds of billions of times, high officials and millions of Germans were blaming the whole thing on a general "shortage of goods"—at the very moment when foreigners were coming in and buying German goods with gold or their own currencies at prices lower than those of equivalent goods at home.

The rise of prices in the United States since 1939 is constantly being attributed to a "shortage of goods." Yet official statistics show that our rate of industrial production in 1959 was 177 per cent higher than in 1939, or nearly three times as great. Nor is it any better explanation to say that the rise in prices in wartime is caused by a shortage in *civilian* goods. Even to the extent that civilian goods were really short in time of war, the shortage would not cause any substantial rise in prices if taxes took away as large a percentage of civilian income as rearmament took away of civilian goods.

This brings us to another source of confusion. People frequently talk as if a budget deficit were in itself both a necessary and a sufficient cause of inflation. A budget deficit, however, if fully financed by the sale of government bonds paid for out of real savings, need not cause inflation. And even a budget surplus, on the other hand, is not an assurance against inflation. This was shown in the fiscal year ended June 30, 1951, when there was substantial inflation *in spite of* a budget surplus of $3.5 billion. The same thing happened in spite of budget surpluses in the fiscal years 1956 and 1957. A budget deficit, in short, is inflationary only to the extent that it causes an increase in the money supply. And inflation can occur even with a budget surplus if there is an increase in the money supply notwithstanding.

The same chain of causation applies to all the so-called "inflationary pressures"—particularly the so-called "wage-price spiral." If it were not preceded, accompanied, or quickly followed by an increase in the supply of money, an increase in wages above the "equilibrium level" would not cause inflation; it would merely cause unemployment. And an increase in prices without an increase of cash in people's pockets would merely cause a falling off in sales. Wage and price rises, in brief, are usually a *consequence* of inflation. They can *cause* it only to the extent that they force an increase in the money supply.

4. A Twenty-Year Record

I PRESENT in this chapter a chart comparing the increase in the cost of living, in wholesale commodity prices, and in the amount of bank deposits and currency, for the twenty-year period from the end of 1939 to the end of 1959.

Taking the end of 1939 as the base, and giving it a value of 100, the chart shows that in 1959 the cost of living (consumer prices) had increased 113 per cent over 1939, wholesale prices had increased 136 per cent, and the total supply of bank deposits and currency had increased 270 per cent.

The basic cause of the increase in wholesale and consumer prices was the increase in the supply of money and credit. There was no "shortage of goods."

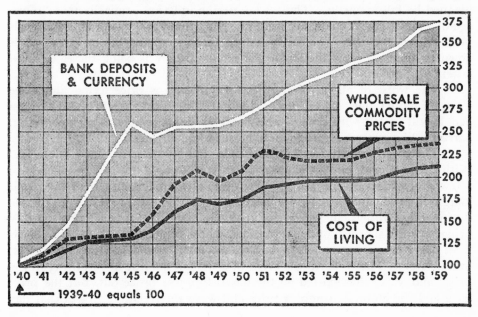

As we noticed in the preceding chapter, our rate of industrial production in the twenty-year period increased 177 per cent. But though the rate of industrial production almost tripled, the supply of money and credit almost quadrupled. If it had not been for the increase in production, the rise in prices would have been much greater than it actually was.

Nor, as we also saw in the last chapter, can the increase in prices be attributed to increased wage demands—to a "cost push." Such a theory reverses cause and effect. "Costs" are prices—prices of raw materials and services—and go up for the same reason as other prices do.

If we were to extend this chart to a total of 24 years — that is, to the end of 1963—it would show that, taking 1939 as a base, the cost of living increased 124 per cent, wholesale prices increased 136 per cent, and the total supply of bank deposits and currency increased 360 per cent in the period.

5 False Remedy: Price Fixing

As LONG as we are plagued by false theories of what causes inflation, we will be plagued by false remedies. Those who ascribe inflation primarily to a "shortage of goods," for example, are fond of saying that "the answer to inflation is production." But this is at best a half-truth. It is impossible to bring prices down by increasing production if the money supply is being increased even faster.

The worst of all false remedies for inflation is price fixing and wage fixing. If more money is put into circulation, while prices are held down, most people will be left with unused cash balances seeking goods. The final result, barring a like increase in production, must be higher prices.

There are broadly two kinds of price fixing—"selective" and "over-all." With selective price fixing the government tries to hold down prices merely of a few strategic war materials or a few necessaries of life. But then the profit margin in producing these things becomes lower than the profit margin in producing other things, including luxuries. So "selective" price fixing quickly brings about a shortage of the very things whose production the government is most eager to encourage. Then bureaucrats turn to the specious idea of an over-all freeze. They talk (in the event of a war) of holding or returning to the prices and wages that existed on the day before war broke out. But the price level and the infinitely complex price and wage interrelationships of that day were the result of the state of supply and demand on that day. And supply and demand seldom remain the same, even for the same commodity, for two days running, even without major changes in the money supply.

It has been moderately estimated that there are some 9,000,000 different prices in the United States. On this basis we begin with more than 40 trillion *interrelationships* of these prices; and a change in one price always has repercussions on a whole network of other prices. The prices and price relationships on the day before the unexpected outbreak of a war, say, are presumably those roughly calculated to encourage a maximum balanced production of *peacetime* goods. They are obviously the wrong prices and price relationships to encourage the maximum production of *war* goods. Moreover, the price pattern of a given day always embodies many misjudgments and "inequities." No single mind, and no bureaucracy, has wisdom and knowledge enough to correct these. Every time a bureaucrat tries to correct one price or wage maladjustment or "inequity" he creates a score of new ones. And there is no precise standard that any two people seem able to agree on for measuring the economic "inequities" of a particular case.

Coercive price fixing would be an insoluble problem, in short, even if those in charge of it were the best-informed economists, statisticians, and businessmen in the country, and even if they acted with the most conscientious impartiality. But they are subjected in fact to tremendous pressure by the organized pressure groups. Those in power soon find that price and wage control is a tremendous weapon with which to curry political favor or to punish opposition. That is why "parity" formulas are applied to farm prices and escalator clauses to wage rates, while industrial prices and dwelling rents are penalized.

Another evil of price control is that, although it is always put into effect in the name of an alleged "emergency," it creates powerful vested interests and habits of mind which prolong it or tend to make it permanent. Outstanding examples of this are rent control and exchange control. Price control is the major step toward a fully regimented or "planned" economy. It causes people to regard it as a matter of course that the government should intervene in every economic transaction.

But finally, and worst of all from the standpoint of inflation, price control diverts attention away from the only real cause of inflation—the increase in the quantity of money and credit. Hence it prolongs and intensifies the very inflation it was ostensibly designed to cure.

6 The Cure for Inflation

THE CURE FOR INFLATION, like most cures, consists chiefly in removal of the cause. The cause of inflation is the increase of money and credit. The cure is to stop increasing money and credit. The cure for inflation, in brief, is to stop inflating. It is as simple as that.

Although simple in principle, this cure often involves complex and disagreeable decisions on detail. Let us begin with the Federal budget. It is next to impossible to avoid inflation with a continuing heavy deficit. That deficit is almost certain to be financed by inflationary means—i.e., by directly or indirectly printing more money. Huge government expenditures are not in themselves inflationary—provided they are made wholly out of tax receipts, or out of borrowing paid for wholly out of real savings. But the difficulties in either of these methods of payment, once expenditures have passed a certain point, are so great that there is almost inevitably a resort to the printing press.

Moreover, although huge expenditures wholly met out of huge taxes are not necessarily *inflationary,* they inevitably reduce and disrupt production, and undermine any free enterprise system. The remedy for huge governmental expenditures is therefore not equally huge taxes, but a halt to reckless spending.

On the monetary side, the Treasury and the Federal Reserve System must stop creating artificially cheap money; i.e., they must stop arbitrarily holding down interest rates. The Federal Reserve must not return to the former policy of buying at par the government's own bonds. When interest rates are held artificially low, they encourage an increase in borrowing. This leads to an increase in the money and credit supply. The process works both ways—for it is necessary to increase the money and credit supply in order to keep interest rates artificially low. That is why a "cheap money" policy and a government-bond-support policy are simply two ways of describing the same thing. When the Federal Reserve Banks bought the government's 2½ per cent bonds, say, at par, they held down the basic long-term interest rate to 2½ per cent. And they paid for these bonds, in effect, by printing more money. This is what is known as "monetizing" the public debt. Inflation goes on as long as this goes on.

The Federal Reserve System, if it is determined to halt inflation and to live up to its responsibilities, will abstain from efforts to hold down interest rates and to monetize the public debt. It should return, in fact, to the tradition that the discount rate of the central bank should normally (and above all in an inflationary period) be a "penalty" rate—i.e., a rate higher than the member banks themselves get on their loans.

Congress should restore the required legal reserve ratio of the Federal

202

Reserve Banks to the previous level of 35 and 40 per cent, instead of the present "emergency" level of 25 per cent put into effect as a war-inflation measure in June 1945. Later I shall discuss other means of preventing an undue increase in the supply of money and credit. But I should like to state here my conviction that the world will never work itself out of the present inflationary era until it returns to the gold standard. The gold standard provided a practically automatic check on internal credit expansion. That is why the bureaucrats abandoned it. In addition to its being a safeguard against inflation, it is the only system that has ever provided the world with the equivalent of an international currency.

The first question to be asked today is not *how* can we stop inflation, but do we really *want* to? For one of the effects of inflation is to bring about a redistribution of wealth and income. In its early stages (until it reaches the point where it grossly distorts and undermines production itself) it benefits some groups at the expense of others. The first groups acquire a vested interest in maintaining inflation. Too many of us continue under the delusion that we can beat the game—that we can increase our own incomes faster than our living costs. So there is a great deal of hypocrisy in the outcry against inflation. Many of us are shouting in effect: "Hold down everybody's price and income except my own."

Governments are the worst offenders in this hypocrisy. At the same time as they profess to be "fighting inflation" they follow a so-called "full employment" policy. As one advocate of inflation once put it in the *London Economist:* "Inflation is nine-tenths of *any* full employment policy."

What he forgot to add is that inflation must always end in a crisis and a slump, and that worse than the slump itself may be the public delusion that the slump has been caused, not by the previous inflation, but by the inherent defects of "capitalism."

Inflation, to sum up, is the increase in the volume of money and bank credit in relation to the volume of goods. It is harmful because it depreciates the value of the monetary unit, raises everybody's cost of living, imposes what is in effect a tax on the poorest (without exemptions) at as high a rate as the tax on the richest, wipes out the value of past savings, discourages future savings, redistributes wealth and income wantonly, encourages and rewards speculation and gambling at the expense of thrift and work, undermines confidence in the justice of a free enterprise system, and corrupts public and private morals.

But it is never "inevitable." We can always stop it overnight, if we have the sincere will to do so.

7 Inflation Has Two Faces

IT MUST BE SAID, in sorrow, that the American public, generally speaking, not only does not understand the real cause and cure for inflation but presents no united front against it. Feelings about inflation are confused and ambivalent. This is because inflation, like Janus, has two opposite faces. Whether we welcome or fear it depends upon the face we happen to look at. Or, putting the matter another way, we are each of us sometimes Dr. Jekyll and sometimes Mr. Hyde in our attitude toward inflation, depending upon how it seems to affect our personal interest at the moment.

All this was once vividly illustrated in a message to a special session of Congress, in 1947, by President Truman. "We already have an alarming degree of inflation," he declared; "and, even more alarming, it is getting worse." Yet he pointed with pride to the results of inflation at one moment and denounced them the next moment. He claimed credit for its popular consequences and blamed his political opponents for its unpopular consequences. Like the rest of us, the President wanted to have his shoes small on the outside and large on the inside.

It should be obvious that high prices, which everybody affects to deplore, and high money incomes, which everyone wants to achieve, are two sides of the same thing. Given the same amount of production, if you double the price level you double the national income. When President Truman boasted in July of 1947 that we had "surpassed previous high records" with a gross national product of $225 billion, he was boasting in large part of the higher dollar totals you get when you multiply volume of output by higher dollar prices.

At one point in his "anti-inflation" message Mr. Truman declared: "In terms of actual purchasing power, the average income of individuals after taxes has risen (since 1929) 39 per cent." But a little later he was asking, inconsistently, how "the cost of living can be brought and held in reasonable relationship to the incomes of the people." Yet if the incomes of the people has in fact already risen so much faster than living costs that the individual could buy nearly 40 per cent more goods than he could before, in what did the alleged inflation "emergency" of 1947 consist?

"Rents are rising," complained Mr. Truman at another point, "at the rate of about 1 per cent a month," and such a rise imposed an "intolerable strain" upon the family budget. But as the average weekly earnings of factory workers had then gone up 112 per cent since 1939, while rents had gone up only 9 per cent, the average worker paid, in fact, a far smaller percentage of his income for rent than he did before the war.

"The harsh effects of price inflation," said Mr. Truman at still another point, "are felt by wage earners, farmers, and businessmen." Clearly this did not refer to the inflation of their own prices, but of somebody else's. It is not the prices they got for their own goods and services, but the prices they had to pay for the goods and services of others, that they regarded as "harsh."

The real evil of inflation is that it redistributes wealth and income in a wanton fashion often unrelated to the contribution of different groups and individuals to production. All those who gain through inflation on net balance necessarily do so at the expense of others who lose through it on net balance. And it is often the biggest gainers by inflation who cry the loudest that they are its chief victims. Inflation is a twisted magnifying lens through which everything is confused, distorted, and out of focus, so that few men are any longer able to see realities in their true proportions.

8 What "Monetary Management" Means

EVER SINCE the end of World War II, the public in nearly ever country has been told that the gold standard is out-of-date, and what is needed in its place is "monetary management" by the experts. It is interesting to notice what some of the consequences of this have been.

When Sir Stafford Cripps, then Chancellor of the Exchequer, announced the devaluation of the British pound on September 18, 1949, Winston Churchill pointed out that Cripps had previously denied any such possibility no fewer than nine times. A United Press dispatch of September 18 listed nine such occasions. A haphazard search on my own part uncovered three more— on September 22 and 28, 1948, and April 30,1949. In corporating these in the UP list, we get the following record of denials:

Jan. 26, 1948—"No alteration in the value of sterling is contemplated by the British Government following the devaluation of the franc."

March 4, 1948—A reported plan to devalue the pound is "complete nonsense."

May 6, 1948—"The government has no intention of embarking on a program to devalue the pound."

Sept. 22, 1948—"There will be no devaluation of the pound sterling."

Sept. 28, 1948—The government has "no idea whatever" of devaluing the pound sterling. Devaluation would "increase the price of our imports and decrease the price of exports, which is exactly the opposite of what we are trying to accomplish."

Oct. 5, 1948—"Devaluation is neither advisable nor even possible in present conditions."

Dec. 31, 1948—"No one need fear devaluation of our currency in any circumstances."

April 30, 1949—"Sterling revaluation is neither necessary nor will it take place."

June 28, 1949—"There has been no pressure on me by America to devalue the pound."

July 6, 1949—"The government has not the slightest intention of devaluing the pound."

July 14, 1949—"No suggestion was made at the conference [with Snyder and Abbott] . . . that sterling be devalued. And that, I hope, is that."

Sept. 6, 1949—"I will stick to the . . . statement I made [July 14] in the House of Commons."

In brief, Sir Stafford emphatically denied at least a dozen times that he would do what he did. The excuse has been made for him that naturally he could not afford to admit any such intention in advance because no one would then have accepted sterling at $4.03. This "defense" amounts to saying that unless the government had lied it could not have successfully deceived the buyers of British goods and the holders of sterling.

For this is what "devaluation" means. It is a confession of bankruptcy. To announce that IOU's hitherto guaranteed to be worth $4.03 are in fact worth only $2.80 is to tell your creditors that their old claims on you are now worth no more than 70 cents on the dollar.

When a private individual announces bankruptcy, he is thought to be disgraced. When a government does so, it acts as if it had brought off a brilliant coup. This is what our own government did in 1933 when it jauntily repudiated its promises to redeem its currency in gold. Here is how the *London Bankers' Magazine* described the 1949 devaluation of the pound by the British Government: "The political technique for dealing with these issues has worn thin. It consists of strenuous, even vicious repudiation beforehand of any notion of revaluation. It insists that the move would be ineffective and utters portentous warning about the dangers. When the unthinkable happens the public is slapped on the back and congratulated on the best piece of luck it has encountered for years."

This is what governments have now been doing for a generation. This is what "monetary management" really means. In practice it is merely a high-sounding euphemism for continuous currency debasement. It consists of constant lying in order to support constant swindling. Instead of automatic currencies based on gold, people are forced to take managed currencies based on guile. Instead of precious metals they hold paper promises whose value falls with every bureaucratic whim. And they are suavely assured that only hopelessly antiquated minds dream of returning to truth and honesty and solvency and gold.

9 Gold Goes With Freedom

THE QUESTION whether or not it is desirable to return to a real gold standard, and when, and under what conditions, and at what rate, and by precisely what steps, has become extremely complicated. But an excellent contribution to the subject was made in a speech of W. Randolph Burgess, then chairman of the executive committee of the National City Bank of New York, before the American Bankers Association in November of 1949. I quote in part:

"Historically one of the best protections of the value of money against the inroads of political spending was the gold standard—the redemption of money in gold on demand. This put a check-rein on the politician. For inflationary spending led to the loss of gold either by exports or by withdrawals by individuals who distrusted government policies. This was a kind of automatic limit on credit expansion. . . .

"Of course the modern economic planners don't like the gold standard just because it does put a limit on their powers. . . . I have great confidence that the world will return to the gold standard in some form because the people in so many countries have learned that they need protection from the excesses of their political leaders. . . .

"There is a group of people today asking for the restoration of the full gold standard immediately in the United States. Today we have a dollar that is convertible into gold for foreign governments and central banks; these people are asking for the same rights to hold gold for our own citizens. In principle I believe these people are right, though I think they are wrong in their timing, and overemphasize the immediate benefits. . . .

"If you try to force the pace by resuming gold payments before the foundations are laid through government policies on the budget, on credit, and on prices, the gold released may simply move out into hoards and become the tool of the speculator.

"Gold payments are only part of the building of sound money, and they are in a sense the capstone of the arch. . . ."

The great virtue of this statement is not only that it recognizes the central importance of returning to a real gold standard but that it takes account also of the formidable difficulties that our past and present errors and sins have placed in the way.

The gold standard is not important as an isolated gadget but only as an integral part of a whole economic system. Just as "managed" paper money goes with a statist and collectivist philosophy, with government "planning," with a coercive economy in which the citizen is always at the mercy of bureaucratic caprice, so the gold standard is an integral part of a free-enterprise economy

207

under which governments respect private property, economize in spending, balance their budgets, keep their promises, and refuse to connive in over-expansion of money or credit. Until our government is prepared to return to this system in its entirety and has given evidence of this intention by its deeds, it is pointless to try to force it to go on a real gold basis. For it would only be off again in a few months. And, as in the past, the gold standard itself, rather than the abuses that destroyed it, would get the popular blame.

In the preceding chapter I recited the shabby record of Sir Stafford Cripps, not as a personal criticism but as an illustration of what typically, if not inevitably, happens under a "managed" paper-money system. For Sir Stafford was not the lowest type of politician likely to be entrusted to manage the people's money; he was the highest type. To millions he had been the very symbol of political integrity and courage. "If gold ruste," as Chaucer asked, "what shall iren do?"

Which reminds us that real gold doesn't rust. As a currency basis it may lack one or two of the perfections that theorists dream of, but it weighs more and can be kept longer than a politician's pledge.

10 In Dispraise of Paper

A SPEECH by Allan Sproul, then president of the Federal Reserve Bank of New York, before the American Bankers Association in 1949, was a startling revelation of official doctrine.

"I perceive," said Sproul, "no moral problem involved in this question of gold convertibility." Let's see whether we cannot perhaps perceive one. Prior to the year 1933 our government pledged itself to pay interest and principal on its bonds in gold of a specified weight and fineness. It also pledged the holder of every currency note that it would redeem that note on demand in gold of a specified weight and fineness. It violated its most solemn pledge. It deprived the rightful owners of their gold. And it made the possession of gold by anybody but the thief illegal.

Now our monetary managers tell us how lucky we are at last to have a system at home of irredeemable paper. Sproul sings paeans in praise of paper. "We use a paper money," he says, "which has the supreme attribute of general acceptability." He neglects to add—at a constantly falling value. The purchasing power of a paper dollar in 1949, according to the Department of Commerce, was only 52 cents, as measured by wholesale prices, in terms of the 1935-39 dollar. It is now only 43 cents by the same measure.

Sproul resorts to flag waving. "The integrity of our money does not depend on domestic gold convertibility. It depends upon the great productive power of the American economy. . . ." Those who recall the disastrous paper money inflations of history must shiver at this argument. Listen to Andrew D. White's report of speeches made in the French Assembly in 1791 to defend the paper assignats: " 'Fear nothing; your currency reposes upon a sound mortgage.' Then followed a glorification of the patriotism of the French people, which, he asserted, would carry the nation through all its difficulties."

The nub of Sproul's defense of our internal irredeemability is that the bureaucrats must be trusted implicitly but that the people cannot be trusted at all. It appears that when you allow the people to redeem their money in gold they always want to do it at the wrong time—i.e., just when it is most embarrassing for the government to meet the demand; in other words, just when the government has connived in an inflationary expansion and issued more paper claims than it is able to honor.

"The principal argument for restoring the circulation of gold coin," Sproul declares, "seems to be distrust of the money managers and of the fiscal policies of government." He couldn't have said it better. What he fails to see is that this mistrust has been richly earned. In addition to the shabby record of Sir Stafford Cripps, we need to remind ourselves that some 30 governments instantly followed the British example. They wiped out overnight, by simple ukase, part of the value of every paper currency unit in the hands of their own people.

Yet in the face of this almost universal record of currency debasement (not to bring up our own sorry record of currency inflation since 1933), Sproul can seriously speak of leaving everything to what he calls "competent and responsible men." Said Sir Stafford Cripps, in explaining his devaluation record: "Even if we had then had some future intention of altering the rate of exchange, which in fact we had not, no responsible minister could possibly have done otherwise than deny such intention." Here, then, is an authoritative definition. A "competent and responsible" monetary manager is one who not only lies to his people regarding the future of their currency but even considers it his *duty* to deceive them.

Sproul's currency theory may be summed up thus: Put your faith in the monetary managers, who have always fooled you in the past.

11 Inflation and High "Costs"

IN AN EARLIER CHAPTER I declared that inflation, always and everywhere, is primarily caused by an increase in the supply of money and credit.

There is nothing peculiar or particularly original about this statement. It corresponds closely, in fact, with "orthodox" doctrine. It is supported overwhelmingly by theory, experience, and statistics.

But this simple explanation meets with considerable resistance. Politicians deny or ignore it, because it places responsibility for inflation squarely on their own policies. Few of the academic economists are helpful. Most of them attribute present inflation to a complicated and disparate assortment of factors and "pressures." Labor leaders vaguely attribute inflation to the "greed" or "exorbitant profits" of manufacturers. And most businessmen have been similarly eager to pass the buck. The retailer throws the blame for higher prices on the exactions of the wholesaler, the wholesaler on the manufacturer, and the manufacturer on the raw-material supplier and on labor costs.

This last view is still widespread. Few manufacturers are students of money and banking; the total supply of currency and bank deposits is something that seems highly abstract to most of them and remote from their immediate experience. As one of them once wrote to me: "The thing that increases prices is costs."

What he did not seem to realize is that a "cost" is simply another name for a price. One of the consequences of the division of labor is that everybody's price is somebody else's cost, and vice versa. The price of pig iron is the steelmaker's cost. The steelmaker's price is the automobile manufacturer's cost. The automobile manufacturer's price is the doctor's or the taxicab-operating company's cost. And so on. Nearly all costs, it is true, ultimately resolve themselves into salaries or wages. But weekly salaries or hourly wages are the "price" that most of us get for our services.

Now inflation, which is an increase in the supply of money, lowers the value of the monetary unit. This is another way of saying that it raises both prices and "costs." And "costs" do not necessarily go up sooner than prices do. Ham may go up before hogs, and hogs before corn. It is a mistake to conclude, with the old Ricardian economists, that prices are determined by costs of production. It would be just as true to say that costs of production are determined by prices. What hog raisers can afford to bid for corn, for example, depends on the price they are getting for hogs.

In the short run, both prices and costs are determined by the relationships of supply and demand—including, of course, the supply of money as well as goods. It is true that in the long run there is a constant tendency for prices to

210

equal marginal costs of production. This is because, though what a thing *has*
cost cannot determine its price, what it *now* costs or is *expected* to cost will
determine how much of it, if any, will be made.

If these relationships were better understood, fewer editorial writers
would attribute inflation to the so-called "wage-price spiral." In itself, a wage
boost (above the "equilibrium" level) does not lead to inflation but to unemployment. The wage boost can, of course (and under present political pressures usually does), lead to more inflation *indirectly* by leading to an increase
in the money supply to make the wage boost payable. But it is the increase in
the money supply that causes the inflation. Not until we clearly recognize this
will we know how to bring inflation to a halt.

12 Is Inflation a Blessing?

THE LATE Sumner H. Slichter, professor of economics at Harvard, was a clear,
vigorous, able, and highly influential writer. He made many instructive con-
tributions, but in the field of money and inflation, to which he mainly devoted
himself in the last years of his life, I cannot believe that his influence was for
the good. I take as one example an article by him in *Harper's Magazine* of
August, 1952, under the title "How Bad Is Inflation?" This article, in fact,
seemed to epitomize all the shopworn fallacies that have been put forward as
apologies for inflation in the last two centuries.

Professor Slichter began by dismissing the conclusions on inflation by the
American Assembly, a group of distinguished economists, as "uncritical and
almost hysterical." The Assembly concluded that "inflation is a continuous and
serious threat to the stability of the American economy and to the security of
the entire Western world." This judgment was not hysterical, but restrained.

It was Slichter who was appallingly uncritical. He not only thought that
it is easy for a government to plan and control "a slow rise in prices"; he
actually believed that an "extreme" inflation "is not easily started." It would
be interesting to learn what his definition was of an "extreme" inflation, and
what his concept was of difficulty. Germany inflated until its mark fell to one-
trillionth of its previous value. Nationalist China inflated until the yuan
reached 425 million to the dollar. In Great Britain prices at the time this
Harper's article appeared were three times as high as they were before World
War II; in the Argentine (with no "war" excuse) prices were already five to

eight times as high; in France, more than 25 times as high; in Italy, more than 50 times as high. None of these countries found it at all difficult to get its inflation going, but most of them were finding it politically almost impossible to stop.

Slichter's argument throughout was based on assumptions that are neither proved nor warranted. One of these is that a rising price level is necessary for prosperity. This is refuted by a wealth of historical experience. The great American boom from 1925 to 1929, for example, occurred in spite of a *falling* price level. And Slichter did not seem to remember that depressions are caused chiefly by the collapse of previous inflations.

Nor did Slichter seem to understand how inflation temporarily works its magic. It does so only as long as prices run ahead of costs (mainly wages). Then the prospective restoration or increase of profit margins may lead to an increase in production and employment. But the jig is up once labor gets on to the game, and wages and other costs begin to rise faster than prices. The apostles of permanent inflation ("continuous slow" inflation) are those who believe that labor can be permanently fooled.

Slichter did not explain in his article by exactly what process a "slow" permanent rise in prices—say 2 or 3 per cent a year—could be produced. He did not understand why no nation has yet succeeded in keeping an inflation, once started, under control. He forgot that you can't afford to tell people in advance that you are *planning* to cheat them. A government can't *plan* a "gradual" increase in prices, because if people *know* that prices will be 3 per cent higher, say, next year, they will bid prices up nearly that much right away. If creditors *know* that the purchasing power of the money they are asked to lend today is going to depreciate 3 per cent within a year, they will add 3 per cent to whatever interest rate they would otherwise demand; so that instead of lending at 5 per cent, say, they will ask 8.

Most astonishing of all, Slichter advocated a continuous inflation to *combat* Communism. One might have referred him to the late Lord Keynes, who wrote a generation ago: "Lenin is said to have declared that the best way to destroy the capitalist system was to debauch the currency. Lenin was certainly right. The process engages all the hidden forces of economic law on the side of destruction, and does it in a manner which not one man in a million is able to diagnose."

Slichter, alas, was not that one man.

13 Why Return to Gold?

FIFTY YEARS ago practically every economist of repute supported the gold standard. Most of the merits of that standard were clearly recognized. It was, for one thing, international. When the currency unit of nearly every major country was defined as a specified weight of gold (previous to 1934 the American dollar, for example, was defined as 23.22 grains of fine gold), every such currency unit bore a fixed relation to every other currency unit of the same kind. It was convertible at that fixed ratio, on demand, to any amount, and by anybody who held it, into any other gold currency unit. The result was in effect an international currency system. Gold was the international medium of exchange.

This international gold standard was the chief safeguard against tampering with the currency on the part of politicians and bureaucrats. It was the chief safeguard against domestic inflation. When credit inflation did occur, it produced a quick sequence of results. Domestic prices rose. This encouraged imports and discouraged exports. The balance of trade (or payments) shifted "against" the inflating country. Gold started to flow out. This caused a contraction of the bank credit based on the gold, and brought the inflation to a halt.

Usually, in fact, the chain of consequences was shorter, quicker, and more direct. As soon as foreign bankers and exchange dealers even suspected the existence of inflation in a given country, the exchange rate for that country's currency fell "below the gold point." Gold started to flow out. Then the central-bank managers of the country that was losing gold raised the discount rate. The effect was not merely to halt credit expansion at home, but to draw funds from abroad from lenders who wanted to take advantage of the higher short-term interest rates. The gold flow was stopped or reversed.

Thus so long as the gold standard was resolutely maintained, a whole set of related benefits ensued. Domestic currency tampering and anything more than a relatively moderate inflation were impossible. As gold convertibility had to be maintained at all times, confidence had to be maintained not only through every year but every day. Unsound monetary and economic policies, or even serious proposals of unsound policies, were immediately reflected in exchange rates and in gold movements. The unsound policies or proposals, therefore, had to be quickly moderated or abandoned.

Because there was a fixed and dependable exchange ratio as well as free convertibility between one currency unit and another, international trade, lending, and investment were undertaken freely and with confidence. And, finally, the international gold standard established (apart from differences

213

caused by shipping costs and tariffs) uniform world prices for transportable commodities—wheat, coffee, sugar, cotton, wool, lead, copper, silver, etc.

It has become fashionable to say that in a major crisis, such as war, the gold standard "breaks down." But except to the extent that the citizens of a country fear invasion, conquest, and physical seizure of their gold by the enemy, this is an untrue description of what happens. It is not that the gold standard "breaks down," but that it is deliberately abandoned or destroyed. What the citizens of a country really fear in such crises is inflation by their own monetary managers, or seizure of their gold by their own bureaucrats. This inflation or seizure is not "inevitable" in wartime; it is the result of policy.

In short, it is precisely the merits of the international gold standard which the world's money managers and bureaucrats decry. They do not want to be prevented from inflating whenever they see fit to inflate. They do not want their domestic economy and prices to be tied into the world economy and world prices. They want to be free to manipulate their own domestic price level. They want to pursue purely nationalistic policies (at the expense or imagined expense of other countries), and their pretenses to "internationalism" are a pious fraud.

14 Gold Means Good Faith

NOTHING has more clearly demonstrated the need for the gold standard than its abandonment. Since that occurred, in Britain in 1931 and in the United States in 1933, the world has been plunged, both in wartime and in peacetime, into a sea of paper money and unending inflation.

Although the inflation everywhere has been blamed on "the war," it has occurred in nations that were never involved in the war (throughout Latin America, for example), and it has continued to rage since the war ended. As an indirect index of this, wholesale prices have increased in this country 73 per cent *since 1945;* in Britain 115 per cent; in France 810 per cent.* And everywhere this result has been due primarily to the increase in the paper money supply.

The monetary managers are fond of telling us that they have substituted

---

* *Before the introduction of the "heavy franc," at the beginning of 1960, at a valuation of 100 old francs.*

"responsible monetary management" for the gold standard. But there is no historic record of responsible paper-money management. Here and there it is possible to point to brief periods of "stabilization" of paper money. But such periods have always been precarious and short-lived. The record taken as a whole is one of hyperinflation, devaluation, and monetary chaos. And as for any integrity in paper-money management, we need merely recall the record of Sir Stafford Cripps, who, in the two-year period preceding his devaluation of the pound sterling on September 18, 1949, publicly denied any such possibility no fewer than a dozen times.

This is what happens under monetary managment without the discipline of the gold standard. The gold standard not only helps to ensure good policy and good faith; its own continuance or resumption requires good policy and good faith. If I may repeat what I pointed out in Chapter 9: The gold standard is not important as an isolated gadget but only as an integral part of the whole economic system. Just as "managed" paper money goes with a statist and collectivist philosophy, with government "planning," with a coercive economy in which the citizen is always at the mercy of bureaucratic caprice, so the gold standard is an integral part of a free-enterprise economy under which governments respect private property, economize in spending, balance their budgets, keep their promises, and above all refuse to connive in inflation—in the overexpansion of money or credit.

So if, as it should, the American government decides to return to a full gold standard, its first step must be to bring inflation to a halt. Without this preliminary or accompanying step any attempted return to gold would be certain to collapse. And once again the gold standard itself, rather than the inflation, would probably be discredited in the popular mind.

How, then, does one halt inflation? The economist Ludwig von Mises has maintained that no increase whatever should be allowed in the quantity of money and bank credit that is not 100 per cent covered by deposits paid in by the public. Although this is basically the result that should be aimed at, it would be politically more acceptable, I think, if this result were brought about by means in accordance with our own best practices and past traditions. I therefore suggest that the halting of inflation should be achieved by these four means:

1—Start balancing the budget.

2—Stop using the banking system either to buy and peg government bonds at fixed rates, or as a dumping ground for huge new issues of short-term government securities. (The peacetime rule, in fact, might be to permit no further net increase in the total volume of government securities held by the country's banking system.)

3—Insist that the Federal Reserve Banks impose discount rates that would penalize borrowing by member banks rather than make it profitable. This means that the rediscount rate should be kept above the rate to prime borrowing customers at the great city banks (or at least above the interest rate borne by the specific securities or "eligible paper" being discounted).

4—Restore the legal reserve requirements of the Federal Reserve Banks (over a reasonable time period) to 40 per cent from their present "war emergency" reserve requirement of only 25 per cent. There is no more effective way in which Congress could register its own opposition to further inflation—if it really is opposed to further inflation.

15 What Price for Gold?

GRANTED that it is desirable, and even imperative, to return to a full gold standard, by what methods should we return? And at precisely what dollar-gold ratio—i.e., at what "price for gold"? These difficult problems have split into dissident groups even the minority of economists who are actively urging a return to a gold standard.

One group, for example, contends that we can and should return to a full gold standard immediately, and at the present price of $35 an ounce. It bases this contention on the arguments that we are already on a limited gold standard at that rate (foreign central banks, at least, are permitted to buy gold from us and sell it to us at $35 an ounce); that we should not suspend this limited gold standard even as a transitional step for a few months; that in the interests of good faith and stability there should be "no further tampering" with this rate; and that at this rate we would in fact have a large enough gold reserve to maintain full convertibility against present outstanding paper currency and deposit liabilities.

These arguments, however, rest on debatable assumptions. Some superficial comparisons, it is true, seem to support them. At the beginning of 1933, the United States money supply (time and demand bank deposits plus currency outside of banks) was $44.9 billion, and the country's gold holdings (measured at the old rate of $20.67 an ounce) were $4.2 billion, or only 9.4 per cent of the country's money supply. At the end of 1963 our outstanding money supply was $265 billion, and our gold holdings against it (measured at the current rate of $35 an ounce) were $15.6 billion, or less than 6 per cent.

Thus our gold reserve ratio is less than in 1933. And we were *thrown off* gold in 1933.

In writing this, I recognize that the run on gold, at the particular moment at which it took place, was at least in part precipitated by the growth of uncontradicted rumors and press reports that the Roosevelt Administration was planning to suspend gold payments. Nevertheless, the relation of credit volume and commodity prices to gold at that time was still such that we had only the choice of going off gold, which we did; or devaluing the dollar and staying on gold (i.e., raising the official gold price); or suffering still further stagnation and deflation. In any case, the run on gold in 1933, before payments were suspended, means that the gold reserves at that time were not in fact sufficient, *in relation to other conditions,* to maintain confidence.

Present gold reserve comparisons with past periods must take account, moreover, of changes in the relative percentage of the world's gold supply held in the United States. In December 1926, the United States held 45 per cent of the world's monetary gold supply (excluding Russia); in December 1933 it held only 33.6 per cent. In 1953 it held 60.8 per cent. At the end of 1959 it held 48.3 per cent. If the United States *alone* returned to gold it could conceivably continue to hold an abnormal percentage for a certain time. But if other countries followed suit within a few years (which would be both desirable and probable), they would presumably attract their previous proportion of the world's gold. More immediately important: in mid-1964, against our gold holdings of $15.5 billion, short-term liabilities to foreigners reported by American banks came to $26.3 billion. And the United States was still showing a heavy deficit in its international balance of payments.

But the real error of those who think we could safely return to a full gold standard at a rate of only $35 an ounce lies in the assumption that there is some fixed "normal" percentage of gold reserves to outstanding money liabilities that is entirely safe under all conditions. This, in fact, is not true of any gold reserve of less than 100 per cent. In periods when public confidence exists in the determination of the monetary managers to maintain the gold standard, as well as in the prudence and wisdom of their policy, gold convertibility may be maintained with a surprisingly low reserve. But when confidence in the wisdom, prudence, and good faith of the monetary managers has been shaken, a gold reserve far above "normal" will be required to maintain convertibility. And today confidence in the wisdom, prudence, and good faith of the world's monetary managers has been all but destroyed. It may take years of wisdom, prudence, and good faith to restore it. Until that is done, any effort to resume a full gold standard at $35 an ounce might lead to a panicky run on gold, while a determined effort to maintain that rate might precipitate a violent deflation.

16 The Dollar-Gold Ratio

THE GOLD-STANDARD SUPPORTERS are divided into three main groups: (1) those who think we could safely return to a full gold standard at $35 an ounce; (2) those who urge return to a full gold standard at some specific higher price for gold (e.g., $70 an ounce) which they claim they already know to be the "correct" one; and (3) those who recommend that we permit a temporary free market in gold for guidance in fixing a final dollar-gold conversion rate.

I have already discussed the main arguments of those who urge a return to gold at $35 an ounce, and what I consider to be some of the shortcomings of those arguments. Those who are urging that we set the price of gold at a higher figure, and who claim to know already what that figure should be, commonly base their conclusion on some comparison of price levels. For example, since 1932, the last full year in which we were on a real gold basis (at $20.67 an ounce), wholesale prices have increased 182 per cent. On the argument that only a corresponding increase in the price of gold could prevent a fall in prices if we went back to a full gold standard, the new price of gold would have to be about $58. Again, the price of gold was set at $35 an ounce on January 31, 1934. For the next seven years wholesale prices averaged only 43 per cent of their present level. If we assume that $35 was the "right" price of gold in those seven years—1934-40—then the price of gold necessary to maintain the present wholesale price level might have to be about $82.

The dubious nature of the assumptions behind such calculations is clear. But the rate at which we return to a full gold standard is not a matter of indifference. Charles Rist, one of the world's leading monetary economists, argued in a powerful article in *Foreign Affairs* in April 1934 that one of the major causes of the world crisis of 1929-33 was the attempt of leading countries, including the United States, to maintain or return to gold convertibility at their prewar rate for gold after having enormously multiplied their paper currency circulation.

The case of Great Britain is clear. It had gone off gold in World War I. The pound had dropped from a gold parity of $4.86 to a low of $3.18 in February 1920, and had returned in late 1924 to approximately 10 per cent below the gold parity. But wholesale prices in Britain in 1924 were still 70 per cent above their prewar level. The British Government decided to resume the gold standard at the old par in 1925. The result was a steady falling wholesale prices over the next seven years from an index number of 171.1 (1913 equals 100) in January 1925 to 99.2 in September 1931, the month in which England abandoned the gold standard. As the British all during this period were unwilling to make corresponding cuts in retail prices and wage rates, the result was falling exports, stagnation, and unemployment. And it was the gold standard itself, not the false rate (or the internal inflexibility of wages), that got the blame.

The British repeated this pattern in essence in the summer of 1947, when they tried to make the pound convertible into the dollar at the wholly unrealistic rate of $4.03. When that experiment broke down within a few weeks, the British once more blamed convertibility itself, and not the false rate, for the breakdown.

It is of the highest importance not only to our own economic future, but to the future of the world, that we do not repeat the British errors by trying to return to gold convertibility at an overvaluation of the paper dollar (which would mean an undervaluation of gold). A temporary free market in gold would give us more guidance regarding what the new conversion rate should be than either an adamant insistence on $35 an ounce or some dubious calculation based largely on hypothetical assumptions.

17 Lesson of the Greenbacks

ONE OF THE worst consequences of inflation is that most of its mischiefs and injustices are irreparable. They cannot be cured by deflation. This merely brings about its own hardships and injustices, which are just as likely to fall upon the previous victims of inflation as upon its beneficiaries. We cannot, for example, cure the inflationary erosion or wiping out of the purchasing power of savings-bank deposits, government bonds and insurance policies by a deflation which may bring about the unemployment or bankruptcy of the very people who suffered from the inflation. So when an inflation has gone beyond a certain amount, the best we can do is to try to stabilize at the new level. When an inflation has gone to the lengths of that in Germany in 1923, for example, or that in France today, a return to the pre-inflation level is inconceivable.

Just what should be attempted, therefore, after an inflation has passed a certain point, becomes an awkward practical problem to which there simply cannot be any completely "just" or satisfactory solution.

We have seen in the preceding chapter what happened in Britain when it tried to go back to the gold standard at the old parity in 1925. But there are many who believe that our own resumption of gold payments on January 1,

1879, at the prewar parity, after the paper money inflation of the Civil War, was an unalloyed success. The fears of a gold drain, they argue, proved quite unfounded. And they attribute the subsequent American recovery of 1879 largely or wholly to gold resumption.

A closer examination of the whole inflationary and deflationary period from 1862 to 1879, however, tells a different story. As soon as the government started issuing irredeemable "greenbacks" in 1862, gold went to a premium on the open market and commodity prices started to soar. In 1864, the greenbacks fell as low as 35 cents on the dollar in terms of gold. From 1860 to 1865, inclusive, though the average of European prices rose only 4 to 6 per cent, average prices in the United States advanced no less than 116 per cent.

But immediately after the end of the war, American prices started downward. At first this was politically popular, because wages had not yet advanced as much as the cost of living. But after 1866 wages had more than caught up with prices. The continued fall in prices soon began to cause bankruptcies and unemployment. Finally came the panic of 1873 which, in the measured judgment of some economists, "left the country's financial and commercial structure almost a ruin." The causes of the panic were complex. But one of them was certainly the continued fall of commodity prices that accompanied the rise of the greenbacks toward parity. By 1873 the greenbacks were only about 15 per cent below parity, and wholesale prices were down to about 30 per cent above prewar levels.

The result of the panic of 1873 was greatly to increase inflationist sentiment. It is true that the Resumption Act was passed on January 7, 1875, but by a repudiated lame-duck Republican Congress that had nothing more to lose. Even more ironic, it was passed, the economist J. Laurence Laughlin tells us, "only under the delusion that it was an inflation measure," because "on its face it looked like a bill to expand the national bank circulation."

Many commentators today think it was foolish and needless for the Resumption Act to put off the actual day of resumption to January 1, 1879—four years after passage of the act. They forget, however, that time, skill, and determination were required to accumulate a gold reserve which would inspire so much confidence that gold would not be demanded when the day of redemption came. And they forget, too, that returning to gold at the original parity involved a still further decline (of about 30 per cent) in American commodity prices to bring them into line with world gold prices. This decline actually took place between 1875 and 1879, and the whole period was one of "economy and liquidation." In 1878, for example, the record of insolvencies far exceeded even that of the panic year 1873.

Many commentators today attribute the recovery that came in the second half of 1879 to the return to gold redemption. The facts do not support them. "With hardly an exception," writes the economic historian, Alexander D. Noyes, "the country's staple industries sank, during the early months of 1879, into complete stagnation." What suddenly turned the tide was an unparalleled coincidence: Europe suffered the worst crop disaster in many years, whereas the American wheat crop reached a new high record. This meant high prices and crop exports unparalleled up to that time.

All this is not to argue that after the greenback inflation of the Civil War this country should have returned to gold at a lower parity for the dollar. It is simply to point out that we had to pay a heavy price for the course we actually took, even though our economy was far more flexible then than now, particularly as regards wage-rates. We must take care that when we return to gold this time we do so at a rate that involves neither inflation nor serious deflation.

18 The Black Market Test

IT MAY PERHAPS be argued that the collapse of the attempted return by Britain in 1925 to the old gold parity, or the hardships involved in the American resumption of specie payments after the Civil War, are irrelevant to the present problem of the United States because (1) we are already on a de facto gold standard at $35 an ounce so far as foreign central banks are concerned, and (2) even in the black market the price of gold bullion has sometimes been no higher than $35 an ounce.

These arguments have some weight, but they are far from conclusive.

As regards the first argument, it may be pointed out that our restricted gold standard at $35 an ounce has been maintained only in a highly abnormal world situation that cannot be counted on to continue. It would, in fact, prove ultimately disastrous if it continued. For even this token American gold standard has been tenable only because the United States has for thirty years been the *least unsafe* place for gold, and because most other leading countries have inflated even more. A slight shift in this situation could easily lead to a heavy drain on American gold. There has been a substantial drain on our gold, in fact, since the high point of $24.5 billion was reached in 1949.

The better the monetary behavior of foreign countries becomes, in other words, the more precarious will become the maintenance even of our closely restricted gold standard at $35 an ounce. And this $35 an ounce standard might give way entirely if private citizens, private businessmen and private bankers, American and foreign, were as free to demand gold for their notes as are foreign central banks. In fact, it is this very fear that is used to justify the present prohibitions against gold convertibility for the private citizen.

As regards the second argument, I do not believe that the "free" (London) market price of gold bullion, or even present black market prices (though gold *coins* are still at a premium), are a reliable guide to anything in particular. There are innumerable possible leaks between the official American buying-and-selling rate of $35 an ounce, and the black market, which make the former dominate and control the latter. (The American Federal Reserve Banks feed out gold to the Bank of England to help it hold down the "free" London market price.)

There are more than a hundred member nations in the International Monetary Fund. How can the American Federal Reserve System, or the I. M. F., supervise and police them all?—not to speak of individual officials in them? Many of these member nations are very poor; it would help their position, or the position of their central banks, if they could buy gold at $35 an ounce from the American Federal Reserve and resell it to private individuals in their own country at a premium. If something like this were going on, even in a few instances, it would mean the existence of "arbitrage" transactions which would prevent more than a moderate spread between the black market and the official market.

I am not framing this as an accusation, but simply as an illustration of one way in which the disappearance of the former black market premium on gold bars could be accounted for. Nicolaas C. Havenga, the South African Minister of Finance, and the eminent French economist, the late Charles Rist, have both implied, in fact, that a sufficient explanation of the disappearance of the black market premium price is that the demand for gold is still subjected almost everywhere to legal restrictions and prohibitions, while the available supply has been becoming more and more abundant. In any case, it would be a very dubious inference to take the absence of a black market premium as any guarantee of the "rightness" or tenability of the present official $35 price.

And certainly any such coincidence of price is not a valid argument for continuing to prohibit a truly free American and world market in gold. The reason free markets in gold do not exist under a full gold standard is not because they are forbidden, but because the universal ability of everyone to buy or sell gold at the official rate leaves no need for a free market. Under a full gold standard, a free market would have nothing to do, no purpose to serve, no function to perform. It is needed only under a paper-money standard, or under a discriminatory and half-fictitious "gold standard" of the sort the United States has had since 1934. It is precisely when a free gold market is needed that most modern governments seek to suppress it. For it reflects and measures the extent of the lack of confidence in the domestic currency; and it exposes the fictitious quality of the "official" rate. And these are among the very reasons why it is needed.

19 How to Return to Gold

IF WE GRANT that there is a great potential danger in trying to return immediately to a full gold standard at $35 an ounce, by what steps are we to return? And how are we to determine the dollar-gold ratio—which would decide the new "price of gold"—at which the return should be made?

It is a sound general principle that unless there are the strongest reasons for change, the dollar-gold ratio, once fixed, ought not to be tampered with. This rule certainly applied to the pre-1933 rate of $20.67 an ounce, because that was a real rate, at which anybody was entitled to demand gold, and got it. But the $35 rate, fixed by Roosevelt-Morgenthau whim in 1934, is not a rate at which real convertibility has existed. It is only foreign central banks, not American citizens, that have been permitted to buy gold from our Federal Reserve Banks at $35 an ounce, and even they have been allowed to do this only under certain conditions. The present $35-an-ounce gold standard is a window-dressing standard, a mere gold-*plated* standard. There is no reason for treating the $35 figure as sacrosanct.

The new dollar-gold ratio that we should aim at is one at which gold convertibility can be permanently maintained, and that will not be in itself either inflationary or deflationary—that will neither, in other words, in itself bring about a rise or a fall in prices.

There are some economists who contend on unconvincing evidence that $35 an ounce *is* that rate. Others profess to have some mathematical formula for arriving at such a rate, and on this basis confidently advocate $70 an ounce or some other figure. Their diverse results in themselves invite suspicion. Values and prices are not set by mathematical calculations, but by supply and demand operating through free markets.

Because of the enormous inflation in the thirty years since we departed from a real gold standard, and the enormous shock to confidence that inflations, devaluations, and repudiations have produced, we must test the state of confidence in a temporary free market for gold—a market that will also give us a guide to a new dollar-gold ratio that we can hold.

The following time schedule of gold resumption is put forward chiefly for purposes of illustration:

1—The Administration will immediately announce its intention to return to a full gold standard by a series of steps dated in advance. The Federal Reserve Banks and the Treasury will temporarily suspend all sales or purchases of gold, merely holding on to what they have. Simultaneously with this step, a free market in gold will be permitted.

2—After watching this market, and meanwhile preventing any further

223

inflation, the government, within a period of not more than a year, will announce the dollar-gold ratio at which convertibility will take place.

3—On and after Convertibility Day, and for the following six months,
any holder of dollars will be entitled to convert them into gold bars, but at a
moderate discount on the paper dollars he turns in. To put the matter the
other way, he would be asked to pay a premium on gold bars above the new
valuation—equivalent, let us say, to ½ of 1 per cent a month. The purpose of
this would be to spread out the first demands for conversion and discourage
excessive pressure on reserves at the beginning. The same purpose could be
achieved also by a wide but gradually narrowing spread between the official
buying and selling prices of gold bars. Of course, the free market in gold would
continue during this period, and if gold could be obtained in this free market
for less than the official premium rates, it would not be demanded from the
government's reserves.

4—Six months after Convertibility Day, the country will return to a full
gold-bullion standard. Conversion of dollars into gold bars, or vice versa, will
be open to all holders without such discounts or premiums and without discrimination.

5—One year later still, on January 1, 19—, the country will return to a
full gold-coin standard, by minting gold coins and permitting free conversion.

A full gold-coin standard is desirable because a gold-bullion standard is
merely a rich man's standard. A relatively poor man should be just as able to
protect himself against inflation, to the extent of his dollar holdings, as a rich
man. The reason for returning to a full gold-coin standard in several stages is
to prevent too sudden a drain on gold reserves before confidence has been re-
established. We achieved this end after the Civil War by delaying actual
resumption for four years after passage of the Resumption Act. A program like
the foregoing would provide a faster schedule.

20 Some Errors of Inflationists

IN EVERY YEAR of the past quarter-century of inflation articulate individuals or
groups have insisted that we were in fact in a depression or a deflation, or on
the verge of one, or at the very least that our "economic growth" was not as
fast as the adoption of their particular inflationist schemes could make it.

A typical example is a "report" of the National Planning Association (a
group of statist planners who frequently manage to get their pronouncements

on the front pages of leading newspapers) in mid-1954. This report declared
that the country must step up its production of goods and services by "at least
$25 billion" over the next twelve months to keep the economy healthy. Why,
as long as they were simply talking about what was desirable, they stopped at a
mere $25 billion, I do not know.

The pronouncement, however, was so typical of current inflationist fallacies that it is worth a little analysis. The NPA firmly believed that what
primarily caused the "recession" from mid-1953 to mid-1954 was a drop in
defense spending, and therefore what could pull us out was a boost in defense
spending. Such a judgment, however, finds no support in either economic
theory or experience. In the fiscal year 1944 the Federal government spent $95
billion; in the fiscal year 1947 it spent $39 billion. Here was a drop in the
annual Federal spending rate in this three-year period of $56 billion. Yet, far
from there being a recession in this three-year period, there was a substantial
increase in employment, wages, and prices.

I may add that there was a very sharp increase in industrial production
and employment between mid-1954 and mid-1955—though in that fiscal year
total Federal spending, instead of being increased (as recommended by NPA),
was further reduced by more than $3 billion.

This fact did not escape the notice of observers at the time. In a column
in *The New York Times* of September 8, 1955, Arthur Krock drew attention to
official statistics which showed that private spending in the United States had
been steadily replacing, and in fact exceeding, the billions cut from the budget
by the Eisenhower Administration over a two-year period. The following table
shows the comparison:

	1953	1954	1955
Gross national product	$369.3	$357.6	$384.8
Federal purchases of goods and services	61.0	48.6	45.2
All other expenditures	308.3	309.0	339.6

What is really compared in the foregoing table is the second quarters of
1953, 1954, and 1955. The figures are expressed, however, in billions of dollars
at seasonally adjusted annual rates. They show that while government spending was running at an annual rate of $3.4 billion less in the 1955 quarter than
in 1954, and $15.8 billion less than in the corresponding 1953 quarter, nongov-
ernmental activity was running in the second quarter of 1955 at a rate $30.6
billion higher than in the same period of 1954 and $31.3 billion higher than in
1953.

There is really nothing astonishing in such figures except to those who
tenaciously hold to a quite erroneous preconceived view. Yet again and again
in recent years we find it stated or assumed by business "forecasters" that the
future of business activity depends primarily on the government's defense-
spending program. If that rises, we are told, business activity and prices will
rise; but if it declines, there is no telling how much business will deteriorate.

This assumption would lead to the absurd conclusion that the more
resources we are forced to devote to making planes, carriers, submarines, nuclear bombs, and guided missiles, the richer we become. Indeed, many amateur

economists have not shrunk from this conclusion, and tell us with a knowing air how lucky we are to have a constant threat of Communist aggression—for if this threat were suddenly and miraculously to disappear, what would become of prosperity, "economic growth," and full employment? Every new Communist act of aggression, on this theory, does us an economic favor.

The fallacy consists in looking only at the government's defense payments and forgetting that the money for these comes ultimately from taxes. If defense payments suddenly dropped from $46 billion to $16 billion, taxes could also be cut by $30 billion. Then the taxpayers would have $30 billion more to spend than they had before, to make up for the $30 billion drop in government spending. There is no reason to suppose that the over-all volumes of output or activity would decline.

The whole theory that defense spending is necessary for prosperity, as I pointed out previously, got a crushing refutation at the end of World War II. Immediately after Japan surrendered in August 1945, there was a sweeping cancellation of war contracts. Government economists predicted that unemployment would reach 8 million by the following spring. Nothing of the sort happened.

In sum, there is no reason whatever to suppose even in theory that wages and employment should depend primarily on the volume of defense spending, or government spending for any other purpose. If the government spends $10 billion less on defense *and reduces taxes by the same amount,* then the taxpayers have as much more to spend as the government has less. The total volume of spending is unchanged. It would be a monstrous as well as a foolish doctrine that we must increase the volume of wasteful expenditure on armament, not for the sake of defense, but for the sake of "creating prosperity."

So far as the inflationary effect is concerned, what counts is not the amount of defense spending or total government spending, but the size of the *deficit* and, even more directly, the amount of new money supply. Even the NPA statement at one point seemed willing to settle for a deficit achieved through civilian public works or even a cut in taxes. It even recognized at one point that private plant and equipment modernization might help to create employment. But it paid scant attention to the fact that only the continuing prospect of profits, and only the ability of the profit-earners to retain enough of these from the income-tax collector, can make possible that continued investment of new capital which is essential to put better and better tools in the hands of the workers and constantly to increase their real wages.

What was typical of the NPA statement was that its proposed statist remedies for unemployment utterly ignored the effects of wage rates. No matter how much we are inflating, no matter how high the absolute level of national income or "purchasing power," we can always bring about unemployment by pushing wage rates too high in relation to prices and productivity.

This points to the error in the Keynesian propensity to look only at such huge over-all money aggregates as "national income" and "purchasing power." Maintenance of employment depends on expectation of profits in each industry. This expectation depends on the *relationship* of costs to prices, which means the relationship of prices to each other and wage rates to prices.

21 "Selective" Credit Control

IN JANUARY 1956, the President's annual Economic Report suggested the restoration of the government's power to regulate the terms of consumer installment credit. The then Secretary of the Treasury, George M. Humphrey, showed political courage as well as excellent sense when he refused to endorse the suggestion.

The Secretary also gave the right reasons why such stand-by powers would be inadvisable. They would put too much discretion in the hands of whoever was to administer them: "You take a great responsibility on yourself when you tell 160 million people what they can afford to buy." Chairman Martin of the Federal Reserve Board also pointed out that "selective controls of this nature are at best supplements and not substitutes for the general over-all credit and monetary instruments."

The most eminent advocate at that time of the imposition of stand-by controls on installment credit was Allan Sproul, then president of the Federal Reserve Bank of New York. In a speech on December 29, 1955, he declared: "I do believe that there is a temptation to abuse consumer credit in boom times, that it can thus become a serious source of instability in our economy, and that we would not jeopardize our general freedom from direct controls by giving the Federal Reserve System permanent authority to regulate consumer credit."

But Sproul's argument indirectly admitted that he wished this power in order to avoid a sufficiently firm control over *general* interest rates and the *total volume* of credit: "If there has grown up a form of credit extension which . . . is introducing a dangerous element of instability in our economy, and if it is difficult to reach this credit area by general credit measures without adversely affecting any of the less avid users of credit, is there not a case for a selective credit control?"

What Sproul was saying in effect is that a handful of government monetary managers should be given the power to discriminate among borrowers; to say which are "legitimate" and which not; to say just who should have credit and on what terms. No government body should have such power. It becomes an implement for political favoritism.

President Eisenhower declared in a press conference on Febrary 8, 1956, that if the government were granted stand-by powers over consumer credit they would not be abused. But the record shows that the "selective" powers over credit which already existed had already been abused. Our Federal Reserve authorities complained of "inflationary pressures." Yet at the very time they were suggesting "selective" credit powers they were keeping the official discount rate down to only 2½ per cent. (Within a year and a half they were forced to raise it three times, to 3½ per cent. In that same year—1957—

227

the Bank of England, to stop British inflation, had to raise its discount rate to 7 per cent.) Early in 1956, also, our Federal Reserve authorities had allowed and encouraged a $12 billion increase in the total volume of money and bank credit since the beginning of 1954.

Government authorities today (1960) discriminate *against* purchase of corporate securities by compelling a minimum down payment of 90 per cent. They have discriminated *in favor of* purchase of houses by pledging the tax-payers' money to allow such purchases for a down payment of only 7 per cent or perhaps only 2 per cent. A Congressional subcommittee, in 1956, raised a storm about even these tiny down payments. It asked for a return to the conditions under which a veteran could buy a $10,000 house without putting up even the $200 cash. The belief that government agencies are above the political pressures which lead to such discriminations among borrowers has been disproved everywhere.

In sum, if general interest rates are allowed to rise to their appropriate level, and if there is a sufficiently firm rein on the total quantity of credit, "selective" credit controls are unnecessary. But if there is not a sufficiently firm rein on the total quantity of money and credit, "selective" controls are largely futile. If a man has $2,500 cash, for example, but can buy a $10,000 house for only $500 down, then he can also buy a $2,000 car with his "own" cash, whereas if he had to pay down his $2,500 for the house he couldn't buy a car even on pretty loose credit terms. This elementary principle of the shifting or substitution of credit seems to have been overlooked by the champions of "selective" credit controls.

22 Must We Ration Credit?

THE PROPOSAL to restore "selective" or "qualitative" credit controls is revived so often by persons who are regarded as monetary authorities, and is so frequently referred to by them as "one of the necessary weapons to combat inflation," that some further analysis is desirable.

The proposal has the sanction of precedent, for whatever that is worth. Our government used "selective" credit controls at various times between 1941 and 1952. They have been widely imposed in Europe. But the results hardly warrant emulation. Selective credit control is merely one more step along the road toward a command economy. It leads logically back to investment control and to price control.

Selective credit controls are, in fact, government control of short-term investments. The pressure for them comes from special groups of borrowers who want to be favored at the expense of the rest. It comes from monetary managers who lack the courage to refuse such demands; who lack the courage to let general interest rates rise to the point where they will halt inflation. When the price of any commodity is held down by government control, the demand soon exceeds the supply, and the commodity is then rationed. Selective credit controls are merely government rationing of credit.

To ration credit is, of course, to discriminate among would-be borrowers. The decision is thrown into politics and determined by political pressures. This has already happened. Buying a house, even if you can't afford it, is considered so laudable that the taxpayers have been forced to guarantee 95 per cent of the purchase price for you. Buying a refrigerator to put into the house, or a car to get to work from it, is considered much less laudable, so that the terms on which the seller was allowed to extend credit even at his own risk were tightened or "liberalized" by bureaucratic decree. Buying shares in Wall Street (i.e., investing in large-scale industries that increase production and create jobs) is considered so antisocial that the government forbids the seller or the lender to accept less than a down payment of 90 per cent of the full price.

Government "selective" credit decisions are made, in short, on the basis of popular pressures and prejudices. Even if the record were better than this, what are we to say of a system which gives a group of government bureaucrats power to encourage borrowing for one purpose and to discourage it for another; to decide that there should be a boom in industry X but that industry Y should be choked to death? The only reason why "selective" credit controls, here and abroad, have not proved intolerably disruptive is that (for reasons explained in the preceding chapter) such controls seldom achieve their aims.

I shall deal here with only one or two of the many arguments that have recently been put forward in favor of selective credit schemes. It is contended, for example, that "over-all quantitative credit control" is "a pretty crude weapon." The truth is that it would be hard to conceive of a more precise and truly selective instrument for allocating the supply of real savings among credit-worthy borrowers than over-all market interest rates that are allowed to reflect the real conditions of supply and demand. It is nonsense to say that a general rise in interest rates hits only "the little fellow" and favors "the big corporations." One might just as well argue that a general rise in wage rates hits only the little project and helps the big project. Any general rise in costs merely shuts off the marginal projects, regardless of size, that do not seem likely to earn the higher costs.

This is the meaning and function of free markets, in the price of loanable funds as in the price of raw materials and in wages.

23 Money and Goods

AMONG the popular ideas which make the inflation of our era so hard to combat is the belief that the supply of money ought to be constantly increased "in order to keep pace with the increase in the supply of goods."

This idea, on analysis, turns out to be extremely hazy. How does one equate the supply of money with the supply of goods? How can we measure, for instance, the increase in the total supply of goods and services? By tonnages? Do we add a ton of gold watches to a ton of sand?

We can measure the total supply of goods and services, it is commonly assumed, by values, But all values are expressed in terms of money. If we assume that in any period the supply of goods and services remains unchanged, while the supply of money doubles, then the money value of these goods and services may approximately double. But if we find that the total monetary value of goods and services has doubled during a given period, how can we tell (except by a priori assumption) how much of this is due to an increase of production, and how much to an increase in the money supply? And as the money price (i.e., the "value") of each good is constantly changing in relation to all the rest, how can we measure with exactness the increase of "physical production" in the aggregate?

Yet there are economists who not only think that they can answer such questions, but that they can answer them with great precision. The late Dr. Sumner H. Slichter of Harvard recommended a 2½ per cent annual increase in the money supply in order to counterbalance the price-depressing effect of an assumed annual 2½ per cent increase in "productivity." Dean Arthur Upgren of the Tuck School of Business Administration at Dartmouth wrote in 1955: "Businessmen, bankers, and economists estimate that the nation requires a money supply growth of 4 or 5 per cent a year." He arrived at this remarkable figure by adding "a 1½ per cent a year population growth, a 2½ per cent yearly gain in productivity, and a gain of 1 per cent in the money supply needed to service the more specialized industries." This looked like counting the same thing two or three times over. In any case, it is questionable whether such estimates and calculations, which vary so widely, have any scientific validity.

Yet a lot of people have come to believe sincerely that unless the supply of money can be increased "proportionately" to the supply of goods and services there will not only be a decline in prices, but that this will bring on "deflation" and depression. This idea will not stand analysis.

If the quantity and quality of money remained fixed, and per capita industrial and agricultural productivity showed a constant tendency to rise, there would, it is true, be a tendency for money prices to fall. But it does not

230

at all follow that this would bring about more net unemployment or a depression, for money prices would be falling because real (and money) costs of production were falling. Profit margins would not necessarily be threatened. Total demand would still be sufficient to buy total output at lower prices.

The incentive and guide to production is *relative* profit margins. Relative profit margins depend, not on the absolute level of prices, but on the relationship of different prices to each other and of costs of production (factor prices) to prices of finished goods. An outstanding example of prosperity with falling prices occurred between 1925 and 1929, when full industrial activity was maintained with an average drop in wholesale prices of more than 2 per cent a year.

The idea that the supply of money must be constantly increased to keep pace with an increased supply of goods and services has led to absence of concern in the face of a constant increase in the money supply in the last twelve years. From the end of 1947 to the end of 1959 the supply of bank deposits and currency increased $79 billion, or 46 per cent. And in the same period average wholesale prices increased nearly 24 per cent, in spite of an increase in the industrial production index of 60 per cent.

24 The Great Swindle

I PRESENT in this chapter a table compiled by the First National City Bank of New York (published in its monthly economic letter of July, 1964) showing the shrinkage in purchasing power of the currencies of 42 countries over the ten-year period 1953-1963. The shrinkage is calculated inversely from the increases in cost-of-living or consumer price index as reported by governments.

It is important to keep this appalling worldwide picture constantly before our minds. It reminds us that inflation is nothing but a great swindle, and that this swindle is practiced in varying degrees, sometimes ignorantly and sometimes cynically, by nearly every government in the world. This swindle erodes the purchasing power of everybody's income and the purchasing power of everybody's savings. It is a concealed tax, and the most vicious of all taxes. It taxes the incomes and savings of the poor by the same percentage as the incomes and savings of the rich. It falls with greatest force precisely on the thrifty, on the aged, on those who cannot protect themselves by speculation or

	Indexes of Value of Money			Annual Rates of Depreciation (Compounded)		
	1953	1958	1963	'53-'58	'58-'63	'53-'63
Guatemala	100	95	95	1.0%	...%	0.5%
Ceylon	100	97	93	0.6	0.8	0.7
El Salvador	100	90	92	2.1	—0.4	0.9
Venezuela	100	97	92	0.6	1.2	0.9
United States	100	93	88	1.5	1.2	1.3
Belgium	100	92	87	1.7	1.2	1.4
Canada	100	92	87	1.7	1.2	1.4
Portugal	100	95	86	1.0	1.9	1.5
Pakistan	100	91	86	1.9	1.2	1.5
Ecuador	100	98	85	0.4	2.7	1.6
Switzerland	100	93	84	1.5	2.1	1.8
Germany	100	92	82	1.7	2.2	2.0
South Africa	100	87	82	2.7	1.2	2.0
Philippines	100	95	81	1.0	3.1	2.1
Australia	100	88	81	2.5	1.7	2.2
India	100	91	78	1.9	2.9	2.4
Austria	100	90	78	2.1	2.7	2.4
Ireland	100	86	78	3.0	1.9	2.4
Netherlands	100	85	77	3.2	1.9	2.5
United Kingdom	100	86	77	3.0	2.2	2.6
New Zealand	100	85	77	3.2	2.1	2.6
Italy	100	88	75	2.5	3.1	2.8
Norway	100	85	75	3.2	2.6	2.9
Sweden	100	84	73	3.4	2.7	3.1
Japan	100	92	72	1.7	4.7	3.2
Denmark	100	86	71	3.0	3.8	3.4
Greece	100	76	70	5.3	1.7	3.6
Finland	100	78	67	4.9	3.1	3.9
France	100	83	66	3.7	4.4	4.0
Mexico	100	66	59	8.0	2.1	5.0
Iran	100	72	56	6.4	4.9	5.6
Spain	100	71	55	6.6	4.9	5.7
Israel	100	72	55	6.4	5.1	5.7
Peru	100	74	50	5.8	7.6	6.7
China (Taiwan)	100	68	46	7.4	7.6	7.5
Colombia	100	66	40	8.0	9.4	8.7
Turkey	100	58	38	10.3	8.2	9.3
Uruguay	100	57	18	10.6	20.6	15.8
Argentina	100	46	9	14.4	27.3	21.1
Brazil	100	42	6	15.9	31.9	24.4
Chile	100	13	5	33.5	18.2	26.3
Bolivia	100	4	3	47.5	7.9	30.5

Note: Depreciation computed from unrounded data and measured by reciprocals of official cost-of-living or consumer price indexes.

by demanding and getting higher money incomes to compensate for the depreciation of the monetary unit.

Why does this swindle go on? It goes on because governments wish to spend, partly for armaments and in most cases preponderantly for subsidies and handouts to various pressure groups, but lack the courage to tax as much as they spend. It goes on, in other words, because governments wish to buy the votes of some of us while concealing from the rest of us that those votes are being bought with our own money. It goes on because politicians (partly through the second- or third-hand influence of the theories of the late Lord Keynes) think that this is the way, and the only way, to maintain "full employ ment," the present-day fetish of the self-styled progressives. It goes on because the international gold standard has been abandoned, because the world's currencies are essentially paper currencies, adrift without an anchor, blown about by every political wind, and at the mercy of every bureaucratic caprice. And the very governments that are inflating profess solemnly to be "fighting" inflation. Through cheap-money policies, or the printing press, or both, they increase the supply of money and credit and affect to deplore the inevitable result.

25 Easy Money = Inflation

In the early summer of 1957, Secretary of the Treasury Humphrey, testifying before a Congressional committee, gave a lucid lesson on the causes of inflation and an impressive answer to the advocates of cheap money.

The inflationists were contending at the time that the Administration had been reducing the volume of credit, and causing "inflation" and higher prices by raising interest rates.

As to the volume of credit, the Secretary had no difficulty in showing that it had actually "expanded substantially in the last four years." "There is more credit outstanding today than ever before." In fact, as the Secretary pointed out, if one counted mortage, consumer, corporate, and other forms of nonbank credit, the total had *increased* over 1952 by the staggering sum of $146.5 billion ($135.8 billion from "savings" and $10.7 billion "from bank credit expansion, or increased money supply"). The "tight money" complaint, as the Secretary showed, merely reduced itself to this—that the government had put some limits on monetary expansion.

Humphrey have the best official answer yet made to the frequent contention that an increase in interest rates raises prices because interest rates are a cost of production. On the basis of the gross sales of all manufacturers, he pointed out that of the cost of an article selling for $100, about 33 cents represented (explicit) interest. During the ten-year period since 1946, "prices of goods that consumers buy rose 27½ per cent, or $27.50 on a $100 item [due to labor and other costs], compared with the 20-cent increase due to higher interest."

His comparisons in home-building were no less impressive. A house that cost $10,000 to build in 1946 would cost $19,000 in 1957. If the interest rate on an FHA mortgage increased from 4 per cent in 1946 to 5 per cent in 1957, then the monthly mortgage payment (on the basis of 15 per cent down and a twenty-year amortization) would increase from $51.51 on the 1946 house to $106.58 on the 1957 house. Only $8.71 of this increase would be due to the higher interest cost; the other $46.36 would be due to the other costs raised by inflation.

But to hold down interest rates artificially is to encourage borrowing, and thereby to increase the money-and-credit supply. It is this increased money supply that raises prices (and costs) and constitutes the heart of inflation.

The real criticism to be made of the Federal Reserve in 1957 (and still) was not that it had kept credit too scarce and interest rates too high, but that it had yielded to inflationist pressure. It had made credit too plentiful and kept interest rates too low. It is precisely because interest rates were still too low in 1957 that the demand for credit still exceeded the supply. A discount rate of only 3 per cent (when 91-day Treasury bills yielded 3.404 per cent) was infla-tionary. The Fed might still be well-advised to follow the example of Canada and keep the discount rate always at least ¼ of 1 per cent above the bill rate. Such a course would not be sufficient to halt inflation, but it would be an indispensable condition. It would also have an important political advantage, for it would show that the Fed was merely following the market, and not arbitrarily raising interest rates.

26 Cost-Push Inflation?

SOMETIME IN EARLY 1957 the theory broke out in several places that we are now confronted with a "new" kind of inflation. As described at the time by Robert C. Tyson, chairman of the finance committee of the U.S. Steel Corpora-tion: "Our new kind of inflation appears to be cost inflation pushing prices up, rather than price inflation pulling up costs through competitive bidding for materials and manpower. We might think of it as a new cost-push type as distinguished from the conventional demand-pull type of inflation."

Going even further, a study by the National Industrial Conference Board declared: "Although money supply has been checkreined by Federal Reserve policy, business is still on the uptrend . . . Since prices have continued to rise, the clear lesson of 1956 is that money and its rate of use are not the sole determinants of price . . . Today, the critical question is: How adequate are monetary controls for coping with price pressures that arise from nonmonetary forces?"

Now such theories seem to me to mix truth with error. The Conference Board attempted to prove its case statistically. But as the U.S. Bureau of Labor Statistics pointed out on May 13, 1957, in a study of productivity, costs, and prices: "Where the figures indicate that prices and unit labor costs showed about the same increase, or that one or the other showed a greater increase during a particular year or period of years, this should be taken as a description of what happened and not necessarily as an explanation of what 'caused' the change. An increase in unit labor costs may lead to an increase in price, but conversely an increase in price can result in strong pressure for increases in wages . . . The answer to the question of whether the wage increases cause the price increase or vice versa cannot be determined from the figures alone."

The BLS report went on to declare: "Average hourly compensation [of workers] in current dollars increased much more than productivity during the postwar period [1947-56]. The former increased by about 61 per cent, the latter by 26 per cent, leading to an increase in employe compensation per dollar of real product of about 28 per cent."

This sounded ominous, but only because it was confusingly stated. Four paragraphs further down, the report declared: "The increase of about 28 per cent in employe compensation per dollar of real product was almost identical with the increase in price between 1947 and 1956." In other words, the word "productivity" in the first quotation must have meant productivity in *real* terms, not in *dollar-value* terms. Multiply the 26 per cent increase in "productivity" by the 28 per cent increase in price level, and we get the same 61 per cent increase as in hourly labor income.

The Conference Board tried to prove that the increase in the money supply could not be the cause of the price rise in the preceding two years, because the money supply had not gone up in this period. But this overlooked longer comparisons, and mistakenly assumed that changes in money supply must reflect themselves exactly proportionately in prices with neither time lag nor anticipations. Expansion of the money (and credit) supply is both the necessary and the sufficient cause of inflation. Without such expansion, an excessive increase in wage rates would lead merely to unemployment.

I regret having to criticize what were otherwise two excellent and informative statistical reports. And insofar as they describe *political pressures*, the "cost-push" theorists are right. Our politicians put irresponsible and irresistible power in the hands of union leaders, and then plead with them not to use it. They remove the natural economic penalties on recklessness, and then beg for restraint. If the Federal Reserve seriously tried to hold the line on money and credit, while the union leaders kept pushing up wage rates, it is the Federal Reserve, not the unions, that the politicians would blame for the consequent unemployment and recession.

As long as the political climate remains this unhealthy, a halt to inflation is impossible. But with understanding and courage, inflation could be halted overnight.

27 Contradictory Goals

IN JANUARY OF 1957, the Guaranty Trust Company of New York, in its monthly Survey, discussed a problem that had already engaged the attention of leading European economists and was becoming urgent here. This involved the clash in the economic objectives of governments which assume "responsibility" for the achievement of certain "goals."

Since the end of World War II governments everywhere have been pursuing three mutually contradictory aims. These are (1) constantly rising wages, (2) stable prices, and (3) full employment.

It should be obvious that these goals cannot all be achieved at the same time. Even in the short run, any two of these goals can be achieved only at the sacrifice of the third. Thus if we try to have constantly rising wages (regardless of productivity), we can have full employment only if we are willing to allow prices to go up to maintain profit margins, and only if we increase monetary purchasing power enough to enable consumers to pay the higher prices. But this is another way of saying that we must give up the goal of stable prices and encourage a continuous inflation.

If we try to have both constantly rising wages and stable prices, we soon arrive at a point where we can have them only at the cost of unemployment, and eventually of mass unemployment. If we want both stable prices and full employment, then the constant annual "rounds" of wage increases, as a result of strikes or strike threats (and regardless of what has happened to productivity), will have to be abandoned.

However, given the pressures from union leaders and other groups, and given the prevailing obsession that government "must assume responsibility" for everybody's economic welfare, the de facto choice of Western governments in the last decade or two has been constantly rising wages and full employment financed by a so-called "creeping" inflation.

There are not lacking, indeed, rationalizations of this very course, among the most candid of which is that of the late Sumner H. Slichter of Harvard. Professor Slichter seemed to think that a "creeping" inflation of some 2 per cent a year would be both necessary and acceptable. It had already been pointed out by Dr. Winfield Riefler of the Federal Reserve that, even if we assume we could control an inflation to a rate of 2 per cent a year, "it would be equal to an erosion of the purchasing power of the dollar by about one-half in each generation." The legalized robbery that such a "solution" would involve of millions of savings-bank depositors, life-insurance policyholders, bond-holders, and of everyone dependent on a fixed or sluggishly responsive income, is itself sufficient ground for rejecting it.

Even so, it would not work. The moment an inflation is planned, ac-knowledged, and *foreseen*, the game is up. Inflation is a swindle. You cannot tell your intended victim in advance that you intend to swindle him. Slichter proposed his plan mainly in order to meet annual wage demands. But union leaders, if the plan were put into effect, would simply add 2 per cent (or whatever the planned annual inflation was) on top of the demands they would have made anyway. In fact, lenders, investors, merchants, speculators would all mark up their demands or change their operations to beat the inflation, which, out of control, would race to a crack-up.

What is still understood only by an appallingly small minority even of the "experts" is that prices, in the early stage of an inflation, usually rise by *less* than the increase in the money supply, but in the later stage of an inflation always rise by *more* than the increase in the money supply.

Yet there is one way in which the three goals of rising wages, stable prices, and full employment (when these goals are reasonably interpreted) could all be achieved. This way is through the restoration of a sound currency and a genuinely free economy. In such an economy, it is true, wages could not for long rise faster than marginal labor productivity, but they would rise *as fast as* marginal labor productivity, though the rise in their real purchasing power might be reflected more in lower prices than in higher wage rates.

28 "Administered" Inflation

GARDINER C. MEANS, an economist who invented the term "administered prices" in the '30s, came up in 1957 with the theory that the current inflation is an "administered" inflation. The solution, he thought, would be for the Presi-dent to call a conference of business and labor leaders and get an agreement from them to "hold the line" for a year or two on wages and prices.

But his theory of causation was and is false. His proposed remedy was not needed, and is not needed now. It would not work, but would greatly aggravate the very evil it is supposed to cure.

Past inflations, he agrees, have been "monetary" inflations—the result of an increased money supply bidding for the available supply of goods and services. This is correct. And it applies to *every* inflation, including the present one (i.e., 1939 to 1960 to ?).

This can be shown by any set of long-term comparisons. At the end of 1939, the total supply of money and bank credit (total bank deposits plus currency outside of banks) was $64.7 billion. In March of 1957 it was $221.5 billion, an increase of 246 per cent. In 1939 wholesale prices were at an index number of 50.1; in 1957 they were at a level of 117.4, an increase of 136 per cent. The chief reason why wholesale prices did not go up even more in this period is that there was also a great increase in production. The increase in the money supply is a sufficient explanation of the present inflation. We do not have a "new kind" of inflation, and we do not need new explanations.

Neither logic nor statistical comparisons give any support to the "administered price" theory of inflation. If sellers can administer prices to any level they choose, why weren't prices as high in 1957, or in 1955, or 1949, or 1939, or 1914, as they are today? Why have prices all been raised now? What has prevented them from going still higher?

Certain prices, it is true, are administered (within narrow limits) at levels different from those that a perfectly fluid competition would bring about. The outstanding directly administered prices are those administered by government. This includes all public-utility rates and railroad rates. But these are administered down rather than up. Farm prices have of course been supported by government above free-market levels. Farm products in 1957 had risen 150 per cent since 1939, whereas industrial products had risen only 116 per cent.

By far the most important administered price is the price of labor. Money wage rates have been administered upward by powerful industrywide labor unions. Since 1939 hourly wages in manufacturing industries had increased in 1957 by 229 per cent.

As a cure for all this, Means in 1957 would have had the President call a conference of business and labor leaders at which he would "get agreement from them to hold the line" on prices and wages. Now such agreements would be extremely harmful if they were uniformly adhered to. They would not allow for the relative changes in particular prices and wages necessary to adjust output to changes in supply and demand.

All hold-the-line legislation or voluntary agreements in the past have broken down under political pressures, chiefly in favor of wage increases. The Means plan left-handedly recognized this. His proposed agreements would have allowed "small" wage increases to take account of increases in productivity, and increases "where a major disparity in particular wage rates required correction." Anyone who remembers our World War II experience must know that such loopholes would be exploited to the point where the hold-the-line agreements would become a farce. But even this would be better than their strict enforcement; for to try to hold a uniform line on prices and wages, particularly if the money and credit supply continued to be increased, would have a disastrous effect on production.

Schemes of the Means type are wholly unnecessary. All that is needed to stop the present inflation is a halt to the expansion of the money-and-credit supply and repeal of the legislation that creates monster unions and gives them a coercive wage-raising power that employers are impotent to resist.

29 Easy Money Has an End

THE MAINTENANCE of short-term interest rates at too low a level, by governments or central banks, is one of the main explanations of the continuance of inflation in Europe and in the United States. Excessively low rates always encourage overborrowing, which means an expansion in the supply of money and credit, which in turn causes commodity prices to rise even further.

It is possible, of course, for a government or a central bank to keep money rates low for a long time, either by printing money directly or by permitting the overborrowing and consequent expansion of credit to which excessively low money rates inevitably lead. What is less well understood is that cheap money cannot be continued indefinitely. It sets in motion forces that eventually drive interest rates higher than if a cheap-money policy had never been followed.

The expansion of money and credit that is necessary to hold interest rates down also raises commodity prices and wages. Higher commodity prices and wages make it necessary for businessmen to borrow correspondingly more in order to do the same volume of business. Therefore the demand for credit soon increases as fast as the supply. Later on, still another factor comes in. When both borrowers and lenders begin to fear that inflation is going to *continue,* prices and wages begin to go up *more* than the increase in the supply of money and credit. Borrowers want to borrow still more to take advantage of the expected further rise in prices, and lenders insist on higher interest rates as an insurance premium against expected depreciation in the purchasing power of the money they lend.

When this happens in an extreme degree, we get a situation like that in Germany in November of 1923, when rates for "call money" went up to 30 per cent per *day*. This phenomenon in mild degree became evident in Britain in 1957. When the U.S. Treasury 2½s were trading around 86 in June of 1957, for example, the British Treasury 2½s issued in 1946 could be bought at 50, or half the original purchase price. Yet corporate shares in Britain had been bid up to levels where returns to the investor were in many cases substantially lower than on gilt-edge bonds. As one London investment house explained the matter: "The argument is, indeed, put forward that, since the pound has been depreciating in the past decade at an average rate of 4¾ per cent per annum, any investment likely to show a total net return on income and capital accounts over a given period of less than this amount is giving a negative yield and should be discarded."

The attractions of easy money were coming to an end. That is why, in September 1957, the Bank of England raised its discount rate to 7 per cent.

30 Can Inflation Merely Creep?

As NEARLY EVERYBODY professes to be against inflation (even those who fervently advocate the very things that cause it), it was refreshing to read a writer like the late Sumner H. Slichter of Harvard, who frankly accepted inflation as a "necessary evil" and did not think we could prosper without it.

He was careful, it is true, to say that he was only in favor of "creeping" inflation, not galloping inflation, though he was often vague concerning the exact point where a creep became a canter. He was at times indiscreet enough to suggest that a price rise of 2 or 3 per cent a year would be about right. It has been pointed out, however, that even if we could control an inflation to a rate of 2 per cent a year it would mean an erosion of the purchasing power of the dollar by about one-half in each generation.

Even so, this would not accomplish Slichter's announced purpose. He thought prices must go up this much in order to meet the unions' annual wage demands. But the moment Slichter's inflation scheme was openly put into effect, as I have already pointed out in Chapter 27, union leaders would simply add 2 per cent (or whatever the planned annual inflation was) on top of the demands they would have made anyway. In fact, lenders, investors, manufacturers, retailers, speculators would all mark up their demands or change their operations to beat the inflation, which would thereupon race to a crack-up. A declining currency must eventually obey the law of acceleration that applies to all falling bodies.

In the *Harvard Business Review* of September-October, 1957, Slichter not only continued to commend a creeping inflation but reprimanded Neil H. Jacoby, a former member of the Council of Economic Advisers, and C. Canby Balderston, vice chairman of the Board of Governors of the Federal Reserve System, for being against inflation. Without going into a detailed analysis of all the confusions in Slichter's article, it may be helpful to cite a few examples.

He declared that it was "incorrect" to believe that "creeping inflation is bound sooner or later to become galloping inflation," because this had not happened in the preceding twenty-five years in the United States. Yet our cost of living had more than doubled in the preceding seventeen years, which was something more than a creep. Slichter might have taken a look at the French franc, which was then already at considerably less than one-hundredth of its 1914 purchasing power; or at the median loss of one-third of their value by 56 different currencies in the preceding nine years alone (as pointed out in Chapter 24).

Slichter seemed to me to take a somewhat callous attitude about the losses suffered in recent years by the thrifty. Of the millions of savings-bank depositors and holders of government bonds who had seen the purchasing power of their holdings shrink by a third or a half, he wrote coolly: "These people have paid the penalty for poor investment judgment." Their poor judgment consisted, in brief, in trusting their country's money and in answering their government's appeal to buy war bonds.

Slichter's proposals were based on his obsessive idea that constant creeping inflation was necessary to maintain full employment. This led him to misstate an argument of Jacoby's as a "suggestion that prices be kept stable by not permitting unemployment to fall below 4 per cent." The truth is that full employment or its absence has no necessary connection whatever with inflation, but depends wholly upon the maintenance of fluid and functional interrelationships between wage rates and prices and profits. Slichter did not seem to understand the argument that unions cannot raise the real wages of the whole body of workers, and his attempted refutation missed the point.

Finally, in his efforts to minimize the harm done by inflation, Slichter failed to see that when employment is reasonably full, further inflation must hurt on net balance as many people as it helps, for the gains in dollar income resulting from inflation must be offset by the losses in dollar purchasing power.

31 How to Wipe Out Debt

WHEN IT WAS POINTED out to the Eisenhower Administration, as it was to its Democratic predecessors, that our huge national debt continues to mount, a favorite defense was that it had not risen as a percentage of the national income.

Such a reply ignores the fact that the national income, has gone up (in dollar terms) in large part because prices have gone up, and that prices have gone up because of the currency debasement brought about partly by the very deficit financing that increased the debt. What this defense amounts to, in short, is a boast that the burden of the national debt has not increased because it can now be paid off in debased dollars.

There are few governments today that cannot make such a boast. At the end of this chapter is a table, taken from the August 1957 issue of *Pick's World Currency Report,* showing what happened in the preceding nine years to the national public debts of a dozen leading countries. Only three of them were smaller in terms of their own currencies; the other nine were all larger in terms of their own currencies. Yet in spite of the fact that they owed more in nominal currency units than a decade previously, the United States, Brazil, France, Sweden, and the United Kingdom owed much less in real terms than a decade previously. Though the U.S. debt increased 24 billion in dollars since 1948, the reduced purchasing power of the dollar wiped out the equivalent of $42 billion of that debt. Though France increased its debt since 1948 from 3,412 billion to 6,506 billion francs, it also wiped out 3,383 billion francs of the 1948 purchasing power of such a debt.

This is the way governments are today cheating their creditors—precisely the citizens who responded to their patriotic appeals for help.

There is nothing new about this process. It was old when Adam Smith denounced it in *The Wealth of Nations* in 1776: "When national debts have once been accumulated to a certain degree, there is scarce, I believe, a single instance of their having been fairly and completely paid. The liberation of the public revenue, if it has ever been brought about at all, has always been brought about by a bankruptcy; sometimes by an avowed one, but always by a real one, though frequently by a pretended payment.

"The raising of the denomination of the coin has been the most usual expedient by which a real public bankruptcy has been disguised under the appearance of a pretended payment. . . . A pretended payment of this kind . . . extends the calamity to a great number of other innocent people. . . . When it becomes necessary for a state to declare itself bankrupt, in the same manner as when it becomes necessary for an individual to do so, a fair, open, and avowed bankruptcy is always the measure which is both least dishonorable to the debtor, and least hurtful to the creditor. The honor of a state is surely very poorly provided for, when, in order to cover the disgrace of a real bankruptcy, it has recourse to a juggling trick of this kind, so easily seen through, and at the same time so extremely pernicious."

Adam Smith then goes on to show how "almost all states . . . ancient as well as modern" have "played this very juggling trick." It may be added that, since the substitution of paper for metallic money, the trick has become much easier and therefore more frequent. It may also be added that the debtor class today, including as it does most corporation stockholders, is probably as rich as the creditor class, which includes savings-bank depositors and owners of savings bonds.

NATIONAL DEBTS
(In billions of currency units)

	1948	1957	1957 Adjusted to 1948
		Nominal Paper Units	Purchasing Power
United States $	252	276	234
Canada $	15	14	10
Argentina p.	18	95	26
Belgium fr.	245	328	279
Brazil cr.	23	67	20
France fr.	3,412	6,506	3,123
Italy l.	2,315	4,805	3,604
Netherlands fl.	26	18	12
Spain p.	53	90	59
Sweden kr.	11	14	10
Switzerland fr.	11	8	7
United Kingdom £	25	27	18

32 The Cost-Price Squeeze

FROM TIME TO TIME during the present inflation (let's say between 1940 and 1964) violent disputes have broken out concerning who or what caused it. "Labor" and "management" blame each other.

Attacks on management have frequently come from Walter Reuther, head of the United Automobile Workers. In 1957, for example, Reuther contended that "exorbitant" profits, not wages, had been the villain promoting inflation. Otis Brubaker, research director of the steelworkers' union, declared at the same time: "Wage increases have not caused a single price increase in twenty years."

These charges provoked replies. In its letter of October 1957, the First National City Bank of New York pointed out: "Regardless of what year is taken as a base [from 1939 on] wages and total employment costs in the steel industry have far outstripped gains in productivity. Measuring from 1940, the gain in productivity of 56 per cent, while substantial, fell far short of increases in hourly earnings and total employment costs amounting to more than 200 per cent. The result . . . was an approximate doubling of unit labor costs with inevitable pressure for higher prices."

A much wider study of the same problem was published by the National Association of Manufacturers in September of the same year. It found that the history of manufacturing since the end of World War II had been one of rising costs per unit of output—particularly labor costs and taxes. Compensation of employes rose 23 per cent per unit of output between 1948 and 1956. Corporate taxes rose 32 per cent on the same basis. But prices of manufactured goods rose only 10 per cent. The result was a reduction of 25 per cent in profit per unit of output between 1948 and 1956.

The decline in the profit margin of manufacturing industries was particularly striking when expressed as a percentage of sales. It dropped from 4.9 per cent in 1948 to 3.1 per cent in 1956. (By way of comparison, the figure for 1929 was 6.4 per cent; for 1937, 4.7 per cent; for 1940, 5.5 per cent.) Thus, concluded the NAM study, "between 1948 and 1956 profit margins as a per cent of sales have fallen from a level characteristic of prosperity years to a level characteristic of recession years." Higher costs cannot automatically be recouped by higher market prices.

These statistical comparisons by the National City Bank and the NAM proved that the inflation was at least not the result of the "greed" of manufacturers for exorbitant profits, as Reuther contended. But they did not prove that "the conclusion is inescapable," as the NAM study put it, "that the current inflationary push is due to the rising costs of labor and the continuing heavy tax burden."

The rise in wages, it is true, as both studies pointed out, exceeded the rise in "productivity." But the studies compared *money* wages to *physical* output. In any inflation, no matter how caused, money wages are practically certain to rise more than physical productivity. This is simply because both wages and prices rise in every inflation. It does not necessarily follow that the rise in prices has been *caused* by the rise in wages. Both may have risen from a common cause.

That common cause is not hard to find. Neither the wage rise nor the price rise since 1939 or 1948 would have been possible if it had not been fed by an increased money supply. The money-and-credit supply (total bank deposits plus currency) increased from $64.7 billion at the end of 1939, to $172.7 billion at the end of 1948, to $226.4 billion at the end of 1956, to $313.8 billion at the end of 1963. There would have been no inflation, in short, in the last ten or twenty years without the cooperation and connivance of the monetary authorities.

This does not mean, of course, that union pressure has had no responsibility for the result. Under present labor laws the government has not merely encouraged but in effect forced the creation of industrywide unions with power to impose continuous wage increases. Unless these excessive union powers are reduced, they must either lead to unemployment by forcing costs above prices, or create political pressure for still more monetary inflation.

33 The Employment Act of 1946

UNDER A GOLD STANDARD the primary objective of a nation's monetary policy was clear: It was to protect the integrity of the currency by maintaining gold convertibility at all times. Under a paper standard and a Keynesian ideology the objectives become confused. The U.S. Employment Act of 1946 declares that "it is the continuing policy and responsibility of the Federal government to use all practicable means . . . to promote maximum employment, production, and purchasing power." Many interpret this as a standing order for inflation. Chairman Martin of the Federal Reserve Board has suggested that Congress should declare "resolutely—so that all the world will know—that stabilization of the cost of living is a primary aim of Federal economic policy."

An infinitely better solution would be simply repeal of the Employment Act of 1946. But if that mischievous law is kept, it should at least be amended to add the requirement of price stability as an offset to the heavy inflationary bias in the law as it now stands.

It is not inherently desirable to make price stability an official goal of government policy. It implies a further extension of statism. But this is the kind of awkward problem we create when we abandon a gold standard.

34 Inflate? Or Adjust?

IN THE MIDST not only of moderate but even of the wildest inflations, there are sudden breaks, slumps, or lulls. Whenever these occur, the inflationists declare that the inflation has ended and that we are now facing recession or deflation unless we immediately adopt their "stabilizing" measures. Such a slump occurred in the late months of 1957 and the early months of 1958. Though wholesale and consumer prices continued to rise, interest rates, industrial production, and employment declined. The proposed remedies started to pour in.

To those of us who had lived through the Great Depression, there was a curious familiarity about these schemes. On June 12, 1931, for example, the Chase National Bank of New York published a pamphlet by its economist, the late Benjamin M. Anderson, called "Equilibrium Creates Purchasing Power." Anderson there drew a contrast between two opposing schools of thought. The school to which he adhered found the cause of the slump in "a disturbance of economic equilibrium." The other found its causes in "deficiencies of purchasing power."

The purchasing-power school was inflationist. It advocated "cheap-money policies," farm price supports, and heavy spending on "public works." It argued that "reductions in wages are on no account to be permitted." "The general picture which the purchasing-power school presents is that of production running ahead of buying power." As against this, Anderson advocated the restoration of equilibrium, mainly through adjustments of free and flexible prices and wages. He called for the restoration of a proper balance among the various types of production, among prices, and particularly between prices and costs of production, including wages, so that profits would be possible and the prospect of them would once more stimulate enterprise.

"When goods are produced in proper proportions," he wrote, "they clear the markets of one another. . . . Production itself gives rise to the income which supports consumption. Production and consumption expand together. The 120 millions of people in the United States consume vastly more than the 400 millions in China, because they produce vastly more. . . . The problem is merely one of keeping the different kinds of production in proper proportion. This is accomplished under the capitalist system by the movement of prices and costs. Labor and capital tend to get out of lines where return is low and to move over into lines where return is better. The smooth working of this system calls for flexible prices, competitively worked out, which tell the truth regarding underlying supply and demand conditions."

Anderson went on to point out that the purchasing-power theory was not working: "We have had extremely cheap money for over a year." Inflexibility of industrial wage-rates, while prices were falling, had led to increased unemployment. "Real" industrial wage-rates between June 1929 and March 1931 had risen 11 per cent, indirectly helping to force down "real" farm wages 17 per cent.

However, as we know, the purchasing-power school—the inflationist school—won out. We had cheap money, inflexible or rising wage rates, and heavy government deficits for the next ten years. As a result, we also had mass unemployment for the next ten years—until World War II finally bailed us out.

Today the chief ideological change is that there can hardly be said to be two schools of thought. Practically everyone in Washington seems to agree that we can easily float ourselves out of slumps through more inflation. We need merely give ourselves a sufficiently big dose—of increased spending, or tax reduction, or anything else that will produce a whopping deficit. The new bible in Keynes's *General Theory*, which denies Say's Law and ignores any need for specific wage and price adjustments. In early 1958, the Republican Administration disagreed with the Democratic inflationists only about the question of timing. It hoped (justifiably, as it turned out) everything would cure itself in the next few months. If it didn't, it promised to take "positive government action"—today's euphemism for more inflation.

Meanwhile, neither political party called attention to the fact that as factory wage-rates had risen, unemployment had increased and payrolls had fallen. Neither party asks today whether even massive inflation can restore employment as long as powerful unions have escalator contracts under which wage-rates soar faster than living costs, preventing restoration of profit margins or lowering of prices. The only remedy proposed is bigger and longer unemployment compensation to help strong unions preserve upward-spiraling wage-rates.

35 Deficits vs. Jobs

I POINTED OUT in the last chapter that, after 1930, we had cheap money, inflexible or rising wage-rates, and heavy government deficits for the next ten years. As a result, we also had mass unemployment for the next ten years—until World War II finally bailed us out.

Inasmuch as today, in every slump or lull, we are being urged to adopt precisely the remedies that failed in the '30s, it may pay us to look at that period in more detail. The deficits, number of unemployed, and percentage of unemployed to the total labor force are tabulated, year by year, in that decade.

	Deficit (billions of dollars)	Unemployed (millions)	Percentage of Unemployment
1931	$0.5	8.0	15.9%
1932	2.7	12.1	23.6
1933	2.6	12.8	24.9
1934	3.6	11.3	21.7
1935	2.8	10.6	20.1
1936	4.4	9.0	16.9
1937	2.8	7.7	14.3
1938	1.2	10.4	19.0
1939	3.9	9.5	17.2
1940	3.9	8.1	14.6

In the tabulation the deficits are for fiscal years ending on June 30; the unemployment is an average of the full calendar year. Spenders, no doubt, will try to find a partial negative correlation between the size of the deficit and the number of unemployed; but the central and decisive fact is that heavy deficits were accompanied by mass unemployment. If we translate the figures into 1959 terms, we find: the average deficit in this ten-year period was $2.8 billion, which was 3.6 per cent of the gross national product of the period. The same percentage of the gross national product of 1963 would mean a deficit of $21 billion. The average unemployment of the ten-year period was 9.9 millions, which was 18.6 per cent of the total labor force. The same percentage of unemployment today would mean 14.4 million jobless. So much for the effect of deficits as a cure for unemployment.

At the end of this chapter the table is continued from 1941 through 1963. It will be noticed that we did, in 1944, get unemployment down to a low point of only 1.2 per cent of the working force. If this is to be attributed to deficit spending, then we must notice that it took a $51.4 billion deficit to do it. Compared with the increase in the gross national product, this would have to be a deficit today of more than $145 billion! (However, the deficits in both 1943 and 1945 were even larger than in 1944; and yet unemployment was also larger in those years.)

Another point to be noticed in this table is that in the ten years from 1948 to 1957 inclusive, average unemployment was 4.3 per cent of the total labor force. Yet this period was one of unusually high employment, even of "labor shortage." But if four persons out of every 100 are "normally" unemployed, "abnormal" unemployment is only the excess above this. Such unemployment is serious, especially for those directly concerned. But it hardly justifies reckless deficit spending or further dilution of the dollar in an effort to cure it. We could more profitably look, in times of abnormal unemployment, at the relation of key wage rates to prices and consumer demand.

THE RECORD

	Employed	Unemployed	Percentage of
		(in millions)	Unemployment
1941	50.4	5.6	9.9%
1942	53.8	2.7	4.7
1943	54.5	1.1	1.9
1944	54.0	.7	1.2
1945	52.8	1.0	1.9
1946	55.3	2.3	3.9
1947	57.8	2.4	3.9
1948	59.1	2.3	3.8
1949	58.4	3.7	5.9
1950	59.7	3.4	5.3
1951	60.8	2.1	3.3
1952	61.0	1.9	3.1
1953	61.9	1.9	2.9
1954	60.9	3.6	5.6
1955	62.9	2.9	4.4
1956	64.7	2.8	4.2
1957	65.0	2.9	4.3
1958	64.0	4.7	6.8
1959	65.6	3.8	5.5
1960	66.7	3.9	5.6
1961	66.8	4.8	6.7
1962	68.0	4.0	5.6
1963	68.8	4.1	5.7

36 Why Cheap Money Fails

THE LATE Lord Keynes preached two great remedies for unemployment. One was deficit financing. The other was artificially cheap money brought about by central bank policy. Both alleged remedies have since been assiduously pursued by nearly all governments. The result has been worldwide inflation and a constantly shrinking purchasing power of monetary units. But the success in curing unemployment has been much more doubtful. In the last chapter we considered the unpromising results of budget deficits. Does cheap money have any better record?

On the next page is a table covering the twelve years from 1929 through 1940, comparing the average annual rate of prime commercial paper maturing in four to six months with the percentage of unemployment in the same year. Both sets of figures are from official sources.

In sum, over this period of a dozen years low interest rates did *not* eliminate unemployment. On the contrary, unemployment actually *increased* in years when interest rates went down. Even in the seven-year period from 1934 through 1940, when the cheap-money policy was pushed to an average infra-low rate below 1 per cent (0.77 of 1 per cent), an average of more than seventeen in every hundred persons in the labor force were unemployed.

Year	Commercial Paper Rate	Percentage of Unemployment
1929	5.85%	3.2%
1930	3.59	8.7
1931	2.64	15.9
1932	2.73	23.6
1933	1.73	24.9
1934	1.02	21.7
1935	0.75	20.1
1936	0.75	16.9
1937	0.94	14.3
1938	0.81	19.0
1939	0.59	17.2
1940	0.56	14.6

Let us skip over the war years when war demands, massive deficits, and massive inflation combined to bring overemployment, and take up the record again for the last eleven years (table following).

It will be noticed that, although the commercial paper interest rate in this period averaged 2.48 per cent—more than three times as high as that in the seven years from 1934 through 1940, the rate of unemployment was not higher, but much lower, averaging only 4.4 per cent compared with 17.7 per cent in the 1934-40 period.

Within this second period, the relationship of unemployment to interest rates is almost the exact opposite of that suggested by Keynesian theory. In 1949, 1950, and 1954, when the commercial paper interest rate averaged about 1½ per cent, unemployment averaged 5 per cent and more. In 1956, 1957, and 1959, when commercial paper rates were at their highest average level of the period at 3.70 per cent, unemployment averaged only 4.4 per cent of the working force.

To bring this record down to date: In the three years 1960, 1962 and 1963, the commercial paper rate was, respectively, 3.85, 3.26, and 3.55 per cent, an average of 3.55 per cent, and the average unemployment in those three years was 5.6 per cent. But in 1961 the commercial paper rate averaged only 2.97 per cent, while the unemployment rate was 6.7 per cent!

In brief, neither deficit spending nor cheap-money policies are enough by

Year	Commercial Paper Rate	Percentage of Unemployment
1949	1.49%	5.5%
1950	1.45	5.0
1951	2.16	3.0
1952	2.33	2.7
1953	2.52	2.5
1954	1.58	5.0
1955	2.18	4.0
1956	3.31	3.8
1957	3.81	4.3*
1958	2.46	6.8
1959	3.97	5.5

* *Unemployment percentages before 1957 are based on Department of Commerce "old definitions" of unemployment; for 1957 and after they are based on the "new definitions," which make unemployment slightly higher—4.2 per cent of the labor force in 1956, for example, instead of the 3.8 per cent in the table.*

themselves to eliminate even prolonged mass unemployment, let alone to prevent unemployment altogether.

The only real cure for unemployment is precisely the one that the Keynesians and inflationists reject—the adjustment of wage rates to the marginal labor productivity or "equilibrium" level—the balance and co-ordination of wages and prices. When wage rates are in equilibrium with prices, there will tend to be full employment regardless of whether interest rates are "high" or "low." But regardless of how low interest rates are pushed, there will be unemployment if wage rates are too high to permit workable profit margins.

37 How to Control Credit

WITHIN A PERIOD of ten days, in 1958, the Federal Reserve authorities illustrated first the wrong and then the right way to control inflation. On August 4 they raised the margin requirements for buying stock from 50 to 70 per cent. (On October 16 they raised them again to 90 per cent.) On August 14 they permitted the Federal Reserve Bank of San Francisco to raise its discount rate from 1¾ to 2 per cent. The first method is what is called "selective" credit control. The second is what is called general credit control. Only the second is equitable and effective.

The targets of selective credit controls are always politically selected. The stock market is the No. 1 target because those with no understanding of its role and function in the American economy regard it as a sort of glorified gambling casino. As G. Keith Funston, president of the New York Stock Exchange, said in a speech in October 1957:

"I sometimes wonder at our sense of proportion. A man can borrow up to 75 per cent to buy a car, 100 per cent to buy a washing machine, and 94 per cent to buy a house. But he can borrow only 30 per cent to buy an interest in the company that makes the car, the washing machine, or the house. We have made it much easier to borrow in order to spend, than to borrow in order to save."

In addition to being discriminatory, these rigid restrictions on stock-buying margins are also in the long run futile. We cannot encourage a *general* inflationary flood and then expect to dam off its effects in one direction. Credit, like water, seeks its level and leaks through every crack. If a man is determined to buy shares, and does not have the required legal margin, he can mortgage his house or other assets and use the proceeds in the stock market.

Raising stock-market margin requirements seldom has the intended effects. No statistics can show, of course, what *might* have happened to stock-market credit or prices if margins had *not* been changed. But most margin increases have shown little effect on stock-market credit.

Nor is it easy to justify the 1958 rise of margin requirements on this ground. As Funston then pointed out, customers' net debit balances on June 30, 1958 (when margin requirements were 50 per cent), totaled $3.1 billion, which represented only 1.4 per cent of the market value of all stocks listed on the New York Stock Exchange on the same date, a ratio almost exactly the same as it was a month earlier or a year before.

Increases in margin requirements have sometimes temporarily halted the upward movement of stock prices, but never for more than a month or two. In fact, in every instance of a margin increase from February 1945 through April 1955, stock prices six months later averaged at least 12 per cent higher than in six months before the margin change. The average price of stocks in October 1958, when the 90 per cent margin requirement was put into effect, was 54.55 on the Standard-and-Poor index; in the following July, with that margin requirement still in effect, it had risen to an average of 59.74.

This is what we might have expected. The price that people pay for stocks is primarily determined by the expected yield from those stocks and the capitalization of that yield as affected by interest rates.

However, because the increases in legal stock margin requirements have not had their *intended* effect, it does not follow that they have done no harm. Their main effect, careful comparisons show, has been to *reduce the volume of trading*—sometimes as much as 25 per cent. This does not merely mean that brokers lose commissions. It reduces the liquidity of the market and throws a damper on the willingness and ability of corporations to raise new money through stock issues.

38 Who Makes Inflation?

OVER THE LAST QUARTER CENTURY the American government has displayed a peculiarly schizophrenic attitude toward spending vs. economy, inflation vs. dollar-integrity.

This has been frequently reflected in the annual Economic Report of the President. A good example is the Economic Report of President Eisenhower transmitted to Congress on January 20, 1959. "An indispensable condition for achieving vigorous and continuing economic growth," he wrote, "is firm confidence that the value of the dollar will be reasonably stable in the years ahead." But most of the report endorsed policies that tended to undermine this confidence.

Describing governmental actions that helped "to bring about a prompt and sound recovery" the President declared: "Monetary and credit policies were employed vigorously to assure ample supplies of credit. Legislation was enacted to lengthen temporarily the period of entitlement to unemployment benefits. Numerous actions were taken to spur building activity. Steps were taken to accelerate Federal construction projects already under way and to speed up projects supported by Federal financial assistance. Activities under a number of Federal credit programs, in addition to those in the housing field, helped counter the recession. And the acceleration of defense procurement . . . exerted an expansive effect."

Every one of these policies was inflationary. All of them meant pouring new money and credit into the system, increasing the supply of dollars, reducing their individual purchasing power. In a later part of the report it was admitted that the Federal Reserve policies enabled the commercial banks "to add nearly $10 billion in loans and investments to their assets" in 1958, largely by "additions to their holdings of U. S. Government securities." This in turn added $13.6 billion to the total money supply (including inflated time deposits), and helped to boost living costs.

Yet the President's report blurred responsibility for inflation and tried to shift it on to consumers, business, and labor. The "individual consumer" was advised to "shop carefully for price and quality"—as if he couldn't be depended upon to do that without urging. The government in effect was saying to consumers: "Here are $10 billion or more additional paper dollars; but don't be reckless enough to spend them, because it will make *you* responsible for raising prices." "Businessmen" were told they "must wage a ceaseless war against costs"—as if self-interest and self-preservation did not ensure that. But nothing was said about Federal labor laws (including compulsory exclusive "bargaining") which rendered the employer all but impotent in resisting excessive demands. And "leaders of labor unions" (after having been granted monopolistic bargaining powers by law) were urged not to ask as much as they could get under these conditions. This meant that they would not last very long as labor leaders.

The President went on to declare: "If the desired results cannot be achieved under our arrangements for determining wages and prices, the alternatives are either inflation, which would damage our economy and work hardships on millions of Americans, or controls, which are alien to our traditional way of life and which would be an obstacle to the nation's economic growth and improvement." What the President seemed to be saying is that it was consumers, businessmen, and labor leaders who threatened to bring inflation by lack of "self-discipline and restraint," and that they might "force" government controls.

But the real culprit was and is government. Government must stop deficit spending, stop flooding the country with more paper dollars, and stop encouraging monopoly in the labor field while blaming "our free competitive economy" for rising wages and prices.

Perhaps the most important recommendation in the Economic Report of January 1959 was that Congress "amend the Employment Act of 1946 to make reasonable price stability an explicit goal of Federal economic policy, co-ordinate with the goals of maximum production, employment, and purchasing power now specified in that act." If the mischievous Employment Act of 1946 is to be retained, such an amendment on net balance would probably make it less mischievous, because the act has been constantly interpreted as a directive to inflate. But an immensely better solution would be to repeal the act altogether.

39 Inflation As a Policy

IN HIS CLASSIC LITTLE HISTORY of fiat money inflation in the French Revolution, Andrew D. White points out that the more evident the evil consequences of inflation became, the more rabid became the demands for still more inflation to cure them. Today, as inflation increases, apologists emerge to suggest that, after all, inflation may be a very good thing—or if an evil, at least a necessary evil.

Until recently, the chief spokesman of this group was the late Prof.

Sumner H. Slichter of Harvard. I should like to discuss here what I consider to be three of his chief wrong assumptions: (1) That a "creeping" inflation of 2 per cent a year would do more good than harm; (2) that it is possible for the government to *plan* a "creeping" inflation of 2 per cent a year (or of any other fixed rate); and (3) that inflation is necessary to attain "full employment" and "economic growth."

We have already noticed, in Chapter 30, that even if the government could control an inflation to a rate of "only" 2 per cent a year, it would mean an erosion of the purchasing power of the dollar by about one-half in each generation. This could not fail to discourage thrift, to produce injustice, and to misdirect production. Actually inflation in the United States has been much faster. The cost of living has more than doubled in the last twenty years. This is at a compounded rate of about 4 per cent a year.

The moment a *planned* "creeping" inflation is announced or generally expected in advance, it must accelerate into a gallop. If lenders expect a 2 or 4 per cent rise of prices a year, they will insist that this be added to the interest rate otherwise paid to them to maintain the purchasing power of their investment. If borrowers also expect such a price rise, they will be willing to pay such a premium. All businesses, in fact, will be forced to offer a correspondingly increased gross rate of return to attract new investment, even new equity capital. If there is a planned price rise, union leaders will simply add the expected amount of that rise on top of whatever wage demands they would have made anyway. Speculators and ordinary buyers will try to anticipate any planned price rise—and thereby inevitably accelerate it beyond the planned percentage. Inflation forces everybody to be a gambler.

The burden of Slichter's argument was that "a slow rise in the price level is an inescapable cost of the maximum rate of growth"—in others words, that inflation is a necessary cost of "full employment." This is not true. What is necessary for maximum "growth" (i.e., optimum employment and maximum production is a proper relationship or *co-ordination* of prices and wages. If some wage-rates get too high for this coordination, the result is unemployment. The cure is to correct the culpable wage-rates. To attempt to lift the whole level of prices by monetary inflation will simply create new maladjustments everywhere.

In brief, if a real coordination of wages and prices exists, inflation is unnecessary; and if coordination of wages and prices does not exist—if wages outrace prices and production—inflation is worse than futile.

Slichter assumed that there is no way to restrain excessive union demands except by "breaking up" unions. Yet we need merely repeal the special immunities and privileges conferred on union leaders since 1932, especially those in the Norris-La Guardia and Wagner-Taft-Hartley acts. If employers were not legally *compelled* to "bargain" with (in practice, to make concessions to) a specified union, no matter how unreasonable its demands; if employers were free to discharge strikers and peaceably to hire replacements, and if mass picketing and violence were really prohibited, the natural competitive checks on excessive wage demands would once more come into play.

40 The Open Conspiracy

MORE THAN THIRTY-FIVE YEARS AGO—in 1928, to be precise—H. G. Wells published a minor propagandistic novel called *The Open Conspiracy*. Though I reviewed it at the time, I've forgotten now exactly what that open conspiracy was. But the description seems to fit with peculiar aptness something that is happening in the United States today. Our politicians, and most of our commentators, seem to be engaged in an open conspiracy not to pay the national debt—certainly not in dollars of the same purchasing power that were borrowed, and apparently not even in dollars of the present purchasing power.

There is of course no explicit avowal of this intention. The conspiracy is, rather, a conspiracy of silence. Very few of us even mention the problem of substantially reducing the national debt. The most that even the conservatives dare to ask for is that we stop piling up deficits so that we do not have to increase the debt and raise the debt ceiling still further. But anyone with a serious intention of eventually paying off the national debt would have to advocate over-balancing the budget, year in, year out, by a sizable annual sum.

Today one never sees nor hears a serious discussion of this problem. We see hundreds of articles and hear hundreds of speeches in which we are told how we can or should increase Federal expenditures or Federal tax revenues in proportion to the increase in our "gross national product." But I have yet to see an article that discusses how we could begin and increase an annual repayment of the debt in proportion to the increase in our gross national product.

When we look at the dimensions the problem has now assumed, it is not difficult to understand the somber silence about it. If someone were to propose that the debt be paid off at an annual rate of $1 billion a year, he would have to face the fact that at that rate it would take 289 years, or nearly three centuries, to get rid of it. Yet $1 billion a year is even now no trivial sum. Republican Administrations, after World War I, did succeed in maintaining something close to such a steady annual rate of reduction between 1919 and 1930; but they were under continual fire for such a "deflationary" policy. Because of such deflationary fears, one would hardly dare mention a higher rate today.

One suspects that there is at the back of the minds of many of the politicians and commentators who sense the dimensions of the problem an unavowed belief or wish. This is that a continuance of inflation will scale down the real burden of the debt in relation to the national income by a constant shrinkage in the value of the dollar, so reducing the problem to "manageable proportions." Such a policy would be indignantly disavowed. But this is precisely what our reckless spending is leading to. On the debt we contracted twenty years ago we are paying interest and principal in 48-cent dollars. Are our politicians hoping to swindle government creditors by paying them off in dollars twenty years from now at less than half the purchasing power of the dollar today?

This trick, alas, has a long and inglorious history. I hope I may be forgiven for repeating part of the quotation from Adam Smith's *The Wealth of Nations* that I made in Chapter 31. "When national debts have once been accumulated to a certain degree," wrote Smith in 1776, "there is scarce, I believe, a single instance of their having been fairly and completely paid. The liberation of the public revenue, if it has been brought about at all, has always been brought about by a bankruptcy; sometimes by an avowed one, but always by a real one, though frequently by a pretended payment [i.e., payment in an inflated or depreciated monetary unit]. . . . The honor of a state is surely very poorly provided for, when, in order to cover the disgrace of a real bankruptcy, it has recourse to a juggling trick of this kind, so easily seen through, and at the same time so extremely pernicious."

Our government is not forced to resort, once more, to such a "juggling trick." It is not too late for it to face its responsibilities now, and to adopt a long-term program that would eventually pay off its creditors with at least the present 48-cent dollar, without plunging us further into inflation or deflation.

41 How the Spiral Spins

FOR YEARS we have been talking about the inflationary wage-price spiral. But Washington (by which is meant both the majority in Congress and officials in the Administration) talks about it for the most part as if it were some dreadful visitation from without, some uncontrollable act of nature, rather than something brought about by its own policies.

Let us see just how those policies, over the last twenty-five years, have produced the wage-price spiral. First of all, under a series of laws beginning most notably with the Norris-La Guardia Act of 1932, followed by the Wagner Act and by its later modification, the Taft-Hartley Act, we decided that labor troubles developed chiefly because there was not enough unionization and because unions were not strong enough.

Therefore we in effect put the Federal government into the union-organizing business. We compelled employers to deal exclusively with the unions thus quasi-officially set up, regardless of how unreasonable the demands of these unions might turn out to be. Though illegalizing all efforts to deny employment to workers who joined unions, we explicitly legalized arrangements to deny employment to workers who did not join unions.

But worst of all, we gave to the unions and union members a privilege not granted to any other associations or individuals—the power of private coercion and intimidation. By the Norris-La Guardia Act we in effect prevented either employers or non-union employes from going to the Federal courts for immediate relief from irreparable injury. We refuse, contrary to legal practice in every other field, to hold a union liable for the acts of its agents. We tolerate mass picketing, which is intimidating and coercive, preventing employers from offering to other workers the jobs abandoned by strikers, and preventing other workers from applying for such jobs. And then we are astonished and indignant when these special privileges, against which we provide no effective legal protection, are "abused."

The inevitable result of these laws is that we have built up huge unions with the power to bring basic national industries to a halt overnight. And when they have done this, we can think of no way of getting an industry started again except by giving in to the demands of the union leaders who have called the strike.

This accounts for the upward push on money wage-rates. But it does not account for the inflationary spiral. The effect of pushing wage-rates above the level of marginal labor productivity, taken by itself, would simply be to create unemployment. But as F. A. Hayek has put it: "Since it has become the generally accepted doctrine that it is the duty of the monetary authorities to provide enough credit to secure full employment, whatever the wage level, and this duty has in fact been imposed upon the monetary authorities by statute, the power of the unions to push up money wages cannot but lead to continuous, progressive inflation."

Soon or late our Federal lawmakers and administrators must face up to the labor-union-boss dictatorship and the wage-price spiral that their own laws and actions have created. But they refuse to do this when each new crisis arises. When, for example, a nationwide steel strike is prolonged, they become panicky. They seek to settle it by the only means that seem possible to them—by giving in once more to union demands, by granting still another wage increase and setting off a new upward wage-price spiral.

Politicians demand that the President appoint a "fact-finding" board to "recommend," i.e., to impose, in effect, compulsory arbitration that would compel the employers to grant another increase to employes. Thus one government intervention begets a further government intervention. Because government has failed in its primary task—that of preventing private coercion—politicians ask, in effect, for price and wage fixing; and we are driven toward totalitarian controls.

42 Inflation vs. Morality

INFLATION never affects everybody simultaneously and equally. It begins at a specific point, with a specific group. When the government puts more money into circulation, it may do so by paying defense contractors, or by increasing subsidies to farmers or social security benefits to special groups. The incomes of those who receive this money go up first. Those who begin spending the money first buy at the old level of prices. But their additional buying begins to force up prices. Those whose money incomes have not been raised are forced to pay higher prices than before; the purchasing power of their incomes has been reduced. Eventually, through the play of economic forces, their own money-incomes may be increased. But if these incomes are increased either less or later than the average prices of what they buy, they will never fully make up the loss they suffered from the inflation.

Inflation, in brief, essentially involves a redistribution of real incomes. Those who benefit by it do so, and must do so, at the expense of others. The total losses through inflation offset the total gains. This creates class or group divisions, in which the victims resent the profiteers from inflation, and in which even the moderate gainers from inflation envy the bigger gainers. There is general recognition that the new distribution of income and wealth that goes on during an inflation is not the result of merit, effort, or productiveness, but of luck, speculation, or political favoritism. It was in the tremendous German inflation of 1923 that the seeds of Nazism were sown.

An inflation tends to demoralize those who gain by it even more than those who lose by it. The gainers become used to an "unearned increment." They want to keep thier relative gains. Those who have made money from speculation prefer to continue this way of making money instead of working for it. I remember once, early in 1929, a conversation between two friends, both of whom held prominent posts as book reviewers but both of whom were heavily in the stock market. They were exchanging stories about their profits. "Today your salary," they agreed, "is just a tip." People do not like to work full time just for a tip. The long-term trend in an inflation is toward less work and production, and more speculation and gambling.

The profiteers from inflation tend to spend freely, frivolously, and ostentatiously. This increases the resentment of those who have been less favored. The incentive to ordinary saving, in the form of savings accounts, insurance, bonds, or other fixed-income obligations, tends to disappear. The spectacle of quick and easy returns increases the temptations to corruption and crime.

It is not merely that inflation breeds the gambling spirit and corruption and dishonesty in a nation. Inflation is itself an immoral act on the part of government. When modern governments inflate by increasing the paper-money supply, directly or indirectly, they do in principle what kings once did when they clipped the coins. Diluting the money supply with paper is the moral equivalent of diluting the milk supply with water. Notwithstanding all the pious pretenses of governments that inflation is some evil visitation from without, inflation is practically always the result of deliberate governmental policy.

This was recognized in 1776 by Adam Smith in *The Wealth of Nations*. Though I have quoted the passage before, it bears repeating: "When national debts have once been accumulated to a certain degree, there is scarce, I believe, a single instance of their having been fairly and completely paid. The liberation of the public revenue, if it has ever been brought about at all, has always been brought about by a bankruptcy; sometimes by an avowed one, but always by a real one, though frequently by a pretended payment."

The pretended payment was inflation. The U.S. government today is paying off in 48-cent dollars the debts it contracted in 1940. Adam Smith went on: "The honor of a state is surely very poorly provided for, when, in order to cover the disgrace of a real bankruptcy, it has recourse to a juggling trick of this kind, so easily seen through, and at the same time so extremely pernicious."

43 How Can You Beat Inflation?

FROM TIME TO TIME I get letters from readers asking how they can protect themselves from the eroding effects of inflation on their savings. Many pamphlets from investment advisers attempt to tell people how this can be done. Schemes are constantly proposed for the issuance of government bonds and other securities with interest payments or redemption values that would increase in the same proportion as the cost of living. Many other schemes are put forward to counter the bad effects of inflation.

Both the advice and the schemes indirectly call attention to one of the worst results of inflation. It steadily wipes out the value of dollar savings, of savings-bank deposits, of bonds, of mortgages, of insurance benefits, of pensions, of fixed-income payments of every kind. It thereby penalizes and discourages thrift and saving, discourages the "safer" and more conservative investments, and forces everybody to be a speculator or gambler. For if, in the midst of an inflation, a man leaves his money in savings banks or mortgages or fixed-interest securities, he faces a certain loss in its real purchasing power.

Can any scheme be devised that would offset this effect? The escalator clauses in wage contracts are an attempt to do this for union labor. Proposals are frequently made that private companies, or the government itself, should issue bonds on which the interest payments, as well as the redemption value at maturity, would increase by the same percentage as the official index of consumer prices.

But the objections to such schemes are very serious. The borrower, whether a private company or the government, would assume an obligation of unknown extent. It would have no assurance, particularly if the subsequent inflation were severe, that its own income would rise proportionately to the cost of living (or, to put the matter another way, in inverse proportion to the drop in the value of the dollar). Such "escalator" bonds, like the escalator wage contracts, would simply increase the number of people with no interest in halting the ravages of inflation against the rest of the population.

What is not understood by those who propose these schemes is that inflation can benefit one group only at the expense of other groups. The price of what you have to sell can go up more or faster than the average price of what you have to buy only if the price of what *other* people have to sell to you goes up less or slower than the price of what *they* have to buy from you. The net amount of any real gain from inflation must be offset by an equivalent amount of real loss. Roughly speaking, one half of the population can gain from inflation only at the expense of the other half. The political appeal of inflation comes from fostering the illusion in the great majority of voters that they will somehow get the better of the swindle, and profit at the expense of a few unidentified victims.

If we grant that it would be possible to devise any scheme by which the gains from inflation would exactly equal the losses, so that nobody would either gain or lose by it, then all the arguments which sustain inflation would collapse. For inflation does not come without cause. It is the result of policy. It is the result of something that is always within the control of government—the supply of money and bank credit. An inflation is initiated or continued in the belief that it will benefit debtors at the expense of creditors, or exporters at the expense of importers, or workers at the expense of employers, or farmers at the expense of city dwellers, or the old at the expense of the young, or this generation at the expense of the next. But what is certain is that everybody cannot get rich at the expense of everybody else. There is no magic in paper money.

It is true that an alert individual can do certain things to protect himself from the eroding effects of inflation on the value of his dollars—but only on the assumption that he acts both sooner and more wisely than the majority.

Even this used to be easier than it is today. In the German inflation which culminated in 1923, for example, a German could always buy American dollars, at whatever the current rate happened to be, as soon as his monthly, weekly, or daily income above current needs became available to him. But as German internal prices went up much slower than the dollar (or, more accurately, as the external value of the German mark fell much faster than its internal value), even this proved an inadequate "hedge" for the German people considered as a whole. As the rush to buy foreign currencies made the external value of the mark depreciate even faster (so that, at the end, it took hundreds of billions of them to buy a single dollar), there was no profit in the operation for the latecomers.

Today, Americans have no completely safe major foreign currency to turn to to protect them against further depreciation of their own dollar. They are prohibited by law from buying and holding gold at home. (This is a left-handed confession by our monetary authorities that the people do prefer gold to paper and would make the exchange if they could.) If they buy gold abroad, they face the risk that our government (following the domestic precedent of 1933), may force them to turn in their gold holdings at an arbitrary value in paper dollars.

They are left, then, in practice, with the choice of buying real estate, common stocks, mink coats and motor cars, television sets and oriental rugs, jewelry—any equity or luxury that is not dollars or a fixed obligation payable in dollars. They are forced, in short, into extravagance and speculation.

An inexpert speculator may, of course, turn to investment trusts or mutual funds which diversify his investment for him and protect him to some extent against his own lack of expert knowledge. But always, the individuals who buy first, or at lower prices, can profit or protect themselves only at the expense of those who buy later or at the top.

It is impossible, in short, for everybody to protect himself against inflation. The early minority can do so only at the expense of the majority, or the early buyers at the expense of the later. And the scramble to get out of money and into things only intensifies the inflation, only increases and accelerates the rise of prices or the fall of the dollar.

This last result must follow whether individuals try to protect themselves against inflation by individual action, or whether they try to do so through such group devices as escalator wage clauses or escalator bond clauses. Even the arithmetic of such schemes is against them. Neither prices nor wages go up uniformly. Suppose some wages and prices do not go up at all, and others go up 100 per cent. The average increase, say, is 50 per cent. Suppose cost-of-living escalator clauses are prevalent, and that wages or prices that have gone up less than 50 per cent are raised to that average. This raises the average increase itself. It may now be 75 per cent. If the prices or wages that have advanced less than this are now raised 75 per cent above the old level, the *average* advance has again been pushed up to, say, 85 per cent. And so on. The process could be stopped only if the monetary authorities refused to supply the added money and credit necessary to sustain successive increases.

There is only one solution—only one sure hedge against inflation that can protect everybody: Don't have the inflation. If you have it, halt it as soon as possible.

44 The ABC of Inflation

SUPPOSE THAT, by a miracle, every family in the United States were to wake up one morning to find four times as much money in its pockets and its bank account as on the night before. Every family would then be eager to rush out and buy things it had previously longed for and gone without. The firstcomers might be able to buy things at the old prices. But the latercomers would bid prices up against each other. Merchants, with their stocks going down, would reorder, raising wholesale prices. Manufacturers and other producers, because they were doing a bigger business, would try to increase their labor force. This would force up wages. Eventually there would be an increase of prices and wages all around the circle.

This picture is, of course, a violent simplification. But it describes what has actually happened in this country, not overnight, but over the last twenty years or so. At the end of 1939 the amount of currency outside of banks was $6.4 billion. The amount of bank deposits subject to withdrawal by check (which is the main part of the "money supply" with which Americans do business) was $29.8 billion. This made a total active money supply of a little more than $36 billion. At the end of 1963 this money supply had grown to more than four times as much—$153 billion.

With this hugely increased supply of money bidding for goods, wholesale prices at the end of 1963 had increased 138 per cent above those at the end of 1939. In the same period the cost of living, as measured by the retail prices paid by consumers, had increased 122 per cent. In other words, the purchasing power of the dollar fell to less than half of what it was in 1939.

When we consider the extent of this increase in the money supply, it is surprising that prices have not risen even further. One reason why they haven't is that the supply of goods in the meanwhile has also been increased. Industrial production at the end of 1963 was running at a rate of about 233 per cent greater than in 1939. While the supply of money has quadrupled, the rate of output of industrial goods has more than tripled.

Let us try to see what inflation is, what it does, and what its continuance may mean to us.

"Inflation" is not a scientific term. It is very loosely used, not only by most of us in ordinary conversation, but even by many professional economists. It is used with at least four different meanings:

1. Any increase at all in the supply of money (and credit).

2. An increase in the supply of money that outruns the increase in the supply of goods.

3. An increase in the average level of *prices*.

4. Any prosperity or boom.

Let us here use the word in a sense that can be widely understood and at the same time cause a minimum of intellectual confusion. This seems to me to be meaning 2.

Inflation is an increase in the supply of money that outruns the increase in the supply of goods.

There are some technical objections to this (as indicated in Chapter 23), but there are even more serious objections to any of the other three senses. Meaning 1, for example, is precise, but runs counter to all common usage. Meanings 3 and 4, though they do conform with common usage, lead, as we shall see, to serious confusion.

Whenever the supply of money increases faster than the supply of goods, prices go up. This is practically inevitable. Whenever the quantity of anything whatever increases, the value of any single unit of it falls. If this year's wheat crop is twice as great as last year's, the price of a bushel of wheat drops violently compared with last year. Similarly, the more the money supply increases, the more the purchasing power of a single unit declines. In Great Britain, for example, the supply of money increased some 226 per cent between 1937 and the end of 1957; at the same time the cost of living increased 166 per cent. In France, the money supply increased about thirty-six times between 1937 and the end of 1957; the cost of living in France, in the same period, went up about twenty-six times.

The rise of prices, which is merely a *consequence* of the inflation, is commonly talked of as if it were *itself* the inflation. This mistaken identification leads many people to overlook the real cause of the inflation—the increase in the money supply—and to think that the inflation can be halted by the imposition of government price-and-wage controls, even while the supply of money continues to increase. Under such conditions, however, government price-and-wage fixing only discourages, distorts, and disrupts production, *without* curing the inflation.

It is sometimes thought that it is "war" that is responsible for all inflations. But a great part of the present inflations in France, Italy, Great Britain, and the United States have occurred *since* the end of World War II. The American cost of living, for example, has gone up 72 per cent since 1945. And some of the most spectacular recent inflations have occurred in countries relatively untouched by the war. Between 1950 and the end of 1959, the money supply in Chile increased nineteen times, and the cost of living there increased twenty times. In Bolivia, between 1950 and 1959, the money supply was increased seventy times, and the cost of living there increased a hundred times. Similar records could be cited for other countries.

Thus we see that the connection between the increase in the supply of money and the rise in prices is extremely close. All the great inflations of earlier and modern times have been primarily the result of reckless deficit financing on the part of governments, which wanted to spend far more than they had the courage or ability to collect in taxes. They paid for the difference by printing paper money.

Most present-day governments are ashamed to pay their bills directly by printing money, so they have developed more sophisticated and roundabout ways of doing the same thing. Typically, they "sell" their interest-bearing securities to the central bank. The central bank then creates a "deposit" in their favor for the face value of the government securities, and the government draws checks against this "deposit." But all this leads in the end to the same result as printing new money directly.

We are often told, however, that we have in America today a "new" kind of inflation, caused by labor unions forcing constant wage increases. This contention contains a political truth but is misleading economically.

Suppose that unions were able to force up their wage-rates, but that the management of currency and bank credit were such that there was no increase in the total money supply. Then the higher wage-rates would either wipe out profit margins, or they would force manufacturers to raise prices to preserve profit margins. If the higher wage-rates wiped out employers' profits, they would lead directly to unemployment. If they forced a rise in prices, and if consumers had no more money to spend than before, consumers would buy fewer goods. The result would be smaller sales and hence less production and less employment.

An increase in wage-rates, in short, without at least a compensating increase in the money supply, would simply lead to unemployment. But very few governments have the courage to sit tight on the money supply and get the blame for the resulting unemployment. They prefer, instead, to try to make the constantly higher wage-rates payable by constantly increasing the money supply. In this way the rise in wage-rates has *politically* led to the continuance of many inflations.

But there is more than one reason why inflation, in spite of all the righteous lip-indignation it calls forth, is not only tolerated by the majority of us over long periods, but actively supported by special pressure groups.

The first of these reasons is "the money illusion." We are so accustomed to measuring our incomes and our economic welfare in purely monetary terms that we cannot break ourselves of the habit. Since 1939 the cost of living in the United States has a little more than doubled. This means that a man whose income after taxes has gone up from $5,000 in 1939 to $10,000 now is no better off, in the things he can buy with his income, than he was in 1939.

He is, in fact, definitely worse off. A study by the National Industrial Conference Board, allowing not only for higher prices but for the higher income-tax bite in the later year, estimated that a man required a gross income of $12,307 in 1960 in order to enjoy a purchasing power equal to that of $5,000 in 1939. His gross money-income had to increase still more as he got into the higher income-tax brackets. It took a gross income of $26,030 in 1960 to give him a purchasing power equal to that of $10,000 in 1939 and a gross income of $77,415 to give him a purchasing power equal to $25,000 in 1939.

A man whose dollar-income has risen from $5,000 in 1939 to only $7,500 today, after taxes, is definitely worse off. Yet so strong and persistent is the money illusion that millions of people who are worse off in terms of the real purchasing power of their incomes probably imagine themselves to be better off because their dollar income is so much higher.

The money illusion will often be found together with what we may call the special-case illusion. This is the belief that the reason my own money-income has gone up in the last five, ten, or twenty years is that I have been personally very lucky or very talented, whereas the reason the prices I have to pay have gone up is just "inflation." I do not understand the inflation process, however, until I understand that the same forces which have pushed up the prices of what other people have to sell (including their labor services) have pushed up the price of what I personally have to sell. Looking at the matter from the other side, the same general forces which have raised my own income have also raised other people's incomes.

Yet the special-case illusion is not *entirely* an illusion. Here we come to one of the main reasons for the political pressure behind inflation. At the beginning we imagined inflation occurring as the result of a simultaneous miracle by which every family awakened to find its money supply quadrupled overnight. Of course no such miracle happens in real life. No actual inflation happens by a simultaneous or proportional increase in everybody's money supply or money income. No actual inflation affects every person and every price equally and at the same time. On the contrary, every inflation affects different persons and different prices *unequally* and at *different* times.

A typical war inflation, for example, starts when the government uses newly created money to pay armament contractors. First, the profits of the armament contractors increase. Next, they employ more workers, and they raise the wages they pay in order to get and hold more workers. Next, the tradespeople that cater to the armament company owners and employes increase *their* sales. And so on, in widening circles.

In the same way, in a "pump-priming" inflation, brought about by a great public works program or housing program, the first group to benefit are the construction companies, the second the construction workers, the third the tradespeople and others who directly cater to the construction workers—and so on.

Inflation always benefits some groups of the population before it benefits other groups, and more than it benefits other groups. And in most cases it benefits these first groups *at the direct expense* of the other groups.

Suppose, to make an extreme simplification, that one-half of the population has its dollar-income and the prices of its goods or services doubled, while the other half still retains the same dollar-income and can only get the same dollar-prices for its goods. The average prices received by the first half will go from 100 to 200. The average prices received by the second half will remain at 100. This means that the average price of *all* goods will now be 150, or 50 per cent higher than before. The first half of the population will then be about a third better off than before, though not twice as well off, even though its dollar-income has doubled. The second half of the population, though its dollar-income has remained the same, will be able to buy only two-thirds as much goods and services.

In any actual inflation, of course, the relative gains and losses will not be thus neatly split between just two distinct halves of the population; they will vary with every group and even, to some extent, with every family. Yet it will remain true that the losers from an inflation will probably be about equal in numbers to the gainers, even though the money illusion hides this from many of the losers.

The fact that there are always those who can relatively profit from an inflation, while it is going on, even though they do it at the expense of the rest of the community, helps to keep up the political pressure for the continuance of inflation.

The losers from an inflation, if they could always identify themselves and make themselves heard, could more than offset in their political strength the forces that temporarily profit from inflation.

Who are the losers? It is customary to identify them as savings bank depositors, holders of government bonds, elderly retired people or widows living on fixed pensions, insurance-policy holders, teachers and similar white-collar workers. The losers from inflation do include all of these, but they include many more.

Have you personally profited from inflation, or are you one of its victims?

Here is a simple way to find out. In the table following, the first column of figures is based on the U.S. Government's Consumer Price Index. For simplicity of calculation this figure has been converted to a base of 100 for 1939. The second column is based on the government's estimate of the per capita "disposable" income (i.e., income after deduction for taxes) in each year. This also has been converted to a base of 100 for the year 1939.

The first thing you want to find out is whether you are better or worse off *absolutely* than in some earlier year. Put down what your take-home pay was in any chosen past year in the table, add two zeros to it, and divide by the cost-of-living figure for that year. Then take your present take-home pay, add two zeros, and divide the result by the last figure in the column.

If your present income (so recalculated) is greater than your income so recalculated from the past year, then your *real* income has increased. Otherwise you have lost.

Let us take an illustration. Your take-home pay in 1963, say, was $5,000 a year. In 1939 it was $2,500. As you both multiply and divide your 1939 income by 100, it remains at the same figure—$2,500. But you multiply, say, your 1963 income by 100 and divide by 220. This leaves you with only $2,270 of "real" income (i.e., in 1939 dollars) in 1963. Your income in terms of what it would buy, therefore, was lower than it was in 1939.

Suppose, now, you are interested in knowing not only whether you are better or worse off now than in some preceding year in what you can buy with your income, but whether you have done better or worse than the average American in the same period. In a progressive economy like ours, not only total production, and hence total real income, but per-capita production and hence per-capita real income, tend to increase year by year, as capital investment increases and machinery and techniques improve. But the income of

| | 1939 average=100 | |
Year	Cost of Living*	Per Capita $ Income**
1939 100		100
1944 127		197
1945 130		200
1946 140		209
1947 161		218
1948 173		238
1949 171		234
1950 173		253
1951 187		272
1952 191		281
1953 193		291
1954 193		291
1955 193		304
1956 196		318
1957 202		326
1958 208		339
1959 210		352
1960 213		361
1961 215		369
1962 218		384
1963 220		396

* Source: U.S. Government Consumer Price Index, as converted from 1957-59 base.
** Source: U.S. Government estimate of per capita disposable personal income in dollars. From table on p. 227 Economic Report of the President, January, 1964. Converted to 1939 base.

some persons has increased much more than that of others. This is partly because, either through ability or good fortune, they hold better positions than formerly; but it may also be because inflation typically benefits some groups at the expense of other groups. As you will notice, unless your dollar income over the last two decades has increased *more* than enough to compensate merely for the increase in living costs in the period, you have not shared proportionately in the increase in the nation's real output.

If you wish to get a closer idea of how you made out relatively to others, you can make the same sort of recalculation of your income in the second column as you made in the first. In this recalculation, however, you would have to take more factors into account (such as full family income, after taxes, relative number of persons in the family in the years compared, etc.). And just how much the operations of inflation can be held responsible for whatever the comparison turns out to be, it is impossible to say without a full knowledge of each individual case. But many a person who thinks he has been one of the special beneficiaries of inflation may sharply revise his ideas after such a calculation.

We have still to look at the strongest reason of all why inflation has such powerful political appeal. This is the conviction that it is necessary to maintain "full employment."

Under special conditions inflation can, it is true, have this effect. If, following a boom, maladjustments of various kinds have caused a collapse of demand and of prices, while labor union leaders have refused to accept any compensating cuts in wage-rates, there will of course be unemployment. In such a case a new dose of inflation may raise monetary purchasing power to a point where the old volume of goods will once more be bought at the old price level, and employment may then be restored at the old money-wage level.

But the restoration of full employment could have been brought about just as well if the powerful unions had merely accepted the necessary wage-rate reductions. This would have involved no real sacrifice, because, as prices had collapsed, the cut in wage-rates would merely need to have been great enough to keep the same relative *real* wage-rates (i.e., wage-rates in terms of purchasing-power) as before.

Nor, to restore full employment under such conditions, would it be necessary to put into effect any *general* or *uniform* cut in wage-rates. Only those wage-rates would have to be cut that had got out of equilibrium and were causing log-jams in the economy.

Moreover, even if we inject greater and greater doses of monetary inflation, and union demands are such that wage-rates continue to run ahead of prices, then though we will certainly have inflation and higher prices, we will not cure the unemployment.

If we continue to try to solve our difficulties by continued fresh doses of monetary inflation, what will be the upshot? Prices will certainly rise further. But this rise of prices will not guarantee the restoration of full employment. The latter, as we have seen, depends on a generally balanced economic situation, and particularly on the proper relationship between prices and wage-rates.

A serious or long-continued inflation is always in danger of getting out of control. Those who naïvely imagine that our monetary managers, or any other group, know any formula by which we could maintain a predetermined "creeping inflation," with prices rising just 2 or 3 per cent a year, are entirely mistaken. Even if it were not extremely difficult to control exactly the supply of money and credit, there is no assurance whatever that a given percentage of expansion of the money supply from year to year will bring a merely proportional price rise each year. On the contrary, the very knowledge of the existence of such a planned inflation would undermine confidence in the value of the dollar. It would bring a racing inflation immediately that could quickly get out of hand.

Whenever any inflation gets beyond a critical point (which can never be known in advance), the social losses and evils it brings about are certain to cancel and exceed any initial gains. Holders of bonds or saving deposits at last become aware that the capital value of their savings is shrinking all the time in terms of what it will buy. This awareness discourages thrift and savings. The whole structure of production becomes distorted. Businessmen and corporations are deceived by the way inflation falsifies their books. Their inventory profits are illusory. Their depreciation deductions are inadequate. It becomes impossible for business managers to know to what extent their paper profits are real. But these profits often *look* bigger and bigger on paper. They provoke charges of "profiteering." Demagogues use them to inflame class hatreds against business.

Inflation makes it possible for some people to get rich by speculation and windfall instead of by hard work. It rewards gambling and penalizes thrift. It conceals and encourages waste and inefficiency in production. It finally tends to demoralize the whole community. It promotes speculation, gambling, squandering, luxury, envy, resentment, discontent, corruption, crime, and increasing drift toward more intervention which may end in dictatorship.

How long will inflation continue? How far will it go?

No one has a sure answer to such questions. The answer is in the hands of the American people. Yet inflation is not necessary and it is never inevitable. The choice between chaos and stability is still ours to make.

THE
GREAT
INTERLUDE

Neglected Events
and Persons from the
First World War to
the Depression

by Francis Russell

Für Karin im Osten
und Irmhild im Westen

Library of Congress Catalog Card Number: 63-22157

Contents

The Strike that Made a President

IF IT HAD NOT BEEN for the Boston Police Strike of September, 1919, Calvin Coolidge would no doubt have ended as just another in the succession of Republican governors of Massachusetts, his name no more remembered than that of his predecessor, Samuel McCall, or Channing Cox, who succeeded him. But that particular set of curious chances made him known all over America. From the blurred perspective of the rest of the country he seemed a courageous Yankee figure of the minuteman stamp who had defied and defeated the violence that had threatened the seventh city of the United States.

For two days Boston's urban core with its more than 700,000 inhabitants was without police protection, and the mob ruled the streets. The city had seen nothing like it even in the draft riots of the Civil War. To find a parallel the historian would have had to go back to Sam Adams' Mohawks. Ordinary Bostonians did not reckon so far. They were shocked by this savagery and dismayed in sensing how thin was the veneer of legal forms by which they had ordered their lives. Conservatives like Henry Cabot Lodge saw the strike as a first step toward sovietizing the country.

The striking policemen, who by descent were for the most part Catholic Irish, would have been astonished at any such notion. They were ordinary Americans with a grievance so engrossing that they gave little thought to the consequences. In the larger analysis, the strike was part of the general pattern of industrial unrest that accompanied the dislocations of the postwar period. Nineteen-nineteen was a year of strikes—the great steel strike, the Seattle general strike, railway and transit strikes, a coal strike, longshoremen's strikes, strikes of actors in New York, even a buyers' strike. Their immediate cause was inflation: the failure of wages to keep up with what was then known as the High Cost of Living. The more underlying cause was, however, that sense of restlessness that runs through every society in the anticlimax following the artificial unity of a war.

As for the policemen's grievances, they were real enough. In spite of a small raise, their minimum pay was still only $1,100 a year—less than half of what many a war worker had been earning—out of which they had to buy their uniforms. Beyond the question of pay there was the even larger grievance of the two-platoon system that kept them on twelve-hour shifts. Station houses were old, crowded, and dirty. To the ordinary Boston patrolman a union seemed the answer. The police in thirty-seven other American cities already had unions.

The Boston Police Strike was not unique. That same year over a thousand London policemen struck, and in Liverpool there was a strike almost as large. Many police strikes before and since then have been passed over or forgotten. In Boston, though, there was no one to replace the police when they struck. That the city was left without protection was due directly to Police Commissioner Curtis. Indirectly, Mayor Peters and Governor Coolidge shared the responsibility. Ironically enough, Coolidge, who did the least, received the final credit for doing everything.

Twenty-four years before becoming Police Commissioner, Edwin U. Curtis had been, at the age of thirty-four, the youngest mayor that the city of Boston ever had. He came from an established and wealthy family, and he felt that in taking public office again he was doing his duty to the community and to his country. His position as commissioner was anomalous. A generation before, when he was mayor, the old-line Bostonians still controlled the city they considered theirs by inheritance. But even then they were being pushed by the Irish offspring of the Famine years. When it became obvious that Irish Democrats would take over Boston politically, the Republican State Legislature engineered a law to place the appointment of the Boston police commissioner in the hands of the governor. Thus the Jim Curleys might possess City Hall, but they would not be able to get their fingers on the Police Department.

Curtis, in his middle age, had become an autocratic Puritan with supercilious eyes and a puffy, disdainful face. His attitude toward the police was that of a general toward his troops. They were "his" men, and in the hierarchy of command his orders were to be obeyed cheerfully and without question. At the core of Curtis' unbending self was a sense of insecurity. The Boston in which he had grown up, the class to which he belonged were being superseded. His class had governed Boston since the Revolution. Now it was being steamrollered by the second-generation Irish. Curtis despised and feared this new emerging group with its alien religion and its eye for political plunder. In his heart he was convinced that Boston would never again be a decent city until the ephemeral Honey Fitzes and Jim Curleys and Dan Coakleys had been replaced by Curtises. That was why, in the period of Boston's decline, he accepted the office of police commissioner from Governor McCall.

During the early summer months of 1919 the policemen began organizing themselves into an unofficial union, the Boston Social Club. Curtis countered with a general order stating that a police officer could not consistently belong to a union and perform his sworn duty. In spite of this warning the Boston Social Club applied for a charter from the American Federation of Labor.

Curtis at once announced the addition to his department rules and regulations that of Rule 35: "No members of the force shall join or belong to any organization, club or body outside the department."

On August 11, the American Federation of Labor granted a charter to the Social Club as Boston Police Union, No. 16807. Curtis then charged the eight leaders and officers of the new union with insubordination and ordered them placed on trial. The union countered by warning him that if these men were disciplined the police would strike. The union also maintained that

Curtis' regulation was "invalid, unreasonable and contrary to the express law of Massachusetts." Curtis found the men guilty but postponed sentence. On August 29, he found eleven more leaders guilty but again suspended sentence —as he later said—to give the men a chance to withdraw from the Federation. He then announced that he would pass sentence on September 4. This was the impasse at the end of August.

No one was more distressed at the prospect of a police strike than the Mayor of Boston, Andrew J. Peters. By nature, Peters was a more conciliatory type than the Commissioner. In addition, he belonged to the same political party as the policemen. He was that rarity, a Yankee Democrat. Here and there they were to be found in Massachusetts, of Colonial descent, of inherited wealth, Harvard-educated, and yet by some twist of family allegiance standing outside the old Bay State Federalist tradition. President emeritus Charles W. Eliot of Harvard was such a Democrat, as were the Russells of Cambridge, Winslow Warren, the President of the Cincinnati and descendant of the Bunker Hill general; and ex-Governor Eugene Foss.

Peters was an interim mayor between the first and second administrations of the flamboyant James Michael Curley. He had been elected with the help of the Good Government Association—Goo-goos to Jim Curley—while Curley and Congressman James Gallivan were at each other's political throats.

To the more optimistic old Bostonians, Peters had seemed a sign of the city's redemption. The new mayor was in the *Social Register*. He was wealthy enough to be personally honest, he was conciliatory as befitted a Democrat, but his dominant quality was ineffectuality. In Woodrow Wilson's first administration he had served casually as Assistant Secretary of the Treasury. In Boston he was lost. While he sat in the mayor's office, bagmen did business in the anterooms and greenbacks were passed routinely in the corridors. Under the rule of Mayor John F. "Honey Fitz" Fitzgerald contractors had a habit of charging the city for each side of a granite paving block. Under Peters they sold the foundations of City Hall.

Peters resembled an aberrant Scot more than a Yankee. He had a domed forehead fringed by rufous hair that gave him the spurious look of a thinker, and curiously tufted, almost Mephistophelian eyebrows. He spoke in a high voice with a precise, exaggerated Harvard accent.

Politics was an avocation rather than a vocation with him. He preferred golf and yachting to long hours at his desk. Somehow he was able to shut both his mind and his eyes to the corruption of his administration. He gave the impression of an easy, superficial man, inclined to bore. Yet beneath his brownstone exterior was a perverse personality, unrecognized at the time and only to come to vague light long afterward.*

With dazed impotence Peters watched the August days recede. The threat of the coming strike was too much for him, and like other weak men in a crisis he looked for some way to shift responsibility. The safest and easiest

---

* For years Peters maintained a Lolita-like relationship with an eleven-year-old playmate of his children. See Morris Markey's "The Mysterious Death of Starr Faithfull" in Isabel Leighton's The Aspirin Age, Simon & Shuster, 1949.

way was, as always, to appoint a committee. So in the last week of the month the Mayor named a Citizens' Committee of Thirty-four to investigate and advise on the situation in the Police Department. The committee was made up of old Bostonians with a lacing of others that included several wealthy Irish and Jewish merchants. It was headed by James J. Storrow of the ultraconservative firm of Lee, Higginson & Company, that somewhat over a decade later was to go to the wall following Ivar Kreuger's suicide.

At the outset the committee opposed the police affiliation with the American Federation of Labor. Except for this they felt a compromise could be worked out, if Curtis did not force the issue. From August 29 to September 2 they met daily with the president and leaders of the Police Union. But the chief obstacle to any settlement was the Commissioner whose adamant personality stiffened the intransigence of the police.

On Wednesday, September 3, the Commissioner refused Storrow's request for a few days' delay in passing sentence, but, when Peters asked formally for a postponement, Curtis finally agreed to put off his decision until the following Monday.

Meanwhile Governor Coolidge sat aloof in his State House office two hundred yards from City Hall. At this point, as Claude Fuess in his definitive life of Coolidge admits, "a single word from him [Coolidge] would probably have led to a compromise, but that word he would not utter."

William Allen White in his *A Puritan in Babylon* tells the story of Calvin Coolidge as a student at Black River Academy. Calvin was in bed one evening in the dormitory while several other boys of a more prankish disposition pitched an old stove downstairs. He remained in bed. When one of the masters asked him next day if he had not heard the noise, he said that he had. When the master asked further why he had not done anything, he replied, "It wa'n't my stove." The looming police strike "wa'n't" his strike: The Commissioner and the Mayor should resolve it as best they could. Since he had not appointed Curtis, he felt no responsibility for him. If a strike should occur it was up to them to safeguard the city. The attempts of the Committee of Thirty-four to get Coolidge to intervene were in vain. As events moved to their climax over that first weekend in September, the Governor left for the western part of the state. No one in Boston knew where he was. He made sure of that.

"Coolidge ran away," my father used to say. "He got scared and cleared out. Just what we expected, but afterward they made a hero of him." At the time my father was in the Massachusetts House of Representatives. Like most of those who came in such close contact with Coolidge, he did not like him. "The laziest man who was ever governor of Massachusetts," my father maintained. "He'd sit in his office mornings with his feet on the desk reading the *Herald* and smoking a cigar. In the afternoon he used to take naps." My mother, meeting Coolidge at the annual reception for legislators and their wives, said that shaking hands with the Governor was like shaking hands with a codfish.

Calvin Coolidge was the product of the Republican escalator system that worked for decades with great smoothness until the depression years destroyed its mechanism. Up the escalator went the more astute and adaptable local politicians under the benevolent surveillance of Boss Murray Crane and the general staff of the Republican State Committee. Coolidge in his typical career went on from mayor of Northampton to become a state representative, state senator, president of the Senate, lieutenant governor, and then governor. Though patricians like Henry Cabot Lodge might be scornful of his bucolicisms, his nasal Vermont accent, and his two-family house on Massasoit Street in Northhampton, Coolidge meshed into the machine. After two one-year terms as governor he could look forward to the sinecure reward of a directorship in some life insurance company or the peace of the First National Bank.

Such were the inducements for those who stayed in line. For those who did not, there was arctic isolation. My father, though a regular Republican, had his maverick side. He once ran for the State Senate before the Republican hierarchy gave him the nod. And he was defeated. Though subsequently he was elected to several additional terms as representative, the escalator entrance was henceforth barred to him. He might sit in the House, but he would never again be appointed to so much as a committee on fish hatcheries. His political career was over.

Storrow and the members of the Citizens' Committee spent a baffling weekend trying to locate the Governor. They themselves wanted no open break with the police. Their compromise plan, approved by Mayor Peters, would have allowed an unaffiliated union. If the men would call off their strike there would be no disciplinary action taken against the leaders, and the various other grievances would be submitted to an impartial board. The counsel for the union urged them to accept. If the Governor and the Commissioner had agreed, the plan would undoubtedly have been accepted by the police. Curtis declined to accept any solution "that might be construed as a pardon of the men on trial." On Monday morning he suspended the nineteen police leaders.

Peters, as fluttery and ineffectual as ever, scurried about trying to find some last-minute solution, although by now he was convinced that the strike was unavoidable. As mayor he had the right in an emergency to call out the units of the State Guard stationed within the Boston area. Characteristically, he was not aware of this.

Coolidge returned suddenly to his office on Monday afternoon in a testy mood at about the same time that the police were voting 1134-2 to strike. The strike was set for the following day at five o'clock. Monday evening Coolidge had dinner with Storrow, Peters, and several members of the Citizens' Committee in a private room of the Union Club. Before the dinner, Storrow and Peters begged him to sponsor the compromise plan as the last hope of averting the strike. He refused. Finally they asked him to mobilize three or four thousand troops of the State Guard. He maintained that the situation could be left safely in Curtis' hands. Curtis was still convinced that the majority of the police would remain loyal to him.

Meanwhile, after a series of calls from Peters, the adjutant general, Jesse Stevens, decided that a certain amount of preparation might be wise after all and sent out verbal orders for the first—and only—mounted squadron of the State Guard to assemble at the Commonwealth Armory. Not until several hours after the Union Club dinner did Coolidge learn of this minor mobilization. Knowing by politician's instinct that to call out the militia prematurely is political suicide, he called Curtis and started at once for the armory, his anger glowing through his pinched features.

With a pale and silent Curtis just behind him, Coolidge strode through the armory arch. A hundred or so troopers were standing about on the lower floor with their newly drawn equipment. They stared in surprise as the irate Governor quacked at their commanding officer, Major Dana Gallup: "Who told you people to come here? Go on home!" With that he stalked petulantly up the stairs to the orderly room, followed by Gallup and Curtis.

Then occurred one of the dramatic (and so far unrecorded) minor episodes of the stirke. Peters, repulsed and desperate, had set out in pursuit of the evasive Coolidge. Ten minutes after the latter had arrived, the rumpled and excited Mayor burst through the armory door demanding to see the Governor, at the very moment that Coolidge was coming down the stairs. The two men faced each other, Peters stammering accusations until Coolidge cut him short with a waspish, "You have no business here!" At that, Peters made a rush for him, swinging his arms wildly and somehow landing a punch square on the Governor's left eye. Coolidge did not attempt to strike back nor did he make any move to retreat, but merely leaned against the balustrade with his hand to his face. Troopers at once seized the gesticulating Mayor. It was fortunate for the Governor that he was not called on to make any public appearances that week, for those who saw him could not fail to notice his shiner.

Peters, Curtis, and Coolidge were all at their desks on Tuesday morning. At one o'clock in the afternoon the Mayor called the Commissioner who assured him he had ample means to protect the city. Four hours later the three key figures held a last acid conference. To Peters' renewed plea to call out the State Guard, Coolidge ironically informed him of the mayor's powers within the Boston limits. Curtis insisted he did not need the State Guard. "I am ready for anything," he told the Governor.

Of the 1544 men in the Boston Police Department, 1117 went out on strike. There was no authority on hand to replace them. Although a force of citizen volunteers had been enrolling in the preceding weeks, the Commissioner did not use them. Years later, Coolidge wrote in his autobiography that he felt afterward he should have called out the State Guard as soon as the police left their posts. "The Commissioner," he added as an apologia "did not feel that this was necessary." Peters, faced with a sudden decision, could not bring himself to call out the local guard. The strike was left to follow its own pattern.

As the police left the station houses, still in uniform but minus their badges, they were cheered by some, and a few furtive adolescents crept up to throw mud against the station doors. At first nothing more happened. Then in the twilight little groups began to start dice games all over Boston Common. Seen from the top of Beacon Hill, they looked like mushrooms springing up on the slope by the Frog Pond as they formed circles to shoot craps under the shadow of the State House. It was harmless enough at first, a naïve gesture against authority. But with the darkness crowds began to gather on the other side of Beacon Hill in the vicinity of Scollay Square with its honky-tonks and flop-houses. For some time they milled about restlessly, as yet uncertain, waiting only for that unifying act of violence that would turn them into a mob. Then it happened. As with all such events no one could be quite sure afterward how it started—a broken store front, an overturned truck, a woman's scream, and the mob was off.

The Boston mob that first night was truculent but aimless. Around Scollay Square plate-glass windows were smashed and stores looted. Pedestrians had their hats knocked off, there were holdups here and there in open view, and later in the evening several women were dragged into doorways and assaulted. Some of the streetcar lines were blocked with mattresses and railroad ties. In the Celtic matrix of South Boston an unfocused rowdyism swaggered and held to such japes as stoning the empty police stations and pulling the trolleys off the wires. But there was a sinister air about the carnival of those streets that made respectable middle-class observers think back uneasily to *A Tale of Two Cities*, read long ago in school. For a few moments the lid was off their stratified social structure, and the glimpse they had of what lay underneath was cold and cruel, something they did not like to think about.

Tuesday night Peters vanished as effectively as had Coolidge over the weekend. Then late Wednesday morning he finally called out the State Guard in Boston, and before the end of the afternoon the guardsmen were patrolling the streets. Peters then issued a statement to the press, remarking plaintively that in this crisis he had "received no co-operation from the Police Commissioner and no help or practical suggestions from the Governor." Now, with the authority he claimed he had found under an old statute, he removed Curtis and began calling up citizen volunteers.

During the day the city remained quiet, but in the evening the mob gathered again, a harder and more menacing mob than the night before, many of its members armed, and reinforced by professional criminals who had been heading toward Boston all the afternoon. Striking policemen moved through the crowd, encouraging the more violent. Behind the closed doors of the banks and the larger stores, blocked off now by barbed wire, employees stood ready with pistols and rifles. In Scollay Square, at the center of the disorders, steel-helmeted guardsmen advancing across the cobbles with fixed bayonets were showered with bricks, stones, and bottles. Not far from the site of the eighteenth-century Boston Massacre, they finally opened fire on their assailants, killing three. Near Cornhill four Harvard undergraduates, acting as volunteer patrolmen, were almost lynched. On the other side of Beacon Hill several guard companies cleared the Common in a flanking movement, rounding up the surly groups still gathered there. Somehow a sailor was killed in the scuffle. Two other men were killed in South Boston. After that the mob melted away.

The Citizens' Committee reported that "by Thursday morning order had generally been restored in the city." The strike was broken. During this interval Coolidge had been consulting with Murray Crane and the Republican elders, all of whom felt it was now time to take a stand. So, nettled by the Mayor's statement and by the removal of the Commissioner, Coolidge belatedly acted. By executive order he called out all the State Guard and assumed full control over the Boston Police Department, instructing Curtis to resume his post at once.

After the rioting the strike overshadowed other news, capturing the headlines and alarming newspaper readers all over the country. By the time it had made its full impact Coolidge had taken over. Out of what seemed to the rest of America a chaotic situation a man had emerged. At once this Yankee governor with the dour expression became a national figure. His pictures papered the land. Even President Wilson sent him a letter of congratulation. And when the Governor replied to President Gompers of the AF of L who had asked for reinstatement of the strikers, he provided a slogan with the copybook phrase: "There is no right to strike against the public safety by anybody, anywhere, any time." Whatever Peters and the members of the committee might think, he became in the words of the Boston *Herald*, "the pilot that weathered the storm."

To those businessmen who as volunteers received badge and revolver from the downtown police stations, the strike was an adventure. For once again, if briefly, the old Bostonians had achieved physical control of their city. As one leafs through the old newspaper files one sees them in faded rotogravure, smiling, self-assured faces, the younger men dressed in trench-coats copied from the war-time British officers. Here and there one finds a sterner note: some Beacon Hill relic of the Civil War days patrolling the financial district with golf cap and night stick. Ex-Harvard athletes-turned-broker are abundant.

My father became a special policeman in Dorchester, but Dorchester Hill where we lived was as placid during the strike as before. Blue Hill Avenue and the Dorchester streets below us were equally calm. It was probably quite a disappointment to my father. His single adventure was in commandeering a private automobile to chase a suspicious character who had been observed boarding a streetcar at Mattapan Square. The character was suspicious because he was foreign-looking and had tried to change a ten-dollar bill at McHugh's drugstore. However, he turned out to be merely an Italian workman, and the bill all that was left of his week's pay.

One of my father's fixed beliefs was that he had a natural talent for things military, a talent under which he now subsumed police work. For several days he directed traffic at the corner of Morton Street and Blue Hill Avenue, the busiest intersection between Franklin Park and Mattapan Square. In those days there were only about a twentieth as many cars on the road as today, but somehow each morning my father managed to create a traffic jam of dimensions previously unknown in Dorchester and not to be seen again until the introduction of traffic lights. He maintained that the tie-up was caused by all the drivers coming in town after the strike, and that no regular policeman could have managed better. Whatever the jam, he enjoyed himself thoroughly.

Badge, revolver, whistle, and white gloves were authoritative symbols that made his law office seem tame when he went back to it a week later.

To my father the police strike was a kind of compensation for not having served in two wars. The World War found him in his late thirties with a wife and two children, and he had to content himself with the second-best of serving in the legislature and being on the Mattapan Legal Advisory Board. Twenty years before, as a boy of seventeen, he had stood in line with my Uncle Charlie at the outbreak of the Spanish-American War to join the Roxbury Horse Guards for service in Cuba. However, somebody tipped off my grandfather in his South Boston office and he whipped down in his buggy to pick up the two of them before they reached the recruiting sergeant's desk. My father never did wear a uniform. The Boston Police Strike was the closest he ever came to being on active service. I expect he regretted that he was not in Scollay Square that second night.

Before the strike, the police of Boston still wore dome-shaped helmets like the English police. They also wore high-necked frock coats above which protruded the ends of a wing collar. With their leather outer belts and long wooden night-sticks they resembled the old Keystone cops.

The only policeman I knew by sight was Mr. Fitzgibbons. His daughter Susy was in our fourth-grade room. Susy was a bright, aggressive little girl who wore paper hair-ribbons, could write in Palmer Method without making blots, and got double promotions. As I look back now at our old fourth-grade picture I can see that she was the most attractive one of our group, but I did not think so then. She was the oldest of seven children.

The Fitzgibbonses lived in a square little two-and-a-half story house down the street from the Martha Baker School. They were all neat, well-behaved children, and though they went to St. Angela's, not like those tough shanty Irish who lived on Mulvey Street. Mrs. Fitzgibbons belonged to the Mothers' Club. There were such a lot of Fitzgibbonses that they used to have benches along the dining room table instead of chairs. People like my mother were dubious about so many children, but they thought Mrs. Fitzgibbons was a wonderful manager.

I can remember Mr. Fitzgibbons coming up over the Hill on the way home from the station, a tall, striding figure in his gray helmet and blue coat with the shining badge and buttons. Even the Mulvey Streeters, who used to yell "Cheese it, the cop!" when they saw other policemen, were quiet when he went by. No one would have dared to challenge his presence. Mr. Fitzgibbons, that proud and handsome man, walking up the street with the sun shining on his helmet, saluting Miss Sykes, the head teacher, as he passed with courtly reserve, was the Law. But on that Tuesday afternoon he went on strike with the others. "If I hadn't been in my last month, I'd have seen that Mike never walked out," Mrs. Fitzgibbons told my mother afterward.

On Friday the striking policemen, dismayed by the reaction against them, voted almost unanimously to return to work on the same basis as before the strike. They had counted on organized labor to back them up, but the two days' rioting had made public opinion too hostile. Commissioner Curtis would

have nothing to do with them. He issued an order that none of the striking
policemen would ever be taken back—and none of them ever were. He also
fixed the minimum wage at $1400 a year and began recruiting a new force.

Meanwhile, the volunteers were sent home and all Boston police duties
were carried on by the State Guard. The Guard was a mixture of overage and
underage men who had joined this temporary organization when the Massachusetts National Guard—the Yankee Division—had been called to active
service in 1917. The guardsmen's aspect was ludicrously unmilitary. They
scarcely knew the manual of arms, and they still wore the laced gaiters and felt
campaign hats of the Mexican Border Campaign of 1916, that had been replaced in the AEF by spiral puttees and overseas caps.

To us in the fourth grade, though, they were impressive indeed, soldiers
in the flesh, objects of military might. It was like having Memorial Day every
day in the week to see so many uniforms. The guardsmen carried rifles with
fixed bayonets rather than revolvers, just like the pictures of soldiers in the
war. That Halloween I was chased by a guardsman who caught me shinnying
up the lamppost to put out the gas light in front of the Sands's. As soon as I
saw him I jumped and tried to get away by ducking through the back yards,
but he ran after me and the fear went down into my legs. I still recall my side
glimpse of that looming khaki figure in his wide-brimmed felt hat, his rifle at
port, and the light sparkling on the bayonet as he chased me across lots and
under clothes lines. At each step he took I could hear the slap of the leather
sling against his rifle butt. I was so frightened I wet myself.

By the end of the year Commissioner Curtis had recruited his new police
force, and the brown uniforms of the State Guard disappeared. Governor
Coolidge was re-elected in November by a tremendous majority and there were
whisperings of him as a dark-horse Presidential candidate. "Jack the Giant
Killer," William Allen White called him. The new policemen had different
uniforms. The long coats and wing collars had been discarded. Caps replaced
the helmets. It was the close of an era: the end of the patrolman in his high
helmet walking his beat under the gas lamps past the corner saloon, the beginning of prowl cars and bootleggers.

Even in the fourth grade I could sense the change. I remember one sunny
October afternoon passing the Fitzgibbons' house on the way from school. The
Fitzgibbonses had a tree in their yard that Susy called an umbrella tree. It had
wide leaves almost two feet long and a pink fruit that ripened in the autumn
and looked like a magnolia bud. Most of the leaves had fallen and the yard
behind the clipped privet hedge was buried under with them. One of the
Fitzgibbons children who was too young to go to school yet was gathering the
leaves in his express wagon. Another, still younger, sat on the edge of the curb
in front of the house playing with an old spoon and a gray policeman's helmet.

The Four Mysteries of President Harding

SEVERAL MONTHS before the Republican National Convention of 1920, the Ohio political boss Harry Micajah Daugherty made the offhand prophecy that none of the leading candidates could muster enough votes to win the nomination, and that after the delegates had reached a dead end a group of fifteen party elders would then get together in some smoke-filled hotel room. There, bleary-eyed and perspiring profusely—at about 2:11 in the morning—they would pick the party's candidate, the almost inevitable next President of the United States. That man, Daugherty predicted, would turn out to be his friend and protégé, Senator Warren Gamaliel Harding of Ohio.

Daugherty's prediction proved uncannily accurate. There have been a number of versions of the "fifteen men in a smoke-filled room," and the casual phrase has taken its place in American political folklore as a synonym for cynical electoral manipulation. Yet when Daugherty made it, his remark seemed no more than a politician's quick quip. Harding was still the darkest of dark horses, a scarcely conceivable candidate. As a favorite son he lacked even the complete Ohio delegation.

The outstanding Republican contender was Major General Leonard Wood. If the nomination had been by popular vote rather than through the maneuverings of the convention, he would certainly have been the party's choice for that year. The most that could be said against him was that he stood out too far for the comfort of politicians. As the ailing boss of Pennsylvania, Senator Boies Penrose, put it, they wanted a man in the White House "who would listen."

The convention, the tinsel-familiar quadrennial spectacle, opened in the barnlike, reverberating Chicago Coliseum on Tuesday, the eighth of June. As usual, there were the bunting-decked balconies filled with strident supporters ready to yammer, the rows of folding chairs in the pit below marked off by state placards, the brass band beyond the speakers' platform. This year the band, in a gesture to modernity, played snappy foxtrots as the delegates straggled in.

Then the ritual began: the chaplain prayed; the band shook the balconies with "The Star Spangled Banner," and the rafters hummed with the atonal attempts of the crowd to sing it. As the brass notes faded, the Director of Community Singing of the Republican League of Massachusetts sprang forward and shouted:

"Now give three cheers and a tiger for the greatest country on earth—the United States of America!"

Obediently three hoarse cheers welled up from several thousand throats: "Hurrah for the United States! And a long-tailed T-I-G-E-R!"

Senator Henry Cabot Lodge, aloof, assured, gray-bearded, gray-haired, and dressed in a gray cutaway, took the rostrum as permanent chairman of the convention. With precise, bitter words he denounced Wilson, the League of Nations, and the Democrats. Then for the next three days the Committee on Resolutions wrestled with a party platform sufficiently straddling to appeal to all men, while the delegates steamed and fidgeted. Not until Friday was the way clear for the balloting to begin, and only then in the afternoon, following interminable nominating speeches for obscure vanity candidates.

Wood's principal and implacable opponent was Frank O. Lowden of Illinois, who had served five terms in Congress and later as governor of his state. Among the many dark horses were Calvin Coolidge and Herbert Hoover. On the opening ballot Wood received 287½ votes for Lowden's 211½. Harding had 65½. By the fourth ballot, Wood had reached 314½ with Lowden close behind at 289. But to the astute bosses it was clear that neither could muster the 493 votes needed to win, that the General and the Governor had canceled each other out. Abruptly the frosty Senator Lodge adjourned the convention until the following morning.

That evening an inner group of senators met in the Blackstone Hotel suite of the enigmatic George Harvey. A former Democrat, as associate of J. P. Morgan, he was editor of the *North American Review* and had formerly edited *Harper's Weekly*, and liked to claim he had "made" Wilson President. Later he had turned against Wilson and Wilson's creation, the League of Nations. Harvey was a man of pontifical solemnity who fancied himself as a statesman behind-the-scenes, a president-maker. For this night's work he would become ambassador to Great Britain. Among the others present were Senator Lodge, the future Vice-President, Charles W. Curtis, Senator Frank Brandegee of Connecticut, Senator James Wadsworth of New York, and Pennsylvania's Joseph Grundy. The man they picked would have the bloc votes they controlled fed to him ballot by ballot until with the disintegration of the Wood and Lowden supporters he would stampede the convention. Such was their plan. Their problem was whom to choose.

As the heat-heavy hours wore away through the blue skeins of cigar smoke, various candidates were discussed and discarded. Harding, by a process of elimination, remained. He was after all innocuous, even if he did talk more about the time he used to play the trombone in his hometown band than about the tariff. As Senator Wadsworth remarked, Harding in the White House could be trusted to sign the bills the Senate sent him and not to send the Senate bills to pass. And he looked like a President. At close enough to 2:11 A.M. to make Daugherty seem clairvoyant, Harvey sent for Harding.

Harding at first glance was an impressive figure. His tall, solid body, his dark complexion, contrasting with blue eyes and white hair, gave the appearance of mental and physical vigor. There were some who compared him to a Roman senator—more justly than they realized, for in his features there lurked the same imbedded sensuality found in Roman portrait busts. William

Allen White remembered him as "a handsome dog, a little above medium height, with a swarthy skin, a scathing eye and . . . the harlot's voice of the old-time political orator."

Behind Harding's senatorial façade fluttered the mind and spirit of a banal smalltown editor. But for his grim-jawed wife—whom he, not wholly in affection, called "Duchess"—and the manipulative Daugherty, he would never have given the Presidency a thought. "I found him," Daugherty remarked afterward, "sunning himself, like a turtle on a log, and I pushed him into the water."

When the late summons came from the Blackstone suite, Harding, disheveled and discouraged, had long since lost faith in Daugherty's brash prophecy. Harvey was waiting for him behind his heavy tortoise-shell glasses. "We think you may be nominated tomorrow," he told the stunned Harding, with the urbanity of an undertaker. "Before acting finally, we think you should tell us, on your conscience and before God, whether there is anything that might be brought up against you that would embarrass the party, any impediment that might disqualify you or make you inexpedient either as candidate or as President." Harding asked for a little time to think it over alone. Ten minutes later he came out of the bedroom to say that there was no impediment.

The following morning was sticky and enervating. The delegates were tired and many of them short of funds. On the fifth ballot Harding received 78 votes to 299 for Wood and 303 for Lowden. On the sixth ballot he had climbed to 89 and on the seventh to 105. William Allen White, who as a delegate would go down voting for Wood to the end, saw the emerging pattern and cried out that to nominate Harding would disgrace the Republican party and bring shame to the country. By the ninth ballot Harding led the list with 374½ votes to 249 for Wood. On the tenth ballot—late in the afternoon of the same day, Saturday, June 12, 1920—it was all over.

Though Harvey had relished his solemn catechising of the night before, he had solid reasons then for playing his portentous role, for there had long been ambiguous rumors adrift concerning Harding. Undoubtedly Harvey had heard them. One concerned something very important in politics, indeed in American life—the color of his skin. The other, no less disturbing, raised a "woman question." To these two mysterious stories, two more mysteries would later be added—the manner of his death, and the fate of his private papers. Over forty years later these four mysteries would still remain.

For campaign purposes the new Republican candidate seemed an embodiment of the American success story. He had started out as a poor boy in Marion, Ohio. At the age of nineteen, with a hundred borrowed dollars, he had managed to take over a moribund newspaper, the Marion *Star,* and over the years had built it up into a prosperous daily. Afterward he had been in turn state senator and lieutenant governor, and in 1914 had been elected to the United States Senate. Now the poor boy was to become President.

But the story bore only a nodding acquaintance with reality. Harding was more a creation of his wife than of himself. Florence Kling De Wolfe Harding, five years older than her husband and as dominating as she was lacking in female charm, had been the driving force behind him. Her aggressive qualities, along with her grimly plain features, she had inherited from her father Amos Kling, a self-made real estate operator and banker who had become one of the richest men in town. At the age of nineteen she had defied her father by marrying the flashy Henry De Wolfe whom she had met at a roller-skating rink. The De Wolfes were almost as wealthy as the Klings, but Henry was the family ne'er-do-well, a small-town sport, aimless, a drinker who would in a few more years die of alcholism. After two years he abandoned his wife and her year-old child.

Ten years later, Flossie Kling De Wolfe married Warren Gamaliel Harding, to the profane rage of her father who preferred even a wastrel of good family to a printer of none. Harding at the time of his marriage had been running the *Star* for almost seven years and had managed to make the paper modestly solvent. Flossie now made it a success, as chief of its business side. Without her neither the *Star* nor Harding would ever have amounted to much. For Harding, jovial and indolent, Marion, Ohio, was the world. He never wanted to be more than just one of the boys whose relaxations were the Saturday-night poker session, the brass rail, and the occasional stag party. As editor he wallowed in the shadow rhetoric of small-town pride. No word of his ever reached beyond the boundaries of Ohio. As a United States senator he had been a popular nonentity. "A cheese-paring of a man," Nicholas Murray Butler described him.

At the convention Daugherty played up the poor-boy-to-President myth where it would do the most good; but another story was also in circulation, one that Harvey must have been aware of when he put his ponderous question to Harding. This counter-myth was derived from a crudely printed circular addressed to the "Men and Women of America" and distributed surreptitiously to the delegates. Harding's family tree was the subject of the circular, which set out to demonstrate through various affidavits that "Warren Gamaliel Harding is not a white man. . . . He is not a creole, he is not a mulatto, he is a mestizo."*

The man responsible for the circular was William Estabrook Chancellor, a professor of economics and social sciences at Wooster College, not far from Marion, and formerly Superintendent of Schools in Washington, D.C. Chancellor was of sufficient intellectual attainments to have had educational and historical books published by such reputable houses as Houghton Mifflin and Macmillan, but—although he had nothing against Harding personally—he was obsessed to frenzy over questions of race. Not only did he believe in strict and complete segregation of whites and Negroes, he advocated the latters' disenfranchisement. Harding's nomination, he maintained, was a plot to

---

* *This one obscure sentence in itself could produce an all-day discussion in many parts of the United States. To most Americans, especially Southerners in Louisiana and along the Gulf Coast,* creole *means a white man of whole or partial French or Spanish ancestry, although it is sometimes used elsewhere to indicate a mixed-blood with various racial admixtures and even to mean a native full-blooded Negro, although in that case the proper expression is* creole Negro. Mulatto, *in its first meaning, indicates a person half-Negro and half-white, but also in broader meanings a mixed-blood in general, including, for example, a Negro-Indian.* Mestizo, *more properly a Spanish word, also means a mixed-blood, although not necessarily containing either Negro or white.*

achieve Negro domination in the United States. Between the nomination and the election thousands more of his circulars were printed. Two hundred and fifty thousand of them were seized by Post Office officials in San Francisco alone.

The rumors that Chancellor unleashed across the country were no novelty in Ohio. They had been current concerning Harding's parents long before his birth. Harding's father was George Tryon Harding, who had served as a drummer in the Civil War and afterward had come back to Blooming Grove, Ohio, where he married and took up the trade of veterinarian. Then, switching from animals to humans, he spent several years picking up what medical knowledge he could by assisting the local doctor on his rounds. Finally he went a few terms to a Cleveland homeopathic college and returned a "paper" M.D. Later "Doc" Harding moved his family to the shabby outskirts of Marion, twenty-five miles away. The Hardings were always itinerant and they remained poor—the mother more successful as a midwife than the father as a physician. Warren was the eldest of their eight children.

Gossip both in Blooming Grove and Marion held that the Hardings were of mixed blood. In 1938 Samuel Hopkins Adams, visiting Marion in search of background material for his book on the Harding era, found that this belief still persisted among the older residents. A reporter who had worked for Harding and the *Star* in the early 1900s told Adams that "it was generally believed that there was Negro blood in the Harding line, but that W. G. had outgrown it."

Professor Chancellor's circular caused such an uproar in Marion County that the Wooster trustees insisted on his resignation. He continued, however, to live in the town and continued his digging into the Harding genealogy. Harding had been President for just over a year when the results of Chancellor's work appeared in a book with the title page:

> Warren Gamaliel Harding
> President of the United States.
> A Review of Facts
> Collected from
> Anthropological, Historical, and
> Political Researches
> by
> William Estabrook Chancellor
> formerly
> Professor of Economics, Politics, and Social Sciences of
> Wooster College, Wooster, Ohio.

Although a casual reader might (and was presumably intended to) assume that the professor was the author, the title was carefully worded and punctuated to make no such claim. Chancellor later denied that he had written it, although no other author has ever been suggested. According to the title page the book was "sold and distributed by agents only. The Sentinal Press."

Like the earlier circular, the book was distributed surreptitiously. Most

of the copies were sold by door-to-door salesmen throughout the main cities of
Ohio. Some copies even reached Washington. In the book Chancellor now
maintained that there were several Negro strains in the Harding clan, but his
chief claim was that Harding's great-grandmother, Elizabeth Madison Harding, born in 1799, was a Negress. Chancellor in his delvings had spent several
weeks in Blooming Grove interviewing the oldest inhabitants, some of whom
claimed to have known Elizabeth Madison Harding.

With Harding's inauguration, Harry Daugherty had attained his own
goal of becoming Attorney General of the United States. When he learned of
the publication of Chancellor's book, he at once sent out agents of the Justice
Department and the Post Office to gather up the whole edition. Agents spread
out all over Ohio buying, borrowing, or even confiscating every copy they
could find. They finally managed to locate the "Sentinal" Press, bought all the
unsold copies, burned them, and destroyed the plates. So thorough was the
Justice Department in its search that this sub rosa volume has become one of
the rarest items in American historical bibliography.

Harding himself was troubled all his days by the shadow across his line-
age. His father-in-law remained for years Harding's bitterest enemy. Just before the marriage, Kling, on meeting Harding in the courthouse, elaborated
profanely on the young man's mixed blood and threatened to kill him. Kling
was responsible for a full-page article that appeared about that time in the
rival *Mirror* alleging that the Harding family had always been regarded and
treated as Negroes in Blooming Grove. Twelve years later, when Harding was
running for lieutenant governor, Kling remarked with open bitterness that he
hoped to God he would never live to see a Negro governor of Ohio.

Whatever Harding's frustrations and anger at these mocking accusations,
he always followed the manly course of disregarding the rumors about his
heredity. He himself did not know whether they were true or not. "How do I
know, Jim?" he once told his old friend James Faulkner of the Cincinnatti
Enquirer. "One of my ancestors may have jumped the fence." Nor, in a day
when such matters have come to be of less concern, is there anything more to
add to that honest comment.

No President of the United States ever suffered such a loss of reputation
in so short a time as did Harding after his death. Aloof insiders like Alice
Roosevelt Longworth might sum him up waspishly as "just a slob," but when
he died suddenly in San Francisco on August 2, 1923, he was as popular and
respected among the mass of people as three years before when he had been
elected by the greatest plurality ever yet given a presidential candidate. Three
million people from cities, hamlets, and open prairie came to watch his funeral
train as it slowly crossed the country; "the most remarkable demonstration in
American history of affection, respect, and reverence for the dead," according
to *The New York Times*. The day of Harding's funeral was proclaimed a day
of public mourning. He would, it seemed, be remembered in history as another
Garfield or McKinley.

Yet within months the scandals long simmering beneath the amiable "normalcy"—the President himself had coined the word—of the Harding administration boiled over. Harding had surrounded himself with his friends, and now it turned out that many of his friends were vultures. Ominous questions arose concerning the Teapot Dome oil leases, resulting in Harding's Secretary of the Interior Albert Fall's being sent to prison for bribery. Secretary of the Navy Edwin Denby retired in disgrace. There were revelations of graft and corruption in the office of the Alien Property Custodian and the Veterans' Bureau. There were suicides. Under Daugherty and his bagman Jess Smith the Justice Department became—in Senator Henry Fountain Ashurst's phrase—the Department of Easy Virtue, with pardons and bootleggers' permits for sale over the counter. Only two hung juries kept Daugherty from going to jail when he retired to Ohio.

As an aftermath to all the other scandals a book appeared in 1927, *The President's Daughter,* published by an organization called the Elizabeth Ann Guild, Inc., and written by a former Marion resident, Nan Britton, who claimed that for years she had been Harding's mistress and that her eight-year-old daughter Elizabeth Ann—whose photograph served as a frontispiece—was Harding's child. By this time, as *The President's Daughter* circulated briskly, although for the most part under the counter, the public found it easy to believe almost anything of Harding. Nan's 440-page book was convincing not only through its elaboration of details but by its very naivety. She was a determined young woman, she had determined to become Harding's mistress, and she had achieved that inglorious goal. She had no regrets.

She was, she wrote, the daughter of a Marion physician. As a schoolgirl of fourteen she had become infatuated with the handsome editor of the *Star.* Since the Britton and Harding families were acquainted, she knew him to speak to. Often she used to wait across the street from the *Star* office just to catch a glimpse of him sitting in the chair with his feet on the desk. Or she would telephone the Harding house in the hope that he would answer so that she could hear his voice. When he ran for governor of Ohio, she covered the walls of her room with his campaign photographs. Her infatuation was so open that it became a mild scandal. Harding was aware of it; so was Mrs. Harding. In 1916, when Nan was nineteen and the forty-nine-year-old Harding a United States senator, she moved from Marion to New York, and from there wrote him a letter asking for a job. He replied with eager cordiality, saying that he would see her on his next visit to the city. Their first meeting in the Hotel Manhattan was the beginning of their liaison. Before he left her, she wrote, "he tucked thirty dollars in my brand-new silk stocking and was sorry he had no more that time to give me."

The gesture symbolized their relationship. For Harding, it would seem, Nan Britton was young, attractive, and available—a pleasure for which he was willing to pay. For her he was the sentimentalized passion of her lopsided life. They lived together off and on, according to Nan, from 1916 to 1922, registering as man and wife at hotels or sometimes staying in borrowed apartments. It was at a rendezvous in the Senate Office Building, she said, that their child, Elizabeth Ann was conceived. Once Harding even took Nan on tour as his niece. She saw him secretly at the 1920 nominating convention. Even when he was President they managed to have occasional trysts in a White House cloakroom.

After Elizabeth Ann was born, Harding always sent Nan money—a hundred or a hundred and fifty dollars each week. At the time of his death she was visiting Europe at his expense. As a girl Nan had had Harding's sister Abigail for a high school teacher, and when she returned from Europe with her money gone, she went to Abigail in Marion and told her story. Abigail, believing it, sent her small sums of money from time to time—in all eight hundred and ninety dollars. But Harding's sister Carolyn and his brother George Harding were less sympathetic and more skeptical. Dr. George Harding, in a cold four-hour interview with Nan, demanded specific dates, specific places, above all letters. Nan had no more than a few impersonal notes. Her love letters—some of which she claimed ran to as long as sixty pages—she said she had destroyed at Harding's request. She now asked for a tenth of Harding's half-million dollar estate—an amount which she claimed he had promised to settle on her and Elizabeth Ann.

When Dr. Harding refused any settlement, Nan brought an unsuccessful court action against the Hardings. It was in preparation for this suit, she claimed, that she began to write *The President's Daughter,* intending it at first as merely background material for her lawyer. With its publication she made well over a hundred thousand dollars.

Following Harding's death she married a Swedish sea captain, mostly with the intention of providing for Elizabeth Ann, but the captain was poorer than anticipated, and the marriage lasted only a few weeks. Financially safe at last after her book was published, she founded and busied herself with the Elizabeth Ann Guild, the purpose of which was to provide legal aid for unmarried mothers.

Defenders of Harding—there were still some left in Ohio—attacked the book as a fraud, pointing out that for all its gossip no clinching evidence, such as a surviving love letter, was offered. Yet Nan Britton herself was no fiction. Her family was as well known in Marion as Harding's. Although her schoolgirl infatuation for the *Star* editor had been Main Street gossip, beyond that everyone had thought well of her. When Samuel Hopkins Adams talked with some of her old high-school classmates, all of them spoke highly of her character and reputation.

It would have taken the most exact documentary proof to connect Harding's successor, the taciturn Coolidge, with any "woman" scandal. Ike Hoover, who had observed much in his decades as chief usher at the White House, noted tartly in his memoirs that whereas Taft was a ladies' man, Harding was "a sporting ladies' man." When such a man is married to a shrill, nagging, older woman, a certain amount of dalliance may be expected. Even in Marion, there was much that the Duchess had to overlook. Editor Harding had once had an affair with the wife of one of the town's leading merchants. Years later when President-elect Harding returned to a Marion decked with flags and bunting, there was one large store front that remained uncompromisingly blank among the red, white, and blue decorations.

There were other such primrose detours from Main Street in Harding's life. And although his affair with Nan Britton could not be documented to the satisfaction of Dr. George Harding, nevertheless the gushing, redundant pages of her book ring true. Such an enthusiastic artlessness could hardly be counterfeited. Subsequently the Secret Service chief, Colonel Edward Starling, who was then in charge of White House security, confirmed in his memoirs that one of the Secret Service detail had, as Nan alleged, carried letters between the President and "a certain young lady, unnamed, in New York," and once brought her to the White House. "This, I suppose," he wrote, "was Nan Britton."

For several years Nan's book gave flourishing support to the Elizabeth Ann Guild. At one point it employed eight staff members to deal with the flood of letters pouring in from unwed mothers from over the country. Boni & Liveright undertook to publish a second edition of *The President's Daughter.* The book was for a time Gertrude Stein's favorite reading.

Nan wrote various articles, gave interviews, and compiled comparative photographs of Harding and Elizabeth Ann. In a 1928 piece for the *Haldeman-Julius Monthly,* she explained:

I based my decision to give my book to the world on a platform of faith built on the eternal rock of love, a higher love than mother-love when mother-love is narrow, fearful and absorbing. Never for a moment have I had the slightest doubt of the rightness of my decision in its relationship to my darling child and Warren Harding's.

In October, 1930, a film company was planning to make what Nan called a "picturization" of her book, until film czar Will Hays—who had been Harding's Postmaster-General—squelched it. In 1932, Nan published her second book, *Honesty or Politics,* more interesting for its assorted pictures of herself, Elizabeth Ann, and Harding than for the 374 rambling pages in which she wrote about her difficulties with the surviving Hardings and with getting *The President's Daughter* into print.

No bills were tucked into stocking tops in *Honesty or Politics.* Lacking the scandal value of its predecessor, the book had only a modest sale. After its publication, Nan and her daughter and the Elizabeth Ann Guild disappeared into anonymity. If Nan is still alive in 1965—the centenary of Harding's birth—she will be sixty-nine years old and Elizabeth Ann forty-six.

It was Harding's good fortune to die when he did, for the scandals of his administration—as he probably knew—could not have remained hidden much longer. He had meant well. With naïve sincerity he had hoped to be America's "best loved" President. He had not consciously sullied his office; indeed his cabinet contained men of unquestioned honor and ability, like Herbert Hoover and Charles Evans Hughes. But his closest friend and associate was still Harry Daugherty; his convivial companions, the Ohio politicians who had trailed him to Washington. With Harding in the White House, with Daugherty attached by a private line, the Ohio gang was all there. Alice Longworth described the presidential poker parties that were an evening feature in the early months of the Harding administration:

No rumor could have exceeded the reality; the study was filled with cronies . . . the air heavy with tobacco smoke, trays containing every imaginable brand of whiskey stood about, cards and poker chips ready at hand—a general atmosphere of waist-coat unbuttoned, feet on desk, and spittoons alongside.

If Harding had lived, it is at least possible that he might have been impeached. By the middle of his term the vultures were beginning to come home to roost. Early in 1923 he discovered that one of his closest poker cronies, Charles R. Forbes, whom he had enthusiastically made director of the Veterans' Bureau, had rigged his department and had robbed the government and the veterans of an estimated 200 million dollars. It was Harding's first experience of treachery. A visitor to the White House, misdirected to the second floor, was appalled as he passed the Red Room to find the President shaking the cowering Forbes by the neck and shouting: "You yellow rat! You double-crossing bastard!" Shielded as the President was both by his office and his incapacity, the last to learn what had long been Washington gossip, he became by 1923 vaguely but increasingly aware of the other leeches about him. There was Daugherty's loose-lipped Jess Smith, master of the revels at the Little Green House on K Street where, it was whispered, appointments and pardons were sold, liquor permits farmed out, and political deals arranged amidst a profusion of poker chips, bootleg liquor, and accommodating women. There was William J. Burns who, as head of the Federal Bureau of Investigation, was using his bureau as a private detective agency to harass the critics of Daugherty and the Ohio gang. There was Secretary of the Interior Fall, suddenly affluent after his leasing of government oil properties to the Sinclair interests, and now resigned from the Cabinet. There were so many others. Harding, the friendly man, was learning tardily to see his friends in their true light. But even as he learned, disaster was rushing toward him.

So timely was Harding's end in the light of the approaching nemesis, that those in the know soon began to whisper that he had committed suicide. Such rumors were stiffened by certain anomalies of his death. There were contradictory reports of his symptoms. It was uncertain, all now said, just who had been with him when he died. Mrs. Harding had refused to allow an autopsy, had refused even to allow a death mask to be made. Even darker rumors followed, hinting that Harding's death had really been a mercy killing and that the iron-willed Duchess had poisoned him to save his reputation. Fifteen years later Samuel Hopkins Adams found a number of people in Ohio—some of them friends of the Hardings—still convinced that Harding had been murdered by his wife. Many Washington insiders accepted that at the time, although the story did not gain nationwide circulation until the publication in 1930 of *The Strange Death of President Harding* by Gaston B. Means.

Means, a perjurer and trickster whose devious career included a trial for murder, was officially an operative in the Bureau of Investigation but his real function was to operate undercover for Burns and Jess Smith. He lived sumptuously in Washington, renting a house at $1,000 a month and owning a $5,000 car driven by a liveried chauffeur—all on a salary of $88.33 a week.

Though his word was always dubious, he maintained in his book that he had also been employed by Mrs. Harding to investigate Nan Britton. Means was to spend two post-Harding terms in a Federal penitentiary, the last (during which he died) for swindling Evelyn Walsh McLean of $100,000 by concocting false clues in connection with the Lindbergh kidnaping. Without saying it in so many words, Means implied that Mrs. Harding had poisoned her husband. Following Nan Britton's revelations, Means's book tore up the last shred of Harding's reputation.

It seemed reasonable enough, after all the other scandals, to believe that Harding had met an unnatural end. Yet the skilled diagnostician Dr. Emmanuel Libman, observing him at a dinner party in the autumn of 1922, had predicted to friends that the President would be dead of a coronary ailment within six months. The year 1923 found Harding oppressed both mentally and physically. He had always played golf with the same compulsive zest that he played cards. Now he tended to become tired after nine holes and often quit at the twelfth or thirteenth. He was unable to sleep except when propped up with pillows. His face aged and grew slack. To his essentially indolent nature the demands of the Presidency had become a relentless burden. With morbid uneasiness he began to doubt himself and to sense the menace to his administration and to his name of the friends he had trusted. Although he still attended the Calvary Baptist Church, he would not go on Communion Sunday, saying that he felt unworthy. He foreswore liquor and gave up his poker parties. For some time he had been thinking of a trip across the continent and to Alaska—"a voyage of understanding," he called it—in which he imagined himself escaping from the isolation of the White House and renewing himself by seeing again the ordinary men and women of America who had elected him.

Originally he had planned the trip as a junket to be made with cronies like Daugherty, Jess Smith, and the court-jester husband of Evelyn Walsh, Ned McLean. The shift to the voyage of understanding developed with the darkening mood of 1923. It was as if Harding were trying to break out of the web of his old associates. Instead of Daugherty, Harding now invited sober-minded men like Speaker of the House Frederick Gillett, Secretary of Agriculture Henry Wallace (father of ex-Vice President Henry Wallace), and Dr. Hubert Work, the former physician who was now Secretary of the Interior. Secretary of Commerce Hoover, then on the West Coast, was asked to join the party there. Dr. Charles Sawyer, the President's personal physician, accompanied him as did a young Navy doctor, Commander Joel T. Boone. Sawyer was a Marion friend, a diminutive country doctor of about the standing of the elder Harding, whom the President had brought to Washington and made a brigadier general. Sawyer cut an absurd figure in his uniform, but he was an honest man. Mrs. Harding of course made the trip, one of her maxims being: Never let a husband travel alone.

The special train with the presidential car *Superb* left Washington on June 20. But before then Harding had had two ominous shocks. In March Charles F. Cramer, Forbes's closest associate in the Veterans' Bureau, had committed suicide. Two months later Jess Smith's improprieties had become so flagrant that they finally reached the President's insensitive ear. Summoned by the White House, Smith confessed, blubbering out the catalogue of iniquities of the Ohio Gang. Harding, aghast, dismissed him with the warning that he would be arrested next day. A few hours later Smith shot himself dead in Daugherty's hotel room.

To the correspondents and those aboard the *Superb* the voyage of understanding seemed more a voyage of doom. Harding in his restlessness insisted on playing bridge steadily, interrupting his game only to make a speech at each town and whistle stop. He prided himself as an orator, but this time his phrases—always resounding platitudes—had lost their resonance. When he spoke in Kansas City, William Allen White noticed that his lips were swollen and blue and his eyes puffed.

Slowly the *Superb* moved across the continent in the rending summer heat. At St. Louis Harding delivered a ghost-written speech on the World Court. Later the wife of former Secretary Fall, obviously much troubled, visited him incognito at his hotel. The veiled elderly woman spent over an hour talking with him, and when she left Harding appeared profoundly disturbed. Afterward on the train, as if he were thinking aloud, Harding remarked that it was not his enemies but his friends who were keeping him awake nights.

On July 3, Secretary Hoover and his wife joined Harding at Tacoma, just before the party embarked for Alaska. Aboard ship the Secretary was forced to play bridge with the President each day beginning immediately after breakfast and continuing until after midnight. So surfeited of cards did Hoover become that he never played bridge again. One evening Harding sent for him and in the privacy of his cabin asked him what he would do if he knew of a great scandal in the administration. Would he for the good of the party expose it or bury it? Hoover replied that the only thing to do would be to publish it and at least get credit for integrity. Harding gave no further details. But Hoover noticed that as the trip continued the President grew increasingly nervous. In Alaska a long coded message came to Harding by plane from Washington. After reading it he almost collapsed, and for the rest of the day seemed half-stunned. He did not recover on the voyage back. His speeches were listless, their banalities no longer covered by his personal magnetism. In Seattle, on a searing afternoon, he faltered and was barely able to finish reading his manuscript.

That night Harding suddenly suffered such pain that Dr. Sawyer was hastily sent for. The doctor announced that the President was suffering from acute indigestion after having eaten crab meat—although later it turned out there had been no crab on the menu. Dr. Boone, noting symptoms of high blood pressure and an enlarged heart that had been passed over by the homeopathic general, insisted over Sawyer's objections that it was much more serious and that Harding had had a cardiac attack.

As the *Superb* moved south all speaking dates were canceled. Boone and Dr. Work arranged to have two specialists meet the train at San Francisco: Dr. Ray Lyman Wilbur, president of Stanford University and afterward president of the American Medical Association; and a well-known heart specialist, Dr.

Charles Miner Cooper. Harding arrived in San Francisco on Sunday, July 29, walking unaided from the train to the street, although reporters noted that he looked "gray and worn." He was taken to the Palace Hotel where Dr. Wilbur and Dr. Cooper examined him and at once diagnosed his condition as a coronary attack aggravated by bronchial pneumonia.

Under treatment the President seemed to improve. On Wednesday Dr. Sawyer announced that the crisis was past. The President's lungs cleared up and on Thursday his improvement continued. He was able to sit up. Then, without warning, at 7:35 in the evening, he suddenly died of what his death certificate described as cerebral apoplexy.

According to the newspaper accounts by reporters at the hotel, his wife had been sitting beside him reading an article about him by Samuel G. Blythe in *The Saturday Evening Post*. It was called "A Calm View of a Calm Man," and it pleased Harding, for he remarked, "That's good! Go on, read some more." And in that instant a change passed over his face, he shuddered and collapsed. Mrs. Harding ran shrieking into the corridor. A few seconds later Dr. Boone and Dr. Sawyer arrived to find him dead. Doctors Wilbur and Cooper were sent for. They, with the other two doctors and Secretary Work, signed the death certificate.

"Nothing could be more absurd than the poison theory," Dr. Wilbur wrote long afterward. And as Samuel Hopkins Adams pointed out, to accept it is to assume that five doctors—four of whom at least were distinguished members of their profession—would violate their ethics to cover up a capital crime. Even if they had done so, there would still be the problem of how either Harding or his wife could have obtained possession of a killing drug without the knowledge of others. As for the suicide hypothesis, Harding for all his faults was not the suicidal type.

After Harding's funeral, Florence Kling Harding wasted no time in unprofitable grief. The Coolidges did not press her, and she spent the first few weeks of her widowhood in the White House gathering up and destroying every bit of her husband's correspondence, official and unofficial, that she could lay hands on. Once back in Marion she performed a similar operation on the files of the *Star*. She employed a corps of secretaries to trace Harding correspondents, to whom she appealed on sentimental grounds for any surviving letters. Her last year of life—she died on November 21, 1924—was a busy one, but her motives were incendiary rather than sentimental. When the publishing house of Doubleday, Page asked if it might publish a volume of Harding letters, she refused to consider it. She admitted to Frank N. Doubleday, the head of the firm, that she had burned her husband's correspondence, saying that she feared some of it might be misconstrued and harm his memory.

What the destroyed letters contained remains as mysterious as the Lincoln correspondence destroyed by his son Robert in the 1920s. Yet there were a number of Harding letters that somehow eluded her.

These letters and papers still exist in possession of the Harding Memorial Association where they are kept in the basement of the old Harding house in Marion. They are at present in the custody of Dr. Carl Sawyer, the president of the association and son of the former White House physician, who has been engaged in sorting and arranging—but not destroying—them. Nothing, however, is open to the public or even to scholars or biographers. Dr. Sawyer maintains that Harding was unjustly treated and that the truth about him will show him to have been "a fine, a wonderful man." But it does not seem to be a truth that anyone in Marion is particularly anxious to hasten before the public. Long ago the association decided not to make the Harding papers public until fifty years after his death, in 1973. Dr. Sawyer is not sure that they will be ready even then. "There's something America doesn't know," he told an interviewer enigmatically in the spring of 1962, "and may not for a hundred years."*

Shortly after Harding's death his friends in Marion formed the memorial association and began to raise money for a tomb splendid enough for their President's body to lie in state forever. Businessmen, workers, schoolchildren, Ohioans from every walk of life—and many outside the state—contributed. At first the money gushed in with fanfares of publicity, but as the Harding scandals darkened the sky over Marion, money and publicity began to run thin. To the press, as to the politicians, the proposed memorial became an embarrassing subject. Eventually, however, the dogged committee of the memorial association succeeded in getting together three quarters of a million dollars.

The cornerstone was laid in 1926 and the dedication set for July 4, 1927. On high ground, in the cemetery on Delaware Avenue south of Marion, the white marble monument loomed up—a beautifully proportioned circle of Tuscan columns joined by an equally austere entablature. Harding's remains and those of his wife were moved there early in 1927 to await the official eulogy. This, according to the etiquette of such things, could be spoken by no one less than the President of the United States. President Coolidge was in any case the honorary president of the memorial association.

Cautious Cal, however, had no intention of getting himself tarred with the Harding brush. At any mention of dedicating the Harding Memorial, Coolidge—according to Herbert Hoover—"expressed a furious distaste."

July 4, 1927, came and went unmarked by any ceremony in the Marion cemetery. So did three more July Fourths. Hoover, succeeding as President, was no more pleased at the prospect of this dubious task than was Coolidge, but he was more the man and less the politician. An article that appeared in the September, 1930, issue of Plain Talk called "Harding's Haunted Tomb" stirred Ohio and bestirred Washington. Hoover finally agreed to take his sour medicine and preside over the dedication.

The Marion memorial was dedicated on June 16, 1931. Chief Justice Charles Evans Hughes spoke first, revealing to his surprised audience that if Harding had lived he would have been a hopeless invalid and that he knew it.

---

* After calling a meeting of the association's Executive Committee on September 30, 1963, Dr. Sawyer finally announced that the Harding papers—including some 300,000 letters and copies of letters—would be released to the Ohio Historical Society. On October 10 the steel boxes containing the papers were removed from the basement of the Harding Home and Museum in Marion and transported in a moving van to the Historical Society building in Columbus. At Dr. Sawyer's insistence the van was accompanied by an armed patrol of state police to protect "against any ambush from the Teapot Dome crowd."

Ex-President Coolidge then cannily accepted the memorial on behalf of the American people, measuring out his words by the teaspoonful. Finally President Hoover stepped before the battery of microphones. Directly behind him, as a member of the committee, sat the gimlet-eyed Daugherty. Hoover might have dodged the issue that was probably alive in the minds of everyone present, glossing it over with meaningless words. But his Quaker conscience faced it squarely. His words were intended to cut home, and they did:

Here was a man [he said, as if he were addressing the man behind him] whose soul was seared by a great disillusionment. We saw him gradually weaken, not only from physical exhaustion but also from mental anxiety. Warren Harding had a dim realization that he had been betrayed by a few of the men whom he had trusted, by men whom he had believed were his devoted friends. It was later proved in the courts of the land that these men had betrayed not only the friendship and trust of their staunch and loyal friend but they had betrayed their country. That was the tragedy of the life of Warren Harding.

The Last Anarchist

ON THE EVENING of January 11, 1943, a tall middle-aged man in a wide-brimmed hat locked the door of his small third-floor office in the building at the corner of New York's 15th Street and Fifth Avenue, then—a little stiffly because of his bulk—walked down the narrow darkened stairs. A scar running down his left cheek showed up even in the shadows, in spite of the pointed gray beard meant to conceal it. From his appearance he might have been Scandinavian. He was accompanied by a smaller, darker man, obviously Italian.

The building had two entrances, one on 15th Street and one on Fifth Avenue. The men walked out of the 15th Street entrance into the dank dimmed-out street and headed eastward for Fifth Avenue. The time was 9:30 P.M. At the corner they stood under a dimmed street lamp, waiting for the traffic light to change. As they stood there, a man stepped up behind them, raised a pistol and fired four shots. The bearded man dropped to the pavement, one bullet in his back, a second in his brain. Before the smaller man could grasp what had happened, the gunman sprang into a dark sedan that disappeared at once down 15th Street. The bearded man died almost instantly. He was Carlo Tresca, the last leader of the American anarchists.

When the police arrived and searched the vicinity, they found a loaded
.38 caliber revolver in an ashcan at the Fifth Avenue entrance to the building.
Since the bullets found in Tresca's body were from a .32 caliber automatic,
they reasoned that there must have been a gunman waiting at each entrance.
After the first gunman had fired, the second had thrown away his pistol and
slipped off.

Two passers-by managed to catch a glimpse of the murderer. He seemed
to them to be between thirty-five and forty, about five feet five inches tall.
Several hours later the police found a Ford sedan abandoned about five blocks
northwest of the murder spot. All four doors of the sedan were open and a
bunch of keys hung from the ignition lock. Tresca's friend Tony Ribavich
recognized the car from its unusual side mirror. The driver of such a car had
tried to run Tresca down two days before as he and Ribavich were walking
past the New School for Social Research on West 12th Street.

The abandoned car had been licensed in the name of a nonexistent man
at a nonexistent Queen's County address. The Con-Field Automobile Company at 1902 Broadway had sold it to "Charles Pappas" on the twenty-second
of December. Two days after the killing the police arrested a thirty-two-year
old paroled convict, Carmine Galante, who had been seen to enter the car only
an hour and a half before Tresca was shot.

On that evening Galante had made his routine weekly report to the
Parole Office at 80 Centre Street. He left the building at 8:10 P.M. Because the
supervisor of parole inspectors had learned that Galante was again associating
with criminals, he assigned two officers to follow him. During this period of
gasoline rationing the officers expected Galante to enter the subway. Instead,
about a block from the parole office, he stepped into a Ford sedan that had
apparently been waiting for him, The officers, on foot, could not follow him
further, but they managed to get the number of the car. It was the number
later found on the plates of the abandoned Ford.

On his arrest Galante denied that he had been in any car that night.
Although the police were convinced that he had killed Tresca, they could get
nothing out of him. He was held in the Tombs for eight months. "Prison wise
and a tough witness to crack," the district attorney described him. Galante had
never known Tresca or anything about him, and he would have had no reason
to kill him (so the police reasoned) unless he had been hired for the job. From
the Tombs, Galante was returned to Sing Sing for violation of his parole.

Eight months after Tresca's murder a second suspect was arrested—Frank
Nuccio, a small-time racketeer who lived less than a block from where the
police had picked up Galante. Nuccio ran an eight-car garage where the escape
car had been kept until the night of the killing. The police had traced the
garage through keys found in the ignition lock of the Ford. A locksmith who
made one of the keys said that he had changed the lock on Nuccio's garage a
few hours before Tresca was shot—persumably to prevent the sedan being
returned there afterward. Nuccio—as uninformative as Galante—was held for
two months, then released.

There the investigation ended. On various unrevealed grounds neither the district attorney's office, the mayor, nor the United States attorney general seemed to be much interested in solving the mystery of Tresca's death. "Is there some political reason?" Tresca's old Boston friend Aldino Felicani asked in an open letter to Mayor La Guardia, published in his miniscule anarchist monthly *Controcorrente (Counter-current)*. "Would it complicate our international relations . . . if the forces which inspired that murder were revealed at this time?"

In his earlier years Tresca had been a doctrinaire anarchist, a believer in—if not a practicer of—the propaganda of the deed. But as he grew older—in spite of his broad-brimmed anarchist hat and black butterfly tie—he became less concerned with anarchist theory and more and more concerned with the rights and freedom of individuals. Fascists and Communists—those who talked of breaking eggs to make omelettes, and who would suppress the individual for the sake of the cause—came to hate him. Others, whatever their politics or religion, could not resist his abounding personality. Even the police who arrested him became his friends—and he was arrested some thirty-six times on charges varying from blasphemy, libel, disorderly conduct, incitement to riot and criminal obscenity to conspiracy, sedition and murder. Even the district attorney who denounced him as an enemy of society would eat and drink at his table. Tresca relished the mere fact of being alive, and he loved to the full the smaller personal things life had to offer him—women and wine, talk, food and song. "Big, bearded, boastful, life-loving," his friend Eugene Lyons saw him, "and as unlike the embittered anarchist of popular traditon as possible. Priest-baiting and spaghetti were among his chief passions, and his hairbreadth escapes from enemy bullets everywhere from Abruzzi to the copper empire of Montana were ample proof of his charmed life." Suzanne La Follette, who served with him on the Dewey Commission, remembered him as "tall, very heavy, with gray hair and beard and the kindest blue eyes twinkling through glasses (if my memory is correct he wore pince-nez with a black cord). He always wore a black hat with rather low crown and wide brim. Altogether a most impressive looking man—warmly affectionate toward his friends, wise and humorous, without a touch of the fanatic about him."

Tresca's funeral was held in the old Manhattan Opera House on 34th Street, and even that building was too small.

It was packed [Suzanne La Follette wrote] and as one looked and listened one knew that these people were no mere sensation-seekers; they were mourners—mourners of all sorts and conditions, sharing a common grief and a common awareness that with Carlo a vital warmth had gone out of their lives that could never be rekindled.

Carlo Tresca was born in 1879 in Sulmonia, an ancient hill town of the Apennines. Like Galleani, Malatesta, and many of the anarchist leaders, he came from an upperclass family, his father being the wealthiest landowner in the vicinity. He became a Socialist before he had left school, and at the age of twenty he organized a local branch of the Socialist party and mustered and marched his father's peasants behind the red flag. Oddly enough, his radical views caused no family conflict, and eventually he was even able to convert his father to a Socialist point of view. At twenty-two the buoyant and irrepressible Carlo had become secretary of the Italian Railroad Workers' Union and made his mark as one of the most popular undesirable citizens in southern Italy. The tone of his revolutionary paper *Il Germe* (The Seed) was scarcely scholastic. He soon found himself indicted for libeling his father's friend, the political boss of Sulmonia. To defend their bright young man, the Socialists sent on two of their deftest lawyers. Tresca was so certain he would go free that while the jury was out he went across the square to a café to celebrate with his friends. While they were drinking a toast to Garibaldi and the new war for freedom, the bailiff appeared on the courthouse steps shouting "Carlo! Carlo!" Tresca dashed over to the courthouse with a bottle of wine in one hand and a piece of cheese in the other—only to hear himself sentenced to a year and a half in prison. His lawyers entered an appeal, he was released—and he then *forgot* to file his appeal.

With jail closing in on him, Tresca left for Switzerland. For a time he joined a group of Italian radicals in Geneva. Among those noisy café exiles, one of the noisiest was a comrade by the name of Benito Mussolini. He and Tresca did not take to each other. Mussolini thought that Tresca was not enough of a radical. Tresca thought that Mussolini talked too much.

In 1904 Tresca sailed for the United States. He still considered himself a Socialist, although in those days the distinctions between Socialists, Communists, and anarchists were much vaguer than they were later to be. For several years in the coal mining region near Pittsburgh he edited *La Plebe* (The People), the paper of the Italian Socialist Federation. Whatever remaining energy he had—and he had much—he spent in organizing and leading his Italian compatriots, the workers who had now replaced the Irish as a source of exploitable labor. The America that he knew in those years was scarcely more than an extension of Italy. He learned only a few words of English, and he would never really master the language. After a few months editing *La Plebe* he found himself in jail for libeling the local priest. On his release he was warned to leave town. Shortly afterward, as he was leaving his office, someone seized him from behind and slashed his face with a razor from the left nostril down to his collar. Instinctively he raised his shoulder and managed to protect his jugular vein. Spurting blood, he staggered into a drugstore. A policeman— one of three who had seen the attack—followed to arrest him. Tresca was still able to muster enough strength to bellow at him: "Why don't you take a dead body to the morgue?" Instead he was carried to the hospital where it took twenty-six stitches to bring his face together. The man who slashed him was caught and tried, but even though the three policemen testified that they had seen him lunge at Tresca with the razor, he was acquitted.

In June, 1905, the one-eyed giant Big Bill Haywood, Daniel DeLeon, "Mother" Jones, and other militants founded the Industrial Workers of the World, soon to be known as the Wobblies. In the decade of their strength the Wobblies organized among the unskilled and migratory workers and led strikes in New England textile mills, Minnesota iron mines, and Pennsylvania steel works, that were as much social rebellions as economic conflicts. The Wobblies were syndicalists whose goal was not the Socialist one of having the state own all the means of production but to have the mines owned and run by the miners' union, the land by a union of agriculture workers, the factories by textile workers, all in a vast non-capitalistic non-nationalist co-operative society. Tresca was attracted to the I.W.W. at once. At this period he considered himself an anarcho-syndicalist.

It was the strike in the textile mills of Lawrence, Massachusetts, beginning on January 12, 1912, that stamped the letters I.W.W. in burning red on the American imagination. The year before, the Massachusetts Legislature—with the best of liberal intentions—had passed a law reducing the working hours of women and of children under eighteen from fifty-six to fifty-four hours. When the law went into effect, the mill owners countered by reducing wages correspondingly. Since many of the juvenile mill workers received five dollars a week or less, the reduction amounted to only about twenty-five cents, but its calculated meanness caused 23,000 workers to strike in aimless anger. They were a polyglot mixture of Italians, Germans, French-Canadians, Poles, Lithuanians, Belgians, and Syrians, with a scattering of Russians, Jews, and Greeks. After a number of riots, the governor called out the militia.

It was then that Joe Ettor of the I.W.W. executive board came on from New York with the radical poet Arturo Giovannitti to give the strike force and direction. The winter was unusually bitter and the workers suffered much from cold and hunger. Sympathy for them grew as the wretchedness of their condition became known. "Their demands were justified," William Allen White wrote in distant Kansas, "and there was no excuse for the violence by police and military."

Clashes between the strikers and the militia became more and more frequent, the Wobblies flaunting red banners reading NO GOD! NO MASTER!, the soldiers replying with bayonets. Finally one afternoon, shots rang out and a girl striker, Annie Lopizza, fell dead. No one ever heard who shot her, but the police welcomed the chance to arrest the "troublemakers" Ettor and Giovannitti.

With the two leaders in jail, the Wobbly hero, Big Bill Haywood, came on from the West to take charge. He arrived in Lawrence at about the same time as did the slim, dark-haired, blue-eyed "East Side Joan of Arc," Elizabeth Gurley Flynn. Decades later, in an antithesis unanticipated by Marx, her almost spherical figure was to be seen waddling in militant complacency across the platform of Communist conventions.*

By March the textile owners capitulated, granting the strikers pay increases of from five to twenty per cent. Ettor and Giovannitti still remained in jail waiting trial. Tresca, who had long been a friend of Giovannitti, hurried to Lawrence to help in organizing mass agitation for his and Ettor's release. Everything that Tresca did had a way of turning into an adventure, and in

---

* In 1961 she became General Secretary of the Communist Party of the United States.

Lawrence he was a marked man. Early one morning a militia squad came to pick him up at the tenement where he was staying, and he escaped out a rear window, dashing through a network of alleys stark naked. At another time when he was leading a parade to lay wreaths on Annie Lopizza's grave the police cornered him, but a group of workers formed a flying wedge to snatch him away. Two policemen were injured, and after that the police preferred to look the other way when they saw Tresca coming.

The Lawrence strike made the I.W.W. famous, and for a while it seemed to the Wobblies and their sympathizers a harbinger of social revolution in the United States. Soon, however, the flame of indignation died down, the textile workers shed their militancy, and Lawrence relapsed into its grubby obscurity.

Lawrence had a more lasting effect on Tresca, for in a May Day parade there he met Elizabeth Gurley Flynn. Her combination of beauty and radicalism he found irresistible. He had married in Italy, but had left his wife with relief. "I no like married life," he once explained to his friend Max Eastman in his not quite basic English. "I like one woman an' then time pass an' I like another. I make many good frien' ship with women because I always say ver' frank: 'Don' trus' me. My character ver' emotional. I have gran' an' real passion now, but when dat gone, I gone too!'" His grand passion for Gurley— as she was called—outlasted all his others. They lived together until 1923.

After Lawrence, Tresca moved to New York and started to publish and edit another anarchist paper, *L'Avvenire* (The Future). He and Gurley were soon involved in a strike of the hotel and restaurant workers, whose degrading working conditions had turned them from the gradualism of the American Federation of Labor to the militancy of the I.W.W. A meeting of the strikers in Bryant Hall on Sixth Avenue, with a squad of hostile police standing by, turned into a riot, and Tresca, as the most conspicious person present, was at once arrested. When a group of strikers tried to rescue him, a policeman pointed his revolver at Tresca's head and stopped the rescuers in their tracks by threatening to shoot him. Somewhere between the hall and the patrol wagon, Tresca lost a copy of Elizabeth Barrett Browning's *Sonnets from the Portuguese* that Gurley had given him with an affectionate inscription and with many of the love passages underlined. Accounts of the "hidden I.W.W. romance" appeared in next day's papers.

After the hotel strike came the silk strike in Paterson, New Jersey. Paterson was known both as the silkweaving center of the United States and as the Red City. Most of the workers were Italians, and the Red City had a long and turbulent anarchist tradition. Luigi Galleani had thundered revolution there in his *Cronaca Sovversiva*. The international anarchist leader Errico Malatesta had been shot at while on a visit. Gaetano Bresci, the editor of an earlier anarchist paper, had left Paterson in 1900 and sailed for Italy to assassinate King Humbert. The city was a dreary, smoke-encrusted industrial hinterland, seared by poverty, belligerently class-conscious.

The strike broke out in February, 1913, when the mill owners attempted to increase the number of looms each weaver had to tend. Before the strike ended, all the leaders and a thousand strikers had been arrested. Two workers were shot dead in clashes with the police. Tresca and Gurley arrived within days of the walk-out. They were picked up by the police at their first platform appearance. Big Bill Haywood came to Paterson, as did the fledgling revolutionary John Reed, lately hatched from Harvard. Reed was soon arrested and spent a dynamic interlude teaching the imprisoned strikers songs of the French Revolution and writing such realistic accounts for the New York papers of imaginary filth and vermin in the jail that the furious sheriff finally had "that writing son of a bitch" ejected to freedom.

In and out of jail, Reed, Tresca, Gurley, and Big Bill kept right on speaking, In addition, Reed, with the help of his friends in the New York theatrical world, organized the Paterson Strike Pageant and staged it in the old Madison Square Garden. New York had never seen anything like this massive spectacle with its cast of 1,029 actual strikers. It was both a pageant and a morality play, and it thrilled its nonproletarian audience in the boxes with the feeling that a new proletarian art form had been born.

On the night of June 7, the letters I.W.W. shone out from the top of the Garden's tower under Diana's statue. To middle-class Manhattanites, those glaring red letters seemed the modern abbreviations for Mene, Tekel, Upharsin.

Unfortunately for Reed, the expenses were heavy, and when after a single performance the Pageant closed, it had added much more to the notoriety of the strike than it had to the strike fund. Some of the disgruntled Paterson workers accused the New York committee of profiting at their expense. The closing of the Pagent was followed shortly afterward by the collapse of the strike.

To enthusiasts like Haywood and Tresca and Gurley and Reed, each new strike in its moment of incandescence seemed a dynamic thrust forward toward a new dawn. The pattern, however, became static—an initial spontaneous walkout; agitation and organization; violence, with more often than not a striker or policeman killed. Sometimes, as in Lawrence, the strikers won; sometimes, as in Paterson, they lost; but in any case the life of the gray industrial communities soon moved much as before, a little better or a little worse, but with no beguiling prospect of revolution just round the corner.

In 1916, Haywood asked Tresca to help organize a strike of iron miners in the Mesabi Range of Minnesota. Haywood's Western Federation of Miners —the genesis of the I.W.W.—had long conducted what was almost a civil war with the feudalistic mine owners of the great western ranges. After the miners struck for an eight-hour day, the companies replied by importing strike-breakers. In that bleak countryside of scarred red earth where even the landscape seemed violent, the law was an irrelevant abstraction. Both sides were willing to fight. No sooner had Tresca arrived with a group of speakers and organizers than he was hustled off to jail.

While he was locked up, four deputies forced their way into a Montenegrin worker's house and, when the man's wife objected, they beat her up. Three boarders jumped to the woman's defence, there was a scuffle, shots were fired, and an instant later a deputy lay dead on the floor. The boarders and the women were held for murder. Tresca and three other organizers were charged with being accessories.

In spite of Tresca's predicament, Haywood did not come to the Mesabi Range. The old direct-action agitator was beginning to show signs of turning into a bureaucrat. At this point he was preoccupied with setting up central offices for the I.W.W. in Chicago. To Gurley and the others in Minnesota, Haywood's interest in the strike appeared unhappily remote. They, on the spot, made what they considered the best deal they could with the state's attorney. Since he wanted to avoid a long, spectacular, and expensive murder trial, he was willing to allow the three boarders to plead guilty to manslaughter. After serving one year of a three-year sentence, the attorney agreed, informally, that they would be released. The Montenegrin wife, Tresca, and the other organizers would be freed. When the boarders appeared before the judge next day, they—to the shock of Gurley and Tresca—received sentences of five to twenty years. From Chicago, with no knowledge of the details, Haywood furiously denounced the outcome. Actually the prisoners were released after three years, but Haywood's arbitrary long-distance reaction to the episode was enough for Tresca who scornfully severed his connection with the I.W.W.

Tresca returned to New York's Little Italy and to editing *L'Avvenire,* his interest in unions now limited to those of predominately Italian membership. From this time on, according to Elizabeth Gurley Flynn, "he wrote and spoke only in Italian and made little or no effort to learn English or to participate in American affairs."

Like all anarchists, Tresca opposed the First World War and America's entry into it. When he wrote flaming editorials in *L'Avvenire* denouncing conscription he found his paper banned from the mails. After President Wilson's declaration of war, the United States government moved against the I.W.W.—Tresca, Gurley, Ettor, Giovannitti, Big Bill Haywood, and 164 others were indicted in Chicago under the 1917 espionage and sedition laws. Ninety-three were sentenced to prison terms. Tresca and Gurley were among those released, since they had broken with the I.W.W. before the new laws became effective.

Undaunted by his narrow escape, Tresca traveled through the Italian enclaves of the East, denouncing Wilson's imperialist war and proclaiming that the real war for freedom was being fought by Lenin and Trotsky in Russia. Because he proclaimed in Italian to Italians, he managed to escape the more assiduous attentions of the monolingual police, although in Canton, Ohio, he came as close as he ever had to dying. As he arrived, the police were waiting for him at the station platform, but he, wise in their ways, managed to drop off the train just outside the station. He made a detour through back alleys to the hall where he had been billed to speak, only to discover that it, too, had been taken over by the police. An anarchist comrade spotted him on the street and took him home. There, among his Italian friends, he was relaxing over a meal in the kitchen when the police burst in, led by the chief with a drawn revolver who fired almost point-blank at Tresca. The men shouted, a woman screamed, but Tresca seemed bulletproof.

"Arrest me," he told the chief, "but stop shooting at my friends!" He did not notice at first that one old friend sitting beside him had slumped forward, mortally wounded. Years before he and that friend had marched behind the red flag in Sulmonia. The young radical had followed Tresca across the ocean to become in middle age, a conservative businessman. Now he was dead because he had merely dropped in with a bottle of wine to chat reminiscently with the friend of his youth.

Such wild and ironic happenings were the very substance of Tresca's life. When Mussolini, after his march on Rome, began to organize the overseas Italians, Tresca organized his own direct-action groups to drive the New York *fascisti* from the streets of Little Italy. It was his boast that from 1925 on he had made it impossible for the fascists to hold meetings in New York. Stung by such obduracy, the Duce arranged to have a New York gunman eliminate his former comrade. But Tresca's apparently bullet-proof figure was so formidable, and his popularity in Little Italy so massive that the gunman hesitated. His hesitation became panic when the Mafia, for inscrutable reasons of its own, "suggested" that Tresca was not to be harmed. Finally, the would-be assassin came to Tresca, confessed his hired intentions and begged forgiveness.

Unlike many of his comrades, Tresca had never felt the need of protecting himself with a weapon. Now, during his struggle with the New York *fascisti,* when for the first time he found himself compelled to move with a bodyguard, he decided to buy himself a revolver. On the very day he bought it he accidentally pulled the trigger and shot himself in the foot, an accident that he considered even more comic than did his friends.

Ever since the Haymarket Massacre of 1886 when six policemen had been killed by a bomb thrown at a Chicago anarchist meeting, the name "anarchist" in America conjured up the cartoonist's image of the bearded foreigner, bomb in hand. Anarchism's own vision was of a golden age when all governments would be done away with and each individual would accept his innate responsibilities in a world of voluntary co-operation. The means to this goal—in Malatesta's portentous words—would be revolutionary destruction; the immediate instrument terrorism, the politics of the deed. By spectacular acts of political assassination, anarchists would stamp their image on the world. One bomb, the anarchist high priest Kropotkin insisted, made more propaganda than a thousand pamphlets, and to demonstrate this the direct-action anarchists had struck down presidents and kings. Denjiro Kotoku had tried to kill the Mikado, Mateo Morral made an attempt on the King of Spain, Luigi Luccheni assassinated the Empress of Austria, Santa Ceserio killed President Carnot of France and Leo Czolgosz had shot President McKinley. Although after the First World War the anarchists lost much of their mass support to the Communists, their individual acts of violence continued. At the Peace Conference in 1919 the anarchist Emile Cottin shot and wounded Clemenceau. Most anarchists—as Emma Goldman in her later days—rejected the politics of the deed, but they were not prepared to reject their comrades who did not. Nor did native Americans, who generally attributed spectacular events like the 1920 Wall Street explosion to anarchists, make any distinction between theorists and bombers.

The year following the war seemed to bring more problems to the

United States, or at least more disillusioning problems, than the war itself—
nationwide strikes, inflation, a crime wave, jobless ex-servicemen. In their wake
came distrust of foreigners and the search for a scapegoat. The scapegoat itself
accommodatingly turned belligerent. Radicals, anarchists, socialists, and the
two nascent American Communist parties saw a great light in the East, and
hailed the Bolshevik Revolution as the harbinger of the second American
Revolution. John Reed expected such an overturn almost momentarily. Even
the mild Eugene Debs announced that he was a Bolshevik "from the crown of
my head to the tips of my toes."

The Attorney General of the United States, A. Mitchell Palmer, shared
with John Reed his belief in the imminence of revolution, which he predicted
for May Day, 1920. Under Palmer's direction large numbers of the foreign-
born, whether naturalized or not, were illegally and often brutally rounded up
and herded into detention centers. Those aliens among them who could be
identified as Communists and anarchists were deported.

To this blunt harassment the direct-action anarchists replied even more
bluntly with dynamite. Bombs were found in the packages mailed to the
Attorney General, the Postmaster General, the Secretary of Labor, the Commissioner of Immigration, J. P. Morgan, John D. Rockefeller, and others. In
May, 1919, when the leader of the American anarchists, the leonine Luigi
Galleani, was deported there were reprisal bombings in eight cities. The chief
target was Attorney General Palmer in Washington. Just as he was going to
bed, a bomb blew in the whole front of his house. Palmer was not injured.
Apparently the bomb had gone off prematurely and killed its carrier, for
fragments of a body were found up and down the street.

In time the Department of Justice concluded that the dead bomber was
Carlo Valdinoce, a former associate of Galleani's. One of the few who knew
this for a certainty was Tresca, who had replaced Galleani as informal leader
of the anarchists in the United States. Without any intention, merely by the
force of his personality, the now-gray and bearded leader assumed the role of a
father figure for comrades and associates who, at least in theory, did not
believe in father figures and leaders. In the sea of troubles that the anarchists
found themselves in, theorists and direct-actionists turned to Tresca almost
automatically. He knew their thoughts and their deeds, he shared their inner-
most secrets. He gave them his skilled and unstinted help. They in turn gave
him their admiring trust.

Flyers calling for the proletariat to smash the tyranny of capitalism,
signed by "The Anarchist Fighters," had been found scattered in the neighborhood of Attorney General Palmer's shattered house. Government agents
traced them to two anarchist printers in Brooklyn, Roberto Elia and Andrea
Salsedo, who had once worked for Galleani. Elia and Salsedo were taken to the
Manhattan offices of the Department of Justice and detained for some weeks.
Tresca and a committee he had formed to aid the Palmer raid victims tried
without success to help the two men. Elia was eventually deported, while
Salsedo—who gave evidence and then regretted it—committed suicide by
jumping out the fourteenth-floor window. While the printers were still con-
fined by the Department of Justice, an inconspicuous Massachusetts anarchist

came to see Tresca. He, Bartolomeo Vanzetti, had been sent by his Boston comrades to inquire about the two prisoners. Nine days before Venzetti's arrival in New York there had been a hold-up murder in South Braintree, Massachusetts. Eight days after Vanzetti returned home, he and a comrade, Nicola Sacco, were—by sheerest chance—plucked off a street car a dozen miles from South Braintree and held on suspicion of this murder.

As soon as Sacco and Vanzetti were arrested, the Boston anarchists hired local lawyers to defend them. Vanzetti was identified by several witnesses as having participated in an earlier robbery attempt at Bridgewater, Massachusetts, where, although there had been much shooting, no one was killed. Vanzetti was tried first on this lesser charge, found guilty of attempted armed robbery, and sentenced to twelve to fifteen years in prison.

Tresca was furious at what he considered the bungling of the Boston anarchists and their local lawyers. He now engaged Fred Moore, a bohemian radical and a former general counsel of the I.W.W., to take over the defense.

If it had been left to Massachusetts lawyers to defend Sacco and Vanzetti, the two obscure Italians, whether convicted or acquitted, would never have shed their obscurity. It was Moore, with his flair for propaganda and his contacts with so many radical labor groups all over the country and even abroad, who took the fate of the two immigrants and made it into a blazing international issue.

Tresca's continuing attacks on the Duce and the Italian monarchy were duly noted by the Italian Embassy in Washington. When in 1923 he printed a small advertisement in his paper *Il Martello* (The Hammer) for a book on birth control, the Embassy complained to the postal authorities and Tresca was prosecuted for sending obscene matter through the mails. He was convicted and sentenced to a year and a day in the Federal Penitentiary in Atlanta. In protest, H. L. Mencken reprinted the advertisement in his *American Mercury* and vainly challenged the government to prosecute him.

Congressman Fiorello La Guardia managed to persuade President Coolidge to pardon Tresca after the impenitent anarchist had spent three months in Atlanta. As soon as it was learned that he was a friend of Eugene Debs, he passed the time like a star boarder. Debs had served his time in Atlanta earlier, and his genial nature and simple goodness had made an unforgettable impression on both guards and prisoners.

On his way North from Atlanta, Tresca stopped off in Washington like any tourist to see the sights. A group of children happened to be standing before the main gate of the White House, and Tresca, as he passed, stopped to talk to them. He was fond of children and, like a benign uncle, soon found himself in the middle of a chattering circle. Then a White House attendant appeared and beckoned to the group to come inside. The children insisted on taking Tresca along on what turned out to be a tour of the White House that ended with everyone shaking hands with President Coolidge. It must have been an incongruous sight when the ebullient Italian grasped the flabby hand of the taciturn Yankee. Reporters thought so when they spotted Tresca on the way out. Next day the headlines announced: CRIMINAL ANARCHIST RELEASED FROM ATLANTA MAKES PEACE WITH PRESIDENT. Tresca's embarrassment was voluble. Coolidge's was not, but the attendant who brought in the anarchist with the children lost his job.

In the twenties, anarchism was an obviously dwindling cause, its more violent adherents absorbed by the Communist wave, the others turning to socialism. In America the emerging second-generation Italians for the most part forsook the radical politics of their fathers to become Democrats and Republicans. Tresca changed too, in emphasis if not in theory. In his middle years, he turned more and more from the heady dream of an international working class to the defense of the individual against oppression.

Just as in the circle of political thought the discipline of fascism and the compulsion of communism come to coincide, so do anarchism and conservatism approach one another with their emphasis on the responsibility of the individual. Tresca, the last great anarchist leader, ended in the conservative belief that the ultimate discipline is self-discipline and that the just society must be built on loving-kindness.

In 1919, as Emma Goldman was deported on the *Buford* she thumbed her nose at receding America. To her Russia was the northern Promised Land. The promise, however, lasted only the few months it took her to find out that the Russian anarchists were being liquidated in the cellars of the Lubyanka. In 1921, after Trotsky's merciless suppression of the anarchist revolt of the Kronstadt sailors, she left Russia. For the rest of her life she remained convinced that the brutalities of the Soviet Union far exceeded anything known in the capitalist world.

Tresca, now chiefly concerned in fighting the imported *fascisti,* did not react as did Emma Goldman. He continued to cooperate with the Communists even when the Boston Sacco-Vanzetti Defense Committee, in the later stages of the case, was bitterly and publicly denouncing them. In 1925 when James Cannon, on orders from Moscow, organized the International Labor Defense Tresca allowed his name to be included among the non-Communist decoy minority on the executive committee. Not until 1934 when the Communists maneuvered to disrupt a strike of New York hotel workers did he break with them, and two years later he was still willing to cooperate with the Popular Front to support the Spanish Republic in the civil war. But word soon came to him of the ruthless Communist control of the International Brigade volunteers and of the Communist liquidation of the anarchist militia. His old friend Camillo Berneri, an Italian anarchist intellectual, was assassinated by OGPU agents in the streets of Barcelona. Communists seized and executed another acquaintance of his, the old Trotskyite Andrés Nin, who had been for a time minister of justice in the Catalan Government.

But whatever the vagaries of politics and policy, Tresca never let them interfere with his emotions. The end of his relationship with Gurley Flynn came not through any political differences but when a man presented her with a package of love letters that Tresca had written to the man's wife. After Tresca had left Gurley he took up with a Communist sculptress, and lived for a while in a *ménage à trois* under her roof, with the roof expenses provided by her husband. OGPU agents often dropped in at the studio, and in that period before the Spanish Civil War Tresca remained on friendly terms with many of them. Subsequently he had a more lasting affair with another Communist, Juliet Stuart Poyntz. She, with a hard veneer of physical attraction, a Daughter of the American Revolution, aristocratic in appearance and revolutionary in ambition, was until 1934 a member of the Communist District Executive Committee. Then she officially dropped out of the party to become a spy for the OGPU. Following the assassination of Stalin's associate, Sergei Kirov in Leningrad in that same year, she was called to Moscow and took part in some of the OGPU interrogations there. The horror of what she saw was too much for her. When she returned to New York, broken in nerve and belief, she refused to take on any new OGPU assignments. Orders to eliminate her came from Yagoda the OGPU chief in Moscow. It was her murder, as the culmination of similar murders in the Spanish Civil War, that set Tresca irrevocably against the Communists.

Juliet Poyntz disappeared in the autumn of 1937, the same year that the Communists drove the anarchists to the wall in Barcelona. She left her room in the American Women's Hotel, an unfinished letter on her desk and none of her friends ever saw her again. Tresca would not let her disappearance rest, although it took him several years to fit together enough bits and pieces of elusive fact to discover what had happened.

She had been enticed from the hotel by a telephone call from one of her former lovers, Shachno Epstein, an editor of the New York *Freiheit*. He, fearful to the point of collapse, had been forced by the OGPU to act as her decoy. The two met at Central Park. Epstein led her along an isolated path close to a large parked car. Then he stopped. Two OGPU agents sprang out of the car, seized her, forced her inside, and drove away, leaving Epstein shaking and alone. With the woman muffled in back, they drove through Westchester and into Dutchess County. Not far from the Roosevelt estate, at Hyde Park in a remote wooded area, they garroted her and buried her body.

Tresca, when he felt that he had gathered enough clues, went to the district attorney's office and demanded an investigation. Communist publications at once began to refer to him as a police spy, and party members hinted that he would be next on the OGPU list. He, through his Italian followers, let it be known that if anything happened to him, the Communist Party Secretary, Earl Browder, would be killed in retaliation.

For the Communists, Tresca committed the ultimate sin when he agreed to serve on John Dewey's commission to sift the treason charges made against Trotsky during the Moscow Trials. After sittings held in New York, Washington and Mexico City, the commission found Trotsky innocent. Tresca was singled out for attack by the *Daily Worker,* and the Italian Communist leader Pietro Allegra published a pamphlet calling attention to Tresca's "moral suicide" and demanding the "elimination from society of beings who are hateful to themselves and to society."

It was of singular and long-standing annoyance to the Communists that Tresca was able to keep them out of the Garibaldi Society, the leading organization of Italian anti-fascists. Even in the hothouse period of Russian-American friendship during World War II, he continued to bar the way to their infiltration. In 1942, the Office of War Information organized the Italian-American Victory Council to arrange overseas broadcasts and prepare for political changes in Italy after the war. So great was Tresca's influence that he was able to exclude Communists as well as ex-fascists from the new organization. For the fellow travelers of the Italian section of the OWI Tresca was as awkward an obstacle as he was to the Communists.

When the awkward obstacle was eliminated that January evening in 1943, it seemed both simple and convenient to let the blame fall on the elusive ex-fascists. Washington was willing to let it go at that. So was New York's Mayor La Guardia, tipped off by his friend Congressman Vito Marcantonio. So was the district attorney. The man who arranged Tresca's murder remained officially unknown.

He had not been unknown to Tresca, however. His name was Vittorio Vidali, alias Carlos Contreras, alias Enea Sormenti, and he had come from Mexico on a special mission to get rid of Tresca. "Where he is, I smell death," Tresca told a friend a few days before he was shot down, when he learned that Vidali had been seen in the city.

Tresca had known him in New York in the twenties. In 1928, Vidali had been deported to Mexico. There he developed his talent for political assassination by arranging the murder of Antonio Mella, a Cuban ex-Communist who had turned against the party and was living in exile.

With the outbreak of the Spanish Civil War, Vidali went to Spain and under the *nom de guerre* of Colonel Carlos Contreras became the political commissar of the Fifth Brigade, which conducted the bloodiest of the Communist-directed purges. It was by his arrangement, and in spite of the protests of the Spanish Republican Prime Minister Juan Négrin, that Andrés Nin was executed. At the war's end Vidali escaped to Mexico where he managed the first attempt on the life of the exiled Trotsky. In May, 1942, Tresca denounced him on the front page of *Il Martello* as a "commandant of spies, thieves and assassins." Within months Vidali took his revenge. He was the type who liked to take his revenge personally. Possibly he was the gunman waiting near the Fifth Avenue entrance to Tresca's office building. Almost certainly he was in the getaway car.*

Carlo Tresca's death marked the end of the great anarchist leaders. Kropotkin, Merlino, Malatesta, Galleani, all were gone. Three years before Tresca was killed, Emma Goldman died. "A mountain of integrity," Rebecca West called her. The same was true of all the anarchist leaders. They were what they said they were, they believed what they said they believed, and no cause or end was for them worthy of a lie.

When Tresca sent Moore on to Boston to represent two unknown anarchists in a local murder trial, he created the Sacco-Vanzetti case. It developed into one of those world-encompassing issues that occur perhaps once in a generation and that polarize a society. Conservative New Englanders defiantly

---

* *Vidali is at present the leader of the Communists in Trieste.*

insisted that the two men were guilty. But in the liberal intellectual world that prevailed outside New England it became a dogmatic conviction that Sacco and Vanzetti were two innocent radicals willfully done to death for their political beliefs by a reactionary and corrupt social order. According to this dogma their innocence was self-evident, the trial a frameup, the jury composed of Yankee bigots, the district attorney a scoundrel, and the judge a senile and profanely biased old man. Massachusetts itself became the arch-criminal when the governor and a special committee appointed by him refused to revoke the death sentences.

Most of the books, pamphlets, plays, articles, and poems about the Sacco-Vanzetti case have all taken the dogma of the men's martyrdom for granted. The dogma long ago became a fixed liberal canon, closed to debate. Yet, ironically, the man who shaped the canon was the man who shattered it.

If there was one man who possessed the ultimate inner knowledge of the Sacco-Vanzetti case, that man was Carlo Tresca. Just as Tresca had known that it was Valdinoce who had blown himself up on the steps of Attorney General Palmer's town house, so he knew the whole hierarchy of direct actionists and their secrets. A few weeks before he died he was talking with Max Eastman, who, whatever his own shifts in politics, had remained his close friend over the years. Some time before, Eastman had written a Tresca "Profile" that appeared in *The New Yorker*. Eastman was perplexed by recent rumors he had heard of Moore's later doubts about the innocence of Sacco and Vanzetti.

"Carlo," he asked his friend suddenly, "would you feel free to tell me the truth about Sacco and Vanzetti?"

Tresca could have answered in many ways. He could have simply said no. He could have said that he did not know the truth. He could have said that the men were innocent. Instead, and without hesitation, he told Eastman: "Sacco was guilty, but Vanzetti was not."

And with the unqualified honesty of his reply, in those seven bare words, he rent the most cherished American liberal myth of the century.

John the Bold: Boston's John F. "Honey Fitz" Fitzgerald

THE THREE-ACT PLAY runs a century: sixty years from the Great Hunger in Ireland to the election of John Francis Fitzgerald—"Honey Fitz" to Massachusetts—as Mayor of Boston; forty more years to see his namesake grandson, the twenty-nine-year-old John Fitzgerald Kennedy, elected to Congress from

Honey Fitz's old district as the first planned step to the Presidency. Those three dates, cut so deeply in Boston's history, mark the beginning, middle, and end of a phenomenon as old as history itself—the superseding of one class by another. Seventy years before the Potato Famine the seaport peninsula had seen it all happen before when on a blustery March day in 1775, Admiral Lord Howe embarked the Boston garrison, and the provincial aristocracy sailed away with the redcoats into exile. Those proudly armigerous Brattles and Vassalls and Dudleys and Hutchinsons abandoned the town to the non-armigerous class below them.

As Boston resumed its pace after the Revolution, the old mansions had new faces in them. "Fellows who would have cleaned my shoes five years ago now ride in chariots," a disgruntled relative of General Joseph Warren observed. The emergents were the sober, hard-faced merchants, men who would never dream of giving up their new counting houses for moth-eaten loyalties. Inheriting the town by default, they—within the limits of their bourgeois sobriety—came to adopt the behavior pattern of their predecessors. One can mark the two eras by comparing the Palladian sophistication of Governor Shirley's Roxbury mansion (1745) with the naïveté of Bulfinch's State House (1795), just as one can mark the next emergence in the contrast of the brick Federalist town houses of Beacon Hill with the Hyannis compound.

It takes about three generations for a new class to consolidate itself, and it took the grandsons of the Federalist merchants to give Boston its literary flowering and its label of the Athens of North America. That moment of flowering was not so much fruition as the pause before the end. And the end came to the self-contained brick town with the waves of Irish immigrants fleeing the Famine.

Between 1846 and 1854 over a million and a half people left Ireland for North America. They were driven out, dispossessed, without hope. Because the Cunard Line terminus was then at Boston, most of them landed there. Sunk in their defeat, they came over like cattle. Five percent of them died aboard the "coffin ships" on the way. The stench of those ships brought back memories of the old slavers; the Boston Harbor Master could recognize the odor of an immigrant vessel when it was still off Deer Island. Often there would be thirty or forty deaths in the course of a voyage on a ship containing 500 to 600 passengers.

The immigrants' memory of that flight and that passage and the desolation of their arrival remained green and bitter for generations. Over half the immigrants were illiterate; three quarters had no trade. In Boston their life-span averaged fourteen years. An able-bodied Irish laborer in the city could not in the 1850s earn enough by himself to keep his family. During the first-year depression of the Civil War the newcomers in their Paddyvilles and Mick Alleys starved. With their arrival they became the solid core of the new urban proletariat, alien in temperament, tradition, and belief to that Yankee plutocracy for whom they were to furnish the cheap labor and from whom later—to the outraged astonishment and moral indignation of the latter—they were to take over Boston.

They were the base of the social pyramid, the unfailing source of exploit-able labor: ditchdiggers, stevedores, hod carriers, and stableboys. Construction bosses from all over America sent to Boston for fresh supplies of Irish workers. The Paddies went as contract laborers in coaches with sealed doors, the curtains nailed across the windows. Along the Erie Canal and the new railroad lines they died like flies.

These unassimilable foreigners with their uncouth solidarity more than doubled the population of static Boston, turning it from a coherent and comprehensive town to an incoherent and incomprehensible metropolis. From the padded perspective of the welfare state, it is easy to condemn the callousness of the Yankee Bostonians toward the newcomers, but the tremendous forced migration had no precedent; there was no mechanism for dealing with it. Beacon Hill felt no sense of responsibility for what was happening in East Boston. Rather, the Yankee epigoni, appalled by the Celtic locust-swarm, withdrew to the Beacon Hill–Back Bay redoubt. Unlike their Tory predecessors they did not quit the fort. For decades yet they would manage to keep political control of what they felt was their city. Its financial structure was and would remain in their hands—the industries, the banks, the stores, the investment houses. It was in reaction to these untouchable newcomers that the tradition of Boston *hauteur* came into being, the proper Bostonian, the myth of the Brahmin—that term the kindly Dr. Oliver Wendell Holmes coined originally to mean no more than a bread-and-water intellectual asceticism and that would now come to mean a class-conscious membership in the Yankee State Street financial oligarchy.

Though exploitable, the Irish seemed to the newly proper Bostonians (in the words of Mayor Lyman) "a race that will never be infused with our own, but on the contrary will always remain distinct and hostile." In the harsh atmosphere of Boston, alienated from the common life of the community both by their background and their religion, the Irish formed a society within a society, an emerging Catholic political bloc of their own against the Protestant Yankee oligarchs. The younger immigrants formed gangs in the spirit of the old Irish Whiteboys. During the seventies and eighties, these gangs and barroom associations controlled the politics of their street and block, gradually spreading out, precinct by precinct, ward by ward, until it was clear that in a matter of time the Irish would capture the city. Politics came naturally to the temperament of the Celts, particularly when all other avenues of mobility were barred to them.

Following the pattern of almost all ethnic groups, the transplanted Irish began by electing their best. Hugh O'Brien was the first Irish immigrant to become mayor. With the support of dissident Yankee Democrats, he was elected in 1884 for the first of four one-year terms. Six years previously he had been chairman of the Board of Aldermen, and this date marks the first break in the Yankee political structure of the city, although the Irish position was not consolidated for another generation. Not until 1902 did Boston receive its second Irish-born mayor, Patrick Collins. Both O'Brien and Collins were outstanding men, able and honest, the type one might expect to find as Lord

Mayor of Dublin or Cork or Limerick. Collins, whose widowed mother had brought him over as a child in the Famine years, started out in life as an upholsterer. After years of struggle he managed to enter the Harvard Law School and received his degree at twenty-seven. As first president of the American branch of the Irish Land League he became a friend of Parnell. In 1880 he was elected to Congress from the newly reapportioned and overwhelmingly Democratic district that included Boston's North and West Ends, and East and South Boston. He served three terms. In 1893 President Cleveland appointed him consul general in London.

Like his poet-friend John Boyle O'Reilly, Collins in his innate mobility tried to pretend away the caste barriers erected against the proletarian Irish. He denied that there was any such thing as an Irish vote, and declaimed passionately: "Americans we are; Americans we will remain." He hoped for the future of the Boston Irish in the light of his own development as a process of accommodation and acceptance, with the Irish conforming to the respectable pattern of their Yankee neighbors. But in the hard emergence of the Fitzgeralds and the Curleys and the Coakleys he saw this hopeful dream dissolve. In his later years, disillusioned, Collins turned to drink, even as O'Reilly in his disillusionment finally ended his own life.

Collins, on his return from England, was urged by Boston Democrats to help reunite the quarreling factions in the party by running for mayor. Reluctantly, he agreed. He was elected in 1901 and re-elected in 1903. Unbribably honest, he disliked the political atmosphere of City Hall. The practical necessities of patronage he detested. While managing to thwart the City Council's periodic raids on the treasury, he preached "caution, prudence and economy" to deaf-eared politicians. In 1905 he died in office. President Cleveland wrote of him: "In public life he was strictly honest and sincerely devoted to the responsibilities involved." With one almost accidental exception he was the last mayor of Boston for half a century of whom this could be said.

After him the practical men took over. The Irish-American politicians, more and more of them now second generation, felt no obligation to observe rules made by the Back Bay ascendancy who had exploited them. The way was open and the trough full. In the autumn of 1905, John F. Fitzgerald was elected Mayor of Boston.

Honey Fitz, he was called, for his mellifluous rendering of "Sweet Adeline" on the hustings and on all possible social occasions except funerals. The song became his trademark. The taking over of City Hall by this dynamic little political buccaneer was as decisive a date in the history of Boston as General Howe's evacuation of the town.

John Francis Fitzgerald was not born with a silver spoon in his mouth, but he was born with a spoon—and this was much in the Irish North End in 1863. His father Thomas had come from Wexford, and like most immigrant Irishmen had worked first as a laborer, but by the time his third son Johnny came into the world, he had become the proprietor of a North End grocery and liquor store. Four more sons were to follow.

A hundred years before, the North End had been a fashionable residential section with an eighteenth-century unsegregated mixture of stout artisan houses like Paul Revere's scattered between the mansions of the aristocracy. Governor Thomas Hutchinson had his elegant town house there, with the English Crown carved on the lintels, where he had written his history of Massachusetts until the house was sacked by the Stamp Act mob in 1765. Encroached on by the business district, the neighborhood had managed to preserve a faded respectability until it was overwhelmed by the Famine immigrants. These ragged illiterates swarmed up from the waterfront to pack the partitioned rooms of decayed mansions, to overflow into the hulls and gutters of the dock alleys and rot away in basement warrens. Copp's Hill with its ancient burying ground was renamed Connemara Hill, Donegal Square's earlier name was forgotten, and Kerry Village came into being. The North End became and stayed a slum.

The Fitzgeralds lived in a four-story, eight-family, red brick tenement near the Old North Church. Their flat had no bath, no modern gas lighting, but no other family shared the few rooms and there was always food on the table. By the standards of the Irish North End the Fitzgeralds were well off, and the boys did not think otherwise. Young Johnny came to love the narrow streets and never developed the bitter sense of alienation that his more savage rival James Michael Curley did.

"Johnny Fitz" the gang called him. He was smaller than the other boys, quicker with his feet than his fists. The teeming streets, littered with horse droppings, crowded with pushcarts and hucksters, were all he at first knew. He tagged after the older boys in their games along the docks. Masts and spars were part of his horizon. On winter days fog would often blanket the North End. In the hot, breathless summer nights the boy, lying in bed with his brothers, listened to the long-drawn wail of steamship whistles, the clang of the East Boston ferry bell. Johnny Fitz felt the sea in his bones. He never forgot it. "My playgrounds," he said years later, "were the streets and wharves busy with ships from every part of the world."

Early he showed that somewhat officious enterprise that is the mark of the embryo politician. The Fitzgerald brood were of course regular attenders at the North End's St. Stephen's, and Johnny was equally regular in attending all the parish social functions. As he grew older he helped the priests run picnics, minstrel shows, suppers, fairs, and dances. At outings he usually won the sprints and always the potato race. So involved did he become in neighborhood affairs, so reliable was he in getting things done, that he was elected president of the Neptune Associates when most of the members were old enough to be his father. The club was the strongest social and athletic organization in the North End.

Yet no one could say that Johnny Fitz was Alger all the way. At a time when most North End boys were considered fitted for life with a grammar school diploma, he attended the Boston Latin School where, as a contemporary of Santayana and Berenson, he received a reasonably classical education. During those years he lost his mother. On graduating from Boston Latin he entered the Harvard Medical School, but at the end of his first year his father died, and he had to turn to and help keep the family together. He left Harvard—still a heretical institution to most of the Boston Irish—and took the examination for a job in the Custom House. "I had to take care of all six of my brothers," he liked to relate tremulously at political rallies in after years, neglecting to add that he was then eighteen and that two of his brothers were several years older. "I washed dishes, scrubbed floors, sifted ashes and brought up scuttles of coal and firewood, climbing three flights of creaky stairs. For some reason it was my trust to boss the family. I even washed the faces of the younger boys every day, and oftentimes dressed them."

He came out near the top of the list on his examination, and for the next three years served as a clerk in the Custom House, where he took the measure of the civil service. Then he resigned to set up an insurance office in the North End, specializing in fire insurance. In those willow years he joined every organization that came his way and made his way to others: The Massachusetts Order of Foresters, the Ancient Order of Hibernians, the Knights of St. Rose, the Red Berry Club, the Heptasophs, the Royal Arcanum, the Charitable Irish Society, the Dorchester Catholic Club, the St. Alphonsus Association, the Catholic Union of Boston, the Young Men's Catholic Association of Boston College, the Franklin Typographical Association, the Knights of Columbus, and still others. He was glib and persuasive in casual talk, he was noddingly acquainted with almost all the North End families, and he knew every voter by name. Although nothing like a generation before, the North End was still a slum. Johnny Fitz sentimentalized it even as he flattered its inhabitants. "Dear old North End" tripped so easily and so frequently from his tongue that his supporters there came to be known as "Dearos." To those who were not his supporters, young Johnny became Fitzblarney. When he was twenty-six he married Mary Josephine Hannon, a young woman whose good looks became one of the inherited characteristics of the Kennedy clan. She had been Johnny Fitz's "girl" for eight years. After their marriage some of the Fitzgerald brothers moved in with them.

Johnny Fitz, with his flourishing insurance business and his face amiably familiar from one end of the North End to the other, was now as ready for politics as a duckling for a pond. Outwardly he suggested more a bantam rooster than a duckling, diminutive and cocky. He was a bouncing, dapper man, so much so that one tended to overlook at first the narrow mouth, the eyes a little too close together, the ready voice pitched just a little too high.

Democratic Boston in the nineties had no consolidating and controlling Tammany Hall as in New York. Power was split among the ward bosses: in the West End, Martin Lomasney—the Ward 8 Mahatma—the most picturesque, the most notorious, yet also the best of the bosses; in East Boston, Patrick Joseph Kennedy, a genial saloon keeper (he would become the paternal grandfather of the future President); in the South End, at a later date, James Michael Curley.

Johnny Fitz now set out to make himself the boss of the North End. In 1892 he got himself elected to the Boston Common Council. It is true there were seventy-four other members in this haphazardly disreputable assembly, but it was a beginning. He hired a secretary and turned over most of his insurance business to his brother Henry. The upstairs office became the Jefferson Club, where anyone in the North End was free to drop in at any time. He was at every dance and caper, expanding the Catholic socials, introducing the first "sunlight dances" to Boston. He kept a card index of everyone in his district who needed a job. At Thanksgiving and Christmas he was on hand with turkey baskets. No wedding took place in the North End without a prominently displayed present from him. Each morning he scanned the death notices in the *Globe,* and he never missed a wake. He had the actor's gift of easy tears. In the summer of 1892 he announced that he was running for the State Senate. The old-time leader of Ward 6 died at this time, leaving the young councilor undisputed boss. "The North End Napoleon," the reporters ticketed him, and Johnny Fitz delightedly began to read up on Napoleon and even adopted some of his mannerisms.

Lomasney's announcement from neighboring Ward 8 that he was supporting Fitzgerald made the latter's election certain. It was politicians' luck that the Mahatma had an old grudge against Honey Fitz's opponent.

All the political, historical, and sociological strands that make up the Boston ward boss were to be seen in the career of Martin Lomasney. Yet of all the bosses, he profited least from his position. An orphan bootblack, he started out in manhood as a lamplighter. Eventually he managed to become a city health inspector, and then, as the first step to controlling his ward, he founded the Hendricks Club (named after Cleveland's Vice President, Thomas A. Hendricks, who had once made a speech defending the Irish). It did not take long before Lomasney was master of the West End. His formula was basic: know every family in the West End; help everyone who needs help. The Mahatma's iron paternalism came to dominate the narrow slum streets. There should be a place, he maintained, where a man could come when he was in trouble, no matter what he had done. That place was for Lomasney the Hendricks Club.

From the standpoint of politics [Lomasney wrote], the great mass of people are interested in only three things—food, clothing and shelter. A politician in a district such as mine sees to it that his people get these things. If he does, he hasn't got to worry about their loyalty and support.

Lomasney's cohorts were on hand to meet each immigrant ship as it arrived. The newcomers were welcomed, given lodgings and jobs, and their names entered permanently in the Hendricks Club's files.

For Johnny Fitz and Jim Curley, being a ward boss was a somewhat slippery stepping stone to something else. For Lomasney it was an end in itself. Day after day he held court in the nondescript hall that was the Hendricks Club. His familiar place was behind a battered rolltop desk, a straw hat, yellow with age, tilted over the baldness of his long head. A drooping handlebar mustache framed the jutting eminence of his pugnacious jaw. One by one the supplicants came to him, and his appraising blue eyes measured them through narrow gold-rimmed spectacles. No one would ever have dared lie to the Mahatma.

Ward 8 was a clean ward in the sense that there was no vice, no gambling, no rough stuff, no trouble about votes. Lomasney, with his filing system, saw to that. The little streets voted to his order. So did former residents who returned in droves as overnight lodgers to vote in old Ward 8. In close elections the dead were known to rise from their graves to vote at the Mahatma's bidding. The Mahatma did not take graft. Money to run the Hendricks Club services came from two sources. Those who got jobs, although it was never mentioned, understood that something was expected in return. Lomasney also accepted donations from all concerns that did business in the West End. The firms made their donations voluntarily, even cheerfully, but they might have found reason to regret it if they had not. Whatever money Lomasney had personally he made in real estate. He was shrewd and he was strategically located. It often happened that when the City of Boston needed to acquire a parcel of land for a school or public building, Martin Lomasney was found to have title to that parcel.

There was surprise among the pols when the Mahatma decreed that he was backing Fitzgerald. "Johnny Fitz must have hypnotized Martin," was the ward-heeler's verdict, and indeed Lomasney would live to regret the leg-up he had given to the North End Napoleon. Fitzgerald was almost unanimously elected. He spent two unspectacular years in the Senate quietly building up his machine for the next leap forward, using his State House opportunities to settle relatives and strategic supporters in plush jobs. With exemplary patriotism he sponsored the April 19 anniversary of the Battle of Concord and Lexington as a local holiday, and with an eye to the Italians now appearing on the waterfront he wangled the same favor for Columbus' birthday in October.

In 1894, moving crabwise but with his eye permanently fixed on City Hall, Fitzgerald announced his candidacy for Congress. The congressional district was made up of the first nine wards of Boston, and was the only sure Democratic district in the state. Again Lomasney backed him, opposing Congressman Joseph O'Neil, who was supported by most of the other ward bosses. It was a rough election as the Irish wards knew elections, with slug fests, mattress voters, and sudden darkness in the occasional close-vote polling place as enthusiasts cut the gas pipes while others rushed in to stuff or steal the ballot boxes. But with the solid support of Wards 6 and 8 Johnny Fitz, "the boy candidate," was not to be beaten.

Three terms Fitzgerald served as congressman. In his first term he was the only Catholic in the House. He made no name for himself, achieving scarcely more than a whimsical reputation as a jack-in-the-box for his insistence on popping up in irrelevant debate. He did sponsor a bill to purchase the frigate Constitution, "Old Ironsides," then rotting away at a pier in Portsmouth, New Hampshire. He managed to get the Charlestown Navy Yard reopened, and helped obtain several million-dollar appropriations for Boston Harbor. His love for the sea and for Boston the seaport was real and would last him all his days, but he also knew how to turn this love to his own ends. His chief concern in Congress was to expand his political power. Brother Henry in the North End kept the machine oiled and saw that supplies of oil were forthcoming. Johnny, during the Washington years, bought a house in rural Concord, but he still kept his legal address in the dear old North End.

In the 1895 election the time was not yet for another Irish mayor. Boston's ward bosses had to go outside the city to Quincy for the Yankee Democrat necessary to defeat Republican Mayor Edwin U. Curtis. The man they picked and elected was Josiah Quincy, after whose ancestors the town had been named. Three bosses—no friends of Lomasney's—did the picking: Smiling Jim Donovan, the chairman of the Democratic City Committee; Judge Joseph J. Corbett, the election commissioner; and East Boston's Patrick "P. J." Kennedy. Impressed by the rise of Fitzgerald, they were willing—if he would turn his back on the Mahatma—to admit the congressman to their circle as the fourth mayor-maker. Honey Fitz was willing.

Then in 1901 the Big Four, still biding their time, managed to persuade the austerely respectable Patrick Collins to be their candidate. Collins was easily if reluctantly elected. He always found the job of mayor distasteful. Smiling Jim he made superintendent of streets, but he refused most other patronage demands. Johnny Fitz galled him.

Meanwhile Fitzgerald had bought a moribund neighborhood paper, *The Republic*, for five hundred dollars. This he turned into an Irish-American social weekly which he both edited and published. Nothing in it was of any great interest, nor did readers flock to it. Nevertheless department stores, public utilities, and contractors hurried to buy half- and full-page advertisements. Despite its small circulation and stiff rates, *The Republic* somehow seemed a desirable advertising medium. Soon it was netting its new publisher $25,000 a year.

In 1903 Fitzgerald moved back from Concord to dearer old Dorchester. The house he bought on Welles Avenue was an ornamental wooden chateau in beer-baronial style, with a scroll-work porch, blank plateglass windows, and a mansard turret. On the stair landing he had a stained-glass window installed with a Fitzgerald coat of arms and the Gaelic motto *Shawn A Boo* (John the Bold.)

John the Bold, full of bounce and pugnacious confidence, knew that the municipal election year of 1905 was his year, that he was on the crest of his political wave, and that the tide was coming in. Every ward heeler and precinct worker sensed instinctively that Johnny Fitz would be a candidate, would be indeed *the* candidate for mayor. Collins had died that September, and the question for the bosses was: Whom should they run against this dynamic challenger they had built up so casually a decade before? Smiling Jim and Kennedy turned to the Mahatma, and the three of them decided on City Clerk Edward Donovan.

Impelled from the clerk's office to the hustings, Donovan scarcely knew what hit him. Johnny Fitz was off like a whirlwind on the most spectacular campaign Boston's twenty-four wards had ever seen. Vacant walls were pasted with his posters twice as fast as opponets could tear them down. Bigger, Better, Busier Boston was emblazoned under the smiling Fitzgerald phiz, retouched to benignity by the photographer. The city, long used to pre-election free-for-alls with brickbats and "alley roses" sailing past a speaker's platform, marveled at the roar of its first political motorcade. Honey Fitz toured the wards in a large red car followed by flying squads of what the reporters described as "Napoleon's lancers," to be met in each precinct by crowds of militant Dearos. Ward 8 itself was invaded and here a zealous Dearo at one point pulled a pistol on several Hendricks Clubbers. Secretly, Fitzgerald solicited the help of younger Democratic hopefuls, the bosses-yet-to-be—and secretly they gave help. Even James Michael Curley, soon to be Fitzgerald's most durable enemy, now planned to back him.

For weeks Johnny Fitz made ten speeches a night denouncing the bosses and the "machine," and on the evening before the primaries he reached the almost breathless climax of thirty. But for Lomasney he would have buried Donovan. Fitzgerald won the nomination, carrying twenty of the city's wards, although it took a dozen wards to make up for what happened to him in Ward 8.

The reform Republicans and the Good Government Association—a civic organization founded two years before by the Chamber of Commerce, the Merchants Association, the Associated Board of Trade, the Fruit and Produce Association, and the Bar Association—had succeeded in nominating the highly respected speaker of the Massachusetts House of Representatives, Louis Frothingham. Unreformed Republicans, with the concealed moral and financial encouragement of Fitzgerald, ran Judge Henry Dewey—already beaten by Frothingham in the primaries—as an independent Republican. The split Republican ticket made Fitzgerald's election a certainty, as wily old Martin Lomasney at once realized. Nevertheless the Mahatma preferred defeat with Frothingham. "That gun play," he remarked, "on top of all the stuff they had been springing on the stump, made me determine to fight."

Frothingham represented all the things that Fitzgerald could ring the sour changes on—Harvard, blue blood, inherited wealth. Honey Fitz also spread the rumor thickly (and unjustifiably) that his opponent was anti-Catholic and anti-Irish. He kept up his whirlwind campaign with variations, visiting department stores and glad-handing the salespeople, even inaugurating a "soda water campaign" with refreshments provided for women's groups in critical wards. Honey Fitz had always been—with prudent impartiality—a ladies' man, and women always thought more of him than did men. They were his most solid supporters, from the days when he used to waltz with the wallflowers at the Irish social clubs.

The battle cost Fitzgerald $120,000—twice as much as it did Frothingham. "But it was not money which won," George Kibbe Turner wrote in *Collier's,* "it was action, ingenuity, and boundless, cheerful effrontery. For thirteen years Johnny Fitz had held Ward 6 obedient and cheerful by public jobs. He extended that one basic system of ward politics over all the city."

The new Mayor took possession of the gray mock-renaissance City Hall on School Street like a conqueror exacting the submission of a taken town. *Enrichissez-vous!* Perhaps Johnny Fitz had read the Napoleonic maxim. His cohorts did not need to read it. The Mayor himself kept control of all the city departments except the schools and the police. He replaced physicians on the board of health with saloon keepers, he appointed another saloon keeper Superintendent of Public Buildings, a whitewasher Superintendent of Sewers, a bartender who had been expelled from the legislature Superintendent of Streets. For deserving Dearos he created such new offices as that of City Dermatologist. Eight additional Deputy Sealers were added to the Department of Weights and Measures—a department soon to erupt in open scandal. The vestiges of civil service were circumvented by the invention of novel job categories—Tea Warmers, Tree Climbers, Wipers, Rubber-boot Repairers, watchmen to watch other watchmen. Brother Henry was given charge of patronage and payments. "See Henry!" was the edict from the Mayor's office.

During Johnny Fitz's first administration, graft was blantant in all departments. "Thieves in the House," John Cutler entitled the chapter on that period in his discreet Fitzgerald biography. During these two years the city lost $200,000 in dealings with a single coal company, whose manager later absconded. In subsequent investigations the Finance Commission discovered that Boston had been paying sixty cents a barrel more than the going price for cement—a $240,000 annual loss. "Bills and vouchers could not be found," Leslie Ainley wrote in his life of Lomasney. "City work was contracted and bids often accepted verbally." There were dozens of strange land deals where the city ended up paying three times more than anyone had imagined a given property was worth. The Finance Commission reported "a steady deterioration in the technical competency and moral strength of the heads of executive departments, until administrative business of this great city was, with few notable exceptions, in the hands either of men without education, training, experience, or technical qualifications of any sort, or of men who had become so demoralized by the conditions which surrounded them as to be unwilling to protest against the most obvious extravagance or graft, if favored by the Mayor. For the first time," the Commission went on to say, "a man was elected to the office of Mayor whose aim was not merely to use or perfect the political machine then in existence, but to become that machine itself."

Meanwhile *The Republic* continued to flourish and expand—its advertising rates were perhaps the highest in the nation in ratio to its circulation. The Boston Elevated Street Railway Company and the American Telephone and Telegraph Company bought up pages, as did the New England Telephone Company, Edison Electric, New England Gas and Coke, Boston Consolidated Gas, the Boston and Maine Railroad, and any number of contracting companies. A list of the paper's advertisers read like a summary of the Boston Stock Exchange. In one special issue the city's banks took fourteen pages.

For most of the time the accumulating scandals seemed secondary to the dynamic ubiquitousness of the little man in the mayor's chair, who might suddenly appear at his office in a black-and-brown checked suit, blue striped tie, and blue-stone scarf pin. During his first term, he is estimated to have attended 1200 dinners, 1500 dances, 200 picnics, and 1000 meetings; made 3000 speeches; and danced with 5000 girls. He thought up Old Home Week and applied it first to Boston—even though Beacon Street held aloof. With his entourage he liked to drop in for a sudden meal, amidst the flattering bustle of the staff, at the various city hotels—the Adams House and the Parker House, Young's, the Democratic politicians' eyrie of the Quincy House on the fringe of the North End, the Winter Palace, and the South End's naughtily Edwardian Woodcock. He excelled as a greeter, entertaining personally such varied visitors as Prince Wilhelm of Sweden and the magician Houdini. Between 1905 and 1907 Johnny Fitz made himself a city institution.

Two years of Fitzgerald, however, brought an inevitable reaction. There were still transplanted Irish in Boston who felt that Patrick Collins was a worthier representative than Johnny Fitz and his Dearos. They could still remember how Collins, as mayor, had welcomed the delegates of the National Municipal League and asked them to report to him if they found anything shady in his administration. What the delegates might have found in the Fitzgerald administration did not bear thinking about.

For the 1907 elections anti-Fitzgerald Democrats nominated Representative John Coulthurst. Coulthurst also had the backing of Hearst's *American* and of all the bosses except Lomasney, who this time returned to Johnny Fitz. The Republicans picked their own variety of boss, George A. Hibbard, the Boston Postmaster. Hibbard was a parrot-nosed, thrifty Yankee who announced he was running for one term only for the purpose of "cleaning up the mess." Fitzgerald conducted his usual bouncing, badgering campaign, adding such bizarreries as circulars in Yiddish to persuade the newly arrived Jewish voters. Most Jewish leaders as well as the more responsible Catholic leaders repudiated him. In a narrow election Coulthrust swung enough Democrats from Fitzgerald so that Hibbard was able to win with a plurality of the votes.

Mayor Hibbard, while looking after needy Republicans, did much of what he had promised. He cut down on municipal workers, halved the cost of street maintenance, and reduced the city's debt. Through departmental efficiencies he managed to save about a million dollars. Toward the end of his administration, and in the hope of more reform mayors to come, the Good Government Association maneuvered the adoption of a new city charter. According to its terms party designations were to be dropped from the municipal ballot. There were to be no more primaries, and nominations for mayor could be made by the petition of five thousand voters. A nine-member council would replace the thirteen aldermen and seventy-five councilors.

Electorates soon weary of reform interludes, and those who are barred from the trough weary even sooner. By 1909 it seemed that the wheel had turned and that the colorless Hibbard would be replaced by the pied Johnny Fitz. To avoid four entrenched Fitzgerald years, Republicans and reformers united on the bluest blood of Beacon Street, James Jackson Storrow. A predestined Harvard man, Storrow had been captain of a crew that had beaten Yale, and now, as New England's wealthiest banker, he was an overseer of Harvard College. With far more civic conscience than most of his kind, he had served as chairman of the Boston School Committee, had been a president of the Boy Scouts, had founded the West End Club for newsboys, and had given much for playgrounds and amenities in the slums. A lean, imposing figure, he was a poor speaker. This was offset, however, by his being that atavistic anomaly, a Yankee Democrat.

Smiling Jim Donovan threw in his lot early with Storrow, impressing on the banker the truism that political campaigns cost money. Storrow was impressed—to the extent of half a million dollars before he got through. Storrow money was loosely plentiful, and Smiling Jim understood its application. Curley, then the visibly rising boss of the South End's Ward 17, said later that he had refused $60,000 to side with Storrow. Fitzgerald knew that without the support of Curley and Lomasney he could not win. The three came to an agreement. The thirty-five-year-old Curley, as junior partner, was to take over Fitzgerald's old congressional seat and bide his time in Washington until the next municipal election. What Lomasney was offered remains a secret, but in spite of personal distaste he stuck with Johnny Fitz.

"Take Storrow's money, but vote for Fitzgerald," was the word the Dearos passed round. Storrow tried to argue about corruption and the issues of municipal government. Johnny Fitz simplified the election to a contest between an Irish-Catholic boy from the slums and a wealth-encrusted Harvard blueblood who was anti-Catholic, anti-labor, anti-Negro and anti anything else Fitzgerald could think of between speeches. He papered the walls with large photographs of City Hall on which was inscribed:

NOT FOR SALE MR. $TORROW

"Manhood against Money" was another Fitzgerald slogan that was used under a touchingly domestic photograph of Johnny Fitz, his wife, and their three boys and three girls. The Storrow forces countered with a photograph of Fitzgerald alone, the word GRAFTER lettered across his forehead. That stung enough to bring tears. Storrow even coined the term *Fitzgeraldism* to describe the antics of Johnny Fitz's administration, but when *Fitzgeraldism* appeared in newspaper advertisements, Fitzgerald countered by running parallel advertisements with slogans: "For Better Streets!" . . . "For Better Schools!"

In a day when a political meeting was for many the most entertaining event of the year, when the catharsis of a campaign could purge the emotions, as in later years films and television never could, when partisans packed the hall for hours to wait for their chosen candidate, Johnny Fitz was a circus and a prophet combined. His campaign is said to have cost somebody, if not him, a quarter of a million dollars. During the frenzied weeks before the election, he led his motorcade through several thousand miles of back streets, shouting his tenor voice hoarse at halls and corners. Storrow, trying in his unfortunate Harvard accent to emulate him, was driven out of South Boston by a mob swinging torches and throwing chunks of ice. Fitzgerald even managed to persuade Hibbard, mortally stricken with tuberculosis of the throat, to run as a token candidate in order to draw votes from Storrow.

The Saturday night before the election Fitzgerald staged his biggest and most bumptious rally in Faneuil Hall in the dear old North End. As an added attraction he had hired a brass band, instructing the leader to play "The Star-Spangled Banner" at his entrance and follow it up with "The Wearing of the Green." The latter song concluded before Fitzgerald and his entourage could manage to hand-shake their way to the platform. Because it was a popular song of the moment, and with nothing more in mind, the band leader had his men strike up "Sweet Adeline." Everybody joined in the chorus. When it came time for the second verse, Johnny Fitz, with deft spontaneity, capered down the platform and sang it solo, then led the crowd again in the chorus. And in that bellowing moment of beaming fair faces, the Honey Fitz legend was born. Ever after that the tenor voice and the treacly song would be harmoniously linked, and whenever at a Democratic meeting the speeches began to run dry, the cry would go up for Honey Fitz to sing "Sweet Adeline."

It was generally admitted by politicians afterward that Honey Fitz's demonic gusto in the last few days of the campaign won him the election. On the final night he spoke at thirty-five rallies and topped it off by singing "Sweet Adeline" from the roof of a hack. Even so, in the largest vote in Boston's history, he barely squeaked through with 47,177 votes to 45,775 for Storrow. The ailing Hibbard, repudiated by the Republicans, received only 1,614 votes —but enough to have swung the election if they had gone to Storrow.

Not much could be said about Honey Fitz's second term as Mayor that was not said about his first, except that Boston grew accustomed to the shenanigans. After four more years of Fitzgerald in City Hall no Storrow would have a ghost of a chance of being elected mayor—or would want to take that ghost's chance. And there were the solid accomplishments, whatever their price tag. Honey Fitz built the City Hall Annex, the City Point Aquarium, numberless public convenience stations memorialized with his name, and the Franklin Park Zoo. He founded the High School of Commerce to prepare boys directly for the business world who could not go to college. One of his more original minor inspirations was the painting of white traffic lines, for which he was accused by proper Bostonians of disfiguring the city's historic streets. With appropriate regard for sentiment he established the local sanctity of Mother's Day and began the custom of having a Christmas tree on Boston Common. He also inaugurated the banned-in-Boston tradition by forbidding the Turkey Trot and the tango as immoral, the opera *Salomé* as sacrilegious, and the red flag in parades as both.

The Mayor's official car was now the *Sweet Adeline II.* In 1911, as he sailed for a tour of Europe on the *Franconia,* he sang his theme song from the bridge. For the voyage he had packed a supply of rockets and other fireworks to set off at the first sight of the Irish coast, with the result that the Irish Coast Guard finally signaled: "Do you need help?"

Greeting and entertaining were his official delight. He welcomed such assorted figures at City Hall as the French actress Gaby Deslys, New Jersey's Governor Woodrow Wilson, William Jennings Bryan, Theodore Roosevelt, Lady Gregory, and the lord mayors of Dublin and London. Sir Thomas Lipton relaxed in his company, visiting him not only in Dorchester but in the wooden-gingerbread ark of Fitzgerald's summer house in Hull, overlooking Boston Harbor. In 1914 Honey Fitz's oldest daughter, Rose, married a brash, up-and-coming young Harvard graduate, Joseph Patrick Kennedy, the son of East Boston's P. J.

Honey Fitz had made a bosses' agreement to leave City Hall at the end of his term. He toyed briefly with the quixotic notion of running for governor or even for United States senator, but as his pleasant and profitable months in the gray School Street building narrowed he began to feel that his earlier renunciation was premature. Meanwhile, Congressman Curley, rounding out his second term in Washington, was regarding the gilt eagle on top of City Hall with an increasingly calculating eye. "You are an old man," he told the fifty-year-old Mayor by way of a Curley-type hint. "Get your slippers and pipe and stretch out in your hammock and read *The Ladies' Home Journal.*"

The lone wolf of Ward 17 was the one opponent whom Honey Fitz feared. Unlike most politicians, Curley never developed a nickname. Even though he had begun by imitating the Ward-6 Napoleon, he had been brought up in a harder school. He had a more commanding presence and a more resonant voice, a crueler tongue, and a quicker fist. Honey Fitz may have been meaner, but Curley was tougher, and he had the instinct for the jugular.

In November, 1913, Curley let it be known, officially, that he would be a candidate for mayor in the January election. A few weeks later Honey Fitz came out with the announcement that he had decided to run for a third term. Next day the *Post* quoted Curley's comment: "Fitzgerald wants a licking, and he will get it." The two were now arch-enemies, and in spite of intermittent superficial political gestures of good will, they were to remain enemies the rest of their long lives.

A few days after Honey Fitz's announcement, Curley announced that he would give three public lectures, contrasting famous characters of history with John F. Fitzgerald. His first lecture, given at the Dorchester High School, was on "Graft in Ancient Times *vs.* Graft in Modern Times," with comparisons between the Rome of the Caesars and Boston of the Dearos. The title of the next lecture was advertised as "Great Lovers: from Cleopatra to Toodles"; but before it could be given, Honey Fitz—on the grounds of ill health—had withdrawn his candidacy.

Toodles Ryan was a cigarette girl at the Ferncroft Inn, one of Honey Fitz's ports of call along the Newburyport Turnpike. He had met her there at a large party some years before. A blur of talk followed about the Mayor and the shapely blonde, and their names became more permanently linked in an anonymous limerick. In later years Honey Fitz righteously insisted in a statement to the *Post* that he had never done more than kiss Toodles casually and publicly at the party, with his wife present. Those close to Honey Fitz have tried to argue away the Toodles stories as no more than malicious jokes. Curley insisted that they and similar Honey Fitz tales long current in Boston were true, and he always maintained that his threat to tell what he knew about Toodles drove Fitzgerald from public life.

After his withdrawal, Honey Fitz and the ward bosses—with the exception of Lomasney—united incongruously with the Good Government Association on an anti-Curley candidate, City Councilor Thomas J. Kenney, an honest but uninspired budget expert who had once served on the School Committee. At the last moment P. J. Kennedy shifted his support to Curley. In spite of the opposition of the rest of the bosses—whom Curley now swore to destroy—the young man from the South End was unbeatable.

Winning inspired no charitable thoughts in Curley. When at his inaugural he had to shake hands with his predecessor, he stared coldly away. Then, with Honey Fitz sitting a few feet from him, he attacked the ex-Mayor so bitingly that the latter's face twitched and reddened. Six hundred of Honey Fitz's supporters employed at City Hall had to walk out the back door the day Curley walked in the front.

With Curley's election, Honey Fitz's political career came to an end. Though he would live on for a third of a century, though he would several times be a candidate, he would never again occupy public office.

For some time he enjoyed his leisure. He could now indulge in his passion for long auto rides, for cruising in Boston Harbor, and for sporting events—baseball, football, and prize fights. With the approach of winter, he sunned himself in Florida. His social life buzzed much as ever. He dined and he danced, he spoke and sang. In 1915 he received an honorary doctorate of laws from Notre Dame University, and liked afterward to have himself referred to as Dr. Fitzgerald. But by 1916 he could feel the old political stirrings in his blood.

That year was the first in Massachusetts for direct election to the United States Senate, and Senator Henry Cabot Lodge, who had served three terms by vote of the Massachusetts Legislature, was now forced to take his chances with the electorate. The chill autocratic Yankee with the gray curls and the gray spade beard was not an endearing personality. Disaffected Republicans and old Roosevelt Bull Moosers would have no part of him. Harvard's President Lawrence Lowell was later to refer to him as "a degenerate son of the University." A Yankee Democrat, in the wake of Wilson's Presidential victory, could probably have defeated Lodge that year. Not, however, Honey Fitz. With Curley occupied at City Hall, Fitzgerald managed to grasp the brass ring of the Democratic nomination. Only his Celtic optimism kept him from seeing that the ring was worthless. *The New York Times* could not understand why Massachusetts Democrats had not put up a worthier candidate against the "gentleman from Massachusetts." From the perspective of New York, Honey Fitz was "an amiable kisser of the Blarney Stone, warbler of 'Sweet Adeline,' rider of Florida sharks, butterfly flitting unconcerned around the solid men of Boston."

The following year brought with it another municipal election, but Honey Fitz had no intention of tangling with Curley again. He preferred to take a temporary step down the political ladder and run for Congress from his old district. The present congressman, Peter Tague, was under a cloud in Boston, or at least in Ward 8. Lomasney had originally given Tague the support that elected him, but turned furiously against him when Tague failed to propose in Congress that the entry of the United States into the war be contingent on England's granting Ireland independence. In spite of the Mahatma's backing, Fitzgerald won the nomination by only fifty votes in a contest memorable even in Boston for the numbers of false registrations, mattress voters, repeaters, burnt ballots, and stolen ballot boxes. Tague refused to accept the result and announced defiantly that he was running on stickers. To counter this, Honey Fitz had blocks of stickers printed without the gum on the

back. On election day dozens of his supporters, pretending to be Tague workers, handed out these stickers at the polls. When the ballots were placed in the
box the ungummed stickers fell off, leaving blank ballots. Fitzgerald won by
238 votes. At once Joseph Kane, Tague's tough professional manager, complained to Washington that the election was a fraud. A Congressional committee came to Boston to investigate Kane's charges. They found enough evidence
of fraudulent voting and "padded returns of alleged residents in cheap lodging
houses" to unseat Fitzgerald and replace him by Tague.

In January, 1922, Honey Fitz announced that he was again a candidate
to oppose Lodge for the United States Senate. As a token of party unity he and
Curley shook hands at the Elks Club and then, to prove their harmony, sang
duets of "Sweet Adeline" and "Tammany." But when the Republicans took to
quarreling among themselves like so many Democrats about a candidate for
governor, Honey Fitz decided he would rather take advantage of their dissension than confront the frosty Lodge. Not for another decade would the Irish
Democrats take over the state, and Honey Fitz's challenge to Republican Governor Channing Cox failed by 60,000 votes. Nevertheless, the *Post* paid tribute
to Fitzgerald's coruscating effort: "Nothing like it has ever been seen in Massachusetts. He is the superman of campaigners, and he is greater in defeat than
he ever was in victory."

Honey Fitz, now in his sixties, was grayer, plumper, his jowls deeper, his
face puffier, but still with the old outrageous bounce. Late in 1925 he let it be
known that he was once more a candidate for mayor. Then, four days later, he
changed his mind, to the relief of his son-in-law Joe Kennedy, who was getting
a little tired of the Toodles stories that were revived with each Honey Fitz
candidacy. Instead of becoming a candidate, the ex-mayor celebrated his birthday by singing "Sweet Adeline" over the radio. The mayoralty contest boiled
up with six others, but somehow a Boston campaign without Honey Fitz lost
half its savor. A reporter wrote nostalgically: "Lovers of the spectacular may
regret that this most colorful personality will not be seen charging up and
down the municipal gridiron, going through for gains, being thrown for losses,
smearing his opponents or being smeared. The battle will not be the same with
the 'doctor' out."

Some time in the mid-twenties Fitzgerald sold the Dorchester château
and moved to a rent-free suite in the Bellevue Hotel, the politicians' Valhalla
beside the State House. The summer house in Hull he exchanged for one in
Wareham on Cape Cod, near the Kennedy compound. For an antidote to
restlessness he took long rides in his chauffeur-driven Locomobile. As he grew
older, that mellowing process took over by which politicians and other way-
ward characters become fixtures, so that in the end even their old enemies are
glad to see them. In 1927 when the Adams House with its memories of so many
political figures closed it seemed fitting that Honey Fitz should ring down the
curtain with "Sweet Adeline."

The year 1930 marked his last real political battle. He announced that
he was a candidate for governor. Massachusetts Republicans were never to
recover from that second Depression year. Boston had been a Democratic city

for a generation, and now it was the turn of Massachusetts to become a Democratic state. If Honey Fitz had won the nomination that year, he would have been elected. But two weeks before the primaries he collapsed, and from his hospital bed he sent word that he was withdrawing from the contest. In one of the strange turnabouts of Boston politics, Curley, who had become his most impassioned supporter and speechmaker, refused to accept the withdrawal—not from any belated affection for Honey Fitz but out of blind hatred for the leading candidate, Yankee Democrat Joseph Ely.

In the 1932 Roosevelt year, Curley was the first Massachusetts politician to sense the swing of the tide and to shift his mercurial allegiance from Al Smith to Franklin Roosevelt, a shift so unpopular among local Democrats that he was dropped from the Ancient Order of Hibernians. Honey Fitz remained an Al Smith man right down to the Democratic Convention, even though his astute son-in-law had become a member of the strategy group, "the Silent Six," touring the country in Roosevelt's campaign train. Nevertheless, the old Dearo was granted the innocuous post-election honor of the presidency of the Massachusetts delegation to the Electoral College.

The mellowing process continued, but now to a point of isolation. P. J. Kennedy had died in 1929. Lomasney followed him shortly after Roosevelt's inauguration. Only the indestructable Curley remained, alternately winning and losing elections. In 1936 Honey Fitz became president of the Clover Club, a local Celtic variation of Washington's Gridiron Club, and took the chair for the first time, dressed as Napoleon. The next year, with wry pride, he saw his son-in-law appointed Ambassador to England. On Honey Fitz's seventy-fifth birthday, 750 guests attended a party for him at the Boston Chamber of Commerce, and he noted with content that the patrician ex-secretary of the navy, Charles Francis Adams, was among them. He was on hand to meet Roosevelt's train when it arrived in Boston in 1940, and the younger charmer greeted the old with: "Welcome, Dulce Adelina!"

One of the few Republican survivors of the 1936 landslide had been Henry Cabot Lodge, Jr., the grandson of the "gentleman from Massachusetts," who had managed to capitalize sufficiently on the accumulated resentments against Curley to defeat him in the contest for his grandfather's old senatorial seat. Senator Lodge came up for re-election in 1942, and Roosevelt picked Democratic Joseph Casey to run against him. Honey Fitz, though now eighty years old and in failing health, decided to have his last political fling by contesting the nomination. For a few weeks he staged a radio counter-campaign with ghost-written speeches and a ghostly voice signing off with "Sweet Adeline." Son-in-law Kennedy consulted with Tague's old secretary, Joe Kane, wise in the ways of pols. Kane was sure that Honey Fitz, in spite of his age, could, by spending a few hundred thousand dollars, beat Roosevelt's dictated candidate. Kennedy wanted to know if the old man could beat young Lodge in the election. Kane said that he could not. Kennedy reached for his hat. "I don't know where you're going," he told Kane, "but I'm going back to the Ritz."

Although no one admitted it openly, it was obvious by the forties that the last of the Dearos was slipping. On his eighty-first birthday party at the Parker House a congratulatory message came from the White House addressed to Boston's Number One Booster. Charles Francis Adams was again present. The climax of the party came just as Honey Fitz was singing "Sweet Adeline," when his grandson Jack—now Naval Lieutenant John Kennedy—whom he had not seen for over a year, suddenly walked into the room, lean and yellow but buoyantly alive after surviving the loss of his P.T. boat and an attack of malaria.

There were bewilderments and there was sadness as well in Honey Fitz's closing years. In the spring of 1944 gossip columns spread the report that his granddaughter Kathleen Kennedy, then in London with the American Red Cross, was about to marry the Marquess of Hartington, the eldest son of the Duke of Devonshire. "Impossible," her grandfather told reporters at the Bellevue. "No grandchild of mine would ever marry outside the Catholic Church." But a few days later Kathleen Kennedy and Lord Hartington, a captain in the Grenadier Guards, were married at a registry office. The best man was Kathleen's brother Joseph, then serving in England as a Navy pilot. Young Joe was to die that August when his plane blew up over the Channel on a bombing mission. Lord Hartington was killed in action a month later. If he and his wife had lived, she would have become the first duchess of England, but she herself died in the crash of a private plane in 1948.

Jack Kennedy, after his discharge from the Navy, came to Boston, took an apartment round the corner from the Bellevue to establish his legal residence, and let it be known that in 1946 he would run for Congress from his grandfather's old district. He set up headquarters in the Bellevue and began to build his organization. Ironically, his chief strategist became that same hard professional, Joe Kane, who had unseated Honey Fitz twenty-seven years before. Grandfather and grandson spent hours together, the Dearo retelling his old political sagas, giving his shrewd old advice. But Jack, with his wealth and his Harvard background and his clipped speech, represented a new breed of Irish-Americans for whom the Dearos and the Smiling Jims and the Mahatmas had become crudely and quaintly obsolete, like gas lighting. The young supporters and strategists who gathered around Jack Kennedy in the Bellevue were Democrats in the liberal New Deal image: lean young men, college educated, most of them ex-officers, many from private schools, with only their surnames to show kinship with the old.

Ten candidates filed for the Democratic nomination—equivalent in that district to the election. Joe Kane saw to it that there were enough to fragment the vote. He paid one candidate $7500 "to stay in or get out," whichever Kane might decide was more useful. When one Joseph Russo threatened to monopolize the Italian vote, Kane dug up a second Joseph Russo to run against him. Kennedy won easily with 43 percent of the vote.

At the Bellevue, Honey Fitz danced a jig on top of a table to celebrate his grandson's victory and followed it with a quavering "Sweet Adeline." Then, with the pride of a grandfather, and perhaps with the prescience of an old pol, he predicted that Jack would be President of the United States.

Honey Fitz lived long enough to celebrate his diamond wedding and to see Jack overwhelmingly renominated for Congress, but not quite long enough to see him triumph over Senator Henry Cabot Lodge, Jr., the grandson of his old Brahmin adversary.

I remember first seeing grandson Jack, Congressman Kennedy, in 1952 when he was running against Senator Lodge. He was on the platform at Springfield, with the members of the Democratic State Committee, welcoming Adlai Stevenson to Massachusetts. Those assembled machine politicians were of the second generation: heavy-jowled, heavy-paunched Neanderthal types. The shoulders of their suits were vast and padded, their ties were handpainted in rainbow tints, and their eyes had that curiously beady look that one finds only in politicians, undertakers, and professional baseball players. Stevenson, the mutely dressed academic Hamlet, and the third-generation congressman in his narrow-shouldered suit and regimental-striped tie seemed from another world. Kennedy looked like what indeed he was, the youngest member of the Harvard Board of Overseers. Curiously enough, he had come to look much as Harvard overseers had always looked in their younger days. Watching him, I suddenly realized that, in this young man moving rather elegantly among the slobs, the consolidation of a new class had—reached its conclusion.

The Last of the Bosses

FOR THE FIRST HALF of this century and beyond, James Michael Curley was the most flamboyant and durable figure on Boston's political scene. Mayor off and on for a total of sixteen years, he spent four terms in Congress and two in jail, and for two Depression years he was Governor of Massachusetts. At his death he lay in state for two days in the State House Hall of Flags, the fourth person in the history of the Commonwealth to be so honored. His seventeen-room neo-Georgian mansion on Jamaicaway, with shamrocks cut in its shutters, was both a landmark of the rise of the immigrant Irish and a nose-thumbing in the direction of Yankee Beacon Hill. He was hated by Proper Bostonians with a proper and ultimate hatred, and held in mindless affection by the slums. His Irish-American political associates alternately embraced and knifed him. Counted out a score of times, he always bounced back. On several occasions and long before his death, he received the last rites of the Catholic Church.

Like his old enemy Honey Fitz, Curley was a transitional figure, a symbol of the emergence of the famine Irish from their proletarian status to political dominance. His father, Michael, came to Boston from Galway in 1865 at the age of fourteen. Sarah Clancy, his mother, arrived that same year—a meager-boned Connemara girl of the type the Irish wit Dr. Gogarty called Firbolg. She was twelve years old and worked first as a maid on Beacon Hill. Michael Curley became a hod carrier at ten cents an hour by the grace of Patrick "Pea-Jacket" Maguire, boss of Ward 17, where Galway men clustered. Michael Curley was good-looking in a stumpy, plodding, impassive way. At twenty-one he married Sarah and took her to a tiny flat in one of the rotting three-deckers off Northampton Street. Along Roxbury Neck there were hundreds of those fetid wooden tenements that had been run up by jerry-builders for the shanty Irish. Beyond Northampton Street lay the North Bay, and at low tide the marsh gas sifting in across the mud mixed with the sour permanent stench of the Southampton Street dump. It was said that in Ward 17 children came into the world with clenched fists. In that Roxbury flat James Michael Curley, the second son, was born in 1874.

The boy's horizon was the waterfront slum. By the time he was five he ran with an urchin gang, pilfering, dodging the cops, wandering along the edge of the Roxbury flats while the herring gulls wheeled overhead, scaling stones at the wharf rats that scuttled across the dumps, selling old whisky bottles they found there to Jakie the Junkie. Daily they would see the cargo schooners coming up the Fort Hill channel from far-off places like Maine or Nova Scotia. In the summer they played about the old Roxbury canal or swam in the murky South Bay. Evenings they could hear the bullfrogs croaking from the marshes. Sometimes, though rarely, they wandered outside the ward. Only a little over a mile to the north was the newly filled area of the Back Bay with its wide avenues and brownstone-front town houses. To tenement boys, these opulent mansions with their turrets and gablings seemed like castles.

By the time Jim reached grammar school he was peddling papers. Afternoons he worked as a delivery boy at the Washington Market. When he was ten his father died. Mike Curley had always been proud of his strength. A workman challenged him to lift a 400-pound edgestone onto a wagon. He managed to raise it but then collapsed. Three days later he was dead.

The Curleys were then living in an alley tenement in Fellows Court. Pea-Jacket Maguire's point of view was limited—no votes, no help. And there was no help for the Curleys.

Sarah kept the family together by scrubbing floors in a downtown office building. Jim and his brother John, two years older, wrapped bundles and served customers at the Washington Market in their free time until the end of grammar school. At twelve, Jim was working in a drugstore an hour and a half before he went to school, and from half past four until eleven after school.

Reared in poverty, corroded with hatred of the Beacon Hill Brahmins, young Jim Curley formed his hard, unwavering, egocentric determination to succeed. Success, the road up from the Fellows Court flat to the imagined great house, was through politics. He knew that when he was still in short trousers. There was no other road for an Irish slum boy. Politics, then, was a game he would play as he found it, not to change the game or reform it, but to win. In the harshness of his own few years he grasped instinctively Boss Martin Lomasney's neoplatonic axiom, that, politically speaking, the mass of people are interested mainly in food, clothing, and shelter. For these they would barter their votes.

At fifteen, after a series of small jobs, he settled for the next eight years as a deliveryman, driving a wagon for C. S. Johnson, Grocers. He was strong like his father, wily and wiry, and except for his somewhat vulpine nose, handsome. He had a resonant voice and soon learned to modify the harshness of his gutter speech. From time to time he would drop in at Curran's livery stable, where the wardheelers gathered, or at One-Armed Peter Whalen's tobacco store, another political hangout of the district.

Meanwhile, he attended the Boston Evening High School two nights a week. In the public library he read Dickens and Thackeray and Shakespeare, and the Boston *Transcript*. He taught Sunday school, ushered and passed the plate at St. Philip's on Harrison Avenue, and joined the Ancient Order of Hibernians. He became chairman of committees for picnics, outings, minstrel shows, and church supper dances. For his straight purpose, games and girls and conviviality had no meaning. Time was too short; life too dear.

He knew the families on his grocery route as if they were his own family; he talked with people—after church, at the Hibernians, at Whalen's, on committees. Always he was obliging and always available. By the time he reached his majority he showed the indefinable air of future success that a sixth-sense pol like One-Armed Peter Whalen could spot at once. In 1898 Whalen tipped him to run for the Boston Common Council against Pea-Jacket's organization, and staked him to his first contribution. Curley won by several hundred votes, but by the time Pea-Jacket's henchmen had finished with the ballot boxes, he found himself counted out. The next year he organized his own strong-arms, and after weeks of pre-election gang fights and corner brawls, he won—too handily for Pea-Jacket to challenge him. So at twenty-six he formally entered political life as one of the three council members from Ward 17.

With his defeat of the aging Pea-Jacket, Curley consolidated himself as the new boss, organizing Ward 17 on the Tammany model of tribute and social services, and even calling his organization the Tammany Club. There was, however, this difference: Curley's organization was personal rather than self-perpetuating. In politics he would always be a lone wolf.

From that time on Curley never lacked for money. Merchants and others who did business in Ward 17 now paid to him on a more regulated basis what they had paid to Pea-Jacket. But from the ordinary people of the ward, deserving and otherwise, whose needs and requests Curley took care of quickly and efficiently, he expected nothing in gratitude but their votes.

The core of his support would always come from the slums. There he was given an allegiance that the Pea-Jackets could never command. But Curley never had a political philosophy beyond that of taking care of himself and his own. With equal ease he would at various times support Al Smith, Franklin Roosevelt, Mussolini, Father Coughlin, and Senator McCarthy. If he had had the vision, he might have become to Boston and Massachusetts what Al Smith was to New York. But his vision was limited to his own drive for power.

With Ward 17 in his pocket, Curley moved on to the Massachusetts Legislature, where he spent one term, more as an observer of the political passing show than as a participant. He was still learning. At the Staley College of the Spoken Word he took elocution lessons, modifying his speech still further to its final form. The Curley accent was unique, with grandiloquent overtones, impressive and at once identifiable, yet underneath synthetic. It achieved the desired effect, but it never rang wholly true. And in an election pinch, it could always be dropped for something more primitive.

In 1903 Curley met his first reverse. He was caught impersonating one of his less talented ward workers at a Civil Service examination and sentenced to sixty days in the Charles Street Jail. Yet, far from being disconcerted by this lapse, he capitalized on it. In later years he often planted stooges in his audience to get up and ask: "How about the time you went to jail?" Curley then liked to draw himself up and announce floridly: "I did it for a friend." Ward 17 understood. While in jail, where he spent a not unpleasant two months reading all the books in the library, he was elected to the Board of Aldermen, the upper chamber of Boston's city government.

Curley remained an alderman until 1909, when he became a member of the new City Council. And all the time he was laying his lines carefully toward his own clear though unexpressed goal—to be mayor and boss of Boston. His retentive mind had the city and its departments catalogued for future use. No one would ever be able to fool Curley.

Established in his thirty-second year, he now found time to marry Mary Herlihy, whom he had met at a St. Philip's minstrel show. With a background much like his own, she was a woman of grace and character, and she became a permanently steadying influence on him. It was a happy marriage for them both and a fortunate one for him. The boys in the back room might make up limericks about Honey Fitz and Toodles Ryan, but no enemy could ever touch Jim Curley that way. His private life was always beyond reproach, though it was to end sadly—only two of his nine children survived him.

In 1880, Mayor Frederick O. Prince had said: "No allegation of municipal corruption has ever been made against any Boston official." By Honey Fitz's time such a remark could be considered a flat, cynical joke. When Honey Fitz was elected to his four-year term in 1909, Curley, willing to wait for the next round, let himself be persuaded to run for Congress by the district incumbent, Bill McNary, who counted on insuring his own re-election by having Curley split his opponent's vote. For the first time Curley stumped outside Ward 17. In a day when political rallies were still a prime source of entertainment, Curley put on a campaign that was a combination of vaudeville, Chautauqua, and the prize ring. No one, his opponents realized too late, could equal him as a showman; no one could talk him down. There was the usual torchlight parade with the bands blaring "Tammany" to celebrate his victory.

He spent two undistinquished terms in the House and his weekends back in Roxbury. In Washington he and his wife mixed in a more sophisticated society than they had known before. They took instruction in etiquette, and this became a source of later jokes in Boston. In his autobiography, Curley maintained that he liked Washington. But Boston—the hard core of the city, the massed wards of the South End—these were his roots, and he never really functioned outside them. Before his second term was up, he resigned to enter the 1913 mayoralty contest.

Young Jim Curley—back from Washington, aggressive and dominating —was like a tidal wave. Honey Fitz, recognizing both the wave and the tide, retreated from the beach. He and the ward bosses finally produced a nonentity as token opposition to the Curley flood.

Curley's campaign for mayor dwarfed his congressional campaign four years before. He stormed the autumn city in racoon coat, "iron mike" on his head, and the gilded voice booming. He promised to clean out City Hall and give it back to the people—whatever that might mean. He savaged the ward bosses and invited the voters to call on him personally at City Hall. He promised more schools and playgrounds and beaches and parks and jobs. Politicians can hear the grass grow, and there was the underground feeling that he was unbeatable.

Incongruous as it might seem in later years, or even months, the newly elected Curley was at first hailed as a reform mayor. Hundreds of Honey Fitz's officeholders were ousted. True to his promise, Curley opened up City Hall. Those who wanted to see him about jobs, favors, or assistance, he received without appointment. A squad of secretaries catalogued each visitor before he was taken to the mayor. Decisions were made on the spot. If a request could not be granted, Curley said so and why. He was the superboss. Ward bosses became obsolete: Curley had destroyed their power, even in Ward 17. He talked to an average of 200 persons a day.

The financial and business community's satisfaction with the new mayor was brutally short-lived. Curley, they soon discovered, had lost none of his old resentments. Assessments were raised all round. A vast construction program such as Boston had never seen before was begun. Streets were ripped up, transit lines extended, beaches and playgrounds laid out, hospitals built, and services expanded. There was a job for every jobless man in the city. Here lay Curley's basic formula, then and in all his administrations: a juggler's act of public works without regard for cost. When the city treasury was empty he would borrow. The outraged Yankees could pay for it all through taxes.

Yet, much of what he did needed to be done. The cost would be excessive, the payrolls padded, a percentage of the contractors' fees would always find its way into Curley's pocket—but without him most of these projects would never have been undertaken. By the end of his first term he had altered the face of the city; by the end of his fourth term the tax rate had quintupled.

Though with him money went as easily as it came, though he liked to be known as the mayor of the poor, he enjoyed lush living. Midway in his first term he built himself the house overlooking Jamaica Pond that would be known as the House with the Shamrock Shutters. It was better than anything on Beacon Street. Some of the trimmings, including the mahogany-paneled

dining room and the winding staircase, came from the recently demolished
Fairhaven house of Henry H. Rogers, the Standard Oil executive. The Finance
Commission and others were to ask in vain how anyone could build a $60,000
house on a $15,000 lot on a salary of $10,000 a year. Such questions never
bothered Curley. In his autobiography he maintained—archly and without
expecting to be believed—that he had made the money for his house on a stock
market tip. Almost everyone in Boston knew that the house had been a dona-
tion from a contractor. The Curley wards felt he deserved it.

In 1917, when Curley ran for re-election, a curious amalgam of businessmen and bosses took the field against him. Martin Lomasney, the only ward
boss to survive unscathed, entered two congressmen with Celtic names as
pseudo-candidates to cut into Curley's Irish-Democratic vote. It was an old
gambit, used many times by Curley himself, and it worked well enough to
defeat Curley.

After several ludicrously unfortunate business ventures—in such matters
Curley would always be both gullible and inept—he became president of the
Hibernia National Bank, within wistful sight of City Hall. But this was for
him only an interlude. His real life was always politics.

The 1921 mayoralty campaign was one of the closest and meanest in the
history of Boston, and Curley fought alone. No political pro in the city was for
him, and the betting against him ran over two to one. But his opponent, a
respected Catholic lawyer named John R. Murphy, was not prepared for what
he now had to face. It was said commiseratingly of him afterward that he was
too much of a gentleman. Among other things, Curley sent some of his workers
to Charlestown dressed in clerical black and carrying prayer books. There they
let it be known that turncoat Murphy had joined the Masons and that he was
divorcing his wife to marry a sixteen-year-old girl. Other Curley supporters
rang doorbells through Catholic South Boston, posing as members of the
Hawes Baptist Club and soliciting votes for John R. Murphy. Curley even
gave a Ku-Klux Klan organizer known as the Black Pope $2000 to campaign
against him.

Against all odds and predictions Curley won, with 74,200 votes to
Murphy's 71,180. For the first time in a Boston election women could vote, and
it was generally felt that Mary Curley's "Personal Appeal to Women Voters,"
an open letter circulated at the last minute, gave her husband the extra votes
that elected him.

Before anyone quite knew what was happening—anyone except Curley—
there were 24 million dollars' worth of building projects under way. Several
times the city treasury gave out. Curley merely borrowed more money against
future taxes. If a banker showed reluctance to lend, Curley would threaten to
start a run on his bank "a mile long." Taxes and assessments, as well as
buildings, went up.

During Curley's second administration, and with Curley pointedly in
mind, the Republican State Legislature passed a law that no mayor of Boston
might succeed himself. Instead, in 1924 Curley ran as Democratic candidate for
governor against Alvan T. Fuller, who would later become widely known in

connection with the Sacco-Vanzetti case. It was a Republican year, and in any case, Massachusetts would not be ready for Curley until after the transvaluations of the Depression. Curley tried to make an issue of the Ku-Klux Klan and his own opposition to it. Wherever he spoke in the rural sections of the state, fiery crosses would suddenly blaze out on nearby hills just in time for him to point to them and say, voice resonant with emotion: "There it burns, the cross of hatred upon which Our Lord, Jesus Christ, was crucified." Later he admitted that the crosses had been touched off by his boys. Fuller won—but the size of Curley's vote gave the state party leaders, whose enthusiasm for Curley was at best limited, something to think about.

In the Presidential election of 1928 the Commonwealth of Massachusetts was one of the eight states carried by Al Smith. To the Irish Democrats of the Commonwealth, Smith was the most creditable man from Irish ranks who had yet appeared in politics. Before the national convention the Massachusetts leaders were solidly for Smith. All of them were at odds with Curley, and they took care that the ex-mayor would have no part in the convention or in the subsequent Smith campaign. They reckoned, however, without Curley.

Shortly after Smith's nomination, Curley opened what he called his Bull Pen in the vacant Young's Hotel near City Hall. He had the walls plastered with Smith signs and photographs. There were loudspeakers in the windows blaring a raucous mixture of speeches and music. Every day was open house in the Bull Pen. Inside it was like an amateur night. Anyone who felt like walking in and speaking his piece about Smith was welcome to use the microphone. And when Al Smith arrived in Boston to ride through the city in a whirl of ticker tape, the excluded Curley was somehow there in the car beside him, to the chagrin of the official members of the party. In the election, when Smith was trailing Hoover by 83,000 votes outside Boston, and the city's roaring majority gave him the state by 17,000, it was Curley's desperate drumming up of the last few thousand votes that made the difference.

After the Hoover sweep, Curley was astute enough to realize that Smith would not have another chance, no matter what Massachusetts Democrats thought. Four years later Curley was the first and in fact the only politician in the state to come out for Franklin Roosevelt before the convention. Massachusetts Democrats, still solidly and emotionally for Smith, were shocked and furious. Curley was a traitor. The wilderness was where he belonged.

The Massachusetts delegation to the 1932 Democratic Convention was headed by Governor Joseph B. Ely, an old Curley enemy. Curley was not to be a delegate to this convention; in fact, if Ely had anything to say about it, he would not even be a spectator. But, as the event again showed, one had better not count Curley out too soon. For directly behind the Massachusetts delegation in the convention hall sat the Puerto Ricans with their chairman—none other than Alcalde Jaime Miguel Curleo. The Alcalde, in a familiarly florid accent, cast the six Puerto Rican votes for Roosevelt; though even after the Roosevelt stampede the Massachusetts delegation glumly and stubbornly held out to the end for Smith. Behind the scenes, Curley had helped arrange with Hearst and Garner the deal that finally gave Roosevelt the nomination.

Public opinion in Massachusetts veered quickly. The emotions that for four years had been bound up with the fortunes of Al Smith were transferred overnight to Roosevelt. Having left Boston as an outcast, Curley came back from Chicago a hero. He arrived in North Station to find that a crowd of 250,000 had turned out to meet him. Streets were jammed all the way to the Common. Inside the station twenty-one bands were blaring at one another. It took a hundred reserve policemen to clear a path for Curley to his car.

From that night until the election all Curley's efforts went into the campaign. He reopened his Bull Pen, this time decorating it with Roosevelt motifs. He mortgaged the House with the Shamrock Shutters. He traveled 10,000 miles through twenty-three western and midwestern states to deliver 140 speeches. For the election he spent a quarter of a million dollars of his own money. With James Roosevelt as an assistant, he was the Roosevelt ringmaster in Massachusetts.

All this activity had not been undertaken just for the Forgotten Man. What Curley now wanted was to set the seal of respectability on his career by becoming Secretary of the Navy. After all, it was a job held recently by a Boston Adams. Shortly after the election, Curley, with his daughter Mary, called on Roosevelt at Warm Springs. There, according to Curley, Roosevelt told him, "Well, Jim, if that's what you want, the job is yours." A few weeks later, however, at Calvin Coolidge's funeral in Northampton, James Roosevelt took Curley aside and told him that a cabinet post was not possible. James went on to tell him that he might instead become ambassador to France or Italy, and suggested that he drop in at the White House to talk it over.

On that visit the President mentioned Italy. Curley asked for a few days to think it over. Whether Roosevelt ever intended to send the boss of Boston to Rome, whether Boston's William Cardinal O'Connell vetoed the idea, or whether Curley was simply being given the Roosevelt run-around, will never be clear. In any event, at Curley's next interview, the smiling President said there were difficulties about Italy and offered him instead the post of ambassador to Poland, remarking that Poland was one of the most interesting places in the world. "If it is such a goddam interesting place," Curley is said to have replied, "why don't you resign the Presidency and take it yourself?" To the newsmen who crowded around him outside the White House, he used a quick term to describe Roosevelt that Truman later reserved for music critics. In Boston a witticism went the rounds that if he had accepted, he would have paved the Polish Corridor.

Between the two conventions Curley had been elected mayor for the third time by a clear majority, and once more with the odds against him. His principal opponent was another respectable Democratic lawyer, Frederick W. Mansfield, silently endorsed by Cardinal O'Connell himself, who had long felt that Curley was a discredit both to the Irish and his Church. The Cardinal, from a slum background similar to Curley's, was of the cast of a Renaissance prelate. He spoke Italian like an Italian, English like a cultivated Englishman. An urbane and aristocratic man, he wanted to see the emergent Irish become respectable and accepted. Politically, the Cardinal was an innocent.

Curley, in his inaugural address, attacked the Republican Good Government Association and the "select and exclusive body of social bounders in the Back Bay." His new administration began with the usual Curley public works projects, the need for which was accentuated now by the onset of the Depression.

Even before his election he knew that his wife was doomed by cancer. She died the following June. Mary Curley's influence on her husband had been stabilizing and restraining. Without her he seemed to lose his balance. He drank too much, he coarsened physically, he grew bombastic and careless, he had less control over his quick temper. Opposing Ely's nomination for governor, he got into a fist fight with the chairman of the Democratic State Committee at radio station WNAC.

The older, less careful Curley now made the political blunder of appointing his friend Edmund L. Dolan city treasurer. Dolan was the legal owner of Curley's 93-foot yacht, punningly named *Maicaway*. As Curley's understudy, Dolan headed the Mohawk Packing Company and the Legal Securities Corporation. Mohawk was organized to provide meat for city institutions —at a third above the usual cost. Through the Legal Securities Corporation, Dolan managed to sell bonds to the city and also buy them from the city to sell to brokers, collecting commissions at both ends. The state-appointed Finance Commission uncovered these and certain aspects of land-takings and other facts sufficient, so it seemed for a while, to send both Curley and Dolan to jail. The younger Curley would never have left himself so vulnerable.

Eventually Dolan was charged with the theft of more than $170,000 from the city. When the case came to trial, he was caught trying to bribe the jury and received two-and-a-half years in jail. At the same time a bill in equity was brought against Curley, and after three years and thirty-four continuances, he was ordered to pay back $42,629 to the city treasury.

Now that he had no more Washington ambitions he badgered Roosevelt for more aid and more money for Boston. He devised new projects for the Civil Works Administration. After all, a CWA was what he had been occupied with all his political life. With Governor Ely, still a disgruntled Smith man, retiring in 1934, Curley had little trouble in getting the Democratic nomination for governor. That election, the second New Deal wave, swept almost the complete Democratic state ticket into office. Boston had taken over Massachusetts at last. The crowd from City Hall moved up Beacon Hill to the State House.

Curley's two-year term as Governor marked both the height and depths of his career. No such turmoil had occurred on Beacon Hill since cynical, droop-eyed Ben Butler had been governor fifty years earlier. Curley would now use the greater resources of the Commonwealth as he had previously used those of the city, but this time with a recklessness and an arrogance he had not shown before. Work there was, projects useful and otherwise, feverishly undertaken from the Berkshires to Cape Cod, and where there was no work there were at least jobs. The State House offices bulged with idle incompetents, the Governor's anterooms swarmed with old City Hall petitioners. When the Finance Commission again threatened to dig up old Curley City Hall scandals, its members were bribed or dismissed. Curley rode roughshod **over the Gover-**

nor's Council, courts, and department heads, his energy as boundless as his activities were unregulated.

Insolence of office trailed him through the state as he scorched the roads in his limousine with its S-1 license plates, preceded by state police motorcycle escorts with sirens wailing, and followed by carloads of his military aides, bright in incongruous blue-and-gold-braid uniforms. S-1 was in a series of accidents. One state trooper was killed, another badly injured. Curley moved across the Massachusetts landscape like a Latin dictator. For the 1936 Harvard Tercentenary, he arrived at the Yard escorted by scarlet-coated National Lancers, drums beating and trumpets sounding, to move ostentatiously past a stony-faced President Roosevelt, while a few Harvard die-hards booed.

Just before he took the oath of office, Curley had swung a parting punch at Governor Ely. That outrageous brawl within the State House became symbolic of his administration. The inauguration ball, held at the Commonwealth Armory, was a monstrous affair to which 14,000 people were invited. During his first year in office the Governor spent $85,206 for taxis, flowers, dinners, luncheons, cigars, refreshments, and trips for himself, his guests, and secretaries. The following winter he moved his entire staff to Florida. In those Depression times his daughter Mary's wedding to Edward C. Donnelly, Jr., of the Donnelly Advertising Company, was the gaudiest ever held in Massachusetts. The bride's trousseau cost $10,000—paid for, and not donated, as anti-Curleyites had hinted. At the packed Cathedral of the Holy Cross, under the dismayed eyes of Cardinal O'Connell, many of those present stood on the pews as the bride and her father came down the aisle. There were 2,300 guests at the Copley Plaza reception afterward. They downed two tons of lobster at thirteen dollars a plate.

Financially buttressed at the end of his Governor's term, Curley determined to revenge himself on Roosevelt. The President had not liked him as Governor, and he would like still less to find him in the United States Senate. For Governor Curley the senatorial nomination was easy to manipulate; the election seemed equally so. His Republican opponent was Henry Cabot Lodge, Jr., the grandson of the old anti-League senator, whose political experience was contained in two terms in the Massachusetts Legislature. Curley liked to refer to him as "Little Boy Blue." Yet in the New Deal landslide of 1936, when every other major Democratic candidate in the Commonwealth was overwhelmingly elected, Curley lost to Lodge by 136,000 votes. All the states except Maine and Vermont went for Roosevelt, but Massachusetts had had enough of James Michael Curley.

In a sense, however, Curley had the last word, for on that day when the cannon boomed across the Common to announce a new governor, he stole the whole show by marrying again. His second wife, Gertrude Casey Dennis, was a widow, a quiet woman without political or social ambitions, who would give him again the domestic stability he had found with his first wife.

The following year he again ran for mayor. He found himself opposed by a "reform" condidate, Maurice Tobin, a handsome and hardy young Democrat from his own district, who in the wheel-spins of politics would twice become mayor, then governor, and finally figurehead Secretary of Labor in Truman's Cabinet. Curley accurately described him as "a protégé of mine who learned too fast." It was to Curley's mind an easy election, but on election morning there appeared on the masthead of the Boston *Post*, whose editorials generally reflected the views of the archdiocese, a brief notice to the voters of Boston that read:

Cardinal O'Connell, in speaking to the Catholic Alumni Association, said, "The walls are raised against honest men in civic life." You can break down these walls by voting for an honest, clean, competent young man, Maurice Tobin, today.

Thousands of copies of the *Post* were distributed free in front of all the churches. The quotation was from an address the Cardinal had made six years before, but few readers noticed that the quotation marks ended before Tobin was mentioned. To the faithful, it seemed that His Eminence had endorsed Curley's opponent. Curley furiously tried to get a retraction broadcast, but the Cardinal could not be reached. It was a maneuver worthy of Curley himself. Enough pious votes were swung to Tobin for him to win.

In 1938 Curley was strong enough to take the nomination away from the Democratic governor, but he was still unable to win the election. His opponent was the long-jawed speaker of the Massachusetts House of Representatives, Leverett Saltonstall, who as a Republican, a Harvard man, and a Brahamin combined the three things that Curley was best at excoriating. Yet Saltonstall was a new type of Old Yankee who represented a *rapprochement* with what Curley liked to call "the newer races." The growing numbers of middleclass Irish liked him. In later years, when he and young Senator Kennedy were colleagues in Washington, they became so friendly that Kennedy refused to endorse Saltonstall's next Democratic opponent. Saltonstall also had the advantage of owning one of the most agreeably ugly mugs in politics. Curley made the mistake of quipping that Saltonstall might have a South Boston face but he would never dare show it in South Boston. Of course Saltonstall walked through the South Boston streets the next day, talking with everyone he met and dropping in at the innumerable bars. He overwhelmed Curley at the polls.

By the time of Boston's next municipal election Mayor Tobin had built a tight political machine of his own. Curley ran against him nevertheless and suffered his fourth defeat in a row. At sixty-seven, after a generation in politics, it looked as if he had come to the end of the road. But that was not the way Curley saw it. He turned again to his solid core of supporters in the close wards of Roxbury, South Boston, and Charlestown. As if he were now going down the ladder he had once climbed, he asked them to send him back to Congress in 1942.

These days he was short of funds, and every week there was the $500 installment on the $42,629 he had been ordered to pay the city. A few months before Pearl Harbor, unlucky as usual in his private ventures, he had run into a Washington promoter named James G. Fuller, who was organizing a fivepercenter corporation to mediate between manufacturers looking for war contracts and the appropriate heads of government agencies. Fuller offered to make Curley president of this organization, to be known as the Engineers' Group, Inc. Later, Fuller was shown to be a confidence man and ex-convict. Curley, in spite of his title, had little to do with Fuller's corporation except to appear on its letterhead. Curley resigned from the company before being elected to Congress.

Two years later the Engineers' Group was one of the concerns investigated by the Truman Committee, and Curley was indicted because of his connection with it. He always maintained that the case against him was directed from the White House. His trial was postponed to allow him to run for mayor of Boston in November 1945.

Tobin had moved on to become governor. The acting mayor was an obscurity, as were the other four candidates. Postwar Boston itself seemed derelict, a fading seaport as drab as the blackout paint that covered the gilt dome of the State House. So much needed doing, from street repairs to housing for veterans, and "Curley gets things done." That, at least, was the campaign slogan spread casually in public by his paid workers and taken up by others. Looking back to the prewar days, it seemed true enough. What if Curley was under indictment for some contract swindle? If he was guilty he hadn't done very much, no more than the rest of them. Anyhow, he got things done!

On election day Curley beat his closest opponent by two to one. For the fourth time he became Mayor of Boston, thirty-one years after his first inaugural. Two months later he was convicted by a Washington jury of using the mails to defraud.

His appeal to the Supreme Court was rejected in 1947. As the date neared for his sentencing he took to his bed. He received the last rites of the Church, and then unexpectedly his health picked up. Finally, the postponed but inevitable day came. He appeared in court in a wheelchair and wearing a collar a size too large. His lawyer produced a certified list of nine ailments from which he was suffering, any one of which might prove fatal. Unimpressed, the judge sentenced him to six to eighteen months at the Federal Correctional Institute at Danbury, Connecticut. "You are sentencing me to die," Curley croaked at him as they wheeled him away. Democratic House Leader John W. McCormack circulated a petition for Curley's release and it was signed by all the Massachusetts delegation in Washington except Senator Kennedy. After five months, President Truman pardoned Curley—because, as the President said later, "he was innocent."

Although it was not known at the time, Curley was shattered by his Danbury experience. There was nothing left of the young man who could shrug off a few months behind bars by reading all the books in the prison library. He now felt his age and a sense of failure, and for the first time he knew self-doubt. On his release, according to his daughter, he was hesitant about facing people again.

It warmed him to be met by a great milling crowd in front of the House with the Shamrock Shutters, welcoming him with "Hail to the Chief." Inside he found familiar faces and a huge cake inscribed "Happy Birthday to Our Beloved Boss." In a few days he was back at City Hall at his old desk, looking fifteen years younger and running the city in his old way.

Yet the city was not the same. His personal open-handedness as boss of old Ward 17, and in his many years as Mayor had now become a more impersonal function of government. Voters were no longer gratefully held in line by a job shoveling snow, by the odd ton of coal, by the perennial Thanksgiving turkey and Christmas basket. Social security and unemployment insurance and the psychiatric social worker had taken over. The Irish were becoming middle class. One couldn't even soak the rich any more. In an almost bankrupt city the tax rate could go no higher. What Boston mostly needed now was an efficient receiver.

In the 1949 election, Curley, to his derisive surprise, was opposed by John B. Hynes, who had served as mayor while Curley was in prison. "A little city clerk," Curley called him contemptuously, but when the ballots were counted, Hynes, the administrator, had won by 15,000 votes. It was the end of Curley's political career.

The next year, by a twist of fate, his daughter Mary and his son Leo both died of cerebral hemorrhages on the same day. Mary, who had been closest to him, had led an unhappy life; her marriage had ended in divorce in 1943. Leo was, at the time of his death, a lieutenant in the Navy. In Curley's loss, even his enemies could feel pity for him.

After Curley got out of Danbury, he had complained to a Boston newspaperman, Joseph Dinneen, that the press had always been unfair to him. Dinneen thereupon offered to write Curley's life story honestly and objectively. Curley agreed, and with his collaboration *The Purple Shamrock* was written. It appeared in 1949. Curley was proud of the book and used to give away autographed copies to City Hall visitors.

The Purple Shamrock, the first attempt to put Curley's career in perspective, was the beginning of the Curley legend. What it told was true and often amazingly frank. Dinneen admitted that money was never a problem for Curley, although Curley could never quite explain where he got it, how his income skyrocketed when he was in office and shrank to a trickle when he was not, or how "there wasn't a contract awarded that did not have a cut for Curley." Yet Dinneen felt that even so, Curley's accomplishments justified the cuts.

Now that Curley was no longer to be feared politically, he began to seem a kind of institution. He had been around for so long. Even the Bostonians who had fought him hardest in the pugnacious City Hall days, now, in the nostalgia for their greener years, felt a certain left-handed affection for him. He in turn was pleased and flattered by the occasional courtesy from a Lowell or a Lodge. Every political figure from Senator Saltonstall to the last South Boston ward-heeler would drop in on the way past the House with the Shamrock Shutters. Curley in his old age could still charm the birds out of the trees.

When Edwin O'Connor's novel *The Last Hurrah* was scheduled to appear in 1956, it was carefully let out in advance that here was a novel about James Michael Curley. The editor of the *Globe* sent Curley a copy with the suggestion that he review it. The next day the book was returned with a note from Curley to the effect that he was consulting his lawyers.

Frank Skeffington, the politician-hero of the book, is undoubtedly Curley, even to his feud with the Cardinal, but he is a retouched Curley, less violent, more urbane. After Curley's first resentment had worn off, he began to see the Skeffington portrait as an asset. The book had toned down his ruthlessness, emphasized his benevolence. The various hints of fraud and peculation were, after all, no more than the admissions of *The Purple Shamrock*. For a while Curley took jokingly to calling and signing himself Skeffington. From originally intending to sue O'Connor, he ended up by congratulating him. As an aftermath he decided to write his autobiography, to out-Skeffington Skeffington by putting into a book what Dinneen had either not known or discreetly omitted.

In the final section of *The Last Hurrah*, when Skeffington is on his death bed, someone standing by the apparently unconscious figure remarks unctuously that if Skeffington had it all to do over again, he'd no doubt do it very differently. The dying man then manages to rouse himself and whisper: "The hell I would!" It was from this episode that Curley took the title of is own book, *I'd Do It Again*.

It is a rambling and uneven book, often dulled by the memory of obscure and forgotten ward-heelers, but on the other hand, enlivened by the brazen candor of Curley's admissions. Though actually written by Honey Fitz's biographer, John Cutler, after conversations with Curley, it preserves Curley's own style of the informal cliché. What runs through the pages as an undercurrent, sensed even when not visible, is the after-feeling of the Famine years, the old Celtic bitterness against the chill Yankee. *I'd Do It Again* is more reticent about Curley's financial background than is *The Purple Shamrock*. There is no mention of his income tax irregularities, and nothing is said of his connection with the Mishawum Manor blackmail scandal of the early twenties in which two district attorney friends of his were disbarred.

The summer after *The Last Hurrah* was published, Curley sold his Jamaicaway house to the Oblate Fathers. Those shamrock shutters, once a gesture of defiance, had become a familiar landmark. The massive furniture, the library, the Georgian silver, the Waterford glass and Crown Derby china, the jade and ivory *bibelots* and pious statuary had been purchased for the most part from auction rooms. Now to auction rooms they would return.

Curley moved to a small suburban-colonial house the other side of Jamaica Pond. He settled down there with his governor's chair and his mayor's chair and a selection of his smaller belongings. Governor Foster Furcolo appointed him to a sinecure job, for Curley was hard up again. The Boston papers always seemed to be printing little human-interest stories about him: photos of him fishing, or being shaved by Sal, the Huntington Avenue barber. Edward R. Murrow ran his Person-to-Person television show from the new house, and on it Curley announced that he was going to live to be 125 years old so that he could bury all his enemies.

Though Curley belittled it, from the time he moved his health began to fail. He was in and out of the hospital for checkups. His face grew gray and flabby. Yet his right hand had not forgotten its cunning. When Columbia Pictures was about to release its film version of *The Last Hurrah,* Curley, after he had viewed the picture privately, filed suit for "irreparable damage to a valuable property"—that is, his life story. Columbia paid $25,000 for the damage. Then it was discovered that the lawyer to whom the check was made out was nonexistent and that the stamp on the release form was that of a nonexistent notary. Curley claimed that his signature was a forgery. Officially, no one knows yet who got the money. When Curley renewed his threat of a suit, Columbia settled for an additional $15,000. The picture was running at a Boston theater when Curley died.

He entered the City Hospital for an intestinal operation on November 4, 1958, election day. Just another campaign, he remarked. For the first few days he seemed to be mending. He was able to walk about and to talk of the great Democratic victory. A week later he had a relapse. The end came quickly.

He lay on a bier in the State House in the great hall where the battle flags of Massachusetts regiments are kept, and in two days 100,000 people filed past. Then, on a warm morning like an aftermath of September, he was buried from Holy Cross Cathedral. It was the largest funeral ever seen in Boston.

According to the Boston papers, Archbishop (later Cardinal) Richard J. Cushing had flown from Washington to deliver the eulogy. The late Cardinal O'Connell had spoken one when Curley's first wife died; the Archbishop himself had eulogized Mary and Leo eight years before. Now he sat silent and dominant in the sanctuary. The celebrant was Curley's youngest son, Father Francis Curley, S.J.

The coffin of polished mahogany glittered in the candlelight that was reflected again on the scabbards of the Knights of Columbus, Fourth Degree, who formed the guard of honor. They stood there, plump and middle-aged, in silk capes, their hands on their sword hilts, white plumes covering their heads. As the Requiem Mass reached its conclusion, the Archbishop approached the coffin. Then he prayed, in the grating, honest, South Boston voice that was his inheritance and that he was too proud to change. High overhead, suspended by a wire from the Reconstruction-Gothic dome and directly over the coffin, Cardinal O'Connell's red hat swung slightly in the air currents.

The prayer ended, and everyone watched the Archbishop's seamed face under its white miter, waiting for him to mount the steps to the pulpit. But the Archbishop did not move. There was no eulogy.

POLITICAL CAUSES OF THE AMERICAN REVOLUTION

by Lord Acton

This essay first appeared in *The Rambler, New Series,* V,
Part XIII (May, 1861) 17-61.

Political Causes of
the American Revolution

AT THE TIME of the utmost degradation of the Athenian democracy, when the commanders at Arginusæ were condemned by an unconstitutional decree, and Socrates alone upheld the sanctity of the law, the people, says Xenophon, cried out that it was monstrous to prevent them from doing whatever they pleased. A few years later the archonship of Euclides witnessed the restoration of the old constitution, by which the liberty, though not the power, of Athens was revived and prolonged for ages; and the palladium of the new settlement was the provision that no decree of the council or of the people should be permitted to overrule any existing law.

The fate of every democracy, of every government based on the sovereignty of the people, depends on the choice it makes between these opposite principles, absolute power on the one hand, and on the other, the restraints of legality and the authority of tradition. It must stand or fall according to its choice, whether to give the supremacy to the law or to the will of the people; whether to constitute a moral association maintained by duty, or a physical one kept together by force. Republics offer, in this respect, a strict analogy with monarchies, which are also either absolute or organic, either governed by law, and therefore constitutional, or by a will which, being the source, cannot be the object of laws, and is therefore despotic. But in their mode of growth, in the direction in which they gravitate, they are directly contrary to each other. Democracy tends naturally to realise its principle, the sovereignty of the people, and to remove all limits and conditions of its exercise; whilst monarchy tends to surround itself with such conditions. In one instance force yields to right; in the other might prevails over law. The resistance of the king is gradually overcome by those who resist and seek to share his power; in a democracy the power is already in the hands of those who seek to subvert and to abolish the law. The process of subversion is consequently irresistible, and far more rapid.

They differ, therefore, not only in the direction, but in the principle of their development. The organisation of a constitutional monarchy is the work of opposing powers, interests, and opinions, by which the monarch is deprived of his exclusive authority, and the throne is surrounded with and guarded by political institutions. In a purely popular government this antagonism of forces does not exist, for all power is united in the same sovereign; subject and citizen are one, and there is no external power that can enforce the surrender of a part of the supreme authority, or establish a security against its abuse. The elements of organisation are wanting. If not obtained at starting, they will not

351

naturally spring up. They have no germs in the system. Hence monarchy grows more free, in obedience to the laws of its existence, whilst democracy becomes more arbitrary. The people is induced less easily than the king to abdicate the plenitude of its power, because it has not only the right of might on its side, but that which comes from possession, and the absence of a prior claimant. The only antagonism that can arise is that of contending parties and interests in the sovereign community, the condition of whose existence is that it should be homogeneous. These separate interests can protect themselves only by setting bounds to the power of the majority; and to this the majority cannot be compelled, or consistently persuaded, to consent. It would be a surrender of the direct authority of the people, and of the principle that in every political community authority must be commensurate with power.

"Infirma minoris
Vox cedat numeri, parvaque in parte quiescat."

"La pluralité," says Pascal, "est la meilleure voie, parcequ'elle est visible, et qu'elle a la force pour se faire obéir; cependant c'est l'avis des moins habiles." The minority can have no permanent security against the oppression of preponderating numbers, or against the government which these numbers control, and the moment will inevitably come when separation will be preferred to submission. When the classes which compose the majority and the minority are not defined with local distinctness, but are mingled together throughout the country, the remedy is found in emigration; and it was thus that many of the ancient Mediterranean states, and some of the chief American colonies, took their rise. But when the opposite interests are grouped together, so as to be separated not only politically but geographically, there will ensue a territorial disruption of the state, developed with a rapidity and certainty proportioned to the degree of local corporate organisation that exists in the community. It cannot, in the long run, be prevented by the majority, which is made up of many future, contingent minorities, all secretly sympathising with the seceders because they foresee a similar danger for themselves, and unwilling to compel them to remain, because they dread to perpetuate the tyranny of majorities. The strict principle of popular sovereignty must therefore lead to the destruction of the state that adopts it, unless it sacrifices itself by concession.

The greatest of all modern republics has given the most complete example of the truth of this law. The dispute between absolute and limited power, between centralisation and self-government, has been, like that between privilege and prerogative in England, the substance of the constitutional history of the United States. This is the argument which confers on the whole period that intervenes between the convention of 1787 and the election of Mr. Davis in 1861 an almost epic unity. It is this problem that has supplied the impulse to the political progress of the United States, that underlies all the great questions that have agitated the Union, and bestows on them all their constitutional importance. It has recurred in many forms, but on each occasion the solution has failed, and the decision has been avoided. Hence the American government is justly termed a system of compromises, that is to say, an inconsistent system. It is not founded, like the old governments of Europe, on tradition, nor on principles, like those which have followed the French Revolution; but on a series of mutual concessions, and momentary suspensions of war between opposite principles, neither of which could prevail. Necessarily, as the country grew more populous, and the population more extended, as the various interests grew in importance, and the various parties in internal strength, as new regions, contrasting with each other in all things in which the influence of nature and the condition of society bear upon political life, were formed into states, the conflict grew into vaster proportions and greater intensity, each opinion became more stubborn and unyielding, compromise was more difficult, and the peril to the Union increased.

Viewed in the light of recent events, the history of the American Republic is intelligible and singularly instructive. For the dissolution of the Union is no accidental or hasty or violent proceeding, but the normal and inevitable result of a long course of events, which trace their origin to the rise of the constitution itself. There we find the germs of the disunion that have taken seventy years to ripen, the beginning of an antagonism which constantly asserted itself and could never be reconciled, until the differences widened into a breach.

The convention which sat at Philadelphia in 1787, for the purpose of substituting a permanent constitution in the place of the confederacy, which had been formed to resist the arms of England, but which had broken down in the first years of peace, was not a very numerous body, but it included the most eminent men of America. It is astounding to observe the political wisdom, and still more the political foresight, which their deliberations exhibit. Franklin, indeed, appears to have been the only very foolish man among them, and his colleagues seem to have been aware of it. Washington presided, but he exercised very little influence upon the assembly, in which there were men who far exceeded him in intellectual power. Adams and Jefferson were in Europe, and the absence of the latter is conspicuous in the debates and in the remarkable work which issued from them. For it is a most striking thing that the views of pure democracy, which we are accustomed to associate with American politics, were almost entirely unrepresented in that convention. Far from being the product of a democratic revolution, and of an opposition to English institutions, the Constitution of the United States was the result of a powerful reaction against democracy, and in favour of the traditions of the mother country. On this point nearly all the leading statesmen were agreed, and no contradiction was given to such speeches as the following. Madison said: "In all cases where a majority are united by a common interest or passion, the rights of the minority are in danger. What motives are to restrain them? A prudent regard to the maxim, that honesty is the best policy, is found by experience to be as little regarded by bodies of men as by individuals. Respect for character is always diminished in proportion to the number among whom the blame or praise is to be divided. Conscience, the only remaining tie, is known to be inadequate in individuals; in large numbers little is to be expected from it."

Mr. Sherman opposed the election by the people, "insisting that it ought to be by the State legislatures. The people immediately should have as little to do as may be about the government."

Mr. Gerry said: "The evils we experience flow from the excess of democracy. The people do not want virtue, but are the dupes of pretended patriots. . . . He had been too republican heretofore; he was still, however, republican, but had been taught by experience the danger of the levelling spirit." Mr. Mason "admitted that we had been too democratic, but was afraid we should incautiously run into the opposite extreme." Mr. Randolph observed "that the general object was to provide a cure for the evils under which the United States laboured; that, in tracing these evils to their origin, every man had found it in the turbulence and follies of democracy; that some check, therefore, was to be sought for against this tendency of our governments."

Mr. Wilson, speaking in 1787, as if with the experience of the seventy years that followed, said, "Despotism comes on mankind in different shapes; sometimes in an executive, sometimes in a military one. Is there no danger of a legislative despotism? Theory and practice both proclaim it. If the legislative authority be not restrained, there can be neither liberty nor stability." "However the legislative power may be formed," said Gouverneur Morris, the most conservative man in the convention, "it will, if disposed, be able to ruin the country."

Still stronger was the language of Alexander Hamilton: "If government is in the hands of the few, they will tyrannise over the many; if in the hands of the many, they will tyrannise over the few. It ought to be in the hands of both, and they should be separated. This separation must be permanent. Representation alone will not do; demagogues will generally prevail; and, if separated, they will need a mutual check. This check is a monarch. . . . The monarch must have proportional strength. He ought to be hereditary, and to have so much power that it will not be his interest to risk much to acquire more. . . . Those who mean to form a solid republican government ought to proceed to the confines of another government. . . . But if we incline too much to democracy, we shall soon shoot into a monarchy." "He acknowledged himself not to think favourably of republican government, but addressed his remarks to those who did think favourably of it, in order to prevail on them to tone their government as high as possible." Soon after, in the New York convention, for the adoption of the constitution, he said, "It has been observed that a pure democracy, if it were practicable, would be the most perfect government. Experience has proved that no position in politics is more false than this. The ancient democracies, in which the people themselves deliberated, never possessed one feature of good government. Their very character was tyranny."

Hamilton's opinions were in favour of monarchy, though he despaired of introducing it into America. He constantly held up the British constitution as the only guide and model; and Jefferson has recorded his conversations, which show how strong his convictions were. Adams had said that the English government might, if reformed, be made excellent; Hamilton paused and said: "Purge it of its corruption, and give to its popular branch equality of representation, and it would become an impracticable government; as it stands at present, with all its supposed defects, it is the most perfect government which ever existed." And on another occasion he declared to Jefferson, "I own it is my own opinion . . . that the present government is not that which will answer the ends of society, by giving stability and protection to its rights; and that it will probably be found expedient to go into the British form."

In his great speech on the constitution, he spoke with equal decision: "He had no scruple in declaring, supported as he was by the opinion of so many of the wise and good, that the British government was the best in the world, and that he doubted much whether anything short of it would do in America. . . . As to the executive, it seemed to be admitted that no good one could be established on republican principles. Was not this giving up the merits of the question? for can there be a good government without a good executive? The English model was the only good one on this subject. . . . We ought to go as far, in order to attain stability and permanency, as republican principles will admit."

Mr. Dickinson "wished the Senate to consist of the most distinguished characters—distinguished for their rank in life and their weight of property, and bearing as strong a likeness to the British House of Lords as possible."

Mr. Pinckney, of South Carolina, said, "Much has been said of the constitution of Great Britain. I will confess that I believe it to be the best constitution in existence; but, at the same time, I am confident it is one that will not or cannot be introduced into this country for many centuries."

The question on which the founders of the constitution really differed, and which has ever since divided, and at last dissolved the Union, was to determine how far the rights of the States were merged in the federal power, and how far they retained their independence. The problem arose chiefly upon the mode in which the central Congress was to be elected. If the people voted by numbers or by electoral districts, the less populous States must entirely disappear. If the States, and not the population, were represented, the necessary unity could never be obtained, and all the evils of the old confederation would be perpetuated. "The knot," wrote Madison in 1831, "felt as the Gordian one, was the question between the larger and the smaller States, on the rule of voting."

There was a general apprehension on the part of the smaller States that they would be reduced to subjection by the rest. Not that any great specific differences separated the different States; for though the questions of the regulation of commerce and of slavery afterwards renewed the dispute, yet interests were so different from what they have since become, and so differently distributed, that there is little analogy, excepting in principle, with later contests; what was then a dispute on a general principle, has since been envenomed by the great interests and great passions which have become involved in it. South Carolina, which at that time looked forward to a rapid increase by immigration, took part with the large States on behalf of the central power; and Charles Pinckney presented a plan of a constitution which nearly resembled that which was ultimately adopted. The chief subject of discussion was the Virginia plan, presented by Edmund Randolph, in opposition to which the small State of New Jersey introduced another plan founded on the centrifugal or State-rights principle. The object of this party was to confirm the sovereignty of the several States, and to surrender as little as possible to the federal government. This feeling was expressed by Mr. Bedford: "Is there no difference of interests, no rivalship of commerce, of manufacture? Will not these large States crush the small ones, whenever they stand in the way of their ambitions or interested views?"

"The State legislatures," said Colonel Mason, "ought to have some means of defending themselves against encroachments of the national government. In every other department we have studiously endeavoured to provide for its self-defence. Shall we leave the States alone unprovided with means for this purpose?"

These speakers may have been good or bad politicians, they were certainly good prophets. They were nearly balanced in numbers, and surpassed in ability, by the centralising party. Madison, at that time under the powerful influence of Hamilton, and a federalist, but who afterwards was carried by Jefferson into the democratic camp, occupied an uncertain intermediate position. A note preserved in Washington's handwriting records: "Mr. Madison thinks an individual independence of the States utterly irreconcilable with their aggregate sovereignty, and that a consolidation of the whole into one simple republic would be as inexpedient as it is unattainable."

In convention he said: "Any government for the United States formed on the supposed practicability of using force against the unconstitutional proceedings of the States, would prove as visionary and fallacious as the government of Congress."

The consistent Federalists went farther: "Too much attachment," said Mr. Read, "is betrayed to the State governments. We must look beyond their continuance; a national government must soon, of necessity, swallow them all up."

Two years before the meeting of the convention, in 1785, Jay, the very type of a federalist, wrote: "It is my first wish to see the United States assume and merit the character of one great nation, whose territory is divided into different States merely for more convenient government."

Alexander Hamilton went further than all his colleagues. He had taken no part in the early debates, when he brought forward an elaborate plan of his own; the most characteristic features of which are, that the State governments are to be altogether superseded; their governors to be appointed by the general government, with a veto on all State laws, and the president is to hold office on good behaviour. An executive, elected for life, but personally responsible, made the nearest possible approach to an elective monarchy; and it was with a view to this all but monarchical constitution that he designed to destroy the independence of the States. This scheme was not adopted as the basis of discussion. "He has been praised," said Mr. Johnson, "by all, but supported by none." Hamilton's speech is very imperfectly reported, but his own sketch, the notes from which he spoke, are preserved, and outweigh, in depth and in originality of thought, all that we have ever heard or read of American oratory. He left Philadelphia shortly after, and continued absent many weeks; but there can be no doubt that the spirit of his speech greatly influenced the subsequent deliberations. "He was convinced," he said, "that no amendment of the confederation, leaving the States in possession of their sovereignty, could answer the purpose. . . . The general power, whatever be its form, if it preserves itself, must swallow up the State powers. . . . They are not necessary for any of the great purposes of commerce, revenue, or agriculture. Subordinate authorities, he was aware, would be necessary. There must be distinct tribunals; corporations for local purposes. . . . By an abolition of the States, he meant that no boundary could be drawn between the national and State legislatures; that the former must therefore have indefinite authority. If it were limited at all, the rivalship of the States would gradually subvert it. . . . As States, he thought they ought to be abolished. But he admitted the necessity of leaving in them subordinate jurisdictions."

This policy could be justified only on the presumption that when all State authorities should disappear before a great central power, the democratic principles, against which the founders of the Constitution were contending, would be entirely overcome. But in this Hamilton's hopes were not fulfilled. The democratic principles acquired new force, the spirit of the convention did not long survive, and then a strong federal authority became the greatest of all dangers to the opinions and institutions which he advocated. It became the instrument of the popular will instead of its barrier; the organ of arbitrary power instead of a security against it. There was a fundamental error and contradiction in Hamilton's system. The end at which he aimed was the best, but he sought it by means radically wrong, and necessarily ruinous to the cause they were meant to serve. In order to give to the Union the best government it could enjoy, it was necessary to destroy, or rather to ignore, the existing authorities. The people was compelled to return to a political state of nature, irrespective of the governments it already possessed, and to assume to itself powers of which there were constituted administrators. No adaptation of existing facts to the ideal was possible. They required to be entirely sacrificed to the new design. All political rights, authorities, and powers must be restored to the masses, before such a scheme could be carried into effect. For the most conservative and anti-democratic government the most revolutionary basis was sought. These objections were urged against all plans inconsistent with the independence of the several States by Luther Martin, Attorney General for Maryland.

"He conceived," he said, "that the people of the States, having already vested their powers in their respective legislatures, could not resume them without a dissolution of their governments. . . . To resort to the citizens at large for their sanction to a new government, will be throwing them back into a state of nature; the dissolution of the State governments is involved in the nature of the process;—the people have no right to do this without the consent of those to whom they have delegated their power for State purposes." And in his report to the convention of Maryland of the proceedings out of which the Constitution arose, he said: "If we, contrary to the purpose for which we were intrusted, considering ourselves as masterbuilders, too proud to amend our original government, should demolish it entirely, and erect a new system of our own, a short time might show the new system as defective as the old, perhaps more so. Should a convention be found necessary again, if the members thereof, acting upon the same principles, instead of amending and correcting its defects, should demolish that entirely, and bring forward a third system, that also might soon be found no better than either of the former; and thus we might always remain young in government, and always suffering the inconveniences of an incorrect imperfect system."

It is very remarkable that, while the Federalists, headed by Hamilton and Madison, advocated, for the soundest and wisest object, opinions which have since been fatal to the Union, by furnishing the democratic party with an irresistible instrument, and consequently an irresistible temptation, Martin supported a policy in reality far more conservative, although his opinions were more revolutionary, and although he quoted as political authorities writers such as Price and Priestley. The controversy, although identical in substance with that which has at last destroyed the Union, was so different in form, and consequently in its bearings, that the position of the contending parties became inverted as their interests or their principles predominated. The result of this great constitutional debate was, that the States were represented as units in the Senate, and the people according to numbers in the House. This was the first of the three great compromises. The others were the laws by which the regulation of commerce was made over to the central power, and the slave-trade was tolerated for only twenty years. On these two questions, the regulation of commerce and the extension of slavery, the interests afterwards grew more divided, and it is by them that the preservation of the Union has been constantly called in question. This was not felt at first, when Jay wrote "that Providence has been pleased to give this one connected country to one united people; a people descended from the same ancestors, speaking the same language, professing the same religion, attached to the same principles of government, very similar in their manners and customs." The weakening of all these bonds of union gradually brought on the calamities which are described by Madison in another number of the same publication: "A landed interest, a manufacturing interest, a mercantile interest, a moneyed interest, with many lesser interests, grow up of necessity in civilised nations, and divide them into different classes, actuated by different sentiments and views. The regulation of these various and interfering interests forms the principal task of modern legislation, and involves the spirit of party and faction in the necessary and ordinary operations of the government. . . . When a majority is included in a faction, the form of popular government enables it to sacrifice to its ruling passion or interest both the public good and the rights of other citizens. . . . It is of great importance in a republic not only to guard the society against the oppression of its rulers, but to guard one part of the society against the injustice of the other part. Different interests necessarily exist in different classes of citizens. If a majority be united by common interests, the rights of the minority will be insecure. There are but two methods of providing against this evil: the one by creating a will in the community independent of the majority, that is, of the society itself; the other, by comprehending in the society so many separate descriptions of citizens as will render one unjust combination of a majority of the whole very improbable, if not impracticable. . . . In a free government the security for civil rights must be the same as that for religious rights. It consists, in the one case, in the multiplicity of interests, and in the other in the multiplicity of sects." That Madison should have given so absurd a reason for security in the new Constitution, can be explained only by the fact that he was writing to recommend it as it was, and had to make the best of his case. It had been Hamilton's earnest endeavour to establish that security for right which Madison considers peculiar to monarchy, an authority which should not be the organ of the majority. " 'Tis essential there should be a permanent will in a community. . . . The principle chiefly intended to be established is this, that there must be a permanent will. . . . There ought to be a principle in government capable of resisting the popular current."

This is precisely what Judge Story means when he says: "I would say in a republican government the fundamental truth, that the minority have indisputable and inalienable rights; that the majority are not everything, and the minority nothing; that the people may not do what they please."

Webster thought the same, but he took a sanguine view of actual facts when he said: "It is another principle, equally true and certain, and, according to my judgment of things, equally important, that the people often limit themselves. They set bounds to their own power. They have chosen to secure the institutions which they establish against the sudden impulses of mere majorities."

Channing was nearer the truth when he wrote: "The doctrine that the majority ought to govern passes with the multitude as an intuition, and they have never thought how far it is to be modified in practice, and how far the application of it ought to be controlled by other principles."

In reality, the total absence of a provision of this kind, which should raise up a law above the arbitrary will of the people, and prevent it from being sovereign, led the greatest of the statesmen who sat in the convention to despair of the success and permanence of their work. Jefferson informs us that it was so with Washington: "Washington had not a firm confidence in the durability of our government. Washington was influenced by the belief that we must at length end in something like a British constitution."

Hamilton, who by his writings contributed more than any other man to the adoption of the Constitution, declared in the convention that "no man's ideas were more remote from the plan than his own," and he explained what he thought of the kind of security that had been obtained: "Gentlemen say that we need to be rescued from the democracy. But what the means proposed? A democratic Assembly is to be checked by a democratic Senate, and both these by a democratic chief magistrate."

"A large and well-organised republic," he said, "can scarcely lose its liberty from any other cause than that of anarchy, to which a contempt of the laws is the high-road. . . . A sacred respect for the constitutional law is the vital principle, the sustaining energy of a free government. . . . The instruments by which it must act are either the authority of the laws, or force. If the first be destroyed, the last must be substituted; and where this becomes the ordinary instrument of government, there is an end to liberty."

His anticipations may be gathered from the following passages: "A good administration will conciliate the confidence and affection of the people, and perhaps enable the government to acquire more consistency than the proposed constitution seems to promise for so great a country. It may then triumph altogether over the State governments, and reduce them to an entire subordination, dividing the larger States into smaller districts. . . . If this should not be the case, in the course of a few years it is probable that the contests about the boundaries of power between the particular governments and the general government, and the momentum of the larger States in such contests, will produce a dissolution of the Union. This, after all, seems to be the most likely result. . . . The probable evil is, that the general government will be too dependent on the State legislatures, too much governed by their prejudices, and too obsequious to their humours; that the States, with every power in their hands, will make encroachments on the national authority, till the Union is weakened and dissolved."

The result has justified the fears of Hamilton, and the course of events has been that which he predicted. Democratic opinions, which he had so earnestly combated, gained ground rapidly during the French revolutionary period. Jefferson, who, even at the time of the Declaration of Independence, which was his work, entertained views resembling those of Rousseau and Paine, and sought the source of freedom in the abstract rights of man, returned from France with his mind full of the doctrines of equality and popular sovereignty. By the defeat of Adams in the contest for the presidency, he carried these principles to power, and altered the nature of the American government. As the Federalists interpreted and administered the Constitution, under Washington and Adams, the executive was, what Hamilton intended it to be, supreme in great measure over the popular will. Against this predominance the State legislatures were the only counterpoise, and accordingly the democratic party, which was the creature of Jefferson, vehemently defended their rights as a means of giving power to the people. In apparent contradiction, but in real accordance with this, and upon the same theory of the direct sovereignty of the people, Jefferson, when he was elected president, denied the right of the States to control the action of the executive. Regarding the President as the representative and agent of a power wholly arbitrary, he admitted no limits to its exercise. He held himself bound to obey the popular will even against his own opinions, and to allow of no resistance to it. He acted as the helpless tool of the majority, and the absolute ruler of the minority, as endowed with despotic power, but without free-will.

It is of this principle of the revolution that Tocqueville says: "Les gouvernements qu'elle a fondés sont plus fragiles, il est vrai, mais cent fois plus puissants qu'aucun de ceux qu'elle a renversés; fragiles et puissants par les mêmes causes."

Hence Jefferson's determined aversion to every authority which could oppose or restrain the will of the sovereign people, especially to the State legislatures and to the judiciary. Speaking of an occasion in which the judges had acted with independence, Hildreth says: "Jefferson was not a little vexed at this proceeding, which served, indeed, to confirm his strong prejudices against judges and courts. To him, indeed, they were doubly objects of hatred, as instruments of tyranny in the hands of the Federalists, and as obstacles to himself in exercises of power."

His views of government are contained in a paper which is printed in Rayner's life of him, p. 378: "Governments are republican only in proportion as they embody the will of their people, and execute it. . . . Each generation is as independent of the one preceding as that was of all which had gone before. It has, then, like them, a right to choose for itself the form of government it believes most promotive of its own happiness . . . it is for the peace and good of mankind, that a solemn opportunity of doing this, every nineteen or twenty years, should be provided by the constitution. . . . The dead have no rights. . . . This corporeal globe and everything upon it belong to its present corporeal inhabitants during their generation. . . . That majority, then, has a right to depute representatives to a convention, and to make the constitution which they think will be best for themselves. . . . Independence can be trusted nowhere but with the people in mass." With these doctrines Jefferson subverted the republicanism of America, and consequently the Republic itself.

Hildreth describes as follows the contest between the two systems, at the time of the accession of Jefferson to power, in 1801: "From the first moment that party lines had been distinctly drawn, the opposition had possessed a numerical majority, against which nothing but the superior energy, intelligence, and practical skill of the Federalists, backed by the great and venerable name and towering influence of Washington, had enabled them to maintain for eight years past an arduous and doubtful struggle. The Federal party, with Washington and Hamilton at its head, represented the experience, the prudence, the practical wisdom, the discipline, the conservative reason and instincts of the country. The opposition, headed by Jefferson, expressed its hopes, wishes, theories, many of them enthusiastic and impracticable, more especially its passions, its sympathies and antipathies, its impatience of restraint. The Federalists had their strength in those narrow districts where a concentrated population had produced and contributed to maintain that complexity of institutions, and that reverence for social order, which, in proportion as men are brought into contiguity, become more absolutely necessaries of existence. The ultrademocratical ideas of the opposition prevailed in all that more extensive region in which the dispersion of population, and the despotic authority vested in individuals over families of slaves, kept society in a state of immaturity."

Upon the principle that the majority have no duties, and the minority no rights, that it is lawful to do whatever it is possible to do, measures were to be expected which would oppress most tyrically the rights and interests of portions of the Union, for whom there was no security and no redress. The apprehension was so great among the Federalists, that Hamilton wrote in

1804: "The ill opinion of Jefferson, and jealousy of the ambition of Virginia, is no inconsiderable prop of good principles in that country (New England). But these causes are leading to an opinion, that a dismemberment of the Union is expedient."

Jefferson had given the example of such threats, and owed his election to them during his contest for the presidency with Colonel Burr. He wrote to Monroe, 15 February, 1801: "If they could have been permitted to pass a law for putting the government into the hands of an officer, they would certainly have prevented an election. But we thought it best to declare openly and firmly, one and all, that the day such an act passed the middle States would arm, and that no such usurpation, even for a single day, should be submitted to."

Shortly afterwards, a conjuncture arose in which Jefferson put his principles into practice in such a way as greatly to increase the alarm of the North-Eastern States. In consequence of Napoleon's Berlin decree and of the British orders in council, he determined to lay an embargo on all American vessels. He sent a pressing message to Congress, and the Senate passed the measure after a four hours' debate with closed doors. In the House the debate was also secret, but it lasted several days, and was often prolonged far into the night, in the hope of obtaining a division. The Bill was passed December 22, 1807. The public had no voice in the matter; those whom the measure touched most nearly were taken by surprise, and a conspicuous example was given of secrecy and promptitude in a species of government which is not commonly remarkable for these qualities.

The embargo was a heavy blow to the ship-owning states of New England. The others were less affected by it. "The natural situation of this country," says Hamilton, "seems to divide its interests into different classes. There are navigating and non-navigating States. The Northern are properly the navigating states; the Southern appear to possess neither the means nor the spirit of navigation. This difference in situation naturally produces a dissimilarity of interests and views respecting foreign commerce."

Accordingly the law was received in those States with a storm of indignation. Quincy, of Massachusetts, declared in the House: "It would be as unreasonable to undertake to stop the rivers from running into the sea, as to keep the people of New England from the ocean. They did not believe in the constitutionality of any such law. He might be told that the courts had already settled that question. But it was one thing to decide a question before a court of law, and another to decide it before the people."

Even in a juridical point of view the right to make such a law was very doubtful. Story, who first took part in public affairs on this occasion, says: "I have ever considered the embargo a measure which went to the extreme limit of constructive power under the constitution. It stands upon the extreme verge of the constitution."

The doctrine of State-rights, or nullification, which afterwards became so prominent in the hands of the Southern party, was distinctly enunciated on behalf of the North on this occasion. Governor Trumbull, of Connecticut, summoned the legislature to meet, and in his opening address to them he took the ground that, on great emergencies, when the national legislature had been led to overstep its constitutional power, it became the right and duty of the State legislatures "to interpose their protecting shield between the rights and liberties of the people, and the assumed power of the general government."

They went further, and prepared to secede from the Union, and thus gave the example which has been followed, on exactly analogous grounds, by the opposite party. Randolph warned the administration that they were treading fast in the fatal footsteps of Lord North.

John Quincy Adams declared in Congress that there was a determination to secede. "He urged that a continuance of the embargo much longer would certainly be met by forcible resistance, supported by the legislature, and probably by the judiciary of the State. . . . Their object was, and had been for several years, a dissolution of the Union, and the establishment of a separate confederation." Twenty years later, when Adams was President, the truth of this statement was impugned. At that time the tables had been turned, and the South was denying the right of Congress to legislate for the exclusive benefit of the North-Eastern States, whilst these were vigorously and profitably supporting the federal authorities. It was important that they should not be convicted out of their own mouths, and that the doctrine they were opposing should not be shown to have been inaugurated by themselves. Adams therefore published a statement, October 21, 1828, reiterating his original declaration. "The people were constantly instigated to forcible resistance against it, and juries after juries acquitted the violators of it, upon the ground that it was unconstitutional, assumed in the face of a solemn decision of the District Court of the United States. A separation of the Union was openly stimulated in the public prints, and a convention of delegates of the New England States, to meet at New Haven, was intended and proposed." That this was true is proved by the letters of Story, written at the time. "I was well satisfied," he says, "that such a course would not and could not be borne by New England, and would bring on a direct rebellion. . . . The stories here of rebellion in Massachusetts are continually circulating. My own impressions are, that the Junto would awaken it, if they dared; but it will not do. . . . A division of the States has been meditated, but I suspect that the public pulse was not sufficiently inflamed. . . . I am sorry to perceive the spirit of disaffection in Massachusetts increasing to so high a degree; and I fear that it is stimulated by a desire, in a very few ambitious men, to dissolve the Union. . . . I have my fears when I perceive that the public prints openly advocate a resort to arms to sweep away the present embarrassments of commerce."

It was chiefly due to the influence of Story that the embargo was at length removed, with great reluctance and disgust on the part of the President. "I ascribe all this," he says, "to one pseudo-republican, Story." On which Story, who was justly proud of his achievement, remarks, "Pseudo-republican of course I must be, as everyone was, in Mr. Jefferson's opinion, who dared to venture upon a doubt of his infallibility." In reality Jefferson meant that a man was not a republican who made the interests of the minority prevail against the wish of the majority. His enthusiastic admirer, Professor Tucker, describes very justly and openly his policy in this affair. "If his perseverance in the embargo policy so long, against the wishes and interests of New England, and the mercantile community generally, may seem to afford some contradiction to the self-denying merit here claimed, the answer is, that he therein fulfilled the wishes of a large majority of the people. . . . A portion of the community here suffered an evil necessarily incident to the great merit of a republican government, that the will of the majority must prevail."

We have seen that in the case of the embargo, as soon as this democratic theory was acted upon, it called up a corresponding claim of the right of the minority to secede, and that the democratic principle was forced to yield. But secession was not a theory of the Constitution, but a remedy against a vicious theory of the Constitution. A sounder theory would have avoided the absolutism of the democrats and the necessity for secession. The next great controversy was fought upon this ground. It exhibits an attempt to set up a law against the arbitrary will of the government, and to escape the tyranny of the majority, and the remedy, which was worse than the disease. An ideal of this kind had already been sketched by Hamilton. "This balance between the national and state governments ought to be dwelt on with peculiar attention, as it is of the utmost importance. It forms a double security to the people. If one encroaches on their rights, they will find a powerful protection in the other. Indeed, they will both be prevented from overpassing their constitutional limits, by a certain rivalship which will ever subsist between them." This was also what Mr. Dickinson looked forward to when he said in the Convention of 1787: "One source of stability is the double branch of the legislature. The division of the country into distinct States forms the other principal source of stability."

The war with England, and the long suspension of commerce which preceded it, laid the foundations of a manufacturing interest in the United States. Manufactories began to spring up in Pennsylvania, and more slowly in New England. In 1816 a tariff was introduced, bearing a slightly protective character, as it was necessary to accommodate the war prohibitions to peaceful times. It was rather intended to facilitate the period of transition than to protect the new industry; and that interest was still so feeble, and so little affected by the tariff, that Webster, who was already a representative of Massachusetts in Congress, voted against it. It was carried by the coalition of Clay with the South Carolina statesmen, Lowndes and Calhoun, against whom this vote was afterwards a favourite weapon of attack. In the following years the increasing importance of the cultivation of cotton, and the growth of manufactures, placed the Northern and Southern interests in a new position of great divergency. Hamilton had said long before: "The difference of property is already great amongst us. Commerce and industry will still increase the disparity. Your government must meet this state of things, or combinations will, in process of time, undermine your system."

The New England manufacturers were awakened to the advantage of protection for their wares. In a memorial of the merchants of Salem, written by Story in 1820, he says: "Nothing can be more obvious than that many of the manufacturers and their friends are attempting, by fallacious statements, founded on an interested policy, or a misguided zeal, or very short-sighted views, to uproot some of the fundamental principles of our revenue policy. . . . If we are unwilling to receive foreign manufacturers, we cannot reasonably suppose that foreign nations will receive our raw materials. . . . We cannot force them to become buyers when they are not sellers, or to consume our cotton when they cannot pay the price in their own fabrics. We may compel them to use the cotton of the West Indies, or of the Brazils, or of the East Indies." About the same time, May 20, 1820, he writes to Lord Stowell on the same subject: "We are beginning also to become a manufacturing nation; but I am not much pleased, I am free to confess, with the efforts made to give an artificial stimulus to these establishments in our country. . . . The example of your great manufacturing cities, apparently the seats of great vices, and great political fermentations, affords no very agreeable contemplation to the statesman or the patriot, or the friend of liberty." The manufacturers obtained a new tariff in 1824, another was carried by great majorities in 1828, and another in 1832 by a majority of two to one. It is the measure of 1828, which raised the duties on an average to nearly fifty per cent on the value of the imports, that possesses the greatest importance in a constitutional point of view. "To it," says the biographer of Mr. Calhoun, "may be traced almost every important incident in our political history since that time, as far as our internal affairs are concerned." At this time the interests of North and South were perfectly distinct. The South was teeming with agricultural produce, for which there was a great European demand; whilst the industry of the North, unable to compete with European manufacturers, tried to secure the monopoly of the home market. Unlike the course of the same controversy in England, the agriculturists (at least the cotton-growers) desired free trade, because they were exporters; the manufacturers protection because they could not meet competition. "The question," said Calhoun, "is in reality one between the exporting and non-exporting interests of the country." The exporting interest required the utmost freedom of imports, in order not to barter at a disadvantage. "He must be ignorant of the first principles of commerce, and the policy of Europe, particularly England, who does not see that it is impossible to carry on a trade of such vast extent on any other basis than barter; and that if it were not so carried on, it would not long be tolerated. . . . The last remains of our great and once flourishing agriculture must be annihilated in the conflict. In the first place, we will be thrown on the home market, which cannot consume a fourth of our products; and instead of supplying the world, as we would with a free trade, we would be compelled to abandon the cultivation of three-fourths of what we now raise, and receive for the residue whatever the manufacturers —who would then have their policy consummated by the entire possession of our market—might choose to give." It seemed a fulfilment of the prophecy of Mr. Lowndes, who, in resisting the adoption of the Constitution in South Carolina forty years before, declared, that "when this new constitution should be adopted, the sun of the Southern States would set, never to rise again. . . . The interest of the Northern States would so predominate as to divest us of any pretensions to the title of a republic." Cobbett, who knew America better than any Englishman of that day, described, in his *Political Register* for 1833, the position of these hostile interests in a way which is very much to the point. "All these Southern and Western States are, commercially speaking, closely connected with Birmingham, Sheffield, Manchester and Leeds; . . . they have no such connection with the Northern States, and there is no tie whatsoever to bind them together, except that which is of a mere political nature. . . . Here is a natural division of interests, and of interests so powerful, too, as not to be counteracted by anything that man can do. The heavy duties imposed by the Congress upon British manufactured goods is neither more nor less than so many millions a year taken from the Southern and Western States, and given to the Northern States."

Whilst in England protection benefited one class of the population at the expense of another, in America it was for the advantage of one part of the country at the expense of another. "Government," said Calhoun, "is to descend from its high appointed duty, and become the agent of a portion of the community to extort, under the guise of protection, tribute from the rest of the community."

Where such a controversy is carried on between opposite classes in the same State, the violence of factions may endanger the government, but they cannot divide the State. But the violence is much greater, the wrong is more keenly felt, the means of resistance are more legitimate and constitutional, where the oppressed party is a sovereign State.

The South had every reason to resist to the utmost a measure which would be so injurious to them. It was opposed to their political as well as to their financial interests. For the tariff, while it impoverished them, enriched the government, and filled the treasury with superfluous gold. Now the Southern statesmen were always opposed to the predominance of the central authority, especially since it lent itself to a policy by which they suffered. They had practical and theoretical objections to it. The increase of the revenue beyond the ordinary wants of the government placed in its hands a tempting and dangerous instrument of influence. Means must be devised for the disposal of these sums, and the means adopted by the advocates of restriction was the execution of public works, by which the people of the different States were bribed to favour the central power. A protective tariff therefore, and internal improvement, were the chief points in the policy of the party, which, headed by Henry Clay, sought to strengthen the Union at the expense of the States, and which the South opposed, as both hostile to their interests and as unconstitutional. "It would be in vain to attempt to conceal," wrote Calhoun of the tariff in 1831, "that it has divided the country into two great geographical divisions, and arrayed them against each other, in opinion at least, if not interests also, on some of the most vital of political subjects—on its finance, its commerce, and its industry. . . . Nor has the effect of this dangerous conflict ended here. It has not only divided the two sections on the important point already stated, but on the deeper and more dangerous questions, the constitutionality of a protective tariff, and the general principles and theory of the constitution itself: the stronger, in order to maintain their superiority, giving a construction to the instrument which the other believes would convert the general government into a consolidated irresponsible government, with the total destruction of liberty." "On the great and vital point—the industry of the country, which comprehends almost every interest—the interest of the two great sections is opposed. We want free trade, they restrictions; we want moderate taxes, frugality in the government, economy, accountability, and a rigid application of the public money to the payment of the debt, and to the objects authorised by the constitution. In all these particulars, if we may judge by experience, their views of their interest are precisely the opposite." In 1828 he said of the protective system: "No system can be more efficient to rear up a moneyed aristocracy"; wherein he is again supported by Cobbett, in the well-known saying, uttered five years later, concerning the United States: "It is there the aristocracy of money, the most damned of all aristocracies." South Carolina took the lead in resisting the introduction of the protective system, and being defeated by many votes on the question itself, took its stand on the constitutional right of each sovereign State to arrest by its veto any general legislation of a kind which would be injurious to its particular interests. "The country," said Calhoun, "is now more divided than in 1824, and then more than in 1816. The majority may have increased, but the opposite sides are, beyond dispute, more determined and excited than at any preceding period. Formerly the system was resisted mainly as inexpedient, but now as unconstitutional, unequal, unjust, and oppressive. Then relief was sought exclusively from the general government; but now many, driven to despair, are raising their eyes to the reserved sovereignty of the States as the only refuge." Calhoun was at that time Vice-President of the United States, and without a seat in Congress. The defence of his theory of the Constitution devolved therefore upon the senator from South Carolina, General Hayne; and a debate ensued between Hayne and Webster, in January 1830, which is reckoned by Americans the most memorable in the parliamentary history of their country. Hayne declared that he did not contend for the mere right of revolution, but for the right of constitutional resistance; and in reply to Webster's defence of the supreme power, he said: "This I know is a popular notion, and it is founded on the idea that as all the States are represented here, nothing can prevail which is not in conformity with the will of the majority; and it is supposed to be a republican maxim, 'that the majority must govern.' . . . If the will of a majority of congress is to be the supreme law of the land, it is clear the Constitution is a dead letter, and has utterly failed of the very object for which it was designed—the protection of the rights of the minority. . . . The whole difference between us consists in this—the gentleman would make force the only arbiter in all cases of collision between the States and the federal government; I would resort to a peaceful remedy."

Two years later Mr. Calhoun succeeded Hayne as senator for South Carolina, and the contest was renewed. After the tariff of 1828 Virginia, Georgia, and North Carolina joined in the recognition of the principle of nullification. When the tariff of 1832 was carried, South Carolina announced that the levying of dues would be resisted in the State. Calhoun defended the nullifying ordinance in the Senate, and in speeches and writings, with arguments which are the very perfection of political truth, and which combine with the realities of modern democracy the theory and the securities of mediæval freedom. "The essence of liberty," he said, "comprehends the idea of responsible power,—that those who make and execute the laws should be controlled by those on whom they operate,—that the governed should govern. . . . No government based on the naked principle that the majority ought to govern, however true the maxim in its proper sense, and under proper restrictions, can preserve its liberty even for a single generation. The history of all has been the same,—violence, injustice, and anarchy, succeeded by the government of one, or a few, under which the people seek refuge from the more oppressive despotism of the many. . . . Stripped of all its covering, the naked question is, whether ours is a federal or a consolidated government; a constitutional or absolute one; a government resting ultimately on the solid basis of the sovereignty of the States, or on the unrestrained will of a majority; a form of government, as in all other unlimited ones, in which injustice and violence and force must finally prevail. Let it never be forgotten that, where the majority rules without restriction, the minority is the subject. . . . Nor is the right of suffrage more indispensable to enforce the responsibility of the rulers to the ruled, than a federal organisation to compel the parts to respect the rights of each other. It requires the united action of both to prevent the abuse of power and oppression, and to constitute really and truly a constitutional government. To supersede either is to convert it in fact, whatever may be its theory, into an absolute government."

In his disquisition on government Calhoun has expounded his theory of a constitution in a manner so profound, and so extremely applicable to the politics of the present day, that we regret that we can only give a very feeble notion of the argument by the few extracts for which we can make room.

"The powers which it is necessary for government to possess, in order to repress violence and preserve order, cannot execute themselves. They must be administered by men in whom, like others, the individual are stronger than the social feelings. And hence the powers vested in them to prevent injustice and oppression on the part of others, will, if left unguarded, be by them converted into instruments to oppress the rest of the community. That by which this is prevented, by whatever name called, is what is meant by constitution, in its most comprehensive sense, when applied to government. Having its origin in the same principle of our nature, constitution stands to government as government stands to society; and, as the end for which society is ordained would be defeated without government, so that for which government is ordained would, in a great measure, be defeated without constitution. . . . Constitution is the contrivance of man, while government is of divine ordination. . . . Power can only be resisted by power, and tendency by tendency. . . . I call the right of suffrage the indispensable and primary principle; for it would be a great and dangerous mistake to suppose, as many do, that it is of itself sufficient to form constitutional governments. To this erroneous opinion may

be traced one of the causes why so few attempts to form constitutional governments have succeeded; and why, of the few which have, so small a number
have had durable existence. . . . So far from being of itself sufficient,—however
well-guarded it might be, and however enlightened the people,—it would,
unaided by other provisions, leave the government as absolute as it would be
in the hands of irresponsible rulers, and with a tendency at least as strong
towards oppression and abuse of its powers. . . . The process may be slow, and
much time may be required before a compact, organised majority can be
formed; but formed it will be in time, even without preconcert or design, by
the sure workings of that principle or constitution of our nature in which
government itself originates. . . . The dominant majority, for the time, would
have the same tendency to oppression and abuse of power which, without the
right of suffrage, irresponsible rulers would have. No reason, indeed, can be
assigned why the latter would abuse their power, which would not apply with
equal force to the former. . . . The minority, for the time, will be as much the
governed or subject portion as are the people in an aristocracy, or the subject
in a monarchy. . . . The duration or uncertainty of the tenure by which power
is held cannot of itself counteract the tendency inherent in government to
oppression and abuse of power. On the contrary, the very uncertainty of the
tenure, combined with the violent party warfare which must ever precede a
change of parties under such governments, would rather tend to increase than
diminish the tendency to oppression. . . . It is manifest that this provision must
be of a character calculated to prevent any one interest, or combination
of interests, from using the powers of government to aggrandise itself
at the expense of the others. . . . This too can be accomplished only
in one way, and that is, by such an organism of the government—and, if
necessary for the purpose, of the community also—as will, by dividing and
distributing the powers of government, give to each division or interest,
through its appropriate organ, either a concurrent voice in making and execut-
ing the laws, or a veto on their execution. . . . Such an organism as this,
combined with the right of suffrage, constitutes, in fact, the elements of constitutional government. The one, by rendering those who make and execute the
laws responsible to those on whom they operate, prevents the rulers from
oppressing the ruled; and the other, by making it impossible for any one
interest or combination of interests, or class, or order, or portion of the community, to obtain exclusive control, prevents any one of them from oppressing
the other. . . . It is this negative power,—the power of preventing or arresting
the action of the government,—be it called by what term it may, veto, interposition, nullification, check, or balance of power,—which in fact forms the
constitution. . . . It is, indeed, the negative power which makes the constitution, and the positive which makes the government. . . . It follows necessarily
that where the numerical majority has the sole control of the government,
there can be no constitution; as constitution implies limitation or restriction;
. . . and hence, the numerical, unmixed with the concurrent majority, necessarily forms in all cases absolute government. . . . Constitutional governments,
of whatever form, are, indeed, much more similar to each other in their struc-

ture and character than they are, respectively, to the absolute governments even of their own class; . . . and hence the great and broad distinction between governments is,—not that of the one, the few, or the many,—but of the constitutional and the absolute. . . . Among the other advantages which governments of the concurrent have over those of the numerical majority,—and which strongly illustrates their more popular character,—is, that they admit, with safety, a much greater extension of the right of suffrage. It may be safely extended in such governments to universal suffrage, that is, to every male citizen of mature age, with few ordinary exceptions; but it cannot be so far extended in those of the numerical majority, without placing them ultimately under the control of the more ignorant and dependent portions of the community. For, as the community becomes populous, wealthy, refined, and highly civilised, the difference between the rich and the poor will become more strongly marked, and the number of the the ignorant and dependent greater in proportion to the rest of the community. . . . The tendency of the concurrent government is to unite the community, let its interests be ever so diversified or opposed; while that of the numerical is to divide it into two conflicting portions, let its interest be naturally ever so united and identified. . . . The numerical majority, by regarding the community as a unit, and having as such the same interests throughout all its parts, must, by its necessary operation, divide it into two hostile parts, waging, under the forms of law, incessant hostilities against each other. . . . To make equality of condition essential to liberty, would be to destroy liberty and progress. The reason is both that inequality of condition, while it is a necessary consequence of liberty, is at the same time indispensable to progress. . . . It is, indeed, this inequality of condition between the front and rear ranks, in the march of progress, which gives so strong an impulse to the former to maintain their position, and to the latter to press forward into their files. This gives to progress its greatest impulse. . . . These great and dangerous errors have their origin in the prevalent opinion, that all men are born free and equal, than which nothing can be more unfounded and false. . . . In an absolute democracy party conflicts between the majority and minority . . . can hardly ever terminate in compromise. The object of the opposing minority is to expel the majority from power, and of the majority to maintain their hold upon it. It is on both sides a struggle for the whole; a struggle that must determine which shall be the governing and which the subject party. . . . Hence, among other reasons, aristocracies and monarchies more readily assume the constitutional form than absolute popular governments."

This was written in the last years of Calhoun's life, and published after his death; but the ideas, though he matured them in the subsequent contest on slavery, guided him in the earlier stage of the dispute which developed nullification into secession, during the tariff controversy of the years 1828 to 1833. Many of those who differed from him most widely deemed that his resistance was justified by the selfish and unscrupulous policy of the North. Legaré, the most accomplished scholar among American statesmen, afterwards attorney-general, made a Fourth-of-July oration in South Carolina, during the height of the excitement of 1831, in which he said: "The authors of this policy are indirectly responsible for this deplorable state of things, and for all the consequences that may grow out of it. They have been guilty of an inexpiable offence against their country. They found us a united, they have made us a distracted people. They found the union of these States an object of fervent love and religious veneration; they have made even its utility a subject of controversy among very enlightened men. . . . I do not wonder at the indignation which the imposition of such a burden of taxation has excited in our people, in the present unprosperous state of their affairs. . . . Great nations cannot be held together under a united government by anything short of despotic power, if any one part of the country is to be arrayed against another in a perpetual scramble for privilege and protection, under any system of protection."

Brownson, at that time the most influential journalist of America, and a strong partisan of Calhoun, advocated in 1844 his claims to the Presidency, and would, we believe, have held office in his cabinet if he had been elected. In one of the earliest numbers of his well-known Review he wrote: "Even Mr. Calhoun's theory, though unquestionably the true theory of the federal constitution, is yet insufficient. . . . It does not, as a matter of fact, arrest the unequal, unjust, and oppressive measures of the federal government. South Carolina in 1833 forced a compromise; but in 1842 the obnoxious policy was revived, is pursued now successfully, and there is no State to attempt again the virtue of State interposition. . . . The State, if she judged proper, had the sovereign right to set aside this obnoxious tariff enactment in her own dominions, and prohibit her subjects or citizens from obeying it. . . . The parties to the compact being equal, and there being no common umpire, each, as a matter of course, is its own judge of the infraction of the compact, and of the mode and measure of redress."

The President, General Jackson, had a strong aversion for the theory and for the person of Calhoun. He swore that he would have him impeached for treason, and that he should hang on a gallows higher than Haman's. One of the nullifying declarations of his Vice-President reached him late at night; in a fit of exultation he had the law officers of the government called out of their beds, to say whether at last here was not hanging matter. He issued a manifesto condemning the doctrine of nullification and the acts of South Carolina, which was very ably drawn up by Livingston, the Secretary of State, famous in the history of legislation as the author of the Louisiana code. Webster, the first orator of the day, though not a supporter of the administration, undertook to answer Calhoun in the Senate, and he was fetched from his lodging, when the time came, in the President's carriage. His speech, considered the greatest he ever delivered, was regarded by the friends of the Union as conclusive against State-rights. Madison, who was approaching the term of his long career, wrote to congratulate the speaker in words which ought to have been a warning: "It crushes nullification, and must hasten an abandonment of secession. But this dodges the blow by confounding the claim to secede at will with the right of seceding from intolerable oppression."

Secession is but the alternative of interposition. The defeat of the latter doctrine on the ground of the Constitution, deprived the South of the only possible protection from the increasing tyranny of the majority, for the defeat of nullification coincided in time with the final triumph of the pure democratic views; and at the same time that it was resolved that the rights of the minority had no security, it was established that the power of the majority had no bounds. Calhoun's elaborate theory was an earnest attempt to save the Union from the defects of its Constitution. It is useless to inquire whether it is legally right, according to the letter of the Constitution, for it is certain that it is in contradiction with its spirit as it has grown up since Jefferson. Webster may have been the truest interpreter of the law; Calhoun was the real defender of the Union. Even the Unionists made the dangerous admission, that there were cases in which, as there was no redress known to the law, secession was fully justified. Livingston gave the opinion, that "if the act be one of the few which, in its operation, cannot be submitted to the Supreme Court, and be one that will, in the opinion of the State, justify the risk of a withdrawal from the Union, this last extremity may at once be resorted to."

The intimate connection between nullification and secession is shown by the biographer of Clay, though he fails to see that one is not the consequence, but the surrogate, of the other: "The first idea of nullification was doubtless limited to the action of a State in making null and void a federal law or laws within the circle of its own jurisdiction, without contemplating the absolute independence of a secession. Seeing, however, that nullification, in its practical operation, could hardly stop short of secession, the propounders of the doctrine in its first and limited signification, afterwards came boldly up to the claim of the right of secession."

Practically, South Carolina triumphed, though her claims were repudiated. The tariff was withdrawn, and a measure of compromise was introduced by Clay, the leading protectionist, which was felt to be so great a concession that Calhoun accepted, whilst Webster opposed it, and it was carried. But the evil day, the final crisis, was only postponed. The spirit of the country had taken a course in which it could not be permanently checked; and it was certain that new opportunities would be made to assert the omnipotence of the popular will, and to exhibit the total subservience of the executive to it. Already a new controversy had begun, which has since overshadowed that which shook the Union from 1828 to 1833. The commercial question was not settled; the economical antagonism, and the determination on the part of the North to extend its advantages, did not slumber from Clay's Compromise Act to the Morrill Tariff in 1861; and in his farewell address, in 1837, Jackson drew a gloomy and desponding picture of the period which is filled with his name. "Many powerful interests are continually at work to procure heavy duties on commerce, and to swell the revenue beyond the real necessities of the public service; and the country has already felt the injurious effects of their combined influence. They succeeded in obtaining a tariff of duties bearing most oppressively on the agricultural and labouring classes of society, and producing a revenue that could not be usefully employed within the range of the powers conferred upon Congress; and in order to fasten upon the people this unjust and unequal system of taxation, extravagant schemes of internal improvement were got up in various quarters to squander the money and to purchase support. . . . Rely upon it, the design to collect an extravagant revenue, and to burden you with taxes beyond the economical wants of the government, is not yet abandoned. The various interests which have combined together to impose a heavy tariff, and to produce an overflowing treasury, are too strong, and have too much at stake, to surrender the contest. The corporations and wealthy individuals who are engaged in large manufacturing establishments, desire a high tariff to increase their gains. Designing politicians will support it to conciliate their favour, and to obtain the means of profuse expenditure, for the purpose of purchasing influence in other quarters. . . . It is from within, among yourselves—from cupidity, from corruption, from disappointed ambition, and inordinate thirst for power,—that factions will be formed and liberty endangered."

Jackson was himself answerable for much of what was most deplorable in the political state of the country. The democratic tendency, which began under Jefferson, attained in Jackson's presidency its culminating point. The immense change in this respect may be shown in a single example. Pure democracy demands quick rotation of office, in order that, as all men have an equal claim to official power and profit, and must be supposed nearly equally qualified for it, and require no long experience (so that at Athens offices were distributed by lot), the greatest possible number of citizens should successively take part in the administration. It diminishes the distinction between the rulers and the ruled, between the State and the community, and increases the dependence of the first upon the last. At first such changes were not contemplated. Washington dismissed only nine officials in eight years, Adams removed only ten, Madison five, Monroe nine, John Quincy Adams only two, both on specific disqualifying grounds. Jefferson was naturally in favour of rotation in office, and caused a storm of anger when he displaced 39 official men in order to supply vacancies for supporters. Jackson, on succeeding the younger Adams, instantly made 176 alterations, and in the course of the first year 491 postmasters lost their places. Mr. Everett says very truly: "It may be stated as the general characteristic of the political tendencies of this period, that there was a decided weakening of respect for constitutional restraint. Vague ideas of executive discretion prevailed on the one hand in the interpretation of the constitution, and of popular sovereignty on the other, as represented by a President elevated to office by overwhelming majorities of the people."

This was the period of Tocqueville's visit to America, when he passed the following judgment: "When a man, or a party, suffers an injustice in the United States, to whom can he have recourse? To public opinion? It is that which forms the majority. To the legislative body? It represents the majority, and obeys it blindly. To the executive power? It is appointed by the majority, and serves as its passive instrument. To public force? It is nothng but the majority under arms. To the jury? It is the majority invested with the right of finding verdicts. The judges themselves, in some States, are elected by the majority. However iniquitous, therefore, or unreasonable the measure from which you suffer, you must submit." Very eminent Americans quite agreed with him in his censure of the course things had taken, and which had been seen long beforehand. In 1818 Story writes: "A new race of men is springing up to govern the nation; they are the hunters after popularity; men ambitious, not of the honour so much as of the profits of office,—the demagogues whose principles hang laxly upon them, and who follow, not so much what is right as what leads to a temporary vulgar applause. There is great, very great danger that these men will usurp so much of popular favour that they will rule the nation; and if so, we may yet live to see many of our best institutions crumble in the dust."

The following passages are from the conclusion of his commentary on the Constitution: "The influence of the disturbing causes, which, more than once in the convention, were on the point of breaking up the Union, have since immeasurably increased in concentration and vigour. . . . If, under these circumstances, the Union should once be broken up, it is impossible that a new constitution should ever be formed, embracing the whole territory. We shall be divided into several nations or confederacies, rivals in power and interest, too proud to brook injury, and too close to make retaliation distant or ineffectual." On the 18th February, 1834, he writes of Jackson's administration: "I feel humiliated at the truth, which cannot be disguised, that though we live under the form of a republic, we are in fact under the absolute rule of a single man." And a few years later, 3d November, 1837, he tells Miss Martineau that she has judged too favourably of his country: "You have overlooked the terrible influence of a corrupting patronage, and the system of exclusiveness of official appointments, which have already wrought such extensive mischiefs among us, and threaten to destroy all the safeguards of our civil liberties. . . . You would have learned, I think, that there may be a despotism exercised in a republic, as irresistible and as ruinous as in any form of monarchy."

The foremost of the Southern statesmen thought exactly like the New England judge. "I care not," said Calhoun, "what the form of the government is; it is nothing, if the government be despotic, whether it be in the hands of one, or a few, or of many men, without limitation. . . . While these measures were destroying the equilibrium between the two sections, the action of the government as leading to a radical change in its character, by concentrating all the power of the system in itself. . . . What was once a constitutional federal republic is now converted, in reality, into one as absolute as that of the autocrat of Russia, and as despotic in its tendency as any absolute government that ever existed. . . . The increasing power of this government, and of the control of the Northern section over all its departments, furnished the cause. It was this which made an impression on the minds of many, that there was little or no restraint to prevent the government from doing whatever it might choose to do." At the same period, though reverting to a much earlier date, Cobett wrote: "I lived eight years under the republican government of Pennsylvania; and I declare that I believe that to have been the most corrupt and tyrannical government that the world ever knew. . . . I have seen enough of republican government to convince me that the mere name is not worth a straw." Channing touches on a very important point, the influence of European liberalism on the republicanism of America: "Ever since our revolution we have had a number of men who have wanted faith in our free institutions, and have seen in our almost unlimited extension of the elective franchise the germ of convulsion and ruin. When the demogogues succeed in inflaming the ignorant multitude, and get office and power, this antipopular party increases; in better times it declines. It has been built up in a measure by the errors and crimes of the liberals of Europe. . . . I have endeavoured on all occasions to disprove the notion that the labouring classes are unfit depositaries of political power. I owe it, however, to truth to say that I believe that the elective franchise is extended too far in this country." In 1841 he described very accurately the perils which have since proved fatal: "The great danger to our institutions, which alarms our conservatives most, has not perhaps entered Mr. Smith's mind. It is the danger of a party organisation, so subtle and strong as to make the government the monopoly of a few leaders, and to insure the transmission of the executive power from hand to hand almost as regularly as in a monarchy. . . . That this danger is real cannot be doubted. So that we have to watch against despotism as well as, or more than, anarchy." On this topic it is impossible to speak more strongly, and nobody could speak with greater authority than Dr. Brownson: "Our own government, in its origin and constitutional form, is not a democracy, but, if we may use the expression, a limited elective aristocracy. . . . But practically the government framed by our fathers no longer exists, save in name. Its original character has disappeared, or is rapidly disappearing. The constitution is a dead letter, except so far as it serves to prescribe the modes of election, the rule of the majority, the distribution and tenure of offices, and the union and separation of the functions of government. Since 1828 it has been becoming in practice, and is now substantially, a pure democracy, with no effective constitution but the will of the majority for the time being. . . . The constitution is practically abolished, and our government is virtually, to all intents and purposes, as we have said, a pure democracy, with nothing to prevent it from obeying the interest or interests which for the time being can succeed in commanding it." Shortly before his conversion he wrote: "Looking at what we were in the beginning, and what we now are, it may well be doubted whether another country in Christendom has so rapidly declined as we have, in the stern and rigid virtues, in the high-toned and manly principles of conduct essential to the stability and wise administration of popular government. . . . The established political order in this country is not the democratic; and every attempt to apply the democratic theory as the principle of its interpretation is an attempt a revolution, and to be resisted. By a democracy I understand a political order,—if that may be called order which is none,—in which the people, primarily and without reference to any authority constituting them a body politic, are held to be the source of all the legitimate power in the state."

The partisans of democratic absolutism who opposed State-rights in the affair of the tariff, and led to the unhappy consequences and lamentations we have seen, were already supplied with another topic to test the power of their principle. The question of abolition, subordinate at first, though auxiliary to the question of protection, came into the front when the other had lost is interest, and had been suspended for a season by the Compromise Act. It served to enlist higher sympathies on the side of revolution than could be won by considerations of mere profit. It adorned cupidity with the appearance of philanthropy, but the two motives were not quite distinct, and one is something of a pretext, and serves to disguise the other. They were equally available as means of establishing the supremacy of the absolute democracy, only one was its own reward; the other was not so clearly a matter of pecuniary interest, but of not inferior political advantage. A power which is questioned, however real it may be, must assert and manifest itself if it is to last. When the right of the States to resist the Union was rejected, although the question which occasioned the dispute was amicably arranged, it was certain to be succeeded by another, in order that so doubtful a victory might be commemorated by a trophy.

The question of slavery first exhibited itself as a constitutional difficulty about 1820, in the dispute which was settled by the Missouri compromise. Even at this early period the whole gravity of its consequences was understood by discerning men. Jefferson wrote: "This momentous question, like a fire-bell in the night, awakened and filled me with terror. I considered it at once as the knell of the Union. It is hushed, indeed, for the moment. But this is a reprieve only, not a final sentence."

In 1828, when South Carolina was proclaiming the right of veto, and was followed by several of the Southern States, abolition was taken up in the North as a means of coercion against them, by way of reprisal, and as a very powerful instrument of party warfare. Channing writes to Webster, 14th May, 1828: "A little while ago, Mr. Lundy of Baltimore, the editor of a paper called The Genius of Universal Emancipation, visited this part of the country, to stir us up to the work of abolishing slavery at the South; and the intention is to organise societies for this purpose. . . . My fear in regard to our efforts against slavery is, that we shall make the case worse by rousing sectional pride and passion for its support, and that we shall only break the country into two great parties, which may shake the foundations of government."

In the heat of the great controversies of Jackson's administration, on the Bank question and the Veto question, slavery was not brought prominently forward; but when the democratic central power had triumphed, when the Bank question was settled, and there was no longer an immediate occasion for discussing State-rights, the party whose opinions had prevailed in the Constitution resolved to make use of their predominance for its extinction. Thenceforward, from about the year 1835, it became the leading question, and the form in which the antagonism between the principles of arbitrary power and of self-government displayed itself. At every acquisition of territory, at the formation of new States, the same question caused a crisis; then in the Fugitive-Slave Act, and finally in the formation of the republican party, and its triumph in 1860. The first effect of making abolition a political party question, and embodying

in it the great constitutional quarrel which had already threatened the existence of the Union in the question of taxation, was to verify the prophecy of
Channing. Webster, who had been the foremost antagonist of nullification in
the affair of the tariff, lived to acknowledge that even secession was being
provoked by the insane aggression of the North. In one of his latest speeches,
in that which is known as his speech for the Union, 7th March, 1850, he
denounced the policy of the abolitionists: "I do not mean to impute gross
motives even to the leaders of these societies, but I am not blind to the
consequences of their proceedings. I cannot but see what mischiefs their interference with the South has produced. And is it not plain to every man? Let any
gentleman who entertains doubts on this point recur to the debates in the
Virginia House of Delegates in 1832, and he will see with what freedom a
proposition made by Mr. J. Randolph for the gradual abolition of slavery was
discussed in that body. . . . Public opinion, which in Virginia had begun to be
exhibited against slavery, and was opening out for the discussion of the question, drew back and shut itself up in its castle. . . . We all know the fact, and
we all know the cause; and everything that these agitating people have done
has been, not to enlarge, but to restrain, not to set free, but to bind faster, the
slave-population of the South."

Howe, the Virginian historian, in principle though not in policy an
abolitionist, says: "That a question so vitally important would have been
renewed with more success at an early subsequent period, seems more than
probable, if the current opinions of the day can be relied on; but there were
obvious causes in operation which paralysed the friends of abolition, and have
had the effect of silencing all agitation on the subject. The abolitionists in the
Northern and Eastern States, gradually increasing their strength as a party,
became louder in their denunciations of slavery, and more and more reckless
in the means adopted for assailing the constitutional rights of the South."

Story writes, 19th January, 1839: "The question of slavery is becoming
more and more an absorbing one, and will, if it continues to extend its influence, lead to a dissolution of the Union. At least there are many of our
soundest statesmen who look to this as a highly probable event."

At that time the abolitionist party was yet in its infancy, and had not
succeeded in combining together in a single party all the interests that were
hostile to the slave States. Lord Carlisle, describing a conversation he had in
1841 with the present Secretary of State, Mr. Seward, says, "I find that I noted
at the time that he was the first person I had met who did not speak slightingly
of the abolitionists; he thought they were gradually gaining ground."

But in the following year the abolitionist policy rapidly grew up into a
great danger to the Union, which the great rivals, Webster and Calhoun,
united to resist at the close of their lives. Commercially speaking, it is not
certain that the North would gain by the abolition of slavery. It would increase the Southern market by encouraging white emigration from the North;
but the commerce of New England depends largely on the cotton crop, and the
New England merchants are not for abolition. Calhoun did not attribute the
movement to a desire of gain: "The crusade against our domestic institution

does not originate in hostility of interests. . . . The rabid fanatics regard slavery as a sin, and thus regarding it deem it their highest duty to destroy it, even should it involve the destruction of the constitution and the Union."

In this view he is fully supported by Webster: "Under the cry of universal freedom, and that other cry that there is a rule for the government of public men and private men which is of superior obligation to the constitution of the country, several of the States have enacted laws to hinder, obstruct, and defeat the enactments in this act of Congress to the utmost of their power. . . . I suspect all this to be the effect of that wandering and vagrant philanthropy which disturbs and annoys all that is present, in time or place, by heating the imagination on subjects distant, remote, and uncertain."

Webster justly considered that the real enemies of the Constitution were the abolitionists, not the slave-owners, who threatened to secede. To appeal from the Constitution to a higher law, to denounce as sinful and contrary to natural right an institution expressly recognized by it, is manifestly an assault upon the Union itself. The South have the letter and the spirit of the law in their favour. The consistent abolitionists must be ready to sacrifice the Union to their theory. If the objection to slavery is on moral grounds, paramount to all political rights and interests, abolition is a peremptory duty, to which the Union itself, whose law is opposed to compulsory abolition, must succumb. It was therefore perfectly just to remind Mr. Seward, that in attacking slavery, and denying that it could be tolerated, he was assailing the law to which he owed his seat in Congress. "No man," said Webster, "is at liberty to set up or affect to set up, his own conscience as above the law, in a matter which repsects the rights of others, and the obligations, civil, social, and political, due to others from him."

Dr. Brownson says, with great truth, as only a Catholic can, "No civil government can exist, none is conceivable even, where every individual is free to disobey its orders, whenever they do not happen to square with his private convictions of what is the law of God. . . . To appeal from the government to private judgment, is to place private judgment above public authority, the individual above the state."

Calhoun was entirely justified in saying that, in the presence of these tendencies, "the conservative power is in the slave-holding States. They are the conservative portion of the country."

His own political doctrines, as we have described them, fully bear out this view. But the conservative, anti-revolutionary character of the South depended on other causes than the influence of its master mind. Slavery is itself in contradiction with the equal rights of man, as they are laid down in the Declaration of Independence. Slave-owners are incapacitated from interpreting that instrument with literal consistency, for it would contradict both their interests and their daily experience. But as there are advanced democrats at the South as well as at the North, and as, indeed, they succeeded in resisting so long the Northern politicians, by using the jealousy of the Northern people against the wealthy capitalists, and the appearance of aristocracy, they find means of escaping from this dilemma. This is supplied by the theory of the original inferiority of the African race to the rest of mankind, for which the authority of the greatest naturalist in America is quoted: "The result of my researches," says Agassiz, "is, that Negroes are intellectually children; physically one of the lowest races; inclining with the other blacks, especially the South-Sea Negroes, most of all to the monkey type, though with a tendency, even in the extremes, towards the real human form. This opinion I have repeatedly expressed, without drawing from it any objectionable consequence, unless, perhaps, that no coloured race, least of all the Negroes, can have a common origin with ourselves." If this theory were not the property of the infidel science of Europe, one would suppose it must have been invented for the Americans, whom it suits so well.

Webster spoke with great power against the projects of the North: "There is kept up a general cry of one party against the other, that its rights are invaded, its honour insulted, its character assailed, and its just participation in political power denied. Sagacious men cannot but suspect from all this, that more is intended than is avowed; and that there lies at the bottom a purpose of the separation of the States, for reasons avowed or disavowed, or for grievances redressed or unredressed.

"In the South, the separation of the States is openly professed, discused, and recommended, absolutely or conditionally, in legislative halls, and in conventions called together by the authority of the law.

"In the North, the State governments have not run into such excess, and the purpose of overturning the government shows itself more clearly in resolutions agreed to in voluntary assemblies of individuals, denouncing the laws of the land, and declaring a fixed intent to disobey them. . . . It is evident that, if this spirit be not checked, it will endanger the government; if it spread far and wide, it will overthrow the government."

The language of Calhoun about the same period is almost identical with Webster's. "The danger is of a character—whether we regard our safety or the preservation of the Union—which cannot be safely tampered with. If not met promptly and decidedly, the two portions of the Union will become thoroughly alienated, when no alternative will be left to us, as the weaker of the two, but to sever all political ties, or sink down into abject submission."

His last great speech, delivered March 4, 1850, a few days before his death, opened with the words, "I have believed from the first that the agitation of the subject of slavery would, if not prevented by some timely and effective measure, end in disunion." And he went on to say: "If something is not done to avert it, the South will be forced to choose between abolition and secession. Indeed, as events are now moving, it will not require the South to secede in order to dissolve the Union."

The calamity which these eminent men agreed in apprehending and in endeavouring to avert, was brought on after their death by the rise of the republican party—a party in its aims and principles quite revolutionary, and not only inconsistent with the existence of the Union, but ready from the first to give it up. "I do not see," said the New England philosopher Emerson, "how a barbarous community and a civilised community can constitute one State."

In order to estimate the extravagance of this party declaration, we will only quote two unexceptionable witnesses, who visited the South at an interval of about forty years from each other; one a Boston divine, the other an eager abolitionist. "How different from our Northern manners! There, avarice and ceremony, at the age of twenty, graft the coldness and unfeelingness of age on the disinterested ardour of youth. I blush for my own people when I compare the selfish prudence of the Yankee with the generous confidence of a Virginian. Here I find great vices, but greater virtues than I left behind me. There is one single trait which attaches me to the people I live with more than all the virtues of New England,—they love money less than we do." Lord Carlisle says, in the lecture already referred to, "It would be uncandid to deny that the planter in the Southern States has much more in his manner and mode of intercourse that resembles the English country gentleman than any other class of his countrymen."

Emerson's saying is a sign of the extent to which rapid abolitionists were ready to go. Declaring that the Federal Government was devoted to Southern interests, against Northern doctrines, they openly defied it. Disunion societies started up at the North for the purpose of bringing about separation. Several States passed laws against the South and against the Constitution, and there were loud demands for separation. This was the disposition of the North at the presidential election of a successor to Pierce. The North threatened to part company, and if it carried its candidate, it threatened the Southern institutions. The South proclaimed the intention of seceding if Fremont should be elected, and threatened to march upon Washington and burn the archives of the Union. Buchanan's election pacified the South; but it was evident, from the growing strength of the republican party, that it was their last victory. They accordingly made use of their friends in office to take advantage of the time that remained to them to be in readiness when the next election came. Secession was resolved upon and prepared from the time when the strength of the republicans was exhibited in 1856. In spite of all the horrors of American slavery, it is impossible for us to have any sympathy with the party of which Mr. Seward is the chief. His politics are not only revolutionary, but aggressive; he is not only for absolutism but for annexation. In a speech on January 26, 1853, he spoke as follows: "The tendency of commercial and political events invites the United States to assume and exercise a paramount influence in the affairs of the nations situated in this hemisphere; that is, to become and remain a great Western continental power, balancing itself against the possible combinations of Europe. The advance of the country toward that position constitutes what, in the language of many, is called 'progress,' and the position itself is what, by the same class, is called 'manifest destiny.' "

When Cass moved a resolution affirming the Monroe Doctrine with regard to Cuba, Seward supported it, together with another resolution perfectly consistent with it, of which he said: "It is not well expressed; but it implies the same policy in regard to Canada which the main resolutions assert concerning Cuba." Nor is this the limit of his ambition. "You are already," he says to his countrymen, "the great continental power of America. But does that content you? I trust it does not. You want the commerce of the world, which is the empire of the world."

When Kossuth was received in the Senate, he was introduced by Mr. Seward, whose European policy is as definite and about as respectable as his American. Speaking of Hungary, he writes, in December, 1851: "I trust that some measure may be adopted by the government which, while it will not at all hazard the peace or prosperity of the country, may serve to promote a cause that appeals so strongly to our interests and our sympathies, viz. the establishment of republicanism, in the countries prepared for it, in Europe." And again, two days later: "Every nation may, and every nation ought, to make its position distinctly known in every case of conflict between despots and States struggling for the inalienable and indefeasible rights of independence and self-government, that when despots combine, free States may lawfully unite."

It is as impossible to sympathise on religious grounds with the categorical prohibition of slavery as, on political grounds, with the opinions of the abolitionists. In this, as in all other things, they exhibit the same abstract, ideal absolutism, which is equally hostile with the Catholic and with the English spirit. Their democratc system poisons everything it touches. All constitutional questions are referred to the one fundamental principle of popular sovereignty, without consideration of policy or expediency. In the Massachusetts convention of 1853, it was argued by one of the most famous Americans, that the election of the judiciary could not be discussed on the grounds of its influence on the administration of justice, as it was clearly consonant with the constitutional theory. "What greater right," says the *North American Review* (LXXXVI, 477), "has government to deprive the people of their representation in the executive and judicial, than in the legislative department?" In claiming absolute freedom, they have created absolute powers, whilst we have inherited from the middle ages the notion that both liberty and authority must be subject to limits and conditions. The same intolerance of restraints and obligations, the same aversion to recognise the existence of popular duty, and of the divine right which is its correlative, disturb their notions of government and of freedom. The influence of these habits of abstract reasoning, to which we owe the revolution in Europe, is to make all things questions of principle and of abstract law. A principle is always appealed to in all cases, either of interest or necessity, and the consequence is, that a false and arbitrary political system produces a false and arbitrary code of ethics, and the theory of abolition is as erroneous as the theory of freedom.

Very different is the mode in which the Church labours to reform mankind by assimilating realities with ideals, and accommodating herself to times and circumstances. Her system of Christian liberty is essentially incompatible with slavery; and the power of masters over their slaves was one of the bulwarks of corruption and vice which most seriously impeded her progress. Yet the Apostles never condemned slavery even within the Christian fold. The sort of civil liberty which came with Christianity into the world, and was one of her postulates, did not require the abolition of slavery. If men were free by virtue of their being formed after the image of God, the proportion in which they realised that image would be the measure of their freedom. Accordingly, St. Paul prescribed to the Chrisitian slave to remain content with his condition.

We have gone at inordinate length into the causes and pecularities of the revolution in the United States, because of the constant analogy they present to the theories and the events which are at the same time disturbing Europe. It is too late to touch upon more than one further point, which is extremely suggestive. The Secession movement was not provoked merely by the alarm of the slave-owners for their property, when the election of Lincoln sent down the price of slaves from twenty-five to fifty per cent, but by the political danger of Northern preponderance; and the mean whites of the Southern States are just as eager for separation as those who have property in slaves. For they fear lest the republicans, in carrying emancipation, should abolish the barriers which separate the Negroes from their own caste. At the same time, the slaves show no disposition to help the republicans, and be raised to the level of the whites. There is a just reason for this fear, which lies in the simple fact that the United States are a republic. The population of a republic must be homogeneous. Civil equality must be founded on social equality, and on national and physiological unity. This has been the strength of the American republic. Pure democracy is that form of government in which the community is sovereign, in which, therefore, the State is most nearly identified with society. But society exists for the protection of interests; the State for the realisation of right—concilia cœtusque hominum *jure* sociati, quae civitates appellantur. The State sets up a moral, objective law, and pursues a common object distinct from the ends and purposes of society. This is essentially repugnant to democracy, which recognises only the interests and rights of the community, and is therefore inconsistent with the consolidation of authority which is implied in the notion of the State. It resists the development of the social into the moral community. If, therefore, a democracy includes persons with separate interests or an inferior nature, it tyrannises over them. There is no mediator between the part and the whole; there is no room, therefore, for differences of class, of wealth, of race; equality is necessary to the liberty which is sought by a pure democracy.

Where society is constituted without equality of condition or unity of race, where there are different classes and national varieties, they require a protector in a form of government which shall be distinct from and superior to every class, and not the instrument of one of them, in an authority representing the State, not any portion of society. This can be supplied only by monarchy; and in this sense it is fair to say that constitutional government, that is, the authority of law as distinguished from interest, can exist only under a king. This is also the reason why even absolute monarchies have been better governors of dependencies than popular governments. In one case they are governed for the benefit of a ruling class; in the other, there is no ruling class, and they are governed in the name of the State. Rome under the Republic and under the Empire is the most striking instance of this contrast. But the tyranny of republics is greatest when differences of races are combined with distinctions of class. Hence South America was a flourishing and prosperous country so long as the Spanish crown served as moderator between the various races, and is still prosperous where monarchy has been retained; whilst the establishment of republics in countries with classes divided by blood has led to hopeless misery and disorder, and constant recourse to dictatorships as a refuge from anarchy and tyranny. Democracy inevitably takes the tone of the lower portions of society, and, if there are great diversities, degrades the higher. Slavery is the only protection that has ever been known against this tendency, and it is so far true that slavery is essential to democracy. For where there are great incongruities in the constitution of society, if the Americans were to admit the Indians, the Chinese, the Negroes, to the rights to which they are justly jealous of admitting European emigrants, the country would be thrown into disorder, and if not, would be degraded to the level of the barbarous races. Accordingly, the Know-nothings rose up as the reaction of the democratic principle against the influx of an alien population. The Red Indian is gradually retreating before the pioneer, and will perish before many generations, or dwindle away in the desert. The Chinese in California inspire great alarm for the same reason, and plans have been proposed of shipping them all off again. This is a good argument too, in the interest of all parties, against the emancipation of the blacks.

The necessity for social equality and national unity has been felt in all democracies where the mass as a unit governs itself. Above all, it is felt as a necessity in France, since the downfall of the old society, and the recognition, under republic, charter, and despotism, of the sovereignty of the people. Those principles with which France revolutionises Europe are perfectly right in her own case. They are detestable in other countries where they cause revolutions, but they are a true and just consequence of the French Revolution. Men easily lose sight of the substance in the form, and suppose that because France is not a republic she is not a democracy, and that her principles therefore will apply elsewhere. This is the reason of the power of the national principle in Europe. It is essential as a consequence of equality to the notion of the people as the source of power. Where there is an aristocracy it has generally more sympathy and connection with foreign aristocracies than with the rest of the nation. The bonds of class are stronger than those of nationality. A democracy, in abolishing classes, renders national unity imperative.

These are some of the political lessons we have learnt from the consideration of the vast process of which we are witnessing the consummation. We may consult the history of the American Union to understand the true theory of republicanism, and the danger of mistaking it. It is simply the spurious democracy of the French Revolution that has destroyed the Union, by disintegrating the remnants of English traditions and institutions. All the great controversies —on the embargo, restriction, internal improvement, the Bank-Charter Act, the formation of new States, the acquisition of new territory, abolition—are phases of this mighty change, steps in the passage from a constitution framed on an English model to a system imitating that of France. The secession of the Southern States—pregnant with infinite consequences to the African race by altering the condition of slavery, to America by awakening an intenser thirst for conquest, to Europe by its reaction on European democracy, to England, above all, by threatening for a moment one of the pillars of her social existence, but still more by the enormous augmentation of her power, on which the United States were always a most formidable restraint—is chiefly important in a political light as a protest and reaction against revolutionary doctrines, and as a move in the opposite direction to that which prevails in Europe.